Real English Grammar

Real English
Grammar

Hester Lott

Intermediate

Marshall Cavendish
Education

© 2005 Marshall Cavendish Ltd

First published 2005 by Marshall Cavendish Education

Marshall Cavendish is a member of the Times Publishing Group

All rights reserved; no part of this publication may be reproduced, stored in
a retrieval system, transmitted in any form, or by any means, electronic,
mechanical, photocopying, recording, or otherwise, without the prior
written permission of the publishers.

Marshall Cavendish Education
32–38 Saffron Hill
London EC1N 8FH

Design and production by Hart McLeod, Cambridge
Editorial development by Ocelot Publishing, Oxford
Illustrations by Yane Christiansen, Andrew Quelch and Noriko Toyama
Printed and bound by Times Offset (M) Sdn. Bhd. Malaysia.

Introduction

To the teacher

This book is designed for both self-study and classroom use by intermediate to upper intermediate level students.

It is organised according to grammatical categories (*nouns, articles, tenses, adjectives* etc), except where some units focus on a lexical area as a more practical way of dealing with specific grammatical problems (for example, the use of certain prepositions and of specific modals such as **would** and **could**).

The book is organised in such a way that the 'fundamental' issues of grammar (*nouns, articles,* and *verbs*) are all dealt with in the first units of the book. Students can work through the book from beginning to end, or they can be asked to dip into it to deal with specific grammatical problems that they are experiencing.

There are passages of real English at the beginning of each unit which are designed to give the student a 'feel' of how the grammatical or lexical area is used in a real context. These texts can be read by students individually, or they can be read aloud to the class, or you can play the audio CD which can be used with this book to hear the texts read by native speakers at a natural speed.

In each unit, there are generally two pages of grammatical explanations with plenty of examples, and then two pages of exercises. All the exercises are set in real contexts, and often with characters that recur throughout the book who students may come to recognise and to identify with.

At the back of the book there are tables of *verb forms, irregular plurals*, a *pronunciation guide*, a guide to the *structure of English sentences*, and a brief look at *American English* for the students to refer to if they need to.

The answers to the exercises are all contained in the booklet inside the back cover of the book which you may let the students keep or not, as you choose.

To the student

This book is for learners of English who have already learnt the basics of English grammar and who need to develop a deeper understanding of how English is used. You can start at the beginning and work through the book if you want to, or you can choose any grammar topic that you think you need to study, as the units are all self-contained. The texts at the beginning of each unit should be read straight through to get a sense of their meaning, and you can also hear them read aloud on the audio CD; then you can look at them more closely to see how the language is used, in terms of the grammar focus of the unit. The grammar explanation boxes all have clear headings so you can choose exactly what you want to work on in each unit.

Most of the exercises tell a story or are a conversation in progress. They test the grammar focus of the unit and they also help you to learn more about how English is used in everyday life. When you have finished them, you can use the handy answer key booklet inside the back cover to check your answers.

At the end of the book there are useful lists of *irregular verbs* and of *plural nouns*. There is also a pronunciation guide and information on the structure of English sentences and of terms such as *adjective* and *modal*, and some brief notes on the differences between British and American English grammar.

I had a lot of fun writing this book, and I hope you will enjoy getting to know the characters and reading about their lives and enjoy getting a better understanding of real spoken and written English.

Contents

'Yes, we haven't got very much letter-writing **paper**, and sticky **tape**. I need two **boxes** of small drawing **pins**, and a **box** of paper **clips**. Oh ... and **glue** ... I'll need a dozen large **bottles** of **glue**. I'd like some of those coloured **labels**, yes, two **packets**, please ... and a selection of those **rubbers** shaped like little **animals**. ... No, I don't want the 'Jungle Book' animals. I want the farmyard animals. ... No. I don't think we need any lined A4 paper at the moment. ... Highlighter **pens**, yes, just one box ... mixed **colours**, please. And I think we've almost run out of black **ink**. We're OK for blue ink, but the black is almost gone. Three dozen **bottles**, yes, thank you. And when will you be able to deliver all that? ... Good, great. I'll see you tomorrow morning then! Bye!'

❶ regular plurals of nouns

Most nouns can be singular or plural. To make the plural, we usually add an **s** to the singular form:

> book → book**s**   pen → pen**s**   house → house**s**   car → car**s**

If the singular ends in **s**, **sh**, **ch**, **x**, or **z**, we add **es** to make the plural:

> bus → bus**es**   watch → watch**es**   wish → wish**es**   box → box**es**   buzz → buzz**es**

Also, some nouns which end in **o** add **es** in the plural:

> echo → echo**es**   hero → hero**es**   potato → potato**es**   tomato → tomato**es**

If the singular ends in consonant + **y**, the plural has **ies**:

> baby → bab**ies**   lady → lad**ies**   party → part**ies**

And if the singular ends in **f**, the plural often ends in **ves**:

> leaf → lea**ves**   loaf → loa**ves**   calf → cal**ves**   wife → wi**ves**

Note: One common exception is **roof** → **roofs**.

Some nouns have no distinct plural form, because the singular ends in **s**:

> series   headquarters   species   means   barracks

❷ irregular plurals of nouns

There are many irregular noun plurals. Some have only one form for both singular and plural:

> sheep   fish   deer   craft   dice

Some nouns coming from Old English have an **en** ending in the plural:

> child → child**ren**   woman → wom**en**   man → m**en**   ox → ox**en**

Some nouns change from the singular **ouse** to the plural **ice**, or from **oo** + *consonant* to **ee** + *consonant*:

> mouse → m**ice**   louse → l**ice**
> goose → g**ee**se   tooth → t**ee**th   foot → f**ee**t

Some words coming from Latin and Greek have a different system of plural endings:

> thesis → thes**es**   curriculum → curricul**a**   medium → medi**a**   nucleus → nucle**i**

(For a complete list of irregular nouns, see page 288.)

❸ multi-word nouns

Many nouns are made up of more than one word. The way that plurals are made depends on the type of words in the noun. To make the plural of nouns made up of a noun and another word (**ing form**, or *preposition*, or *adverb*) we add **s** or **es** to the noun:

> sitting room → sitting room**s**   running track → running track**s**
> flying fox → flying fox**es**   passer-by → passer**s**-by   runner-up → runner**s**-up

But we make the plural of a ***noun + noun*** by making the second noun plural:

bread bin → bread bin**s**   egg box → egg box**es**   dog lead → dog lead**s**

Note: When we talk about containers containing things we use *container*(**s**) + **of** + *plural noun*:

a tin of beans → two tin**s** of beans   a packet of biscuits → three packet**s** of biscuits

❹ countable nouns

Countable nouns have a singular and a plural form, and you can say how many there are:

a book → two books   the song → the songs   this window → these windows

We can use **some** or **any** with the plural of countable nouns:
- ▧ Sheila bought **some** curtains.
- ▧ She couldn't find **any** curtain hooks.

(For more information on **some** and **any**, see unit 4.)

❺ uncountable nouns

Uncountable nouns refer to *things that we see as one unit, and not made up of separate parts or items.*
They have no plural form. We don't use **a** or **an** with uncountable nouns, but we can use **the**, or
some, or **any**. We use a singular verb with uncountable nouns.
Types of things that are uncountable are:

substances – water, milk, ink, syrup, butter, flour:
- ▧ **Water** was pouring out of the tank.

materials – glass, cotton, stone, plastic:
- ▧ Kevin's jacket was made of **cotton**.

abstract ideas – hope, fear, information, war:
- ▧ **Fear** often makes people unreasonable.

collections of things – luggage, equipment, furniture, rubbish:
- ▧ I left my **luggage** at the station.

things we do not think of as made of separate objects – flour, sand, grass, money, hair:
- ▧ There was **flour** all over Robin's clothes.

❻ nouns with countable and uncountable uses

Some nouns can be used as either countable or uncountable nouns. The meaning often changes:

countable	uncountable
a coffee (*a cup of coffee*)	**coffee** (*coffee beans, powder,* or *liquid*)
▧ Would you like **a coffee**?	▧ **Coffee** is made from roasted beans.
the paper (*a newspaper*)	**paper** (*sheets of paper*)
▧ **The paper** is delivered every morning.	▧ There is **some paper** in the printer.
a glass (*a container for a drink*)	**glass** (*the transparent material*)
▧ David broke **a glass**.	▧ **The glass** in the mirror is cracked.

A lot of *abstract* nouns have a countable and an uncountable use:

countable	uncountable
▧ She had **a fear** of spiders.	▧ **Fear** makes you selfish.
▧ Paul's **hopes** were very high.	▧ We all need to have **hope**.

The names of types of *media* are usually uncountable when we are talking about them generally,
and countable when we are talking about the object or place where they are seen or heard.

countable	uncountable
▧ We're going to buy **a new television**.	▧ I'm very interested in **television**.
▧ She's in **the cinema** on the High Street.	▧ I wanted to work in **cinema**.
▧ They sell amazing clockwork **radios**!	▧ **Radio** is a very interesting medium.

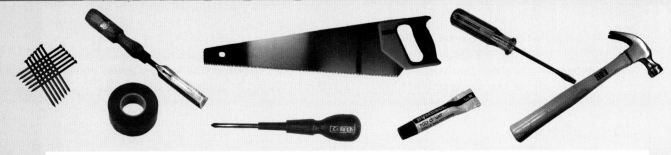

1 EXERCISES

nouns (book, books)

A Read the text and decide if the underlined nouns should be plural or singular. Put a tick if the word is correct; if it is not correct, write the correct form on the line.

French and Sons

'We can fix anything'.

Instructions for new employees

To work in the Repair Department you must have the right ⁰equipment. You must get all the following ¹item from the store:

- a ²hammer
- a packet of ³nail, (mixed ⁴size)
- two ⁵screwdriver (one Phillips screwdriver, one flat screwdriver)
- a ⁶tools bag
- a small ⁷saw
- three ⁸roll of insulation tape
- a chisel
- three ⁹tube of glues (wood, plastic, and metal)
- four ¹⁰box of screw (small, medium, and large).

0 ✓
1
2
3
4
5
6
7
8
9
10

B Look at the words in the box. Write down in the correct column all the uncountable nouns. Then write, in the next column, the plurals of all the countable nouns. Remember, some nouns can be either countable or uncountable, so some words will appear in both columns!

~~tomato~~ ~~glass~~ child swimming pool headquarters fear window greenhouse match policeman ice wool tea furniture chapter curriculum deer love television snow library box shelf stone doorbell

uncountable nouns	plurals of countable nouns	
glass	tomatoes	
	glasses	

4

C Read the following pairs of sentences and underline the noun that occurs in both. Now put a 'U' beside the sentence with the *uncountable noun* in it, and a 'C' beside the one with the *countable noun*.

0 (a) The old <u>theatre</u> burnt down last year. ....*C*.

  (b) Gary is training to work in the <u>theatre</u>. ...*U*..

1 (a) In the afternoon the actors have a break for tea and cake. ....

  (b) There's a walnut cake and a Swiss roll today. ....

2 (a) The café sells more coffee than anything else. ....

  (b) Bob Collins drinks about 8 coffees a day! ....

3 (a) The glass in the entrance to the theatre is broken. ....

  (b) We need to order some more glasses for the bar. ....

4 (a) They are going to deliver the paints for the stage set this afternoon. ....

  (b) Gloss paint is very expensive. ....

5 (a) Karen gave Steve a chocolate. ....

  (b) He is allergic to chocolate! ....

6 (a) He bought two papers this morning. ....

  (b) There's an enormous pile of paper on Mr Collins' desk. ....

7 (a) Gary prefers working in the theatre to film or TV. ....

  (b) Bob Collins has a TV in his office. ....

8 (a) Gary wanted to be an actor but he had a fear of speaking in public. ....

  (b) Miriam thinks fear is very important for an actor. ....

9 (a) The costumes for the next play, 'The Tempest', are all made of plastic. ....

  (b) There are many different kinds of plastics, some hard and some soft. ....

10 (a) Miriam has her own dressing room. ....

  (b) There isn't much room for her costumes. ....

D Read the following recipe and find all the errors in the use of nouns. Then write the incorrect form in brackets and the corrected word(s).

Recipe for Blueberry Pancake

Ingredient	Quantity
wholemeal flour	500 gram
egg	2
baking powder	1 1/2 teaspoon
milk	200 millilitre
blueberry	200 gram
butter	50 grams
salt	a large pinches
oil for frying	

Method:
Sift the flours into a bowl and add the bakings powders. Add the eggs and some of the milk. Mix gently. Add the rest of the milks and mix until the mixture is smooth. Add the blueberries and mix gently. Heat the frying pan until the oils are smoking and pour in about 3 tablespoon of the mixture. When bubble appear on the surface, turn it over and wait until it is firm to the touch. Serve the pancake with maple syrup and melted butters.

0 *(pancake) pancakes*....

1 ....

2 ....

3 ....

4 ....

5 ....

6 ....

7 ....

8 ....

9 ....

10 ....

11 ....

12 ....

13 ....

14 ....

15 ....

PHYLLIS:	Jasmine – don't look now, but I think …
JASMINE:	I know! I saw him too. It's **the actor** … oh, what's his name … Orlando Bloom. I'm sure it is!
PHYLLIS:	It can't be! I knew he was acting in **a film** near here but here he is, in **the café** we always go to … it's amazing!
JASMINE:	Can you see what he's eating?
PHYLLIS:	I don't want to look. I think he ordered **a coffee**, and something else …
JASMINE:	Oh, go on! I can't turn round. I'm too embarrassed!
PHYLLIS:	I think he looked better with blond **hair**. Did you see him in **the film** 'Lord of the Rings'?
JASMINE:	He was brilliant! … and in 'Pirates of **the Caribbean**'.
PHYLLIS:	Shall we go and ask for **an autograph**?
JASMINE:	No, that's just embarrassing. I know. I'll go to **the bathroom** and accidentally knock **a cup** or something off **the table**, as I walk past him.
PHYLLIS:	Don't be stupid. That'll just annoy him.
JASMINE:	I just want to get **a** closer **look**.
PHYLLIS:	Oh my goodness, he's getting up … he's turning round …

❶ uses of the indefinite article (**a** / **an**)

We use **a** before a noun beginning with a consonant sound, and **an** before a noun beginning with a vowel sound:

■ Jonathan ate **a sandwich** and Peter had **an apple**.

We use **a** / **an** when we want to talk about something countable and when *it doesn't matter (or we don't know exactly) which person or thing we are talking about*:

■ There's **a man** on the phone. (*I don't know who.*)
■ Can I have **an orange**, please? (*It doesn't matter which.*)

(For more on countable and uncountable nouns, see unit 1.)

We use **a** / **an** when we are talking about *a job* or *a profession*:

■ Keith's son is training to be **a doctor** and his daughter is **an actor**.

If we want to talk about a unit of something that is an uncountable noun, we must use a phrase with **of** (e.g. **a piece of news, a drop of water**) to describe it:

a piece / **an item of** furniture / news / information
a grain / **a bag** / **a kilo of** flour / sugar / sand / rice
a drop / **a glass** / **a bottle of** water / ink / milk / oil

❷ uses of the definite article (**the**)

We use **the** when *there can be no doubt what we are talking about*, and we don't need to specify which one:

■ Put the shopping in **the kitchen**. (*There is only one kitchen in the house.*)
■ You need to turn on **the heater**. (*The one which will warm you.*)

We also use **the** when *we <u>specify</u> what we are talking about*:

■ She lives in **the house** <u>at the top of the hill.</u>
■ He's **the kind** <u>of person that I really like.</u>

We use an indefinite article (**a** / **an**) the first time we mention something, and then we use the definite article (**the**) afterwards, because our listener knows what we are referring to:

■ There was **a parcel** waiting for me at home. **The parcel** was from my sister in France.

We use **the** when we're talking about *something unique* (something that there is only one of):

■ **The moon** is full tonight.
■ I once met **the head of Fiat**.

We also use **the** when we are *defining someone by saying what they do*:

■ That's Sian Edwards, **the lawyer**, and that's Howard Haigh, **the guitarist**.

We use **the** with superlatives:
  - ▦ Wasim is **the most** successful salesman we have.
  - ▦ The Alpha Romeo went round the circuit **the fastest**.

We use **the** with adjectives like **last**, **first**, **only** etc. to make them *absolute*:
  - ▦ That's **the last** time I trust you!
  - ▦ Geraldine is **the only** person I know in Dublin.

We use **of the** after a *quantifier* like **some**, and before a plural or uncountable noun, if we are talking about a *specific group or quantity*:
  - ▦ A few **of the** people have bought most **of the** pictures in the show.

In formal or academic English, we use **the** with a singular countable noun to mean *all examples of*:
  - ▦ The most intelligent sea mammal is **the dolphin**. (*all types of dolphin*)

We also use **the** with musical instruments when we are talking about them *generally*:
  - ▦ Dan is learning to play **the piano**. BUT I'm going to buy **a piano**.

❸ when to use **no article**

Articles are examples of ***determiners***; these are words which come before the noun and tell us which thing we are talking about. If we use another determiner (e.g. **this**, **that**, **my**, **his**, **another**) before the noun, we don't need an article as well:
  - ▦ **These colours** are more popular.
  - ▦ It's **his turn** to wash up.

We don't use an article when we are talking about *something abstract* and uncountable:
  - ▦ **Love** is a wonderful thing. ▦ I wish you **happiness** and **success**.

We don't use an article with uncountable nouns, that are not abstract, when we are talking about *something in general*:
  - ▦ Do you take **sugar**? NOT ~~Do you take the sugar?~~
  - ▦ This bag is made of **leather**. NOT ~~The bag is made of the leather.~~
(For more on countable and uncountable nouns, see unit 1.)

We don't use an article when we are talking about *things generally*, using a plural noun:
  - ▦ There were **cherries** in the cake.
  - ▦ **Roses** are my favourite flowers.

We don't use an article with *sports*, *academic subjects*, and *games*:
  - ▦ Jenny is good at **tennis** but she failed **biology** at school.

We don't use an article after a quantifier (**some**, **any**, **lots of** etc.), when we are *not talking about a specific group or quantity*:
  - ▦ There were **some people** in the room making **lots of noise**.

❹ common expressions with **a**, **an**, and **the**

After the quantifiers **all** and **both**, we use **the** (or **of the**) before a noun:
  - ▦ **All the** milk is gone! = **All of the** milk is gone.
  - ▦ **Both the** girls were late. = **Both of the** girls were late.

We use **a** in quantifiers such as **a few**, **a lot of**, **a ton of**:
  - ▦ Sarah bought **a few** books for her course.
  - ▦ There's **a ton of** old clothes in the cupboard!
(For more on quantifiers, see units 49 and 50.)

We use **a / an** + *noun* after **what**, **such**, **quite** etc:
  - ▦ **What an** awful mess!
  - ▦ It was **such a** tragedy.

A Mark and Diego are going shopping together in Melbourne. Read their conversation and put **a**, **an**, or **the** in the gap, if you need to.

DIEGO: I must get (0) ......*a*.. present for my Dad. He's really hard to buy (1) .... presents for.

MARK: I got (2) .... wallet for my Dad in Adelaide. It was made of (3) .... kangaroo skin!

DIEGO: That's (4) .... good idea! That shop sells (5) .... leather goods. Let's have a look in there.

MARK: I hope it's air-conditioned. (6) .... last shop we went into was nice and cool.

DIEGO: Have you got something for your Mum? I got my Mum (7) .... lovely set of table mats with (8) .... Aboriginal designs on them.

MARK: Yes, I got my Mum (9) .... picture of Sydney harbour, with (10) .... famous bridge all lit up.

DIEGO: This shop looks great! Come on, open (11) .... door.

B Answer the following questions. Use a noun and (if necessary) **a**, **an**, or **the**. You can use the words at the bottom of page 9 to help you.

General Knowledge Quiz

0 What do we call the development of animals and plants over history? ......*evolution*..........

1 What is the opposite of a hill? ....

2 What is the title of the head of the Australian government? ....

3 What do you call a person who designs houses? ....

4 What do car engines run on? ....

5 What is the name of the part of an engine that moves up and down inside a cylinder? ....

6 What are windows made of? ....

7 In a football match, there are two teams on the pitch and one other person. Who is it? ....

8 My father had to have .... to repair his broken collar bone.

9 What instrument do you hold under your chin and play with a bow? ....

10 What are wedding rings made of? ....

11 Which game do you play with a ball, a bat, and two teams of eleven people? ....

12 What do you call a flying craft with no wings but large, rotating blades? ....

13 In what piece of furniture do we hang our clothes? ....

14 Where has all the energy on the earth come from? ....

Choose and circle the best option to fill each gap in the following text.

'The Lodge', Trinidad

When you arrive, get (0)(a) / — taxi from (1) an / the airport to 'The Lodge'. It is (2) — / a vegetarian guest house up in (3) — / the hills outside (4) a / the capital. (5) The / — owners are two musicians from Swansea, who wanted to create (6) a / the kind of holiday that they had always wanted to have. The guest house costs less than (7) a / — hotel, and (8) the / an air is clean and the food is fresh and healthy. You can hire (9) the / a bicycle and go down to (10) — / the beach. It's (11) the / a simple but very relaxing way to spend (12) — / a few days.

architect   petrol   violin   valley   piston   ~~evolution~~
referee   sun   wood   glass   helicopter   gold
operation   Prime Minister   wardrobe   cricket

ADELAIDE HOTEL

AMY: How many are in our group, then? ... I've got twelve names; is that right?

PAUL: Yes, I've got twelve, too, but three of them are couples – **Mr** and **Mrs Grant**, **Mr** and **Mrs Giulliani**, and **Dr** and **Mrs Heath**. That makes fifteen people in all.

AMY: Yes, that's right. And there's **Amy**, Mr and Mrs Grant's daughter. Have you got her on your list?

PAUL: Yes, so that's sixteen. Phew! OK, now, let's decide where to go first. We need to visit **Victoria Square**, and **the museum** and **gallery** on **North Terrace**, and then have a look at the **River Torrens**. We could have lunch at **the Mall** on **Rundle Street**. Then in the afternoon we could take them down to **Port Adelaide** and have a look at **the dockyard**.

AMY: We could take them for dinner in that nice restaurant with a view of **the Gulf of St Vincent** ... and let them relax a bit.

PAUL: OK, I'll phone and book for eighteen. Then tomorrow we could go up into **the Mount Lofty Range**. Is there anything to see up there? I've never been there myself.

AMY: Oh yes! If we go to **Stirling**, we could go to the **Organic Market** first, then take the coach to **Mylor** – there's a brilliant nature reserve there. In the afternoon we could go on to **Strathalbyn**, it's really lovely.

PAUL: You obviously know this area of **Australia** pretty well!

AMY: Yes, I love it. It's so beautiful and unspoilt.

❶ place names without **the**

We do not use the *definite article* (**the**) before:
the names of *planets*, except **the Earth** and **the Moon**:
- There is water on **Mars**.

geographical areas:
- Finland is a beautiful part of **Europe**.

states (US) *or counties* (UK):
- **Dorset** is a county in southern England.

the names of most *countries*:
- Dulcy went to **Romania** last year.

Note: Exceptions are **the Netherlands** and **the Congo**.

We don't usually use **the** with the names of *mountains, islands, lakes,* and *particular places*:

Mount Fuji	Mount St Helen
Mount Everest	Table Mountain
Sardinia	Prince Edward Island
Lake Windermere	Lake Ontario
Chelsea	Stonehenge	Botany Bay
Ayers Rock	

We do not use **the** with the names of *cities* or *towns*:
Managua   Cape Town   Oxford
Note: An exception is **the Hague**.

Most *street names* have no article:
- **Oxford Street** crosses **Regent Street**.
- **Times Square** is in central New York.

The names of *palaces, castles, churches, schools and universities, stations, zoos,* and *airports* don't usually have a **the**:
- This week we're going to see **Buckingham Palace**, **Warwick Castle**, and **Durham Cathedral**.
- We went to **Victoria Station** and took the underground to **London Zoo**.

❷ place names with **the**

We do use **the** with *groups of states or islands*, or when the name contains the words **United**, or **Kingdom**, or **Republic**:
the Philippines   the Azores
the United States / the USA   the UAE
the United Kingdom / the UK
the Kingdom of Brunei
the Republic of Ireland
the Czech Republic

We often use **the** with *regions within countries*:
the Midlands   the Cotswolds
the Dordogne   the Ruhr   the Riviera

We use **the** with the names of *mountain ranges, deserts, seas,* and *rivers*:

> **the** Pyrenees   **the** Andes   **the** Alps
> **the** Sahara   **the** Gobi Desert
> **the** Pacific Ocean   **the** Baltic Sea   **the** Mediterranean
> **the** Rhine   **the** Amazon

The names of *museums, galleries, libraries,* and *hotels* often have a **the**, particularly if the word **museum, hotel** etc. is included in the name:

> **the** Tate Gallery   **the** British Library
> **the** Randolph Hotel

Cinemas and *theatres* usually have a **the**:

> ■ I'm going to **the** Apollo to see 'Fight Club'.
> ■ Have you been to **the** Odeon?

Note: With some very famous theatres we do not use **the**, but usually we do:

> ■ **Covent Garden Opera House** is a beautiful theatre in London.
> ■ **Madison Square Garden** holds concerts as well as sporting events.

We often use **the** before:

> names with an *__adjective__*:
> ■ **the** Indian subcontinent   **the** Great Lakes   **the** White House   **the** Organic Market
> names with **of**:
> ■ **the** Isle **of** Wight   **the** Cape **of** Good Hope   **the** Houses **of** Parliament
> the expression **north / south / east / west / centre + of**:
> ■ I've never been to **the south of** India.
> ■ Leona was staying in **the centre of** Australia.

❸ institutions (**school, hospital, bank** etc)

We don't use an article to talk about a *school, college, university, hospital,* or *place of worship* (e.g. *synagogue, church, mosque*) when it is used for the purpose it was made for:

> ■ The children went to **school** – to learn.
> ■ My aunt is **in hospital** – she is ill.

But if we want to talk about them as *places*, rather than as institutions, we use **the**:

> ■ They are going to knock down **the school**.
> ■ **The hospital** is very crowded.

If we are talking about *other institutions* (*bank, Post Office, hotel, garage, museum, airport* etc), we use an article (**a** or **the**):

> ■ I went to **the Post Office** this morning.
> ■ **The garage** was closed.

❹ people's names with **the**

People's names do not take an article, even with a title:

> ■ **Mr** and **Mrs Dearlove** arrived this morning.
> ■ **Pia** and **Gregory** came with them.

If we refer to *two or more people by their family name* we use the definite article:

> ■ I've invited **the Carters** to lunch.
> ■ **The Harris sisters** live down the street.

A Read the text and put in the article **the** where it is necessary, or write a dash (–) where you don't need **the**.

[untitled email window]

Send Now   Send Later   Save as a Draft   Add Attachments

From:
To:
Cc:
Bcc:
Subject:
Attachments: none
Font ▽   Text Size ▽   **B** *I* U̲ T   ≡ ≡ ≡

Hi Lucy, :-)

Phil and I are having a great time here in (0) ...–... Scotland. Yesterday we went to (1) .... Edinburgh Castle. It was really cool! Our hotel is called (2) .... Old Castle Hotel, and it's very comfortable. You won't believe it, but this morning we met (3) .... Mr and Mrs Grant from down our street! It's amazing! They are here with their daughter (4) .... Katherine, who is studying medicine at (5) .... Edinburgh University. Tomorrow we are going to (6) .... Loch Ness, the lake with the famous monster. I hope we see the monster.

Last night we ate at a typical Scottish restaurant, and met some lovely people from (7) .... Hanover in (8) .... north of (9) .... Germany. (It's a pity that none of us liked haggis!!!) Jane wanted to see the exhibition of traditional Scottish clothing at (10) .... museum. The tartan kilts were fabulous. We each bought a kilt. You will laugh when you see me in a skirt!

This evening we are going to see a play at (11) .... Edinburgh Playhouse.

Hope you're having a great holiday, too,

Mark

B Answer these quiz questions. All the answers are in the box, but you may need to add **the**.

Grand Central   USA   Po   Globe
Prince Phillip   Oxford and Cambridge
~~Buckingham Palace~~   Indian subcontinent
Congo   Andes

---

0 'What is the name of the Queen's palace in London?'
'It's called *Buckingham Palace.*'

1 'What is the name of the river that flows through Florence, Italy?'
'It's called ....'

2 'What country is Chicago in?'
'It's in ....'

3 'Brazzaville is the capital of which country?'
'It's the capital of ....'

4 'Which continent is Bangalore in?'
'It's in ....'

5 'What is the name of the husband of the Queen of England?'
'He's called ....'

6 'Which two universities are the oldest in Britain?'
'.. are the oldest.'

7 'What is the name of the main station in New York?'
'It's called ....'

8 'What was the name of Shakespeare's theatre?'
'It was ....'

9 'Which mountain range runs down the border of Peru?'
'..'

Cape Town Holiday Itinerary

Depart – UK – late afternoon/evening.
Day 1
Arrive – Cape Town – morning. Coach – Leeuwenvoet Hotel.
Day 2
Explore – Visit National Museum.
Day 3
Take cable car – Table Mountain. Views of: city, Cape of Good Hope.
Day 4
Travel east – Visit Hermanus (small town by the sea).
Return via Winelands – a visit to a vineyard or two.
Day 5
Visit lighthouse – at Cape of Good Hope.
On the way there – visit to penguin colony at Boulder Bay.
Day 6
Relax and shop – go by boat – visit Robbin Island (the place where Nelson Mandela was in prison).
Day 7
To airport – evening departure – UK.

Imagine you have been on this holiday. Now answer the following questions as if you are a couple (use **we**). Use **the** if it is necessary.

0 'Where did you depart from?'
   '...... *We departed from the U.K.* ......'

1 'Where did you arrive the next morning?'
   '..'

2 'Where did you stay?'
   '..'

3 'Where did you go on the second day?'
   '..'

4 'Where did you go in the cable car?'
   '..'

5 'What could you see from there?'
   '..'

6 'What place did you visit to the east of Cape Town?'
   '..'

7 'What do they call the region where they grow grapes for wine?'
   '..'

8 'Where was the lighthouse you visited?'
   '..'

9 'Where is the penguin colony?'
   '..'

10 'What is the name of the island where Nelson Mandela was in prison?'
   '..'

11 'Where did you go to return to the UK?'
   '..'

4

Islamabad, March 17th

Dear Qasim,

I am very glad to hear the business is going so well, and that Ahmed is giving you **some** help. He is a good boy and **any** father would be very proud to have such a son. **Some** people say that young people today are bad, but I don't agree. They aren't **any** worse than we were when we were teenagers.

Anyway, I'm writing to tell you that I have bought **some** land at Kallar Kahar, about 25 kilometres from Chakwal. Do you remember the place? I'd like **some** advice on what to do with it. It doesn't have **any** houses on it, but there are **some** old farm buildings and a small lake. I haven't got **any** money left to develop it, but I could borrow **some** from the bank. **Some** of my friends say that I should build **some** holiday cabins and rent them to tourists, and **some** say I should start a commercial orchard. Do you have **any** ideas?

I hope you will all be able to come and visit me **some** day soon.

Love and kisses to Anisha and all the children,
Mridul

❶ some as a determiner

We use **some** with *plural countable nouns* to mean *a number of something*:
- There were **some rabbits** in the field.

We also use **some** with *uncountable nouns* to mean *a quantity of something*:
- There is still **some tea** in the pot.

Although we usually make questions with **any**, we use **some** in questions when we are talking about a *quantity of something rare or unusual, or a specific quantity*:
- Have you got **some** fresh **figs**? That's great!
- Would you like **some coffee**?

❷ some as a pronoun

We can use **some** without a noun when it is clear from the context what we are talking about:
- I've got some money. Would you like to borrow **some**? (**some** = *some money*)
- Get yourself a cup of tea. There is **some** in the kitchen. (**some** = *some tea*)

We can use **some + more** without a noun:
- There are lots of strawberries left. Would you like **some more**?

We also use **some** as a pronoun to mean *some people*, often with **say** or **think**; this is more common in writing than in speech:
- **Some say** Robin Hood was a hero.
- **Some think** he was a criminal.

We use **some + of + determiner + plural / uncountable noun** when we are talking about *a quantity of something*:
- My teacher gave us **some of the** old exam **papers** to do.
- **Some of the lemonade** was spilt on the table.

❸ idiomatic expressions with some

In informal conversation we use **some + singular countable noun** to mean *an unknown item*:
- Paul's talking to **some woman** in the office. (*I don't know who she is.*)

We use *noun + of some kind* to mean *something of an unknown type*:
- He says there's **a problem of some kind.** (*I don't know what kind of problem.*)

14

Some time, with the two words separate, is used to mean *a long period of time*. It is often used with **for** or **ago**:

■ The Dawsons have been living in Australia **for some time**.
■ They left America **some time ago**.

❹ any as a determiner

We use **any** with *plural countable nouns* in questions and negatives:

■ Have you read **any books** about Charlemagne?
■ We did**n't** see **any eagles** in America. (= *We saw no eagles.*)

We also use **any** with *uncountable nouns* in questions and negatives:

■ Is there **any paper** in the printer?
■ There is**n't any ink** left.

We can use **any** with a *singular noun* to mean *an example of something, and it doesn't matter which*:

■ I'd like **any** CD by Bjork. I like them all.

❺ any as a pronoun

We also use **any** without a noun in negative sentences and questions, when it is obvious what we are talking about because of the context:

■ I had some tea but Jane did**n't** have **any**. (= *Jane had no tea / Jane had none.*)
■ John needs a good grammar book. Have you got **any**? (**any** = *any grammar books*)

We use **any** + **of** + *determiner* + *plural noun* when we are talking about *one, or none, of something*:

■ I didn't have **any of** those grapes. (= *I had no grapes.*)
■ Have you met **any of** my friends? (= *Have you met one of my friends?*)

❻ idiomatic expressions with any

We use **hardly any** to say *almost none of something*:

■ I've got **hardly any** spare time this week.
■ There's **hardly any** tea left.

We use **any** + **will do**, to mean *it doesn't matter which thing, anything is acceptable*:

■ I'm really hungry. **Any** sandwich **will do**. (= *I can eat any of the sandwiches.*)
■ **Any** bus going north **will do**. It doesn't matter which one.

We sometimes use **any** + **old** to mean *it doesn't matter which thing*:

■ Give me **any old** blanket. I'm freezing!

We use **not any** with a *comparative adjective* to mean *no more*:

■ The Toyota was**n't any more expensive** than the Ford. (= *was no more expensive*)
■ My cold is**n't any better** but at least it is**n't any worse**.

We often say something is **not any use**, or **not any good**, to mean *not useful* or *not effective*. We also use **any use / good** in questions:

■ I'm trying to lose weight. Is it **any use** giving up chocolate?
■ It isn't **any good** arguing with Stephen. He's very stubborn.

We use **not** + *verb* + **any more** / **any longer** to mean *something used to be the case but is not now*:

■ I do**n't** eat meat **any more**.
■ Paul is**n't** working **any longer**. He's retired.

A

Look at the picture and make questions and answers about what you can see, using the words in brackets. Remember to use **some** and **any**.

0 (be / there / ducks / on the pond?)

Are there any ducks on the pond? - Yes,
there are some ducks on the pond.

1 (be / there / flowers / in the garden?)

2 (be / there / people / playing tennis?)

3 (be / there / families / having picnics / on the grass?)

4 (be / there / boats / on the water?)

5 (be / there / children with / big red balloons?)

6 (be / there / rubbish / on the grass?)

7 (can / you / buy / food / in the park?)

8 (can / you / see / policemen / in the park?)

9 (be / there / boys / playing football?)

10 (be / there / ice / on the water?)

B

Write either **some** or **any** in each of the gaps in the following conversation.

ANNIE: I think I need (0) _some_ changes in my life. I don't seem to get (1) .... pleasure from my job (2) .... more. I'm thinking about starting a business of (3) .... kind.

JOSH: Business? I always thought you were quite happy as a journalist.

ANNIE: Well, I was, but (4) .... of the stories I have to cover are just so depressing. And (5) .... of them are so boring – and I'm bored with sitting at my desk all the time. I never meet (6) .... new people. I want to open a shop!

JOSH: A shop! That's cool! What would you sell?

ANNIE: Well, don't laugh, but I've always loved hats! I've got about ten of them! And there aren't (7) .... good hat shops in this town. Everyone needs a hat of (8) .... kind, for a wedding, or a special garden party, or just for (9) .... time, when it's cold.

JOSH: Do you think you could make (10) .... money from hats?

ANNIE: Well, I wouldn't make very much money, probably, but (11) .... things are more important than money! I'd love to have my own smart, little shop and I saw (12) .... shops for rent in Clayton Crescent.

JOSH: That's a really smart area. Aren't there (13) .... cheaper properties?

ANNIE: It wouldn't be (14) .... good having a shop in a poor area. Only rich people buy expensive hats!

C

Read the following passage and correct the errors. Some of the examples of **some** and **any** are correct. Tick the ones which are right. Circle and correct the ones which are wrong.

✔ *some*
⁰**Some** years ago I decided to go and visit ⁰(any) friends in Australia. After spending a couple of weeks with them in the city, I went travelling in Central Australia with ¹**any** local men as guides. The land we were travelling through was ²**some** of the driest in Australia, and there weren't ³**some** rivers or even streams for many miles. We had all brought flasks of water and, after a week, we still had ⁴**some** left. But our Land Rover also needed ⁵**any** water. It was steaming and hissing and, when we checked it, there was hardly ⁶**any** water left. We decided it wasn't ⁷**some** good continuing because the men said there wasn't ⁸**some** water for miles. What could we do? Well, the Australians have ⁹**any** amazing methods of getting water, but even they hadn't ¹⁰**some** suggestions. There weren't ¹¹**some** plants, nor ¹²**any** maggots to suck, so the only thing to do was to phone the nearest town on my mobile phone and to ask the police to send a helicopter with ¹³**any** water and other supplies. When the police arrived, they wanted me to go back with them and it wasn't ¹⁴**some** use arguing.

ANDREW: It's absolutely amazing – I had forgotten that **this** place was so incredible!

GRAHAM: I've never been here before. **This** is far bigger than I imagined. And look at **that** wall painting! It's so beautiful.

ANDREW: Wow! Let's look in the guidebook. ... Yes, **that**'s the House of the Small Fountain, and **this** one here is the House of the Large Fountain.

GRAHAM: **That**'s right. I was reading about **that** last night. But **this** is so much better than the book! You really get a feel of what Roman life was like!

ANDREW: Come on, let's go and look at the House of the Vettii. They say **that** it's the most complete and impressive example of a real Roman home.

GRAHAM: Oh, sure! Then I want to go and see the Amphitheatre. **This** is great!

❶ **this** and **these**

We use **this** with a singular or uncountable noun and **these** with a plural noun:
- I like **this** bright yellow **shirt** better than **these** dark green **shirts**.

We use **this** and **these** for *something that we are showing, or holding, or that is close to us*:
- **This car** is very fast. (*I am driving the car now.*)
- I bought **these shoes** in Venice. (*I am wearing the shoes now.*)

We use **this** and **these** to talk about *something closer to us than something else*. We often use **this** and **these** with **here**:
- **This house** is nicer than the house next door.
- I like **these ties here** better than those ties there.

We often say **this one** or **these ones** when we are referring to *another example of something* that we have already named:
- That book is better than **this one**. (**this one** = *this book*)
- Now those dancers run in front of **these ones**. (**these ones** = *these dancers*)

We use **this** and **these** when we are talking about *a time which is now, or close to the present*:
- I'm going to the theatre **this evening**.
- **This year** has been really hard for farmers.

We can use **this** and **these** without a noun when *it is clear from the situation what we are talking about*:
- **This** is cool! I love surfing. (= *This sport is such fun.*)

We also use **this** without a noun to refer to *the situation we are in now*:
- One of the tyres on the car is flat. **This** is very dangerous.

❷ idiomatic uses of **this**

When we speak informally, especially when we are telling a story, we often use **this** and **these** with a noun to mean *something important in the story*, when it is first mentioned:
- There was **this** man, and he was carrying **this** huge bag …
- … and then **these** planes flew right over the house.

We use **this** to *say who we are* on the telephone:
- Hello. **This** is Jake. Can I help you?

or to *introduce someone* to someone else:
- Phoebe, **this** is Mark. He works in the office with me.

❸ that and those

We use **that** with a singular or uncountable noun and **those** with a plural noun:
> ■ I love **those** beautiful, white **roses**.

We use **that** and **those** to refer to *something that is some distance away;* (often with **there**):
> ■ **Those** boots **there** in the hall are John's.

We often say **that one** or **those ones** when we are referring to *another example of something* which we have already named:
> ■ This laptop is cheaper than **that one**. (**that one** = *that laptop*)
> ■ I didn't want the red apples so I bought **those ones**. (**those ones** = *the green apples*)

We use **that** and **those** when we are talking about *a time which is in the past*:
> ■ My new mobile phone's much better than **that** big, old **thing** I used to have.

We can use **that** without a noun *when it is clear what we are talking about*:
> ■ **That**'s my **bike**, **there**, at the end of the street.
> ■ He said he wasn't angry, but I didn't believe **that**.

We often use **that** to *comment on something that someone has just said to you*:
> ■ 'Pompeii is wonderful.' '**That**'s true!'
> ■ 'There's been an earthquake!' '**That**'s terrible!'

We also use **that** to *comment on something amazing or surprising*:
> ■ Look at the sunrise. **That**'s wonderful!
> ■ This book costs £25. **That** is very expensive!

We use **that** in *relative clauses*:
> ■ I really enjoyed the book **that** you lent me.

We also use **that** when *reporting what people say or said*, or after expressions like **I'm sure** and **I'm afraid**:
> ■ They **say that** life begins at forty.
> ■ Maria **said that** she wanted a new dress.
> ■ **I'm sure that** I put my mobile phone in this bag.

(For more on relative clauses, see unit 62. For more on reporting speech, see unit 60.)

❹ idiomatic uses of that

When we are speaking informally and refer to *someone or something we all know about*, we often use **that + noun**:
> ■ Keith met **that boy** who used to work in the library.
> ■ Would you like to borrow **that book** I was reading last week?

We also use **not + that + *adjective***, informally, to mean *not very*:
> ■ Karen said that the ring was**n't that expensive**.
> (= ... *wasn't very expensive*.)
> ■ Don't be angry with Jerry! He was**n't that rude**.

We use **that** in questions when we *ask who or what someone or something is*.
> ■ 'Who's **that**?' 'It's my sister Gabriella.'
> ■ 'What's **that**?' 'It's a mouse.'

We use **who's that**, very informally, to *ask who we are speaking to* on the telephone:
> ■ I'm sorry I didn't hear what you said. **Who's that**?

A Read the following passage and circle the best alternative from the underlined words.

Susan is with her kids in a computer games shop ...

'I really like the design of (⁰those) / that new games packs. Look at ¹these / this one! The red and blue look really good together, and ²this / that silver one over there … it's great. And they're not ³these / that expensive. ⁴This / These prices are lower than in our local shop. It's worth travelling a bit when you can save ⁵that / those much money. Which one shall we buy? Do you like ⁶those / these platform games here, or ⁷those / these sport games there? I don't really like ⁸those / this fighting games very much. I'm sure ⁹that / this it isn't a good idea for people to play with violent games … though some people say ¹⁰this / that it isn't true that violent games are bad for people. They say ¹¹this / that it's a good way to use aggression safely. Oh look, let's buy ¹²these / this classic game from Gargantuan Games – *Dinah Dynamite*! It's not violent at all!'

B Andrew and Graham are looking in the motorcycle showroom for a new bike. Put the words in the box in the correct gaps.

that's	that	that one	this one	those	that	those	that	this man	~~this one~~
	that	that reliable	these		not that	this is	that old		

ANDREW: I really like the new Kawasaki range. What do you think of (0) *this one* ?

GRAHAM: Wow! It's massive! I can't afford such a big bike.

ANDREW: Neither can I! What about (1) ....? This is only a 250cc, but it looks pretty fast.

GRAHAM: It's cool! How much is it? I don't believe it! (2) .... very expensive!

ANDREW: Maybe we should go and have a look at (3) .... second-hand bikes over there. There are some nice classic bikes there. What do you think of (4) .... Norton there?

GRAHAM: It's a beauty! How much is it? Oh dear me! (5) .... is very expensive too! I suppose they are quite rare now.

ANDREW: I still prefer (6) .... bikes that we used to ride back in the seventies. (7) .... modern ones are too vulgar. And the colours! They're a bit bright.

GRAHAM: Oh, look! Here's an old Honda just like (8) .... that I used to ride! It's the same colour, too. Do you remember (9) .... summer when we went all the way down through Europe together?

that and those

ANDREW: Don't remind me! Your bike was great but mine was a disaster! It was (10) .... silver Enfield bike – it broke down every day! It looked great but it wasn't (11) .... Still, we met lots of nice people. I think it took us three weeks to get down to Greece!

GRAHAM: I met (12) .... yesterday who has a Motoguzzi. He said (13) .... it was the best bike he had ever had! Maybe you should get one, as they're (14) .... expensive.

ANDREW: No way! I don't want such a sporty bike. Now look at this Yamaha – (15) .... a fine bike.

C Read the telephone conversation between Peter Ross and Frank, the manager of a local restaurant. Find the wrong words and replace them with either **this**, **that**, or **those**. Some lines have two wrong words.

FRANK: Hello? I can't hear very well. Who's ~~here?~~ (0) _that_

PETER: Hello. I is Peter Ross, from Oakley Farm. (1) ....

FRANK: Oh, hello Mr Ross. What's your noise? (2) ....

PETER: That is just the noise of the packing machine. I'm calling from the packing room. I wanted to ask you about any cheque here. (3) ....

FRANK: What's there? I'm sorry, I can't hear you. (4) ....

PETER: Sorry. I'll turn off the machine. … Can you hear me now?

FRANK: Yes, I can, thanks. I had a message which said how you wanted to talk to me. Is he a bad time to talk? (5) .... (6) ....

PETER: No, it's fine. I just have the problem with your cheque. (7) ....

FRANK: Oh? What is the problem?

PETER: I'm afraid so it's not enough. I mean, I sent you 4 kilos of mushrooms and the cheque is for £3.60. (8) ....

FRANK: £3.60? Oh dear, that isn't enough money.

PETER: Yes. They weren't ordinary mushrooms! It were wild, organic mushrooms. (9) ....

FRANK: I'm terribly sorry, Mr Ross. We should have paid £36. We usually pay you £9 a kilo, don't we? Obviously it should have been £36. All is very embarrassing. (10) ....

PETER: Oh, I see! Don't worry. Here was an easy mistake to make. If you like, my wife and I could come and collect the money. Do you have a table for two this evening? (11) ....

6

It's a cold, miserable day here at the Rotherfield Stadium, but the match so far has been really exciting. Both teams are playing tremendously well. **They** are passing the ball with a lot of skill and imagination. **They** are giving **us** a real demonstration of magical football.

So far the score is still 0–0, but **we**'ve had a couple of exciting moments from Mark Hardcastle, **who** is playing particularly well today. ... Oh, and now Tim Franks is making a strong run down the right wing – **he** passes the ball to Hardcastle again - **he** really is the man of the match so far – and the ball shoots past **him** and ... oh ... **it** goes out of play.

Oh well, the fans are getting a lot of excitement today and **they** are obviously enjoying **it**! Can **you** hear **them** roar?

❶ what are pronouns?

A **pronoun** is a word that we use in place of a noun or noun phrase, *if it is clear who, or what, we are talking about.*

Pronouns often refer back to something that someone has just said:

> ■ Both teams are playing tremendously well. ~~Both teams~~ **They** are passing the ball with a lot of skill and imagination.
> ■ The fans are getting a lot of excitement today. Can you hear ~~the fans~~ **them** roar?

But often we also use pronouns to refer to people or things when it is obvious what we mean:

> ■ They are giving **us** a real demonstration of magical football. (**us** = *me and the other spectators*)

❷ subject pronouns

Subject pronouns are the subject of a sentence or a clause:

	singular	plural
first person	**I**	**we**
second person	**you**	**you**
third person	**he, she, it**	**they**

It is used for things; **they** is used for things or people; the rest are used for people:

> ■ My car is in the garage. **It** is ready to collect.
> ■ The mechanic phoned. **She** said it was ready.

We can use **you** to talk about people generally, meaning *everyone*:

> ■ **You** have to be very careful cycling in a city. (= *Everyone has to be careful ...*)

We can use **they** to talk about *someone* or *some people*:

> ■ **They**'ve stolen the radio from my car. (= *Someone has stolen ...*)

We only need one subject or one subject pronoun in each clause:

> ■ NOT ~~Mr Slater he is~~... **Mr Slater** is arriving at four. OR **He**'s arriving at four.

We often use **it** as the subject of a sentence (the **empty subject**) when we are talking about *time, weather, distances,* and *emotional responses to things*:

> ■ **It** wasn't time for the lesson yet.
> ■ **It**'s very hot today.
> ■ **It**'s a great pity you can't come to the party.

We use **there** as an *empty subject* when we are saying that *something exists*:

■ **There** was an awful smell of burning.
■ **There** are fifteen players in the team.

(For more on the empty subjects **there** and **it**, see unit 10.)

We can use **who**, **what**, and **which** as a subject pronoun in questions:

■ **Who** wants a chocolate?
■ **What** caused the accident?
■ **Which** costs more?

We use **who** and **which** for people, and **what** and **which** for things.
(For more on questions, see unit 58.)

We use **who**, **that**, and **which** to introduce a relative clause:

■ She's the person **who** walked all the way along the Great Wall of China.
■ There's the dog **that** bit my daughter.
■ Do you remember the restaurant **which** closed last year?

We use **that** for people or things.
(For more on relative clauses, see unit 62.)

❸ object pronouns

We use object pronouns as the object of a verb:

	singular	plural
first person	**me**	**us**
second person	**you**	**you**
third person	**him, her, it**	**them**

■ Have you seen my screwdriver? I need **it**.
■ I'm going to give **you** some advice. Don't give **him** anything!

In short answers, we use an object pronoun after **It is** / **was** or the object pronoun on its own:

■ 'What was that?' 'It was **him**.'/ '**Him**.' NOT ~~It was he~~.
■ 'Who's there?' 'It's **me**.'/ '**Me**.' NOT ~~It's I~~.

We also use **some** and **one** as object pronouns.
We use **some** to refer to *something that is uncountable or plural*:

■ I'm having some coffee. Would you like **some**?
■ Harry has got lots of books. He could lend us **some**.

We use **one** for a *single thing or person*:

■ I'm having a muffin. Would you like **one**?

❹ prepositions with object pronouns

We use object pronouns after *prepositions* (**at**, **to**, **with**, **for** etc):

■ 'Don't wait **for me**,' he said **to her**.
■ Frances went **with him** to the theatre.
■ Jill threw the water **at them**.

Look at these sentences:

■ Tom gave the flowers **to her**.
■ Ian bought a ring **for her**.

In sentences like these (*verb + object + to/for + object*) we can often put the second object pronoun immediately after the verb and leave out **to** or **for**:

■ Tom gave **her** the flowers.
■ Ian bought **her** a ring.

(For more on direct and indirect objects, see page 284.)

A Write the correct pronoun for each underlined noun in the following passage.

Andrew Markham wants to start a new hobby, so ⁰<u>Andrew Markham</u> goes to his local Adult Education College and looks at the brochure. ¹<u>The brochure</u> lists all the classes that are available this term. He sees something called Gamelan, but he doesn't know what ²<u>Gamelan</u> is. The description in the brochure says that ³<u>Gamelan</u> is an Indonesian musical form, that uses gongs and drums and a type of xylophone. ⁴<u>The brochure</u> says that students don't need to be experienced musicians, but that ⁵<u>students</u> need a good sense of rhythm and be prepared to take off their shoes and sit on the floor. He thinks this sounds just right for ⁶<u>Andrew</u> so he phones his wife, Sheila, and asks ⁷<u>Sheila</u> if ⁸<u>Sheila</u> would like to come with ⁹<u>Andrew</u> and try Gamelan.

'I think ¹⁰<u>Sheila</u> would love Gamelan,' he says to ¹¹<u>Sheila</u>. 'Go on! Why don't ¹²<u>Andrew and Sheila</u> sign up for the course?'

'But what about the children?' says Sheila, '¹³<u>Andrew and Sheila</u> would have to find a babysitter for ¹⁴<u>the children</u>.'

'That won't be a problem,' he says. 'It's really time we did something just for ¹⁵<u>Andrew and Sheila</u>!'

0 *he*	6	12
1	7	13
2	8	14
3	9	15
4	10	
5	11	

B Mary and Peter are looking through some brochures and planning a holiday. They haven't been away for over a year because they work very hard on their farm. They want a really good holiday now. Some subject and object pronouns are missing from their conversation. Put the right one from the box in each gap.

me   you   ~~it~~   we   he   him   us   who   me   it   you   we

MARY: I think (0) ...*it*... would be nice to go somewhere in the mountains.

PETER: (1) .... could go and visit my Uncle Thomas in Auckland.

MARY: Oh no! I don't get on with (2) .... very well. He doesn't like (3) .... either.

PETER: That's not true! He does like you. I don't know where (4) .... got that idea! He's a bit serious, but his wife and (5) ....are really very kind.

MARY: I'd rather stay in a hotel. And this holiday is supposed to be for (6) ....

PETER: Yes, but think of the money (7) .... could save!

MARY: I know, but (8) .... suggested this holiday? I think it was (9) ....

PETER: OK. Sorry. (10) ....'re right. You did suggest this holiday. What about this one, then, in the mountains?

MARY: Oh, it looks wonderful! And (11) ....'s very near where they filmed 'Lord of the Rings'! Let's go there!

(I, me, who)

C Paul and Steve are trying to make a chest of drawers from a kit. Read their conversation and put in the missing pronouns in the gaps.

0 STEVE: It says 'Fragile' on the box.
PAUL: Be careful with ......*it*...... !

1 STEVE: Are all the pieces there?
PAUL: Yes, I think ....'re all here.

2 STEVE: Where is my screwdriver?
PAUL: Here .... is.

3 STEVE: I can't find the large screws!
PAUL: I think you're sitting on .... !

4 STEVE: I hope this isn't going to be too difficult.
PAUL: .... looks quite simple.

5 STEVE: What's this bit for?
PAUL: I don't know what ....'s for. The instructions aren't very helpful.

6 STEVE: Have we got any wood glue?
PAUL: There was .... in the box.

7 STEVE: Put some glue on this long section first.
PAUL: I hope .... is enough glue!

8 STEVE: There seem to be three pieces like this.
PAUL: There should be four of ....

9 STEVE: Wow! This is really hard!
PAUL: They never told us ....would be so difficult.

D Put the underlined words in the correct order to complete Bob's answers.

0 ANN: Isn't it boring living in the country?
BOB: Oh no! / are / there / lots / to do / of / interesting / things /.

.....*There are lots of interesting things*..... .....*to do.*.....

1 ANN: What is there to do?
BOB: Well, there's the local farmer's market, / which / every Friday morning / is /.

2 ANN: What's that?
BOB: It's the market / that / go to / farmers / to sell what / they produce /.

3 ANN: What can you buy?
BOB: You can buy lovely fruit and vegetables / cheap / are / and fresh / that /.

4 ANN: What else?
BOB: Some farmers make their own sausages and bacon, and / are / who / cheese / some farmers / there / make /.

5 ANN: Do you like their home-made cheese?
BOB: Oh yes, / it / I / really love / !

6 ANN: Is it very expensive?
BOB: No! It costs less than cheese / buy / which / you / the / supermarket / in /.

7 ANN: Shall we go along tomorrow and have a look?
BOB: That would be great – and / our lunch there / could / we / buy /.

8 ANN: My mother is coming to visit tomorrow.
BOB: That's OK. / can buy / we / some flowers / for her /.

9 ANN: Can you get bread and cakes?
BOB: / organic bakery / there / a / fabulous / 's /.

10 ANN: It sounds amazing! What time shall we go?
BOB: / at / starts / a.m. / it / 6.30 / !

25

Peter Ross runs an organic farm with his wife Mary, producing fruit and vegetables, and dairy products. He is talking about his life on a local radio farming programme ...

INTERVIEWER: What was your childhood like?

PETER: Well, I remember **my** father carrying me on **his** back around **our** family farm, in Devon, explaining everything to me. And I remember that he drove **his** tractor, with me on **his** knee. I'm sure that's completely illegal now! He had **his** own particular smell – animals, and grain, and engine oil. It was great! I wonder if I smell like that now?

INTERVIEWER: And what about **your** mother?

PETER: She worked very hard, too, but mostly in the dairy and the kitchen. I don't think **my** wife Mary would like that! She's involved in everything on **our** farm.

INTERVIEWER: Why did you decide to run an organic farm?

PETER: It started when I was at agricultural college. **My** ambition was to run a small, organic farm. I believed that more and more people would want to pay a bit extra to protect **their** health and the environment. And when we saw **our** farm on the market we fell completely in love with it, and bought it. It was really cheap, because **its** doors and windows were all rotten – in fact, we had to replace all the wood, including the floors! But the view is absolutely wonderful and the people around here are great. **Our** neighbours – that's **their** field over there – are organic farmers too, so there's no danger of contamination.

INTERVIEWER: And now, the most important question – can you make a living like this?

PETER: Oh yes! We're doing quite well now. Some of **our** customers are the big stores and restaurants in Exeter and Plymouth. It hasn't been easy, but all farming is hard. But we are very proud of **our** business. It's **our** life's work, and the market is growing fast. There's plenty of room for more organic producers!

❶ what are possessive adjectives?

Possessive adjectives are words that go before a noun. We use them to talk about:

- *belongings*: Have you seen **my screwdriver**?
- *relationships*: Mike says that **his sister** is a film actress.
- *features*: **Your fingernails** are dirty.

They are:

singular	plural
my (= *belonging to me*)	**our** (= *belonging to us*)
your (= *belonging to you*)	**your** (= *belonging to you*)
his, her (= *belonging to him or her*)	**their** (= *belonging to them*)
its (= *belonging to something*)	

Note: Possessive **its** does not have an apostrophe (NOT ~~it's~~). We use **it's** to mean *it is*.

We also use **your** when we are talking about something belonging to *anyone* or *everyone*:

- At a job interview **your** clothes are very important. (= *Everyone's clothes are important.*)

The possessive adjective is singular or plural depending on the <u>possessor</u>, not on the noun that follows it:

- <u>Mary</u> keeps **her hats** in the top cupboard.
- <u>The students</u> put **their essays** on the desk.

The possessive adjective always goes before other adjectives:

- I really like **his** old, French, theatre **posters**.

❷ possessive adjectives with a / an and the

We don't use **the** before a possessive adjective:

- Do you know **her** friend? NOT ~~Do you know the her friend?~~
- **His** house is the biggest in the street. NOT ~~The his house is the biggest in the street.~~

We don't use **a** / **an** before a possessive adjective. To talk about *an example of something, not the only one*, we can use:

> **one of** + **my** / **your** / etc. + *noun*:
> - I've lost **one of my** shoes. NOT ~~I've lost a my shoe.~~
> - **One of our teachers** has left the school. NOT ~~An our teacher has left ...~~
>
> or, **a** + *noun* + **of** + *possessive pronoun* (*mine* / *yours* / etc):
> - I've lost a **shoe of mine**.
> - **A teacher of ours** has left the school.

❸ possessive adjectives with **this**, **that** etc.

We don't use a possessive adjective immediately after *this*, *that*, *these*, or *those*; we must make another clause or sentence:

> - This is my brother. He's called Simon. NOT ~~This my brother is called Simon.~~
> - That's his wife, who's called Flora. NOT ~~That his wife is called Flora.~~

But with questions with *be* we can use *this*, *that* etc. followed by a possessive adjective to *ask about the identity of something*:

> - Are **these our** seats?

❹ possessive adjectives with quantifiers (**a few**, **some**, **both** etc)

If we want to use a *quantifier*, we must use **of** before the possessive adjective:

> - **Some of their** friends are Welsh.

But we can usually use **both** and **all** before a possessive adjective, with or without **of**:

> - **Both her** cousins are here. = **Both of her** cousins are here.
> - They've spent **all their** money. = They've spent **all of their** money.

(For more on quantifiers, see units 49 and 50.)

❺ possessive adjectives with parts of the body

When we are talking about parts of the body, we use possessive adjectives:

> - John said that **his legs** were aching.
> - When the children came in from the snow, **their faces** were very red.

When we are talking about a problem with a part of the body, such as an injury or an illness, we don't always use the possessive adjective. In some expressions we use **on** / **in** + **the** + *noun*:

> - Paul has a cut **on his foot**. = Paul has a cut **on the foot**.
> - Philip hit Andy **in his face**. = Philip hit Andy **in the face**.

❻ possessives with **own**

When we want to stress that *something belongs to someone*, we use **own** after the possessive adjective:

> - I've got **my own** pencil, thank you.
> - Karen doesn't have to share her room with Laura. Laura has **her own** room, next door.

We can use a *possessive adjective* + **own** like a pronoun:

> - You can read that newspaper. I've got **my own**. (= *my newspaper*)
> - We don't need to borrow sheets. We've brought **our own**. (= *our sheets*)

A There are 15 possessive adjectives in the following passage. Write down who, or what, each one refers to, at the bottom.

Graham Hampton writes:

[0]<u>My</u> favourite new book this week is 'The Sari', by Professor Daniel Miller and Dr Mukulika Banerjee. The two authors have different specialisations: [1]<u>his</u> field is culture studies, while [2]<u>her</u> interest is in politics, but both authors felt that [3]<u>their</u> book would be an excellent way to teach people about contemporary Indian women and [4]<u>their</u> daily lives.

'We wanted the book to be a serious academic work, but also we wanted it to be interesting to [5]<u>our</u> non-academic readers,' said Prof Miller.

Dr Banerjee said, 'Putting on the sari is just the beginning. Because of [6]<u>its</u> flexibility you can wear it in different ways during the day to change [7]<u>your</u> appearance and to respond to different environments. There is a kind of conversation between a woman and [8]<u>her</u> sari.'

[9]<u>Their</u> book is very original because one aspect of [10]<u>its</u> subject is people and [11]<u>their</u> clothes – what makes people feel comfortable and stylish, and how a simple thing like choosing clothes can be very significant in many ways.

Prof Miller said, 'We think that a book about how people feel about [12]<u>their</u> clothing will appeal to almost anyone. I think that some people will buy the book for the quality of [13]<u>its</u> photography and design alone, and then they may become interested in [14]<u>our</u> text.'

0 *Graham Hampton's*   8 ....
1 ....   9 ....
2 ....   10 ....
3 ....   11 ....
4 ....   12 ....
5 ....   13 ....
6 ....   14 ....
7 ....

(my, his)

B Mr Patterson, Managing Director of *Gargantuan Games Plc*, has called a meeting. Read the conversation and circle the correct word.

MR PATTERSON: Now, as you know, we aren't doing very well and (0) **our** / **us** sales figures have been going down and down. We need to look very carefully at (1) **ours** / **our** development methods and marketing. Now, Heinrich, will you and Francis work together? OK, (2) **you** / **your** team will study (3) **our** / **us** design and development process.

HEINRICH: Fine. Can I also ask Penny to join (4) **me** / **my** team as she's more experienced in software development?

MR PATTERSON: Yes, of course. That's a great idea. (5) **Her** / **She's** experience on the 'Starfighter' project will be really useful. And we need someone to look at (6) **ours** / **our** marketing methods. Alice?

ALICE: I'd like to do that. (7) **I'm** / **My** interest is mainly in advertising and market research. ... But can I have Gerry in (8) **my** / **her** team?

MR PATTERSON: Would you like to work on (9) **she** / **her** team, Gerry? I think it would be great to have a salesperson in Alice's team.

GERRY: Sure. That would be fine. And we need a third person ... what about Steve? I heard he was bored with (10) **he's** / **his** job.

MR PATTERSON: No, I don't think (11) **her** / **his** experience would be useful. Now, let's discuss a schedule for the reports.

C Choose the right possessive adjective from the box to write in each gap in the text.

| my   our   ~~his~~   their   my   his   their   my   her   your   his   their |

Andrew Markham is a teacher of electronic engineering at the University of Pentland. Last night he took home a lot of (0) *his* students' exam papers to mark, but Bob, (1) .... son, knocked the whole pile of papers off the table onto the floor.

'Oh Bob! What have you done to (2) .... papers? They're all mixed up on the floor,' he shouted, trying to pick them all up again.

'Be careful, Dad – some of (3) .... papers have got mixed up with (4) .... students' essays! The robotics teacher just gave us (5) .... assignment and I've just started working on it! And we have to hand it in next week,' he said, 'How many essays did you have, Dad?'

Andrew looked at his list. 'I don't know. I think my students all handed in (6) .... essays – so there must be 12. And the essay had to be 3,000 words – so that's at least two pages ...' he tried to remember.

'They should have put (7) .... name on each page, shouldn't they?' asked Bob.

Andrew laughed. 'They should – but I don't know if they have. And they used computers, so you can't even recognise (8) .... handwriting.'

'I'm really sorry, Dad. I'll help you sort them out,' said Bob, picking up some of the papers.

'OK, Derek Smith, page 1, and here's (9) .... second page, ... and this one is Jenny Franklin's. Is this (10) .... second page?'

Andrew groaned. 'I should have put them all in a box file. I suppose it's (11) .... fault really.'

29

Sharks

*I've always thought sharks are like robots. They don't seem to have a soul. **Sharks'** eyes are cold and mechanical, just looking around for something to eat. They have no predators, so they fear nothing but hunger. A **shark's** teeth are perfectly formed to catch whatever is most common in the waters where it lives, and the teeth hook the prey so it can't get away. A shark has an extra sense – it can pick up electrical pulses in the water using a sensor on its nose. It can't stop swimming; it needs to move all the time because otherwise it will drown, so it can never sleep or even rest. The skin **of the shark** is cold and smooth and dull, and its fins are smooth and pointed and cruel. I think this is why the **shark's** reputation is so bad. It looks so absolutely evil!*

❶ possessives with people

When we want to say that *someone has something*, we add **'s** to the end of the name of the person:
- I like **Steve's** new haircut. (*Steve has a new haircut.*)

If the name has a final **s** in the singular, we usually add **'s**:
- **Dennis's** badminton racket was broken.

But with some *foreign or old-fashioned names* that end with **s**, we just add **'**:
- **Socrates'** reputation is growing.
- That was Guy **Fawkes'** house.

We can add **'s** to a name made up of *more than one word*:
- I met the **supermarket manager's** wife.
- **My mother-in-law's** house was burgled.

When we want to talk about *things owned by two or more people*, we add **'** to the final **s**:
- The **students'** papers were all handed in. (= *the papers belonging to all the students*)
- The two **girls'** luggage was in the hall. (= *the luggage belonging to the two girls*)

But if we talk about more than one person by name, we use **'s** on the last name:
- **Marc and Yvette's** house is near Toulouse.

If the noun has an *irregular plural* (i.e. doesn't end in **s**) we use **'s**:
- Have you ever been to The **People's** Palace?
- The **children's** room has been decorated.

If we want to describe *something unusual and different* about a person, we can use the **of** form to indicate something special:
- Pavarotti has the voice **of an angel**!
- Stephanie has the hands **of an artist**.

We can choose to put the noun before the person if we want to *stress who the item belongs to*:
- The ring is **Frank's**. (= *It's Frank's ring.*)

and we can answer a question with just the name and **'s**:
- 'Whose is this letter?' **'Madeleine's.'** (= *It's Madeleine's letter.*)

If we want to say that *someone owns more than one of something*, we can use two possessives – **of** and **'s**:
- Robin was reading a novel of **Peter's**. (*Peter has several novels.*)
- I borrowed a pair of gloves of **Sue's**. (*Sue has more than one pair.*)

❷ possessives with animals

When we want to talk about *parts of an animal* or *something belonging to an animal*, we usually use **'s** after the name of the *animal* or **'** after the *animals*:

- Your **dog's tail** is very long.
- The **donkeys' field** is behind the house.

We can use **of** + **a** / **an** + *animal*, if we are talking generally about a *species* and not about a particular individual animal, or if we are writing scientific English:

- This bag is made from **the skin of a muskrat**. (= *It's made from a muskrat's skin.*)
- The **brain of a dolphin** is bigger than a man's. (= *A dolphin's brain is bigger than a man's.*)

❸ possessives with things

When we want to talk about *a part of something or something belonging to something*, we usually use **of** + **a** / **the** / **my** etc. + **noun**:

- The **handle of the drawer** is damaged.
- The **branch of a tree** had fallen on the roof.

When we speak informally about *a part of a specific thing*, we can often use the **'s** ending after the particular thing (e.g. **the car**, **the book**):

- The **car's rear wheel** came off. (= *The rear wheel of the car came off.*)
- I spilled coffee on **the book's cover**. (= *I spilled coffee on the cover of the book.*)

When we are talking about a common object we often use two nouns (**shoe lace, door handle**) without **'s** or **of the**, and with the first noun describing the second:

- The **bathroom window** is open. NOT ~~The bathroom's window ...~~
- I've lost my **pen lid**. NOT ~~... my pen's lid.~~

If we want to talk about *one of several things that are a part of something*, we use **one of the** + *plural noun* followed by **of** + *article* + *noun*:

- **One of the pages of the book** was missing.

If we are talking about *the position of something or a part of something*, we use **of**:

- The vase is in **the middle of the table**. NOT ~~the table's middle~~ NOR ~~the table middle~~
- Gavin sat in **the back of the car**. NOT ~~in the car's back~~ NOR ~~in the car back~~

We use **'s** or **s'** with things *connected with particular times*:

- I bought **yesterday's newspaper**.
- Dana is still wearing **last year's fashion**.

and also when we want to say *how long things take*:

- It's **five minutes' walk** to the station.
- Penny is taking **ten days' holiday**.

❹ pronunciation of possessive endings (**'s** and **s'**)

The pronunciation of **'s** follows the same rules as plural noun endings:

- I trod on the **cat's** tail. (pronounced kæts)
- I've lost the **dog's** collar. (pronounced dɒgz)
- This is the **mouse's** cage. (pronounced maʊsɪz)

(For more on the pronunciation of noun plurals, see page 290.)

The pronunciation of **s'** is usually the same as that of **'s**:

- The **cooks'** aprons were covered in flour. (pronounced kʊks)
- Sam was marking the **pupils'** work. (pronounced pjuːplz)

But note that when we say the possessive form of names ending with **s** or **z**, we pronounce the ending **ɪz**:

- I like Mrs **Jones's** new car. (pronounced dʒəʊnzɪz)
- **Cortez'** ship was sunk. (pronounced kɒːtezɪz)

A Read the following story and write the correct form of the possessive ('s, s', or of), if needed, using the words in brackets. More than one answer may be possible, and sometimes the order of the words must be changed.

It's ⁰(**my sister / birthday**) next week and I decided to organise a surprise birthday party for her. I used ¹(**Paul / computer**) to print out invitations. I put a picture of a cat on the invitations, because my sister loves cats, and the ²(**tail / cat**) had a bow around it. ³(**The printer / his computer**) had run out of ink, so I had to take the floppy disk over to ⁴(**Harry / house**) to print them out on his printer. I printed out 25 invitations and he showed me how to put in a list of names so I didn't have to put in ⁵(**everyone / name**) separately. It would have taken me hours! They looked great when they were done and he even printed out all the envelopes with all the ⁶(**addresses / guests**). I went out to the postbox to post them, and on the way I met the ⁷(**next door neighbour / daughter**). In the end I had to invite her too, and her boyfriend. When I came back I went round to the ⁸(**back / the house**) so I wouldn't meet any more neighbours! Only I didn't have the ⁹(**key / back door**) so I tried to climb in through the ¹⁰(**kitchen / window**) – and just as I was lying there with my legs sticking out of the window I heard a ¹¹(**man / voice**) shouting 'Eh, what do you think you're doing!' and I felt ¹²(**hand / someone**) grabbing my foot. I couldn't move either way so I tried to explain the situation. He let me go eventually and I went and opened the door, and sure enough, there was my neighbour! He expected me to thank him for his thoughtful act! They are a terrible family.

0 *my sister's birthday*
1
2
3
4
5
6

7
8
9
10
11
12

B Sarah phones her friend Angela. Rewrite the underlined phrases correctly.

SARAH: Hello Angela? Oh, thank goodness you're at home. I really need some help!

ANGELA: Sarah? What's the matter?

SARAH: ⁰A tree's branch has fallen on my car. They've taken the car to the garage to repair it, and I've lost ¹the coat of Jack. He must have left it ²in the car back. It's ³half an hour walk to the garage and he hasn't got another coat. I can't leave him at home on his own, and it's freezing today.

ANGELA: Do you want me to go to the garage? I'm afraid I can't take ⁴Paul car.

SARAH: No, no, I just wondered if you could lend me one of ⁵the coats of Sam. They're about the same size, aren't they?

ANGELA: Oh yes, of course you can! Was any other damage done when the branch fell onto the car?

SARAH: Well, it was the ⁶big oak tree's branch at ⁷my house the front. It almost fell onto the ⁸conservatory of our neighbour. The only other damage was to the ⁹kennel of the dog, by the porch, but fortunately the dog was in the kitchen at the time.

ANGELA: You were very lucky there wasn't more serious damage! Anyway, don't worry, I'll bring Sam's coat over right away! It's only ¹⁰<u>two minutes walk</u> to your house. We can have a cup of coffee before you go out, if you like!

SARAH: Oh yes, that would be lovely. Thank you so much! See you soon!

0	*A tree branch / The branch of a tree*	7	
1		8	
2		9	
3		10	
4		11	
5		12	
6			

Look at the pictures of Ian and Therese's house and say what each thing belongs to, or is part of, using either **'s, s', of the,** or **of a.**

0 the double-bass?
   It's Ian's double-bass.

1 the music?
   It's .... music.

2 the fur
   ....

3 the leg?
   ....

4 shoes?
   ....

5 glasses?
   ....

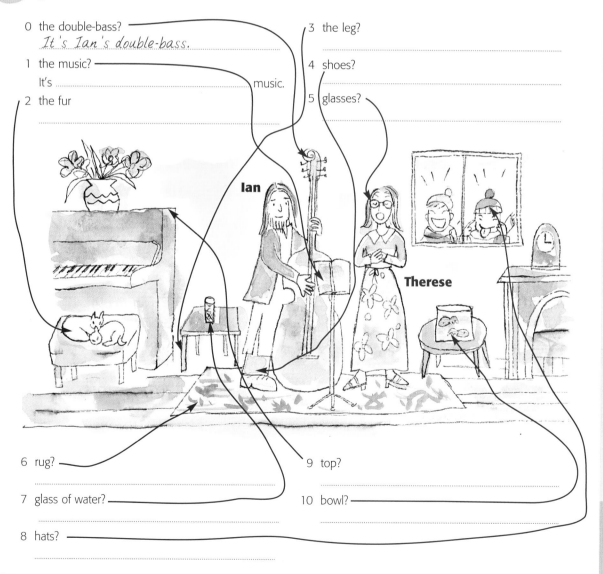

6 rug? ....

7 glass of water? ....

8 hats? ....

9 top? ....

10 bowl? ....

9

I'm singing to **myself**, wondering whether she's **mine**.
You're sitting by **yourself**, hoping she's **yours**.
He's looking at **himself** in the mirror, talking to his reflection.
She's thinking about **herself**, knowing she'll soon be **his**.
We all want to be loved, and we all need to belong to someone,
but we need to be **ourselves** ...

❶ possessive pronouns (mine, yours etc)

We use possessive pronouns (e.g. **mine**, **yours**, **his**) in the place of a noun phrase (e.g. **my house**, **his shoe**), usually to talk about *something that belongs to someone*:

- This house is **mine**. (= *This house is my house.*)
- Is this Sarah's camera? Yes, it's **hers**. (= *Yes, it's her camera.*)

These are the possessive pronouns:

	singular	plural
first person	**mine**	**ours**
second person	**yours**	**yours**
third person	**his, hers**	**theirs**

Note: We don't use **its** as a possessive pronoun, because a thing does not actually possess anything:

- 'Is this CD case for this CD?' 'Yes, it is.' NOT '~~Yes, it's its~~.'

The possessive pronoun is singular or plural depending on the possessor:

- Are those children <u>Jane</u>'s? Yes, they're **hers**.
- Is this game <u>Tom and Michael</u>'s? Yes, it's **theirs**.

When we want to say that *something is one of a number of things belonging to someone*, we say **one / some / two** etc. + **of** + *possessive pronoun*:

- That sock is **one of his**. (*He has more than one sock.*)
- I think these are **two of yours**. (*You have more than two.*)

We can also use a possessive pronoun as the subject of the verb:

- **Mine** was the blue car. (= *My car was the blue car.*)
- **His** was the one with the massive tyres.

If we want to stress the fact that something is owned by someone, we can use a possessive adjective (**my**, **your**, **his**, **her**, **our**, **your**, **their**) with **own**, in the place of a possessive pronoun:

- The DVD player is **my own**. (= *The DVD player is mine.*)
- The flat is **her own**. (= *The flat is hers.*)

(For more on possessive adjectives, see unit 7.)

❷ reflexive pronouns (myself, yourself etc)

We usually use reflexive pronouns (e.g. **myself**, **yourself**, **himself**) as an object when the <u>subject</u> and the object refer to the same person or thing:

- <u>Jack</u> must learn to control **himself**. (= *Jack must learn to control Jack.*)
- <u>We</u> washed **ourselves** in the waterfall.
- <u>That oven</u> cleans **itself**!

These are the reflexive pronouns:

	singular	plural
first person	**myself**	**ourselves**
second person	**yourself**	**yourselves**
third person	**himself, herself, itself**	**themselves**

Note: There are no reflexive verbs in English as there are in some other languages. We only use a reflexive pronoun when we want to specify that the object of the verb is the same as the subject.

Some common verbs can be used without a pronoun because we know that the meaning is reflexive:

> ▧ I always **wash** and **dress** before breakfast. (= *I wash and dress myself.*)

But with most verbs we need to use a pronoun after the verb to show that we are using the verb reflexively. Compare these examples:

reflexive	not reflexive
▧ David convinced **himself** that he was right.	He convinced **me**, too.
▧ Andy and Helen surprised **themselves** by winning.	They surprised **us**, too.

❸ reflexive pronouns in idiomatic phrases

The following are some verbs which are used idiomatically with a reflexive pronoun:

> **behave yourself** = *be polite, do the appropriate things*:
> ▧ I hope the kids will **behave themselves**!
> **enjoy yourself** = *be happy, have fun*:
> ▧ Dan really **enjoyed himself** at the barbecue.
> **help yourself to** = *give yourself* (*food and drink*):
> ▧ **Help yourselves to** more pudding!
> **not let yourself** = *not allow yourself to*:
> ▧ Jane **didn't let herself** get too worried when she couldn't find her keys.

To talk about *things people do for themselves*, we use **to** / **for** + *reflexive pronoun*:

> ▧ He bought a cup of coffee **for himself**.

We can leave out the preposition **to** or **for** before the reflexive pronoun if we put the reflexive pronoun immediately after the verb. We can only do this if it is obvious that we are not using the verb reflexively:

> ▧ I bought **myself** a cup of coffee. (*Obviously I did not buy myself!*)
> ▧ Sam cooked **himself** some pancakes. (*Obviously he did not cook himself!*)
> ▧ We gave **ourselves** a reward. (*Obviously we did not give ourselves!*)

We can use the reflexive pronoun, idiomatically, after a preposition with certain words:

> ▧ We must learn to **think for ourselves**. (= *to not accept other people's opinions without thinking.*)
> ▧ You will need to **look after yourself**. (= *to not rely on others doing things for you.*)
> ▧ Geraldine always **pays for herself**. (= *She does not let anyone buy things for her.*)
> ▧ Yuri is very **sure of himself**. (= *He is confident and knows his own value.*)

By myself / **yourself** / etc. is an idiom meaning *alone*:

> ▧ Lucy goes swimming **by herself**.
> ▧ My nephew and niece travelled to Cologne **by themselves**.

If we want to *stress the identity of the person we are talking about*, we use the reflexive pronoun at the end of the sentence. In this case the pronoun is not necessary except for emphasis:

> ▧ I don't really like chocolate, **myself**.
> ▧ Keith paid for it **himself**.

We also use reflexive pronouns to *stress the identity of the person we are talking about*, after *comparing words* (e.g. **like**, **except for**):

> ▧ I arrived late. There was a seat for everyone, **except** (**for**) **myself**.
> ▧ Well, sir, this car was designed for drivers **like yourself**.

possessive and reflexive pronouns (mine, myself)

A Write in the correct pronoun in the gaps in the following text.

It's Friday afternoon and Karen is ready to go home ...

'Oh good! The wages are here. Now which envelope is (0) _mine_? It's great! My very first wage packet! And I earned it all (1) .... Which one is (2) ...., Annie? The other one must be for Steve. Yes, this one's (3) .... It's much bigger than (4) .... because he earns more than we do. Everyone else seems to be working late. They're crazy! They don't enjoy (5) .... enough! What shall we do this evening? Shall we go to the cinema? I don't want to go by (6) .... We could have something to eat at your house, or at (7) .... if you don't want to cook. I think we should give (8) .... a treat as it's the end of our first week. Shall we have a lovely big plate of spaghetti? You can forget about your diet tonight. I forget about (9) .... every Friday!'

B Mark is trying to sort out the belongings of the guests at the end of a party. Lucy replies to what Mark says. Write what she says, using the clues in brackets and a possessive pronoun.

0 MARK: This hat belongs to Kate.
LUCY: (yes)
Yes, it's hers.

1 MARK: The green coat belongs to Ian.
LUCY: (yes)
....

2 MARK: I think the white scarf belongs to Harry.
LUCY: (no)
....

3 MARK: Do these gloves belong to you?
LUCY: (no)
....

4 MARK: ... and look at these bright pink shoes! Are they Polly's?
LUCY: (no, me)
....

5 MARK: This bag looks like it might belong to Anthea.
LUCY: (yes)
....

6 MARK: Are these two sweaters Sanjit and Halima's?
LUCY: (no)
....

7 MARK: Maybe they belong to us?
LUCY: (yes)
....

8 MARK: Is this furry hat the one your mother gave you?
LUCY: (no)
....

9 MARK: And these black gloves – who do they belong to?
LUCY: (you)
....

10 MARK: Do these boots belong to Phil?
LUCY: (yes)
....

pronouns (mine, myself)

C Read the dialogue. Underline the mistakes and write the correct word on the right.

0 STEPHEN: My exam results come out today. You've already got <u>your</u>. I'm really nervous! I'm not at all sure that I've passed. ....*yours*....

1 MARIE: Oh don't be silly! I'm sure your results will be better than my. ....

2 STEPHEN: Jenny has got her, too. Oh, I hate waiting. I really don't want to have to take the exam again. ....

3 MARIE: I know! I was worried about that. I didn't want to have to do the exams again by my, when everyone else is on holiday. ....

4 STEPHEN: Oh thanks, you're really cheering me up! What about Rajiv's exams? Did he pass himself? ....

5 MARIE: Oh, I don't know. I think he did alright, but not great. He doesn't let him get too upset about exams. ....

6 STEPHEN: My sociology course was great, and I really enjoyed me this term. It was nice to do something a bit different. ....

7 MARIE: I prefer medicine, my. I can't see the point in Social Sciences. ....

8 STEPHEN: I don't think you can be a very good doctor if you don't know anything about people. I want to help other people; I'm not doing it for my.
....

9 MARIE: We all have to make our own choices. Your is to be a family doctor, and mine is to be a surgeon. ....

D The girls are trying to pack to go home but their belongings are all mixed up. Match the sentences in the two columns.

0 Do these shoes belong to Susie?

1 Look at this horrible red and green sweater.

2 Are these Jane's trousers?

3 I'm sure this shirt is yours.

4 That sweater is mine.

5 No one wants this coat.

6 Which of those socks are mine?

7 Pick up all those sheets and pillows!

8 This soap came from the boys' room.

9 These towels belong to Paula and Georgina.

10 What about these packets of sweets?

A. No, that shirt's definitely not mine.

B. Yes, I think it's theirs.

C. They must be ours!

D. Don't be rude! My mother knitted that herself.

E. No, it's not yours, it's mine – I packed it myself.

F. Do it yourself!

G. Yes, I think they're hers.

H. But you were wearing it yourself in the rain yesterday.

I. I think these blue ones are yours.

J. No. Hers were the ones with the thick soles.

K. They should fold them themselves.

0	*J*	3	......	6	......	9	......
1	...	4	......	7	......	10	.....
2	...	5	......	8	......		

NEWTONIAN PHYSICS

At the beginning of the 20th century **there** were six assumptions that physicists made about physics. Because of these assumptions, **it** was very difficult for them to accept new ideas. Here's a list of what they were sure of:

1. **there** is a framework of absolute time and space, and the universe exists within it, like a giant machine.

2. **there** is always a cause for motion. If something moves, you can always discover what is causing the motion.

3. **if** you know how something is moving, **it** is possible to know how it was moving in the past or will be moving in the future. This is 'determinism'.

4. **there** are two physical models which represent energy in motion: one is as a particle, and the other is like a wave. **It** is impossible for anything to have both properties.

5. **it** is possible to measure the properties of anything, like its temperature or speed. They thought atomic systems were the same.

It was discovered eventually that all six assumptions were wrong. The group of physicists in the photograph were the first to realise this. **There** was a meeting at the Metropole Hotel in Brussels on 24th October 1927 which they all attended. After that, physics has never been the same!

❶ there with be

We use **there**, as a subject pronoun, with a singular or plural form of **be** when we say that *something exists*. **There** doesn't add anything to the meaning of the simple sentence:

- **There is** a big green beetle on your hair! (= *A big green beetle is on your hair.*)
- **There are** lots of insects in the forest. (= *A lot of insects are in the forest.*)
- **There was** a dog barking inside the house. (= *A dog was barking inside the house.*)

We also use **there** when we are saying *how many things* there are:

- I hope **there are** 52 cards in the pack.
- **There are** 12 people coming for dinner.

We can use **there** as the subject, when *we are not talking about a specific thing or person*, with **no**, **anyone**, **someone** etc:

- **There** are **no** empty chairs in the hall.
- Is **there anyone** listening to me?

❷ there with other verbs

We can use **there** as the subject of the verbs **seem** or **appear**, with **to be** + *noun phrase*:

- **There seems to be** some misunderstanding.
- There **doesn't appear to be** any paper in the photocopier.

We can also use the empty subject **there** with *modal verbs*, with **be** + *noun phrase*:

- **There might be** snow tonight.
- I think **there should be** equal pay for women.

When we are talking about what we think about the future, we often use there after a verb like **hope**, **wish**, **expect** etc:

- **I hope there** won't be any violence in the film.
- **I expect there** will be a storm this evening.

❸ it with be

We use **it** as the subject of a singular form of **be**, when we are talking about *distance*, *the weather*, *temperature*, or *time*:

- **It's** six or seven miles to the nearest town.
- **It was** very sunny last week.
- **It'll be** too hot if we shut the door.
- **It was** about three o'clock when the boat arrived.

We often use **it** with **be**, at the beginning of a sentence, to refer to <u>something</u> *later in the same sentence*:

- 'Who was that person on the phone?' '**It** was <u>my uncle</u>.'

We use **it** + **be** + *adjective* to give *our opinion* or to emphasise *how we feel about something later in the sentence*:

- **It's important** to tell the truth.
- **It was terrible** to see how thin he was!
- **It was** really **lovely** when he gave me those flowers!
- I think **it's great** that he's decided to have a long holiday from work.

❹ it with other verbs

We can use **it** as the empty subject with the verbs **rain** and **snow**, describing the *weather*:

- **It rained** all last night.
- I think **it's going to snow** this afternoon.

We can also use **it** as an empty subject with verbs describing a *perception* or *impression* (e.g. **looks as if**, **sounds as if**, **smells of**, **feels as if**):

- **It looks as if** the train is late.
- **It smells of** incense in here.

We use **it** with **looks like**, **seems**, or **appears** to talk about *something probable*:

- **It looks like** it's going to rain.
- **It seems** that he was a spy!

We can use **it** as an empty subject with **is said**, or **is thought**, or **is believed** to talk about *what other people say or think about something*:

- **It was thought that** Picasso lived here for a while.
- **It is said that** the Yeti really exists.

We often use *verb* + **it** + **when** when we comment on *how something makes us feel*:

- **I loved it when** he asked her to marry him!
- James **hated it when** the clowns came in!

A

Put either there or it in the gaps in the following text.

(0) *There* was a circus in our town last week.
(1) .... was really exciting to see the lorries and caravans driving down the High Street. The circus people set up their camp on some rough land at the edge of town and (2) .... was amazing to watch them set up the enormous tent for the show.
(3) .... were about twenty caravans, and, as
(4) .... was really hot, they put all their animals out in the open. (5) .... were some beautiful white Arab horses, some tiny dogs and some ducks.
(6) .... weren't any lions or elephants as
(7) .... is illegal to make wild animals perform for people now. I think (8) .... 's good that it's illegal, because I can remember seeing a bear dancing and I remember thinking that (9) .... was horrible to see a wonderful, big animal suffer like that! I don't know what the ducks did in the show, but I think (10) ....
must have been very funny to watch them!

B

Read the following dialogue and choose the right phrase, from the box, to put in the gaps after it or there.

rains   not too late   were a lot of   ~~cruel to make~~
easy to feed   's a picture   aren't any
horrible to keep   were some lovely   seems to be
so frightening

Sam and Keira are talking outside the circus tent ...

SAM: Are you going to the circus?

KEIRA: I want to, but my mum says it's (0) *cruel to make* animals perform.

SAM: But there (1) .... animals! Only horses and dogs! That's not cruel!

KEIRA: She says it's (2) .... them shut in caravans all the time.

SAM: But when I went past the field I saw all the animals out on the grass. There (3) .... white horses!

KEIRA: There (4) .... ducks too! What do they do?

SAM: I don't know. Ducks aren't very clever. I think it must be a comedy act.

KEIRA: I doubt if you could train them to do anything. I wonder where they keep them if it (5) ....?

SAM: There must be a special tent for them to live in. It's (6) .... animals that eat grass!

KEIRA: I love the jugglers and the trapeze artists! It's (7) .... when they climb so high up. There (8) .... of trapeze artists swinging on a rope on the poster.

SAM: There (9) .... a queue at the box office. I hope it's (10) .... to get a ticket.

there and it

C Sam and Keira are talking about the circus after they have seen it. Make sentences using the words in brackets and **there** or **it**. Sometimes you may need to add another word.

0 (really funny / when the ducks came in)

   It was really funny when the ducks came in.

1 (enormous tent / in the field)

2 (very exciting / when the trapeze artist climbed to the top)

3 (I / not / like / when the clowns were fighting)

4 (lots of people / watching the show)

5 (looked as if / the trapeze artist was going to fall)

6 (ice creams / for sale in the interval)

7 (three girls / on a trampoline)

8 (quite expensive / to sit at the front)

9 (fantastic / when the horses walked on their back legs)

10 (I'm glad / not / any wild animals in the circus)

D Read the text and circle the correct word.

The circus started in Roman times, when (0) **there** / **it** were shows held in a circular arena. These consisted mainly of fighting between men, and between men and animals. (1) **It** / **There** were also displays of skill and strength. (2) **There** / **It** was a very violent and horrific spectacle. The fighters were called gladiators, and were as popular as footballers are now. Although most gladiators were men, (3) **there** / **it** were some female gladiators. In fact, in 200 CE the emperor Septimus Severus banned women from the arena. This proved that (4) **it** / **there** had been women gladiators before this date.

(5) **There** / **It** is a very interesting grave in a Roman cemetery in south London. A young woman's body was buried there, and (6) **there** / **it** is believed that she was a popular gladiator because (7) **there** / **it** are lots of valuable objects in her grave that give clues to her identity. (8) **There** / **It** is, for example, a dish decorated with a scene of a fallen gladiator, and (9) **it** / **there** are several lamps with images of the Roman god, Mercury. (10) **It** / **There** is significant that the people who came to take away the dead from the arena were always dressed as Mercury.

(11) **It** / **There** are some references to female gladiators in some Roman poems and letters, and (12) **it's** / **there's** certain that people admired women in this role.

Mark and Diego are arriving back in Britain with their ice-dance **team**. The **team is** very tired. The **orchestra have** lost most of their instruments in transit; they are going to have to wait at the airport to see if their instruments will appear on the next flight from Canberra. The **staff** at the airport **are** trying to help, but they can only wait to see if the airline **company have** put the instruments on the next flight. Mark's **family have** come to meet him, but there is such a big crowd that they can't get through to the arrivals gate. The **BBC are** there, and some other TV companies, with all their cameras and crews, all fighting for a position near the arrivals gate. Mark's **family hear** someone saying that Silchester United, the football **team**, **are** arriving by private jet at any minute. Suddenly there is a loud cheer; the crowd pushes forward, and Diego sees Brian Stillness, the famous footballer! He is very rich and successful but his **clothes are** very ordinary; he is wearing **jeans** and a sweatshirt, and **a pair of trainers**. His **jeans have** holes in them! But his **sunglasses are** cool, though. The camera crews go crazy! After this Mark and Diego can't see anything because there **are** too many **people**.

❶ singular and plural

Most nouns have a singular form and a plural form. The plural form usually ends in **s**. We usually use a singular verb after a singular noun, and a plural verb after a plural noun:

singular	plural
▪ The **cat is** in the garage.	The **cats are** in the garage.

But there are a number of common nouns which are unusual:

some *plural nouns* only have a plural form and use: e.g. **the clothes are ...**
other *plural nouns* have a singular form but are used with a plural verb: e.g. **the people are ...**
pair nouns describe one thing but are used with a plural verb: e.g. **the shoes are ...**
group nouns have a singular form but are often used with a plural verb: e.g. **the team are ...**
uncountable nouns don't have a plural form: e.g. **physics is ...**

(For more on uncountable nouns, see unit 1.)

❷ plural nouns: plural form only

Some nouns have no singular form:

clothes   belongings   goods   earnings   contents   remains   savings
surroundings   outskirts   congratulations   thanks   arms   troops   customs

These nouns always take a plural verb:

▪ The **contents** of the suitcase **were** all over the floor.

❸ plural nouns: singular form only

Some nouns only have a plural meaning and use. One member of the group has a different name. Here are some examples of this:

police:
▪ The **police are** looking for a dangerous man. (= *the whole police force*)
▪ A **police officer is** knocking at the door.
cattle:
▪ How many **cattle were** in the field? (= *cows, bulls, and bullocks*)
▪ There **was a cow** and (there were) three **bullocks**.

youth:

- European **youth** are much richer than they were. (= *the young people of Europe*)
- A **young person** was working in the shop. (Note: **A youth** is a *young boy*, not a girl.)

people:

- **People** are ready for a change. (= *everyone*)
- A small **person** was sitting on the doorstep.

(Note: **A people** are *all the people who come from a particular place*.)

❹ pair nouns

Pair nouns only have a plural form, though the meaning may be singular. They are used for *things with two distinct parts to them*. Some examples of pair nouns are:

        jeans   tights   trousers   pants   pyjamas   shorts   sunglasses   scissors

With pair nouns we use a plural verb even when we are talking about one item:

- Leo's **jeans are** hanging on the line.   ■ Those **sunglasses don't** cost much.

If we want to talk about *more than one item*, we can use **the**, **some**, **these**, or **those** as determiners, but then it is not clear if we are talking about one pair or more than one pair because the verb is always plural:

- Where are **those shorts** I bought yesterday? (*They could be one or more pairs*.)
- **The scissors** weren't very sharp. (*They could be more than one pair*.)

If we want to make it clear that we are talking about *one item*, we say **a pair of** before the pair noun:

- Andre bought **a pair of** designer **sunglasses** at the airport.
- Jane wants to buy **a pair of** blue **jeans**.

If we want to make it clear we are talking about *more than one pair of things*, we must use **pairs of** before the pair noun:

- Where are the **pairs of shorts** I bought yesterday?
- Those **pairs of scissors** weren't very sharp.

We also use **a pair of** and **pairs of** with *things that usually exist in twos* (e.g. **shoes**, **trainers**, **gloves**):

- That **pair of gloves** is / are mine.   ■ There are **six pairs of trainers** in the hall!

❺ group nouns

Group nouns are nouns which refer to a *group of people*. Here are some examples:

        team   committee   crew   orchestra   family   government   staff   class
        school   firm / company   the BBC   Manchester United

With group nouns we can use either a plural or a singular verb. If we are talking about *the group as a unit*, we use the singular verb:

- The TV **crew works** very hard. (*the crew as a group*)

If we use a group noun to refer to *each member of a group*, we use a plural verb:

- **The crew** of the yacht **work** really well together. (*all the individuals in the crew*)

❻ irregular nouns ending in s

News always goes with a singular verb:

- The **news** from Toronto **is** very positive.

The names of many *academic subjects* and *games* end in **s** but take a singular verb:

        physics   economics   logistics   mathematics   politics   electronics   cybernetics
        genetics   billiards   darts   bowls   athletics

and these diseases, which end in **s**, are singular:

        measles   rickets   mumps   AIDS

(For more on irregular noun plurals, see page 288.)

A Read the following sentences and choose which word in brackets to put in which gap.

When Diego starts to unpack, he realises he hasn't got the right suitcase. He obviously picked up another person's suitcase at the airport, by accident.

0 (person / people)

Lots of ......*people*...... have dark blue suitcases. This suitcase isn't locked so he opens it to see if he can find the name of the ......*person*...... who owns it.

1 (belongings / contents)

Diego tips out the .... of the suitcase onto the floor and starts looking though the owner's ....

2 (shirts / jeans)

Inside he finds two pairs of .... and several ....

3 (darts / athletics)

There is a set of .... and an .... shirt with the number '8' on it.

4 (economics / glasses)

There are some .... textbooks and a pair of ....

5 (person / youth)

He thinks it must belong to a young .... , but obviously quite a serious ....

6 (belongings / shorts)

Among his .... there are four pairs of ....

7 (customs / scissors)

He also finds some .... , and he wonders how he got those through .... !

8 (earnings / savings)

There's also a pay cheque, which looks like his .... and a .... book from a bank in Switzerland.

9 (the staff / the airline company)

He phones .... who say his case has arrived and that he should bring the other suitcase to give it to .... at the left luggage office.

10 (congratulations / thanks)

A month later he gets a letter of .... from the owner of the case, which is full of .... for his honesty.

group and pair nouns

Here is a letter from David to his friend Sam.
Look at the underlined words. Some of them have an s and shouldn't, some of them don't have an s and should. Some of them are correct. Rewrite them all, so that they are all correct.

> 98 Grantham Lane
> London NE 15
>
> Dear Sam,
>
> The ⁰new is that we've moved into our new flat at last! I had to use all my ¹saving to pay the ²rent, as it's a bit expensive! The flat is on the ³outskirts of the city, and it takes half an hour to get to ⁴works, but the ⁵surrounding are lovely so it's worth it. Bob has started working at his company ⁶headquarter, which is just down the ⁷roads, and his ⁸earnings have doubled!
>
> There is much more space here, so there's plenty of room for my ⁹belonging.
>
> ¹⁰Thank for your letter with all the ¹¹news from back home. I'm amazed to hear that Kate is studying ¹²politic and ¹³economics! I always thought she would do ¹⁴athletics, or something sporty. Give her my love, and say I'm sorry to hear about her illness. ¹⁵Measles is a horrible disease! I hope she's better now.
>
> I must go now, as we're all going to have a game of ¹⁶billiard in a few minutes.
>
> Lots of love,
>
> David

0	_news_
1	
2	
3	
4	
5	
6	
7	
8	
9	
10	
11	
12	
13	
14	
15	
16	

Read the following sentences and circle the correct form of the underlined verbs.

0 The news (is)/ are terrible!

1 The roof of my house has fallen in and the contents is / are damaged.

2 It's been raining and all my belongings has got / have got ruined!

3 My savings isn't / aren't enough to replace them.

4 Luckily the outskirts, where I live, isn't / aren't very crowded, …

5 …. so the surroundings is / are mostly gardens, and no one was hurt.

6 Did you know that a rare species of bat lives / live in my garage?

7 The remains of my roof has / have been cleared away now.

8 I can't stay with my brother because he has measles and measles affects / affect some people very seriously.

9 I am trying to study, and even though electronics interests / interest me a lot …

10 … the mathematics makes / make my head ache.

45

12

Dear Mum,

It is ten o'clock in the evening and I am in the library at the medical school. Lots of other students are working. It is quite silent, except when someone turns a page or scratches their head. Tomorrow the end-of-term exams start. Everyone is very frightened and no one sleeps much at the moment.

The weather is a lot better now. I like living in a country which has seasons. Although the winter is horrible, it's really exciting when the first leaves appear on the trees and the bulbs start to push up through the earth. However, I do miss the Caribbean with its blue sky and warm breeze! And the food – I specially miss that!

I have got a new girlfriend. Her name is Sophie and she is also a medical student. I really like her. Her mum comes from Jamaica and her dad is Scottish, and she cooks almost as well as you!

I have some more good news – I have found a nice little flat near the hospital and my friend Bob and I hope to move in at the weekend! I really hate the room I live in at the moment.

I'd better get back to work now.

Wish me luck with my exams – and the new flat.

Lots of love and hugs to you and Therese,

Stephen

❶ form

The form of the present simple does not change, except for **he**, **she**, and **it** when we add **s**; after **I**, **you**, **we**, and **they** the verb has the same form as the infinitive:

infinitive	singular	plural
(to) smile	I / you **smile**	we / you **smile**
	he / she / it **smiles**	they **smile**

If the verb ends in **o**, we add an **e** before the **s**:

go → go**es**   do → do**es**

If the verb ends in *consonant* + **y**, we change it to *consonant* + **ies**:

carry → carr**ies**   worry → worr**ies**

The verb **be** has a different present simple form from the infinitive:

infinitive	singular	plural
(to) be	I **am**	we **are**
	you **are**	you **are**
	he / she / it **is**	they **are**

In British English we usually use **have got** instead of **have** when we mean *possess something*:

■ Sue **has got** three dogs. (= *Sue has three dogs.*)

(For more on **have** in US English, see page 292.)

❷ questions and negatives

To make questions with **be**, we put **am / is / are** before the <u>subject</u>:

■ **Are** <u>you</u> hungry?

■ Why **is** <u>the bus</u> so late?

To make questions with other verbs in the present simple, we use **do / does** + <u>*subject*</u> + *infinitive*. We use **do** with **I**, **we**, **you**, and **they**; we use **does** with **he**, **she**, and **it**:

■ **Do** <u>you</u> **work** for Harrington's?

■ What time **does** <u>the meeting</u> **finish** today?

To make short answers to **yes / no** *questions*, we repeat the auxiliary **do / does**:

■ '**Do** you like pizza?' 'Yes, I **do**.'

(For more on questions, see units 58 and 59.)

To make the negative of **be**, we can add **not** or **n't** to the verb:

   ■ **I'm not** very good at chess.
   ■ The boots **aren't** as expensive as the shoes.

Note: We don't use **n't** after a contracted form (e.g. **I'm**, **she's**) and after **am**:

   ■ NOT ~~I'mn't very good at chess~~. NOR ~~I amn't very good at chess~~.

To make the negative of other verbs, we add **do not / don't** or **does not / doesn't** before the infinitive:

   ■ Jenny **doesn't eat** meat.

❸ present simple for facts and descriptions

We use the present simple for *facts* (*things that are true now and that we don't expect to change*):

   ■ I **am** British.
   ■ Paul **likes** Chinese food.

We also use it for *situations that we don't expect will change*:

   ■ Tom **lives** in Durham.
   ■ Sue **works** for a German bank.

We can also use the verb **be** and other *state verbs* (**have**, **seem**, **want** etc) in the present simple when we are describing a *current situation*:

   ■ Jacob **is** in the swimming pool.
   ■ Sue **wants** to stay at home today.

(For more on state verbs, see unit 17.)

❹ present simple for frequent events

We use the present simple to talk about *something which happens frequently* or *regularly*, often with a *frequency adverb* (**often**, **always**, **usually** etc) or when the time is specified:

   ■ Lorna **always arrives** late for work.
   ■ Lorna's mother **visits** her every **Sunday**.

❺ present simple for the future

We use the present simple with *future* meaning when we are talking about a *timetable* or *schedule*. We usually use it for things and not people:

   ■ The coach **leaves** at 6.30 in the evening.

We use the present simple with *future* meaning for *personal plans*, if the event is *part of a schedule*:

   ■ Mr Collins **gets** here at 2, and the meeting **starts** at 2.30.

After **if** and **when** and **after**, we use the *present simple* to talk about a *future event*:

   ■ **If** you **see** Mike tomorrow, ask him to phone me please.
   ■ Tom wants to live in Mexico for a year **after** he **leaves** school.

❻ present simple for jokes and stories

When we are telling *a story* or *a joke* we often use the present simple, even to talk about the past:

   ■ This man **goes** into a shop and **says** to the shopkeeper ...

Note: This is only used in informal conversation, and is not strictly 'correct' English.

A Read the following text and look at the present simple verbs underlined. Decide if each one is used to describe:
(a) a frequent event
(b) a fact or a situation
(c) the future
(d) a story or a joke

B Read this description of a hermit crab. Most of the verbs are missing. Choose the right verb from the box and put it, in the right form, in each gap.

lose	belong	go	~~live~~	find	use	eat
	let	have	be	be		

Hermit crabs (0) *live* in the sea around coral reefs. The hermit crab (1) .... to the animal group called 'crustaceans'. Crustaceans (2) .... a shell called an exoskeleton. The joints in the exoskeleton (3) .... the crab move. The joints (4) .... clearly visible on the pincers and legs. The hermit crab (5) .... unusual among crustaceans because the back part of its body is not covered. So the crab (6) .... into an empty mollusc shell, in this case a conch shell, and (7) .... the shell to protect its soft rear end. Each year, the crab (8) .... its exoskeleton and (9) .... a new, larger shell to hide in. Hermit crabs (10) .... small fish and shrimps.

MRS HARRIS: Who's your doctor? My doctor's name [0]is Dr Gupta. Do you [1]know her? She's really nice!

MRS KAMAL: No. My doctor is called Jacobs and he [2]works near my house. He's quite nice, but I think he [3]likes cars more than people! He's got a beautiful old Jaguar which he [4]drives to work every day.

MRS HARRIS: Dr Gupta is so popular; [5]it's often difficult to get an appointment with her. She runs a maternity clinic every Friday which I usually [6]go to. I [7]am seven months pregnant now. How many months are you?

MRS KAMAL: Nearly eight. I [8]go into the hospital in five weeks. [9]I'm really uncomfortable now. I'm getting really tired now.

MRS HARRIS: I know! Oh, it's so boring waiting here! Do you [10]know any good jokes?

MRS KAMAL: Well, I'm not very good at telling jokes, but I'll try. ... Have you heard the joke about the woman who [11]goes to see her doctor? She says 'Doctor, doctor, I've swallowed my pen!'

MRS HARRIS: So the doctor [12]says, 'Don't worry. You can use mine!' ... I've heard that one.

conch shell   pincers

exoskeleton (shell)   legs

0 _b_	4	7	10 ....
1	5	8	11 ....
2	6	9	12 ....
3			

TIME	PLACE	EVENT
	Trip to Northcott Theatre, Exeter, to see 'The Tempest', Monday 14th January	
9.00	Bus Station	Board coach, number 147
9.30	Bus Station	Departure
11.00	Bristol Service Station	Stop for toilets and refreshments
12.30	Exeter	Arrival
12.45	Belmont Hotel *****	Allocate rooms
13.15	White Hart Inn	Lunch (sandwiches or pizza)
14.30	Exeter Museum of Rural Life	Museum visit
16.00	Exeter Museum	Tea in the museum café
17.00	Belmont Hotel	Change / Rest
18.00	Northcott Theatre restaurant	Dinner (Vegetarian food available)
19.30	Northcott Theatre	Performance starts
21.45	Northcott Theatre	Performance ends
22.00	Belmont Hotel	Back to the hotel
09.30	Tuesday 15th, return coach leaves Exeter Bus Station	

C Look at the tour schedule for a trip to Exeter next week; make questions using the words in brackets, and then give the answers.

0 (What time / we / meet / the bus station / ?)
'What time do we meet at the bus station ?'
'We meet at nine o'clock.'

1 (Where / we / eat / lunch / ?)
'..?'
'..'

2 (How long / be / the journey / ?)
'..?'
'..'

3 (we / stop / on the way / ?)
'..?'
'..'

4 (the restaurant / have / vegetarian food / ?)
'..?'
'..'

5 (we / have / time to change our clothes / before the performance / ?)
'..?'
'..'

6 (What time / be / the performance / ?)
'..?'
'..'

7 (Which museum / we / visit / ?)
'..?'
'..'

8 (What / be / the hotel / called / ?)
'..?'
'..'

9 (be / the hotel / nice / ?)
'..?'
'..'

10 (we / come back / after breakfast / ?)
'..?'
'..'

49

JULIE: Keith **is making** a lot of noise! What **is** he **doing**?

ADAM: I don't know. He**'s working** in his room. You know he**'s studying** electrical engineering, and I think he**'s trying** to build a robot, or something.

JULIE: He**'s** always **working** these days.

ADAM: That's because he**'s taking** his final exams next week.

KIM: Yes, and then he**'s going** home.

JULIE: What **are** you **making** for dinner tonight, Kim?

KIM: I**'m not cooking** again tonight! I'm sure it's Keith's turn to cook.

JULIE: I hope he**'s making** us a robot that can cook dinner. I hope so because Keith is a terrible cook!

❶ form

We make the present continuous with the auxiliary verb **be** (**am** / **is** / **are**) and the **ing** *form* of the main verb:

singular	plural
I **am working** (I'm working)	we **are working** (we're working)
you **are working** (you're working)	you **are working** (you're working)
he / she / it **is working** (he's working)	they **are working** (they're working)

We usually use the contracted form (**I'm**, **he's** etc), especially in speech.

If the main verb ends in *consonant* + **e**, we cut off the **e** and add **ing**:

place → **placing**   lose → **losing**
place → **placing**   file → **filing**

If the main verb ends with a *single vowel* + *single consonant* (e.g. **rob**), we usually double the consonant and add **ing**:

tip → **tipping**   rob → **robbing**
fit → **fitting**   drum → **drumming**

Note: We don't double **w** and **y**:

throw → **throwing**   say → **saying**

It is possible to use the same auxiliary with more than one **ing** *verb* if the subject of the verbs remains the same:

■ We **are walking** down the road, **talking**, and **eating** chips.

❷ questions and negatives

To make a question, we usually put the auxiliary verb **be** (**am** / **is** / **are**) before the <u>subject</u>:

■ **Is** <u>Graham</u> **listening** to the news?
■ **Are** <u>you</u> **coming** to the match this afternoon?
■ What **are** <u>you</u> **planning** to do after you leave school?
■ 'Who **is** <u>Helen</u> **talking** to?' 'She's talking to Antonio.'
■ Where **are** <u>you</u> **going** for your holidays this year?

But if **what**, **who**, **how many** etc. is the subject, then we put the <u>subject</u> before the auxiliary:

■ <u>Who</u> **is making** all that noise?

- 'Who **is talking** to John?' 'Maria is.'
- How many people **are coming** to your party?

(For more on questions, see unit 58.)

The negative is made by adding **not** or **n't** between the auxiliary verb **be** and the **ing**-verb. Notice the different contracted forms:

singular	plural
I **am not** / **'m not** working	we **are not** / **'re not** / **aren't** working
you **are not** / **'re not** / **aren't** working	you **are not** / **'re not** / **aren't** working
he / she / it **is not** / **'s not** / **isn't** working	they **are not** / **'re not** / **aren't** working

❸ present continuous with present meaning

We use the present continuous to talk about *things which are happening now*:

- **I'm having** lunch right now. Can I phone you back in half an hour?
- Lucy **is talking** on the phone at the moment.

We also use it for *things which are happening during this period in time*, but not necessarily at this moment. In this case we often use a time phrase, such as **this week**, **this month**, **these days**:

- Ros **is studying** hard this week, as she has an exam on Friday.
- The band 'Slipperslap' **are spending** a lot of time in the studio this month. They **are making** a new album.
- The staff **are working** very hard this year.

❹ present continuous for repeated events with **always**

We use the present continuous with **always** to talk about *something which happens frequently during this period*; it usually has a negative and critical meaning:

- Howard **is always telling** me what to do. (*I don't like it.*)
- Pete and Debbie **are always fighting**. (*It makes them and me unhappy.*)

❺ present continuous with future meaning

We can use the present continuous to talk about the *future*, when we are talking about *things which people are definitely doing in the future* because they are planned:

- Hurry up! The guests **are arriving** at 7!
- Jane**'s starting** her French course next week.

(For more on the future, see units 23–26.)

❻ present continuous for refusal

In informal speech we use the negative present continuous in the first person (**I**) when we are talking about *refusing to do something*:

- She told me to cheat in the exam, but **I'm not doing that**!
- **I'm not going** to her party even if she invites me!

❼ present continuous for stories and jokes

We use the present continuous in very informal narrative, such as funny stories or jokes. We use the present continuous to describe the scene and the present simple for the events:

- So, this dog **is walking** down the road, when he sees a monkey on a bicycle …
- I **am sitting** on the bench, when this man comes up to me …

A Use the present continuous to make sentences about the picture, using the words in brackets.

0 (a dog / run / across the road)
A dog is running across the road.

1 (a pigeon / sit / on the traffic light)
....

2 (a taxi / stop / at the traffic lights)
....

3 (some customers / look / at some jewellery)
....

4 (the policeman / arrest / a thief)
....

5 (a bank clerk / give / some money to the nurse)
....

6 (a young woman / send / an email)
....

7 (the baby / throw / his bottle on the ground)
....

8 (some passengers / stand / in the bus)
....

9 (the newspaper vendor / sell / a magazine)
....

10 (a businessman / do / a deal on his mobile phone)
....
....

B Find the ten verbs in the present continuous in this conversation and list them below. Beside each one, indicate whether they are describing:
(a) what is happening now
(b) what is happening during the present period
(c) what is happening in the future

JOSH: Are you having a break?

KAREN: Yes, I'm waiting for the kettle to boil. Would you like a coffee?

JOSH: No thanks. I'm only drinking herbal tea these days.

KAREN: Is anyone using the fax machine at the moment?

JOSH: Yes, John's trying to send all those papers to Nigeria. It's taking a long time. Sorry!

KAREN: That's alright. I think the phone on my desk is ringing. ... Hello? ... Yes, who am I speaking to? ... Oh, Mr Fanshaw! ... Yes. ... No. I'm going home at 5.30. ... Oh yes, I'm really enjoying the training course, thank you. ... Yes, I'm doing the extra class this evening. ... See you later! Bye.

0 *Are you having (a)*
1 ....
2 ....
3 ....
4 ....
5 ....
6 ....
7 ....
8 ....
9 ....
10 ....

C Fill in the missing word or part of a word.

0 Hello! I 'm trying to contact John Franklin at Gargantuan Games.

1 .... I speaking to the sales department?

2 Who am .... talking to?

3 Oh, hello Kerry! Are .... working in the sales department now?

4 Yes, ... 'm still working as Susan Jarrod's secretary.

5 Oh, yes! But .... 're moving to a new office next week.

6 No, Susan .... visiting the Tokyo office at the moment.

7 The directors are hav .... a meeting at three o'clock today.

8 They' .... meeting in the conference room on the third floor.

9 OK, is Mr Franklin com .... in tomorrow?

10 Thanks. Oh, someone .... calling on the other line. Bye!

D Look at the picture. Now look at the replies below and write the questions to match them, using the words in brackets. You may need to use **how many, where, what,** or **who.**

		questions	replies
0	(people/ travel / in the train)	' *How many people are travelling in the train* ?'	'Six.'
1	(people / eat / sandwiches)	'..?'	'Two.'
2	(people / wear / hats)	'..?'	'Three.'
3	(train / go / to)	'..?'	'Chicago.'
4	(train / come / from)	'..?'	'New York.'
5	(read / a newspaper)	'..?'	'The man.'
6	(the two women / drink / coffee)	'..?'	'Yes, they are.'
7	(look out of / the window)	'..?'	'The boy.'
8	(talk / to the boy)	'..?'	'The boy's mother.'
9	(she / carry / a bag)	'..?'	'Yes, she is.'
10	(check / the tickets)	'..?'	'The ticket inspector.'

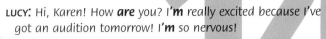

LUCY: Hi, Karen! How **are** you? I**'m** really excited because I've got an audition tomorrow! I**'m** so nervous!

KAREN: That**'s** brilliant! What **is** it for?

LUCY: It**'s** for a part in a new show which **opens** in the autumn. It**'s** about the start of jazz music in New Orleans. There**'s** a really big cast, so I've got a pretty good chance of getting a small part.

KAREN: What **do** you **have** to do? I've never done an audition!

LUCY: I**'m doing** a jazz solo, and you always **have** to do a 'routine' – that **means** they **teach** you a sequence of steps and you all **do** them together.

KAREN: That **sounds** really hard!

LUCY: Oh no! That**'s** fine! I **do** routines all the time. I**'m doing** two dance classes a week at the moment. Actually, I**'m feeling** more nervous about singing! I**'m not** very good at that. Anyway, how**'s** your new job?

KAREN: Oh, it**'s** OK. I'm **working** at Gargantuan Games now. I left my old job and started there last week. They**'re** very nice but they all **work** really hard! But they**'re paying** me quite well.

LUCY: What **are** you **doing** now? **Are** you busy?

KAREN: Actually I**'m** just **cooking** myself some supper, and then I**'m going** to bed early.

LUCY: I **have** to go to bed early too. I **have** to be at the theatre at 9 o'clock.

KAREN: Well, good luck! Phone me after the audition! Bye!

LUCY: Bye!

❶ present simple with present meaning

We use the present simple for *facts and situations in the present that we do not expect to change*:

- My brother **is** a rock musician.
- Mae Ling **has** a big house in the suburbs.
- The River Seine **flows** through Paris.
- Maria **speaks** English better than me.
- 'Gargantuan' **means** 'enormous'.

We also use the present simple for *frequent or regular events*:

- The river **floods** every spring.
- Mark always **walks** to work.

(For more on the form and use of the present simple, see unit 12.)

❷ present continuous with present meaning

We use the present continuous when we are talking about *something that is happening at this moment*:

- Sam **is reading** the Mitsubishi manual and trying to repair his engine.
- **Are** you **listening** to me?

We also use the present continuous to talk about *things which happen during the present period of time*, but not necessarily at this particular moment:

- Phil **is doing** Spanish lessons this term.
- I'm afraid we**'re spending** more than we should!

(For more on the form and use of the present continuous, see unit 13.)

❸ verbs rarely used in the continuous

Note that some verbs are not usually used in a continuous form. These are verbs describing a *state* (**be**, **have**, **look**, **need**, **seem**, **sound**, **smell** etc) and verbs describing *feelings* and *thoughts* (**have to** [= *must*], **hope**, **feel**, **like**, **trust** etc). With these verbs we use the simple form to talk about something that is happening now:

- Gary **is** very tired today. NOT ~~Gary is being very tired~~ ...
- He **seems** to think that there isn't a problem. NOT ~~He's seeming~~ ...
- I **have** to finish this report tonight. NOT ~~I'm having to~~ ...
- I **hope** you are enjoying yourselves! NOT ~~I'm hoping~~ ...
- I really **like** this cappuccino. NOT ~~I'm really liking~~ ...
- The people **trust** the government. NOT ~~The people are trusting~~ ...

A few verbs that describe *feelings*, such as **enjoy** and **feel**, can be used in the continuous to talk about what is happening now:

- I**'m enjoying** this music – what is it?
- I**'m not feeling** very well. I think I'll sit down for a bit.

Some verbs have one meaning where they describe a *state* and another meaning where they describe an *action*; we can use a continuous form for the *action*:

- That boy **looks** ill. (*state*)   That boy **is looking** at the plane. (*action*)
- Jack **has** three cars. (*state*)   Jack **is having** a shower. (*action*)

(For more on verbs not usually used in the continuous, see unit 17.)

❹ present forms with future meaning

We use the ***present simple*** with future meaning when we are talking about *something which is scheduled*. We usually don't use this tense when we are talking about people:

- The bus **leaves** in half an hour.
- Don't be late for the meeting. It **starts** at 2.

We use the ***present continuous*** when we are talking about *something which is planned in the future*. We usually use this form when we are talking about what people are planning to do:

- Sarah **is coming** for dinner tonight.
- I**'m taking** my mother to the airport tomorrow morning.

Note: After **when** / **before** / **after**, we use the present simple to talk about people's plans:

- Dan and Vanessa are visiting Pisa **before** they **fly** back to America.

❺ present forms in stories and jokes

When we are telling a story or a joke in a very informal, idiomatic way, we often use the present tense even when we are talking about something that happened in the past.
We use the ***present continuous*** to give the *background information* and the ***present simple*** for the *main events*:

- It's raining and my friend is running, and then she slips on the pavement ...
- I'm walking through the gate and a ticket inspector is standing there and he says 'your ticket isn't valid!'

A Read the passage and choose which verb form is better. Draw a circle around it.

Mary Ross (0) **works** / (**is working**) in the packing room today. She (1) **is packing** / **packs** strawberries, and they (2) **smell** / **are smelling** very sweet and delicious. She (3) **is being** / **is** really tired. Peter (4) **doesn't help** / **isn't helping** her this afternoon because he (5) **'s** / **'s being** in the office. He (6) **phones** / **'s phoning** the bank manager to ask for some advice. They (7) **have** / **'re having** a bit of a problem as they (8) **employ** / **are employing** a new packer and they (9) **are needing** / **need** to borrow some money from the bank. Mary (10) **hates** / **is hating** talking about money. She (11) is **preferring** / **prefers** to work on the farm. But she (12) **'s not working** / **doesn't work** very hard at the moment!

B Read the following data about Warren Daly, then look at the questions. Write the questions and correct the verbs in the questions if they are incorrect, and then answer the questions.

NAME: Warren Daly

AGE: 37

PROFESSION: Film actor

HAPPY?: Yes

HOME: New York

HOLIDAY HOME?: Yes. Beach house on Martha's Vineyard

MARRIED?: Yes

WIFE'S NAME: Anthea

CHILDREN: Jake, Delilah, and Star

WIFE'S JOB: Film editor

HOLIDAYS: England – stay with friends there

PRESENT JOB: Film of life of the balloonist Montgolfier

CHILDREN AT SCHOOL?: Jake studying at High School in Greenwich Village; Delilah at kindergarten; Star at home

HOBBIES: Golf, scuba diving, sailing

PRESENT ACTIVITY: Rehearsing for a new film

0 How old is Warren Daly being?
   How old is Warren Daly?
   He's 37.

1 What is his wife's name?

2 What is his job?

3 Is he liking it?

4 Where are they living?

5 Have they got a holiday home? Where?

6 How many children are they having?

7 What are their children called?

....

....

8 Does his wife have a job? What?

....

....

9 Where are they going on holiday usually?

....

....

10 Where do they stay when they go to England?

....

....

11 Where is Jake going to school?

....

....

12 What hobbies is Warren enjoying?

....

....

13 Is Star being at school?

....

....

14 What is Warren doing right now?

....

....

C Look at the notes Chi-Nan is making about the holiday he is planning. He is going with his friend, Guo-Fu. Make sentences to explain their plans, using the verbs in brackets and the present simple or the present continuous.

0 flight from Heathrow – 13.05 → Hong Kong – 8.00, the next morning

(leave / arrive) *The flight leaves Heathrow at five past one, and arrives in Hong Kong at eight o'clock the next morning.*

1 local flight from Hong Kong – 9.00 → Taipei – 10.35, on Wednesday

(leave / arrive) The flight ....

....

2 whole journey time – 21.5 hours

(take) The whole journey ....

....

3 Hotel Taipei Fortuna – for five days

(stay) They ....

....

4 single room – £47 per night

(cost) Each room ....

....

5 the National Palace Museum, on Thursday

(visit) They ....

....

6 if possible, the Fulong Seaside Park, on Friday morning

(go) ....

....

7 boat trip to the islands, on Saturday

(take) ....

....

8 boat to islands, 10 a.m.

(go) ....

....

9 the train to Wulai – to see the hot springs

(take) ....

....

10 two nights, with Guo-Fu's parents, near Wulai

(stay) ....

....

11 the Long Shan Temple, before return to the UK

(visit) ....

....

When Gloria Cross was a girl, she **loved** reading. She **had** three brothers and a younger sister and **lived** in the most beautiful bay just south of Bridgetown in Barbados, where her father **used to run** the local post office – he's retired now. She **had** a very happy childhood, and **was** very lucky to have a kind and clever school teacher, Mr Grant, who **recognised** her ability. He **helped** her to pass her exams, and to get into the University of the West Indies, at Cave Hill Campus. She **studied** Law, but then **decided** to become a teacher; so, she **did** a postgraduate degree in Education at Erdiston Teacher's College. In 1995 she **got** the job as head teacher of the Primary School at Holetown, and she and her two children, Stephen and Therese, **moved** to Paynes Bay on the West Coast of Barbados. When Stephen **left** to go to study medicine in London, she and Therese **missed** him terribly at first, but he **promised** that he would come back to work in Barbados when he **qualified** as a doctor. After all, he thinks it's the most beautiful place in the world!

❶ form

We make the past simple of regular verbs by adding **ed** to the infinitive of the verb:

infinitive	singular	plural
(to) look	I **looked**	we **looked**
	you **looked**	you **looked**
	he / she / it **looked**	they **looked**

If the infinitive ends in **e**, we add a **d**:

bake → **baked**   type → **typed**

The verb **be** has a different past simple form:

infinitive	singular	plural
(to) **be**	I **was**	we **were**
	you **were**	you **were**
	he / she / it **was**	they **were**

Many of the most common verbs are also irregular. They have one different past tense form:

make → **made**   go → **went**   have → **had**   begin → **began**

(For a list of irregular verbs, see page 286.)

❷ questions and negatives

To make questions with **be** in the past simple, we usually put the verb before the <u>subject</u>:

- **Was** <u>Graham</u> in the army?
- **Were** <u>Mark and Jim</u> friends?
- When **were** <u>you</u> in Thailand?

To make questions with other verbs in the past simple, we usually use **did** + <u>*subject*</u> + *infinitive*:

- **Did** <u>Jane</u> **like** the film?
- **Did** <u>your friends</u> **pass** their exams?

To make the negative of **be** in the past simple, we add **n't** or **not** to the verb:

- Graham **wasn't** in the army.
- Mark and Jim **were not** friends.

To make the negative of other verbs in the past simple, we use the auxiliary **did** with **n't** or **not** and the infinitive of the main verb:

- Jane **didn't like** the film.
- They **did not** all **pass** their exams.

❸ use

The past simple is used to talk about *an event that happened in the past and finished*. We usually use the past simple when we say <u>when something happened</u>:

- Margaret **went** to Holland <u>last Monday</u>.
- The boys **bought** some drinks <u>when they were in the shop</u>.

We also use it for *regular, repeated events in the past*:

- I always **took** my car to the same garage.
- Helen **cycled** to the swimming pool every Sunday.

It is also used for *things that continued for some time but then ended*:

- My brother **worked** for ICI for a few months. He works for another company now.
- The snow **fell** all morning. In the afternoon the sun came out.

We usually use the past simple when we are telling a *story*, or describing a sequence of events:

- The phone **rang** and I **went** to answer it …
- Dave **put** the video on the shop counter, **took** out his wallet, and **gave** the man a five pound note …

We use the past simple when the action or situation we are talking about is *the main focus* of the sentence. The background or less important situation or actions are described using the past continuous (**was falling**, **was working**):

- Rain **was falling** and the car **skidded**. (The car skidding *is the focus*.)
- Paul **worked** for Reuters while Jane **was working** for Thompson. (Paul's job *is the focus*.)

(For more on the use of the past continuous and past simple, see unit 16.)

❹ used to

To talk about *past habits and long-term situations <u>which do not exist now</u>*, we can use **used to** + *infinitive*:

- Mr Patterson **used to go** to the gym three times a week, but <u>he doesn't have time to go now</u>.
- Karen **used to think** opera was boring, but <u>now she loves it</u>.

To make questions we use an auxiliary (**did**, **didn't**) with **use to**:

- **Did** we **use to spend** so much money every month?
- **Didn't** you **use** to have a Buick?

To make the negative we use **did** + **n't** / **not** + **used to** or **used not to**:

- Karen **didn't use to like** opera.
- Jack **used not to eat** meat at all.
- Liam's parents **did not use to live** in London when he was a boy.

Remember: We use the *present simple* for present habits and long-term situations.

A Here is a brief biography of F.M. Alexander, the inventor of the Alexander Technique. Some of the verbs are missing. Write the past simple form of the correct verb in the box in each gap.

| invent | decide | ~~be~~ | publish | begin | go | die |
| breathe | want | use | notice | have | move | |

F.M. Alexander (0) ....was.... an Australian actor, born in 1869. His career as an actor was not very successful because he (1) .... problems with tension in his voice. Doctors couldn't understand why his voice failed, so he (2) .... to try and solve the problem himself. He made a study of his acting using mirrors to watch exactly how he (3) .... his body, and he (4) .... a system for improving his posture and the way he (5) .... his body, and the way he (6) .... when he spoke. The improvement in his voice and movement was so great that other people (7) .... it and they (8) .... him to show them how he managed it. That is how he (9) .... teaching and soon doctors started sending their patients to him. Eventually he (10) .... to London to teach doctors there. Now, all over the world, teachers recognise the *Alexander Technique* as essential training for actors and musicians.

He (11) .... his most successful book, 'The Use of the Self', in 1932. He (12) .... in 1955, aged 88.

B Look again at the text about Gloria at the top of page 58. Now look at the replies and write the questions, using the past simple and the words in brackets.

questions	replies
0 (what / love / doing)	
'*What did she love doing?* ?'	'She loved reading.'
1 (How many / brothers and sisters / have)	
'................. ?'	'She had three brothers and a sister.'
2 (What / Mr Grant / do)	
'................. ?'	'He helped her to pass her exams.'
3 (Where / study)	
'................. ?'	'The University of the West Indies.'
4 (What / study)	
'................. ?'	'Law.'
5 (Where / learn / to teach)	
'................. ?'	'Erdiston Teacher's College.'
6 (When / get / the job of head teacher)	
'................. ?'	'In 1995.'
7 (How many / children / have)	
'................. ?'	'Two – a son and a daughter.'
8 (Where / move to)	
'................. ?'	'To Payne's Bay.'
9 (Where / Stephen / go to study medicine)	
'................. ?'	'He went to London.'
10 (What / Stephen / promise)	
'................. ?'	'That he would go back to Barbados to work.'

used to (I worked, I used to work)

C Read the following text and underline all the past simple verbs. Now list the infinitive of each verb in two columns of regular and irregular past forms.

When Peter Ross <u>was</u> at college, he worked with his parents on their farm in the vacations. But in the third year of his course he had the opportunity to go to Africa for the summer to learn about different climates and farming methods. While he was there he learnt a lot – not just about farming, but also about people and community. He met a young man the same age as him who worked on a farm in Zambia. His name was Adam. Peter wrote to Adam when he got back to England, and they became very good friends. Peter went back to Africa for a while after he graduated and stayed with Adam's family. When he bought his organic farm, he invited Adam to come and see his farm. Yesterday Peter got a letter from him saying that he is coming to stay next month! Peter and his wife Mary are very excited.

regular verbs

irregular verbs
be

D Annie has just finished her studies at university and is now working for the magazine 'Home and Health'. She's talking to a friend in the office. Complete the sentences, using the words in brackets, with **used to, didn't use to,** or **use to,** or the present simple.

ANNIE: When I was at university, I (0) ....*used to get up*.... (get up) at about 9 o'clock in the morning. Now I (1) .... (get up) at about 7, because I have to catch a train into the city at 8.

SAM: And then you stay here till 6 or 7 in the evening! Did you (2) .... (work) so hard when you were at university?

ANNIE: Oh no! I only (3) .... (study) for about an hour a day! But the work here (4) .... (be) much more interesting. It's weird, but I (5) .... (enjoy) working hard here.

SAM: I (6) .... (not / like) working for 'Home and Health' magazine because everyone seemed really unfriendly. I (7) .... (feel) really lonely, but then lots of new people joined. Now everyone here (8) .... (seem) really friendly. A few years back I (9) .... (think) a lot about leaving, but now I really (10) .... (want) to stay.

61

16

It was 9.45 a.m. on January 23rd, 1916. Private Michael Donnelly **was sitting** miserably in his trench in the Somme valley and an icy rain **was falling**. It was his birthday. He was 23. To his left, he could hear the pounding of the guns. His heavy boots were full of water and the rain **was trickling** down his neck and **soaking** into his rough, wool, jacket collar. He **was thinking** about his family, back in Ireland, and particularly about his fiancée, Kathleen. The shell hit Michael's trench at 9.46 a.m.

Kathleen O'Connor **was sweeping** the stone kitchen floor of her white-painted cottage in County Cork at 9.45 in the morning. She **was singing** while she worked, and a kettle **was whistling** on the fire. She **was thinking** about Michael and **wishing** that she could give him the sweater she had made for him for his birthday. Suddenly she heard a noise behind her in the passage and stopped sweeping. She thought that someone **was whispering** her name 'Kathleen' and **saying** 'I'm coming home, Kathleen...'; but when she went to look in the passage the whispering stopped and she couldn't see anyone there. She shivered and went back to work.

❶ form

We make the past continuous by using the past of the auxiliary verb **be** (**was**, **were**) and the **ing form** of the main verb:

singular	plural
I **was talking**	we **were talking**
you **were talking**	you **were talking**
he / she / it **was talking**	they **were talking**

- The judge **was putting on** his wig.
- Tim and Frank Dealy **were standing** in the waiting room.

We can use one auxiliary with more than one **ing form**, if the subject of the verbs remain the same:
The rain **was trickling** down his neck and **soaking** into his jacket collar. (= *the rain was soaking*)

❷ questions and negatives

We usually make questions by putting the auxiliary verb (**was** / **were**) before the <u>subject</u>:

- **Was** <u>I</u> **snoring** last night?
- **Were** <u>the students</u> **working** in the library?
- Why **was** <u>the dog</u> **barking** all night?

The negative is formed by adding **not** or **n't** to **was** / **were**:

- Terry **wasn't walking** very fast.
- We **were not feeling** very happy about the election result.
- **Weren't** you **living** in Toronto in 1996?

❸ past continuous for situations in progress in the past

We use the *past continuous* to talk about *things which were in progress at, or during, a particular time in the past*:

- At 9 o'clock **I was watching** a film on the TV.
- The car **was running** well during the journey.

The past continuous is often used to talk about *something that was in progress when an event happened*. We use the *past simple* to describe the event, and the *past continuous* to describe the unfinished situation:

- The soldiers **were cleaning** their rifles. The sergeant shouted at them to hurry up.
- The wind **was blowing** very hard outside. The door slammed shut.

Two sentences like these can be joined using **when**, **while**, or **as**, usually before the continuous clause:

- When the soldiers **were cleaning** their rifles, the sergeant shouted at them to hurry up.
- Paul studied sculpture when he **was living** in Paris.
- The army attacked while the enemy **was sleeping**.
- As the car **was speeding** away, the man stepped out of the shadows

(For more on **when**, **while**, and **as**, see unit 70.)

When we want to say that *one thing followed the other*, we use the *past simple* for both events:

- The soldiers **cleaned** their rifles. They **were** ready for the parade.
- The wind **blew** into the room. The door **slammed** shut.

We can do the same thing within one sentence, using **when** or **as soon as** for the first event:

- When he **saw** the man, he **recognised** him immediately.
- He **closed** his umbrella as soon as the rain **stopped**.

(For more on the past simple, see unit 15.)

❹ past continuous for repeated actions or changing situations in the past

We also use the *past continuous* for:

repeated actions over a past period of time:

- Henry **was going** to evening classes in Greek when I knew him.
- He **was trying** to find a job in Greece at that time.

something that was changing at a particular time in the past:

- Tom saw that it **was getting** light.
- The leaves **were beginning** to change colour.

❺ verbs not often used in the continuous

Be and other *state verbs*, like **have** and **want**, are not usually used in the past continuous:

- When I **was** eighteen, I had a Ford Escort. NOT ~~When I was being eighteen, ...~~
- Robert **was** very ill during the voyage. NOT ~~Robert was being very ill ...~~

(For more on state verbs, see unit 17.)

We sometimes use the past continuous with state verbs like **wonder**, **hope**, **think**, **expect** etc. when we are describing our feelings about something uncertain:

- I **was hoping** to finish the essay yesterday afternoon.
- She **was wondering** if she should go to the library.
- The staff **were thinking** of moving their office.

We can use a small number of state verbs that describe *feelings*, such as **feel** and **hurt**, in the past simple or past continuous with no difference in meaning:

- I **felt** really happy yesterday. = I **was feeling** really happy yesterday.

63

A Look at the picture and describe the scene, using the words in brackets, and the past continuous or the past simple.

0 (a waitress / carry / a tray)

A waitress was carrying a tray.

1 (the manager / talk / to a barman)

2 (the tablecloths / be / crisp and white)

3 (candles / burn / on all the tables)

4 (Mrs Fitzhugh / wear / all her diamonds)

5 (the Duke of Rotherhythe / laugh / with his sister)

6 (the Fitzhugh twins / be / very bored)

7 (they / look / at the menu)

8 (the chef / cook / crème brûlée)

9 (Lord Winstan / order / his meal)

10 (The Fitzhugh twins / not eat / soup)

B Put a circle around the correct option in each sentence.

0 In 1777 the British prisons (were) / were being terribly overcrowded.

1 The government decided / was deciding to send prisoners to a new colony.

2 Captain Arthur Phillips was / was being the captain of the first convict ship to land in Australia.

3 While the convicts travelled / were travelling to Australia, their suffering was terrible.

4 They did not have / were not having enough food or clean water.

5 When they reached the coast of Australia, they started / were starting to look for a safe harbour and some good farmland.

6 When they were arriving / arrived in Botany Bay, they found / were finding that it was not suitable for a settlement.

7 The convicts got / were getting desperate after so long in the ship.

8 A lot of them were suffering / suffered from starvation and disease.

9 While they were disembarking / disembarked, there was a tremendous thunderstorm.

10 They decided / were deciding to call the place where they settled 'Sydney'.

(I was working)

C Choose the best second half to the following sentences.

0 In September Graham Segalowitz lost his job

1 Sally, his wife, was worried about him,

2 He was watching lots of videos

3 Sally was getting up early to go to work

4 He was reading lots of books because

5 He decided to do some evening classes

6 Andrew Markham came into Graham's office

7 Andrew advised him to do a course in car maintenance

8 Andrew was feeling very jealous

9 When Graham and Andrew were talking,

10 Tim asked to use Graham's phone

A … but Graham was thinking of taking a course in Italian.

B … while he stayed in bed till 11.

C … but he was enjoying himself.

D … and relaxing.

E … because he still had to go to work every day.

F … while he was studying the brochure.

G … because his company was failing.

H … he wanted to try lots of new things.

I … because his own phone wasn't working.

J … so he got the college brochure.

K … their friend Tim came into Graham's office.

0 _G_   1 ....   2 ....   3 ....   4 ....   5 ....
6 ....   7 ....   8 ....   9 ....   10 ....

D Read this interview with a chef. The past tense verbs have been left out. Write in the correct past simple or past continuous form of the verbs in brackets.

Last Saturday I (0) _went_ (go) to the famous restaurant, Tomassini's. I (1) .... (hope) to interview the famous Italian chef, Giovanni Tomassini. I (2) .... (choose) to interview him there because I (3) .... (want) to see exactly how the restaurant worked. While we (4) .... (talk), the waiter (5) .... (serve) us with a very varied and delicious menu.

'Does your choice of menu come from your childhood in Italy?' I asked Giovanni.

'Oh yes, definitely! I (6) .... (be) born in Tuscany and when I (7) .... (be) a child, my mother and grandmother worked in our family trattoria. They (8) .... (teach) me how to cook and also how to eat! I mean, they showed me how to appreciate really good Tuscan food.'

'(9) .... you always .... (cook) Tuscan food?'

'Oh no! When I (10) .... (train) in Rome and Paris, I (11) .... (learn) other styles of cooking. While I (12) .... (run) a restaurant in Brighton in the late 90's, we served mainly British cuisine. When I (13) .... (live) in Australia, I (14) .... (have) the opportunity to try new fish and fruits that (15) .... (not / be) available in Europe at the time. I (16) .... (think) it was important to be flexible and absorb what was best from each environment and I still think that.'

'Our society relies on electricity. The traditional way to make electricity is to burn fossil fuels such as coal or oil. Unfortunately we are burning up all the reserves in the earth and if we don't stop soon they will all be finished. The other way we make electricity is by using nuclear power. This is unpopular and dangerous as we don't know how to dispose safely of nuclear waste. Scientists are busy developing alternative solutions now. One of these is wind power. Building wind turbines on the top of hills and out at sea is a good way of producing a lot of very low cost electricity. The problem is that wind turbines are very big and not very beautiful!

Another source of cheap energy is the sun. Lots of people now own solar panels and are saving a lot of money by using them for their heating and lighting. Many people buy them on the Internet. The only problem is that some countries (like Britain) don't have very much sunshine!

Another great source of energy is the sea. The sea is moving all the time, both in waves and in tidal action, and if that energy could be converted into electricity cheaply we could produce enough electricity to continue living as we want to without destroying our planet.

What we need in order to solve the energy crisis is a combination of all these alternatives, depending on which is the best for the local environment.'

❶ what is the 'continuous'?

Verbs in the continuous have an auxiliary (**am**, **was** etc) and an **ing** form (**looking**, **watching** etc). We usually use verbs in the continuous to talk about *actions in progress*:

- I **am looking** for my keys. (*present continuous*)
- He **was watching** the TV news. (*past continuous*)
- Mark **has been reading** all afternoon. (*present perfect continuous*)

❷ action verbs and state verbs

We can use *action verbs* in simple or continuous forms, depending on what we want to say:

- *present simple*: I **watch** the TV news every day. (= *a repeated action*)
- *present continuous*: Shhh, please. I**'m watching** the news. (= *an action in progress*)
- *past simple*: I **watched** the news yesterday. (= *a past action*)
- *past continuous*: I **was watching** the news at 6 o'clock yesterday. (= *a past action in progress*)

State verbs (which describe *states*, *feelings*, and *thoughts*) are not usually used in the continuous. We usually use these verbs only in simple verb forms:

possession verbs	emotion verbs	thinking verbs	describing verbs	sense verbs
have	like	matter	be	see
own	dislike	deserve	cost	smell
possess	fear	impress	look	taste
include	hate	think	appear	hear
belong to	love	believe	seem	sense
contain	please	know	fit	
	prefer	imagine	consist of	
	satisfy	realise	owe	
	surprise	recognise		
	want	remember		
	wish	suppose		
		understand		

- Harry doesn't possess a dinner jacket. NOT ~~isn't possessing~~
- Rosemary knew my brother. NOT ~~was knowing~~
- That skirt doesn't fit you. NOT ~~isn't fitting~~
- The roses smell wonderful. NOT ~~are smelling~~

❸ modal verbs

Modal verbs (**must**, **can**, **will**, **should** etc) do not have continuous forms. Other verbs used like modals (**have to**, **need to** etc) are usually used in the simple form:

- We **must** take some money with us. We **have to** buy lunch while we're there.
- David **will** send the company a letter. He **needs to** get a refund for the camera.

❹ verbs with *state* and *action* meanings

Some verbs have one meaning that is a *state* and another meaning that is an *action*. We can only use the continuous form with the *action* meaning:

have:
- He's **having** a shower right now. (*action*)
- They **have** a shower but not a jacuzzi in their bathroom. (*state*)

think:
- I'**m thinking** about our next holiday. I've got some brochures. (*action*)
- **Do** you **think** we should go to Africa or Spain? (*state*)

remember:
- 'Why were you smiling?' 'I **was remembering** the old days.' (*action*)
- I **remember** the name of the street where you used to live. (*state*)

appear:
- Maria **is appearing** at the Apollo theatre tomorrow evening. (*action*)
- The concert **appears** to be sold out. (*state*)

smell:
- Phillys **is smelling** all the perfumes in the shop. (*action*)
- The room **smells** of coffee. (*state*)

❺ continuous and simple forms with the same meaning

We can use a small number of verbs that describe *feelings* in the simple or continuous with no significant difference in meaning:

feel:
- I **feel** really tired. = I'**m feeling** really tired.

hurt:
- Keith's knee **hurts**. = Keith's knee **is hurting**.

ache:
- Diana's back **ached**. = Diana's back **was aching**.

hope:
- I **hope** you won't be late. = I'**m hoping** you won't be late.

look:
- Geraldine **looked** very tired yesterday. = Geraldine **was looking** very tired yesterday.

A Read the following sentences and circle the best form of the verb.

0   Keith is in his room this evening. He studies /(is studying) for an exam tomorrow.

1   He is studying electrical engineering and really is liking / likes robotics.

2   His tutor, Dr Markham, is teaching / teaches at the University of Pentland, where Keith studies.

3   He is drinking / drinks a cup of black coffee to keep him awake.

4   His flatmate Annie plays / is playing her music very loud so he can't concentrate.

5   He wears / is wearing a pair of earplugs.

6   He is trying / tries to remember what he learnt about scanners.

7   There is being / is a lot of mess on his desk.

8   He has / is having a very expensive computer.

9   No one else knows / is knowing how to use his computer.

10 Keith wants / is wanting to do well in his exam.

B All the verbs in the following email are in the continuous form. Some of them should be in the simple form. Underline the verbs that should be in the simple form and write a correct version underneath.

Hi Andy,

I'm really loving my new car! It was only costing me £4,000. I am hoping it isn't breaking down straight away!

Are you remembering that car which we were seeing in Brighton last week, the bright yellow Ford? Well, it's looking a bit like that, but it is having flames down the side. When I am driving it, I am feeling like a racing driver. It is being really cool. Of course it isn't going very fast as it is being very old. But it is making a very loud roaring noise, so it is seeming like a racing car.

I am wanting to come and visit you in my new car this weekend. Will you be being at home on Saturday morning? Phone me to say if you are being able to meet me then,

See you soon,

Trevor (Schumacher)!

Hi Andy,
I really love my new car!

in the continuous

C Read the following conversation. Correct all the underlined errors.

SAUL: Well, what ⁰<u>are you thinking</u> of this painting?

DEREK: Hmm. I don't know. I ¹<u>am really liking</u> the colours …

SAUL: But ²<u>does the artist try</u> to tell us something in this picture?

DEREK: That's not what this kind of art ³<u>is being</u> about. It just expresses a feeling … a mood.

SAUL: Oh. I ⁴<u>am not understanding</u> modern art. Sometimes you ⁵<u>are having</u> to think and sometimes you don't.

DEREK: I know. I ⁶<u>am preferring</u> sculpture. I want to see the Rodin exhibition. His work is really easy to understand.

SAUL: I don't like Rodin very much. He ⁷<u>is being</u> too sentimental for me.

DEREK: Are you feeling hungry? ⁸<u>I'm thinking</u> the restaurant is good here.

SAUL: I hope it's not expensive. ⁹<u>I'm not having</u> much money.

0   *do you think* ....

1   ....

2   ....

3   ....

4   ....

5   ....

6   ....

7   ....

8   ....

9   ....

18

MRS KHAN: Hello Dave, **I've been** away for a couple of weeks and you should have finished the work on my house by now. **I've** really **enjoyed** staying with my daughter and grandchildren, but **I've been** a bit worried about my house.

DAVE: Nice to see you, Mrs Khan. Well, **I've had** a few problems with suppliers, you know, but actually I'm quite happy with everything …

MRS KHAN: Does that mean that you **haven't finished** the work in the bathroom?

DAVE: Oh, the bathroom … well, we **haven't** exactly **finished** it, but you can use it.

MRS KHAN: What have you **finished**? What about the kitchen?

DAVE: Oh yes, the kitchen is almost finished, but we **haven't finished** the ceiling yet.

MRS KHAN: Do you mean you **haven't painted** it yet?

DAVE: **I've had** some problems, as I said … and Jim, my bricklayer, **has broken** his leg, so he **hasn't been able** to climb ladders or carry anything heavy …

MRS KHAN: So **have you done** anything?

DAVE: Oh yes! **I've built** the conservatory and **converted** the attic. It's going really well.

❶ form

We make the present perfect simple by using the present of **have** with the *past participle* of the main verb:

singular	plural
I **have talked** (I've talked)	we **have talked** (we've talked)
you **have talked** (you've talked)	you **have talked** (you've talked)
he / she / it **has talked** (he's talked)	they **have talked** (they've talked)

We often use the contracted form of the auxiliary (**'s** / **'ve**), particularly after pronouns (e.g. **I**, **he**, **they**):

- He**'s written** a long letter to the manager.
- They**'ve** often **said** they didn't like the music in the lift.

When we speak informally, we often use the contracted form with names and other noun subjects; we don't normally do this when we write:

- Your wet umbrella**'s dripped** water all over the floor.
- Tim and Nicky**'ve taken** all the toffees!

Remember, many common verbs have irregular past participles.
(For a list of irregular past participles, see page 286.)

The verb **go** changes to **has been to** in the present perfect when we mean *has visited*:

- Mr Conway **has been to** Venice. (= *He has visited Venice. He is not there now.*)

but we use **has gone to somewhere** to mean *is visiting*:

- He **has gone to** Venice. (= *He is in Venice now.*)

❷ questions and negatives

To make a question in the present perfect, we usually put the auxiliary verb (**have** / **has**) before the <u>subject</u>:

- **Have** <u>you</u> **found** your scarf?
- Why **has** <u>James</u> **left** the door open?

We make the negative by adding **not** or **n't** after the auxiliary **have** / **has**:

- Robin **has not seen** the film 'Titanic'!
- They **haven't mended** the computer yet.

We often reply to a present perfect question with a short **yes** / **no** *answer* using the auxiliary **have** / **has** or **haven't** / **hasn't**:

- 'Has Graham arrived yet?' 'Yes, he **has**.'
- 'Have the girls bought their bus tickets?' 'No, they **haven't**.'

❸ use

We use the present perfect when we are talking about the past in relation to the present. We use it for:

something which began in the past and is still the case:
- Andy **has been** friends with Paul since they were six. (*They are still friends.*)

something which has continued up to the present moment but has now finished:
- I**'ve been** away for a couple of weeks. (*I have just come back now.*)

something in the recent past which has direct consequences in the present:
- Woody **has bought** a new motorbike. (*He has got a new bike now.*)
- They **haven't finished** painting the hall. (*The hall is half painted.*)

We also use the present perfect when we talk about *repeated actions in a present period of time* (e.g. **today**, **this week**):
- I**'ve been** to the new sports centre every day **this week**.

We often use **so far** meaning *up till now*:
- Joe **has had** three driving lessons **so far this month**.

Note: For single, complete events, we usually use the past simple with **today**, **this week** etc:
- I **saw** Thomas **today** in the office.

❹ present perfect with adverbs (**never**, **often**, **just**, **already** etc)

We often use adverbs, such as **never**, **often**, **just**, **only**, **almost**, and **already**, with the present perfect. They go between the auxiliary and the main verb:
- Phil has **never** been to Portugal.
- Jean has **just** left for the airport. (= *She left a moment ago.*)
- Tom has **only** been here for a few minutes.

We use **ever** in questions and **not ever** or **never** in negative statements:
- 'Have you **ever** learnt to skydive?' 'No, I haven**'t ever** wanted to.'
- 'Has Jane **ever** been to our house?' 'No, I've **never** invited her.'

We use **still**, **yet**, and **quite** with **not** to talk about something that *has not happened*. **Still** goes before the auxiliary, **quite** after it, and **yet** usually goes at the end of the sentence. **Still not** indicates *concern* or *impatience*; **not yet** is more *neutral*; **not quite** means *almost*:
- I **still** haven**'t** finished this book. (*When will I finish it!?*)
- I haven**'t** finished this book **yet**. (*I will soon.*)
- I haven**'t quite** finished this book. (*I have almost finished it.*)

We use **yet** in positive and negative questions:
- Have you finished editing that film **yet**? = Have**n't** you finished editing that film **yet**?

❺ since and for

We often use the present perfect and **since** with *a specific time* to talk about something which has continued *up till now*:
- Paul has been here **since nine o'clock**.
- We've been studying 'Midsummer Night's Dream' **since the spring**.

And we use **for** with *a length of time* to talk about something which continued for *some time in the past, or up till now*:
- Miss Busia has only worked **for about half an hour** today. (*She has gone home.*)
- The doctor has stayed awake **for three days**. (*He is still awake.*)

71

A Read the text and put in the correct form of the words in brackets. Use the present perfect simple.

Yes, we (0) *'ve recently received* (recently / receive) a new work from Harland Strange. I (1) .... (not / see) it yet, but he says a reviewer (2) .... (write) a nice review of it in the newspaper. (3) .... (you / ever / see) any of his work? ... No? Well, it's just like his name – strange! I think the public (4) .... (often / find) modern art shocking, surprising, difficult, but this ... well ... let's say, I (5) .... (hear) it described as 'ghastly'. Another word people (6) .... (use) is 'horrible'. Isn't it exciting! The tickets for the private showing (7) .... (only / be) on sale since yesterday and Harland (8) .... (already / sell) 150 tickets. Some people (9) .... (be) wildly enthusiastic about this new work. ... No, we (10) .... (not / decide) how much we should charge for it yet. ...

B Diego and Mark are taking part in a skating competition. They are having a conversation in the dressing room. Complete each gap with the correct word from the box.

yet	quite	almost	still	just	ever
always	since	never	yet	~~already~~	

0 DIEGO: Hi Mark! You've *already* changed!

1 MARK: I've been here .... four o'clock.

2 DIEGO: I've .... arrived – only a minute or two ago. I missed the flight connection.

   MARK: I was wondering where you were!

3 DIEGO: I've .... done that before! It was terrible!

   MARK: Don't worry. You've got plenty of time to get ready.

4 DIEGO: But I've .... missed the deadline for registering for the competition!

   MARK: Calm down! You've still got a few minutes to sign up.

5 DIEGO: Up till now I've .... managed to get to the rink at least an hour early, so I have time to change.

   MARK: Pass me your cloak. I'll fix it for you.

6 DIEGO: Thanks. Have you seen any of the competitors ....?

   MARK: Yes. I've met the girls from Lithuania. They're very nice. Come on, let's go and register and watch the first round.

7 DIEGO: Just a minute. I haven't .... finished doing up my skates.

   MARK: Sorry. Your hands are really shaking!

8 DIEGO: Oh, I haven't .... felt so nervous before a competition!

   MARK: It's just because you're in a rush.

9 DIEGO: Have they put up a list of competitors ....?

   MARK: No, they haven't put up a list yet. Come on, let's go and register.

10 DIEGO: Sorry, I .... haven't finished doing up my skates!

Look at the picture and read and answer the questions. Write complete sentences with contractions ('s, 've etc) if you can.

0 'Has the concert started yet?' '*No, the concert hasn't started yet.*'

1 'Have they finished setting up the show?' 'No, ...'

2 'Has the girl finished sweeping the stage?' '..'

3 'Have the electricians connected the TV screens?' '..'

4 'Has Rob Grant ever won a prize for his music?'..'

5 'Where have they put the portable toilets?' '..'

6 'Have all the tickets been sold?' '..'

7 'Has the singer arrived yet?' '..'

8 'Have the security staff started work yet?' '..'

9 'Has the hamburger van arrived?'..'

10 'What have they stuck over the Rob Grant poster?'..'

My dear wife Elsbeth,
I landed on this island last night in darkness. To be honest, we did not intend to land here, and I'm not exactly sure which island we are on. I made a small error in my navigation and we hit a coral reef and the ship sank. I haven't found any other survivors, but I'm sure some of the men have landed safely because I have seen smoke coming from the other side of the island … unless other people live here. I haven't explored the island yet as I hurt my leg when the ship went down.

Don't worry about me. I have managed to find coconuts and breadfruit, and I've tried fishing but so far I haven't caught anything. I've seen a lot of fish, though, and I'm sure to catch one soon.

How are you, my dear? I hope you have not been too lonely since I left. I have thought a lot about our dear daughter, Matilda, and I regret that I have lost the watch she gave me. It had a piece of her lovely, brown hair in the back

❶ use

present perfect use	past simple use
We use the present perfect to talk about *a* **state** *or* **situation** *which started in the past and continues to now*: ■ I**'ve known** Jeremy for many years – *and I still know him.* ■ He **has thought** a lot about his daughter, Matilda, since he left England.	We use the past simple to talk about *something which was the* **situation** *in the past and is finished*: ■ I **knew** Tom for many years – but then he moved to South Africa. ■ I **thought** Mary was in Mexico, but apparently she's in Canada.
We use the present perfect when we are talking about *an* **action** *or* **event** *which affects the present*: ■ Oh look! The cat **has eaten** the goldfish. ■ Yvette **has sold** her car – *and she doesn't have one now.* ■ I**'ve found** my car keys! Let's go!	We use the past simple when we are talking about *an* **action** *or* **event** *that occurred at some time in the past*: ■ The cat **ate** the hamster last month. ■ Mike **sold** his old car in September and bought an Alfa Romeo. ■ When I **found** my keys, we immediately drove to the hospital.
We use the present perfect for *repeated events in a period of time from the past to now*: ■ John **has played** a lot of squash this month. ■ I **have seen** that film twice already. (For more on the present perfect simple, see unit 18.)	We use the past simple for *repeated events during some period in the past*: ■ Jake often **played** football for his school when he was a teenager. ■ We **saw** a lot of dolphins when were on a cruise last year. (For more on the past simple, see unit 15.)

present perfect and past simple

GARGANTUAN GAMES

A Read the passage and then the questions below. Write the answers, using the present perfect simple, or the past simple. Write in brackets which tense you are using with the initials – *PP* (present perfect), or *PS* (past simple).

Jim Patterson is a very successful man. He is 36. He started Gargantuan Games when he was only 24, because he was a great fan of computer games and wanted to invent some new games. He studied computer science at university for three years, until 1992, and then went to work for a big computer-software company. He worked there for a year, but he didn't like working for a big company. He left the company in 1993 and started his own company. He had to borrow a lot of money, but he paid it all back after three years and now he is making a lot of profit. He started his company with one other person, but they employed three other people after two years. Since then he has employed several other people, and now has a staff of about twenty-five. He got married in 2002. His wife, Leanne, has never worked for Gargantuan Games. She is a teacher, and hates computers!

He works very hard – in fact, today, he has had meetings all day and has missed his lunch again, so he's feeling hungry and tired.

0 How long has Jim been the Director of Gargantuan Games? *He has been the Director of Gargantuan Games since 1993. (PP)*

1 Why did he decide to start the company? ....

2 How long did he study computer science at university? ....

3 Did he like working for the big computer software company? ....

4 Has he always loved computer games? ....

5 How long has he been an employer? ....

6 How long did it take to pay back the money he borrowed? ....

7 When did he employ the first three other staff members? ....

8 How long has he been married? ....

9 Has Leanne worked for Gargantuan Games? ....

10 Has Jim missed his lunch again today? ....

B Read these sentences and circle the best form of the verb in each sentence.

0 Nabila (got) / has got home from school at 3.45.

1 She practised / has practised the violin for an hour, and now she's just finishing her favourite piece of music.

2 Her mother isn't at home because she didn't finish / hasn't finished work yet.

3 Yesterday Nabila didn't go / hasn't gone to school because she was ill.

4 During the last school holidays she worked / has worked in her father's stationery shop.

5 She had / has had a lot of experience of working in a stationery shop.

6 This evening she is going out, as a schoolfriend invited / has invited her to the cinema.

7 They are going to see 'The Talented Mr Ripley' even though she saw / has seen it before.

8 She likes Jude Law – and he once has given / gave her his autograph!

9 She met / has met him once at the première of one of his films and he signed her book.

10 He seemed / has seemed smaller than she expected.

Imran Khan **has been playing** the guitar in his band since he was 14. He has always loved music and has given up almost everything for his career as a rock star. His band is called *Rizzible* and he has decided to change his name to Izzy. His parents have always been very helpful and **have been paying** for his lessons and for his guitar strings for many years. Up till now he **has been playing** an old guitar that doesn't look very glamorous but now he wants a really funky, new instrument. He has found a second-hand guitar in a local music shop, which is deep blue with silver stars all over it. He took his dad to have a look at it, but Mr Khan didn't seem very impressed. He hasn't ever been to hear the band and he hasn't liked the boys who **have been coming** to the house. He said that Imran must pay for the new guitar himself.

His mother is not very happy with his attitude to study and work, and she **has been trying** to make him understand that he needs to have some qualifications. He says that he hasn't ever wanted to do anything else but play in his band, and that that is not going to change now. Poor Imran! He**'s been having** a bad time recently!

❶ form

We make the present perfect continuous with **have / has + been** with the **ing** *form* of the main verb:

singular	plural
I **have been swimming** (I've been)	we **have been swimming** (we've been)
you **have been swimming** (you've been)	you **have been swimming** (you've been)
he / she / it **has been swimming** (he's been)	they **have been swimming** (they've been)

We often use the contracted form of the first auxiliary (**'s** / **'ve**), after pronouns (e.g. **I**, **he**):
   ▪ He**'s been practising** the guitar this morning.
   ▪ Lucy and I**'ve been talking** for over an hour.
When we speak informally, we can often use the contracted form of the auxiliary with names and other noun subjects; we don't normally do this when we write:
   ▪ Anthony**'s been looking** for his dog.

To make the **ing** *form*, if the main verb ends in *consonant* + **e**, we cut off the **e** and add **ing**:
   take → **taking**   lose → **losing**
If the main verb ends with a *single vowel + single consonant* (e.g. **rob**), we usually double the consonant and add **ing**:
   drum → **drumming**   rob → **robbing**
Note: we don't double **w** and **y** when we make an **ing** *form*.

❷ questions and negatives

We make questions in the present perfect continuous by reversing the <u>subject</u> and the first auxiliary verb **has / have**:
   ▪ **Has** <u>Margaret</u> **been playing** golf this morning?
   ▪ **Have** <u>the children</u> **been drawing** pictures?
We often reply to a question with a short **yes / no** *answer* using the auxiliary **has / have**:
   ▪ 'Has Graham **been living** here long?' 'Yes, he **has**. About ten years.'

We make the negative with **not** or **n't** after the first auxiliary verb **has / have**:
   ▪ Peter **hasn't been working** very hard.

❸ present perfect continuous: use

We use the present perfect continuous to talk *about an activity or situation which started in the past and continued up till the present*. We often use a **_time clause_** to say *how long something has happened for*:

- We **have been playing** bridge <u>for hours</u>. (*We're still playing now.*)
- Paul **has been working** on his computer <u>all day</u>. (*He's still working now.*)

We also use it for *something that began in the past and has very recently finished*; often there is now some evidence of the event:

- Mary **has been painting** her nails. (*Her nails are red and shiny.*)
- The cat **has been eating** the cheese. (*The cheese is nearly gone.*)

We use **go** + **ing** *form* for sports and recreational activities (e.g. **go swimming**, **go skating**, **go dancing**, **go jogging**), but to make the present perfect continuous we don't use **go**:

- I **have been swimming** today. NOT ~~I've been going swimming today~~.

❹ present perfect continuous with **for, since, how long, just**

We often use **since** and **for** with this verb form, in the same way as with the present perfect simple, to specify *how long* an activity or situation has occurred.
We use **for** with a period of time to talk about *how long something has been in progress* to now:

- I've **been waiting** for the bus **for hours**. (*I am still waiting.*)

We use **since** with a time or date to talk about *when something*, which is in progress now, *started*:

- Mr and Mrs Hamley **have been living** in Darlington **since 1958**.

We use **how long** at the beginning of questions when *we want to know the duration of something* which is still in progress:

- **How long have** you **been working** for the college? (*You work there now.*)

We use **just** after the first auxiliary to say that *something happened* and *stopped very recently*:

- Andrea and Sue **have just been arguing**. (*They stopped arguing a minute ago.*)

❺ present perfect continuous or simple

If we are talking about *a single event or a short action*, we usually only use the **_present perfect simple_**:

- Helen **has put** on her coat and is about to leave.

For *longer actions* (*activities*) we can use the present perfect simple or continuous:

- We **haven't been listening** to the lecture. OR We **haven't listened** ...

There is a difference of focus between the use of the continuous and simple forms:
where *the activity is more important than the result*, we choose the **_present perfect continuous_**:

- Linda **has been washing** the dog. (*That's why there is water everywhere.*)

where *the result is more important than the activity*, we choose the **_present perfect simple_**:

- Linda **has washed** the dog. (*That's why the dog is very clean.*)

For *repeated actions* in the past to now, we use the **_present perfect continuous_**:

- Mary **has been performing** in a show for the last two months.

But remember, we do not use the present perfect continuous to talk about <u>every</u> *time that something has happened*. We usually use the present perfect simple:

- <u>Every</u> time I**'ve gone** to the market, I**'ve spent** too much money!
- We **have bought** something in <u>every</u> shop that we **have gone** into.

There are some verbs, called **_state verbs_**, which are not often used in the continuous. These are verbs of *possession* (**have, own**), emotion (**like, love, enjoy**), *thought* (**think, understand**), *description* (**be, seem**), and *sense* (**see, feel**). With state verbs we usually use the simple form:

- Harry **has loved** June for many years. NOT ~~... has been loving...~~

Some verbs have *action* meanings (e.g. **have, see**) where they can be used in the continuous.

A Lucy has been looking after her niece, Jamila. She is on the phone to Jamila's mother, her sister May. Write in what Lucy says, using the words in brackets, and the present perfect simple or continuous.

0 MAY: What has Jamila been doing?

 LUCY: She *has been cooking* (cook).

1 MAY: Has she made something nice?

 LUCY: Well, no, she .... (not / make) anything, exactly.

2 MAY: What do you mean?

 LUCY: She .... (try) to make a cake.

3 MAY: Has she made a terrible mess?

 LUCY: Yes, she .... (cover) the kitchen with food!

4 MAY: But has she been having fun?

 LUCY: Yes, I think she .... (have) a brilliant time.

5 MAY: I'm really sorry she's made so much work for you.

 LUCY: That's OK. I .... (really / enjoy) looking after her.

6 MAY: What about you? What have you been doing recently?

 Lucy: Oh, I .... (dance) in a show at the Phoenix Theatre.

7 MAY: That's great! Have they been paying you?

 LUCY: Well, no, but it .... (be) a very useful experience.

8 MAY: Have you met some important people?

 LUCY: I .... (meet) someone, but I don't know if you would call him important!

9 MAY: Lucy! Do you mean you've got a new boyfriend?

 LUCY: No, we .... (not / go out) together yet. But I'm hoping …

10 MAY: I'm so glad! It's been ages since you went out with anyone.

 LUCY: You .... (not / come) to see me dance for ages. Why don't you come this evening? Then you can meet Mark!

B Read the descriptions and write a sentence about what has happened, or what has been happening, using the words in brackets. Use the present perfect continuous wherever you can. Only use the present perfect simple when you have to.

0 Bob is walking on the golf course. He is wearing golfing shoes and carrying a set of golf clubs. He started his game three hours ago.

 (play / for) *He has been playing golf for three hours.*

1 It is 11 p.m. and Stephen is sitting in the library. He has a book on cardiology open on the table and is writing notes in an exercise book. He came to the library at 5 p.m.

 (study / for) ....

2 Delia is putting on her coat at the health centre, preparing to go home. Her shift began at 9 a.m.

 (work / since) ....

3 Sally is in the gym. She is on the rowing machine and still has ten minutes before she finishes her routine. She rows for twenty minutes.

 (row / for) ....

4 Phyllis is in the bathroom putting on her make-up. It is 8.30. She started half an hour ago.

(put on / for) ....

5 Qasim Khan is on his way to work. He is stuck in a big traffic jam. He left home at 7.00.

(drive / since) ....

6 Andrew is Professor of Electronic Engineering. He was made a professor in 2000.

(be / since) ....

7 Diego is a prize-winning skater. He has competed in the local ice-dance competition for seven years.

(compete / for) ....

8 Diego won the first prize four years ago and has won it each year since then.

(win / for) ....

9 Mary Ross started farming when she was 23. She is now 30. She is still a farmer.

(farm / for) ....

10 Mr Patterson is having a meeting with his staff at Gargantuan Games. He called the meeting at 2.00 and it is now 4.15.

(have a meeting / for) ....

Read the email and put in the best form of the verbs. Use contracted forms.

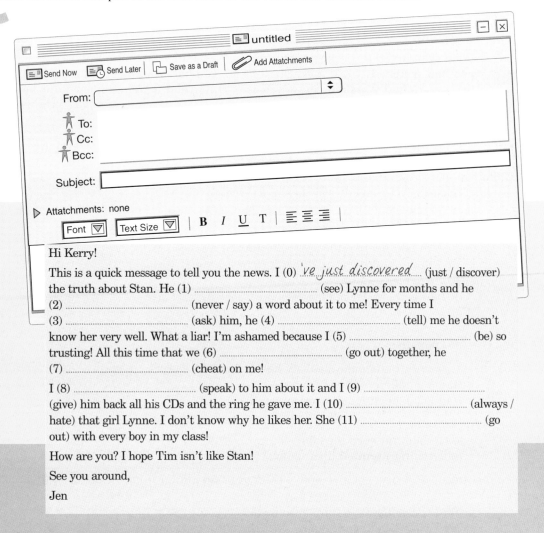

Hi Kerry!

This is a quick message to tell you the news. I (0) _'ve just discovered_ (just / discover) the truth about Stan. He (1) .... (see) Lynne for months and he (2) .... (never / say) a word about it to me! Every time I (3) .... (ask) him, he (4) .... (tell) me he doesn't know her very well. What a liar! I'm ashamed because I (5) .... (be) so trusting! All this time that we (6) .... (go out) together, he (7) .... (cheat) on me!

I (8) .... (speak) to him about it and I (9) .... (give) him back all his CDs and the ring he gave me. I (10) .... (always / hate) that girl Lynne. I don't know why he likes her. She (11) .... (go out) with every boy in my class!

How are you? I hope Tim isn't like Stan!

See you around,

Jen

21

In 1943 Bridge Farm was the home of William and Matilda Gibbons and their son Jack. Jack remembers that life was harder then, with no car, and no telephone or electricity in the house. On October 8th it was a quiet, calm night and the family **had** all **gone** to bed early, as farmers always did in those days. At 3.30 a.m. the family were woken up by a terrible noise. A plane, which **had been** on its way back to its airbase in Norfolk, **had lost** control and **crashed** into two trees, and the branches **had torn** off both wings. William Gibbons ran to where the plane **had crashed**. He saw the airmen climbing out of the plane; fortunately no one **had died** in the accident. After the family **had invited** the shocked crew into their house for tea, they immediately sent little Jack off on his bicycle in the dark to the next village. When he got to the village, he woke up the post-mistress and asked her to phone the police. Jack then bicycled back to his house and went back to bed. It **had been** one of the most memorable nights of the war for Jack and his parents.

❶ form

The past perfect simple is made with the past of **have** (**had**, **'d**) and the *past participle* of the main verb:

singular	plural
I **had watched** (I'd watched)	we **had watched** (we'd watched)
you **had watched** (you'd watched)	you **had watched** (you'd watched)
he / she / it **had watched** (she'd watched)	they **had watched** (they'd watched)

In formal contexts and writing we use the full form **had** + *past participle*:
■ I signed the contract after I **had read** it carefully.
In speech we usually use the contracted form of the auxiliary (**'d**) after pronouns (**I**, **you**, **he** etc):
■ It was six o'clock and we**'d waited** for hours for the bus.
In very informal speech we use the contracted form after names and nouns as well:
■ Peter**'d** never **played** rugby before he went to university.
Remember, many common verbs have irregular past participles, such as **been**, **taken**, and **gone**. (For more on irregular verbs, see page 286.)

The verb **go** changes to **had been** in the past perfect when we mean *had visited*:
■ Mr Conway **had been to** Jamaica. (= *He had visited Jamaica.*)
but we use **had gone** to mean *was visiting*:
■ He **had gone to** Jamaica. (= *He was in Jamaica at that time.*)

❷ questions and negatives

We make the questions by putting the auxiliary **had** before the <u>subject</u>:
■ **Had** <u>Sue</u> **taken** her bag with her?
■ **Had** <u>Frank</u> **been** too busy to answer the email?

We make the negative by adding **not** or **n't** after the auxiliary **had**:
■ Robin **had not seen** the film.
■ John **hadn't mended** the computer yet.

We often reply to a past perfect question with a short **yes** / **no** *answer* using the auxiliary **had** or **hadn't**:
■ 'Had Graham arrived yet?' 'Yes, he **had**.'
■ 'Had Jane found her passport?' 'No, she **hadn't**.'

❸ use

We use the past perfect to make it clear that *something happened before <u>something else happened</u>*:

- Pat **had cooked** breakfast <u>when Sally got up</u>. (= *Pat cooked breakfast and then Sally got up*.)
- <u>When Mike arrived</u>, Dan **had** already **left** the house. (= *Dan left the house and then Mike arrived*.)
- After they **had finished** the plastering, <u>they started painting the walls</u>.
- As soon as John **had mended** my computer, <u>he phoned me</u> to tell me it was ready for collection.
- <u>They put a big stick in the ground</u> to show where they **had found** the box of old coins.
- <u>When Brendan got home, he saw</u> that someone **had taken** his expensive stereo.
- <u>We waited three weeks</u> for the books which we **had ordered** to arrive.

We use the past perfect to talk about *something which happened in the past but which had consequences <u>at the time we are talking about</u>*:

- Toni**'d bought** a new computer <u>so she was selling her old one</u>.
- <u>I couldn't concentrate in the lesson</u> because I **hadn't slept** enough that night.

We use the past perfect to talk about *a state or situation which started in the past and was still the case at the <u>time we are talking about in the past</u>*, usually with a time phrase (e.g. **for ten years**):

- <u>When he was 15</u>, Phil **had known** his friend Ross for ten years.
- <u>When the doorbell rang</u>, James **had been** in the bath for half an hour.

We use the past perfect when we talk about *things which happened or existed in a period of time up to <u>the time we are talking about</u>*:

- He**'d watched** sixteen films <u>by the end of January</u>.
- The police **had made** ten arrests <u>by the time the match ended</u>.
- She **had become** very rich but <u>she still wanted to be more successful</u>.
- <u>After the bombing</u>, where there **had been** streets <u>there was nothing but rubble</u>.
- <u>Before Mary joined the company</u>, it **had not been** very successful.

❹ in reported speech

We often use the past perfect when we are saying *what someone said or thought*,

when they used the <u>present perfect</u>:

- Tom thought he**'d left** his wallet on the bus. (= *Tom thought '<u>I've left</u> my wallet on the bus!'*)

when they used the <u>past simple</u>:

- Robert said that he**'d enjoyed** the party. (= *Robert said 'I <u>enjoyed</u> the party.'*)

when they used the <u>past perfect</u>:

- Jane said that Dan **had** already **left**. (= *Jane said 'Dan <u>had</u> already <u>left</u>.'*)

Note: We can also report the past simple with the past simple:

- Robert said that he **enjoyed** the party. (= *Robert said 'I <u>enjoyed</u> the party.'*)

(For more on reporting speech, see units 60 and 61.)

❺ past perfect with adverbs (**never, often, already** etc)

With the past perfect we often use **never**, **often**, **just**, **really**, and **already** before the main verb:

- When Phil was 21, he had **never** been to a football match.
- Daisy had **often** forgotten her appointments before she got a diary.
- Sam had **just** finished his meal when the restaurant closed.
- Paul had **already** left when I arrived.

A Read the following text.

Adelaide Hall was a very popular jazz singer in Britain during the war years. Before she came to Britain, she **had been** a successful singer in America for a number of years. She **had come** to London in 1938 to perform in 'The Sun Never Sets' at the Drury Lane Theatre, and she loved London and the British loved her. She very quickly became one of Britain's best-loved entertainers and she decided to stay in England. She stayed for over fifty years until her death in 1993. She was important partly because she **had been** the first black star to sign a long-term contract with the BBC. Later, she also signed a recording contract with Decca. By the time of her death she **had recorded** over seventy discs. During the war she **had worked** very hard, and she **had sung** on the radio, in the theatre, in the movies, and in nightclubs. Unfortunately a bomb destroyed the club which she had bought in 1940, and she had to move out of London and live in the Surrey countryside. She often helped on her neighbours' farms during the summer!

By the end of 1941, she **had become** the best-paid entertainer in Britain! If there was an air raid during a concert, she always continued with the performance. On one occasion, when she was performing in Lewisham, and the siren **had started**, she asked the audience if anyone wanted to leave the theatre. They all shouted 'no', and she continued to sing for the next four hours, while bombs fell around them.

When the war ended she was in Hamburg singing to the soldiers, and she went immediately to Berlin. She was shocked by the devastation. Where there **had been** streets there was nothing but rubble; she saw that people **had put up** wooden boards with the street names written on them to show where the streets **had** once **been**. When she left Berlin, she was feeling very sad.

Refer back to the text about Adelaide Hall and join the following two sentences, using the past perfect in one of them. Use the word in brackets. Sometimes it goes at the beginning and sometimes in the middle.

0   Adelaide Hall came to Britain. She was already famous in America for a number of years. (when)
    When Adelaide Hall came to Britain, she had already been famous in America for a number of years.

1   She decided to stay in England. She became one of Britain's best-loved entertainers. (because)

2   She died in 1993. She lived in England for over fifty years. (when)

3   She signed a long-term contract with the BBC. She signed a recording contract with Decca. (after)

4   She died in 1993. She recorded over seventy discs. (when)

5   She moved out of London. A bomb destroyed her club in Mayfair. (because)

6   She became the best-paid entertainer in Britain. She still worked on her neighbours' farms. (but)

7   She continued her performance. The air-raid siren started. (after)

8   She asked the audience if they wanted to leave. She continued her concert for another four hours. (after)

9   People wrote the names of the streets on wooden boards. They showed where the streets were before the bombing. (to)

10 When Adelaide left Berlin, she felt very sad. She was shocked by the devastation. (because)

B

Read the following text and put in the right phrases from the box in the gaps.

> had changed   had selected
> had finished decorating   had improved   had sold
> had signed   ~~had never worked~~   had been
> had promised   had looked   had ordered

When Annie decided to open her own hat shop, she (0) *had never worked* in a shop before. After she (1) .... at a lot of shops to rent, she chose a small shop in a nice area of the city centre. Josh came to see it and thought it looked great. As soon as she (2) .... the lease, she took the train to Paris to visit a hat factory. There were hats of all kinds, and she had a lot of difficulty choosing the perfect hats for her shop. She loved the elegant, little, ladies' hats, but she (3) .... herself that she would be sensible and practical and choose hats for the English weather and the British lifestyle. After she (4) .... the hats that she wanted for her shop, she paid for them and then returned to England. While waiting for the hats which she (5) .... to arrive, she decorated her shop herself. The shop was very small, and before she rented it, it (6) .... cards and posters. She decided to paint it in very pale, pastel colours and, where the counter (7) ...., she put a modern sofa and a small table with a mirror on it, so the customers could sit in comfort to try on their hats. When she (8) .... the shop, it seemed much smarter and bigger. Josh came to visit the shop and saw that she (9) .... it completely. He said that he thought she (10) .... it enormously, and that he was sure it would be a huge success.

C

Forrest Clark was an American airman in Europe during the Second World War. Read his story, and then imagine that you have interviewed him. Read the questions and then report what he said, using the underlined phrases. Use the past perfect in your answers.

I was in England in 1945, because I'd escaped from France to England that spring. That summer I was in Brighton on holiday with some other American airmen. We were in the Brighton skating rink when an air-raid siren started. We were all very frightened, so we ran out of the rink and skated down the street, with bombs falling all round us.

I woke up the next day in a hotel by the beach with my skates still on, and there were some Australians in the hotel as well. I had a bad cut on my head, but I wasn't badly injured. I don't remember what happened that night, but I think the Australians saved my life.

I was very happy when the war ended and I went back to America because I hated the weather in England!

I've never been back to England, but I'd love to go and see the Brighton skating rink again. Brighton is great – I really enjoyed my holiday there – until that air raid!

0 When was Forrest Clark in England? – He said he
   had been in England in 1945.
1 Why was he in England? – He said he
   ....
2 What was he doing in Brighton? – He said he
   ....
3 Where were he and his friends when the air-raid siren started? – He said they
   ....
4 What did they do? – He said they
   ....
5 Where did he wake up? – He said he
   ....
6 Was he injured? – He said he
   ....
7 Who saved his life? – He said that he thought
   ....
8 How did he feel when the war ended? – He said he
   ....
9 Has he been back to England since the war? – He said he ....
10 Did he like Brighton? – He said he
   ....

LAWYER: When you saw the accused man steal the sweater from the shop, **had you been watching** him for some time?

MISS JENKINS: No. **I'd been shopping** in the store and I was walking past the sweater section when he picked up the sweater and put it in his bag.

LAWYER: Had you seen the man before?

MISS JENKINS: No, I'd never seen him before. I only noticed him because he was behaving oddly.

LAWYER: I think you knew the man, and had known him for some time! I think you **had been following** and **watching** him ...

MISS JENKINS: It's not true! I was just walking past.

LAWYER: Isn't it true that you not only knew this man, but that, in fact, you had been engaged to this man?

MISS JENKINS: Oh dear. Yes. It's true. We were engaged. We **had been going out** for three years when we got engaged.

LAWYER: And had he ever been in trouble with the police before?

MISS JENKINS: No. Not as far as I know. He'd never been in trouble with the police or anything.

LAWYER: So what made you think he **had been shoplifting**?

MISS JENKINS: I didn't! I admit it. I **had been feeling** angry with him for years for breaking off the engagement and I was just trying to punish him! He didn't really do anything wrong in the shop!

❶ form

We make the past perfect continuous with the past of **have** (**had**, **'d**) + **been** and the **ing** *form* of the main verb:

singular	plural
I **had been running** (I'd been running)	we **had been running** (we'd been running)
you **had been running** (you'd been running)	you **had been running** (you'd been running)
he / she / it **had been running** (he'd been running)	they **had been running** (they'd been running)

(For more on the spelling of the **ing** *form*, see unit 13.)

In speech we usually use the contracted form of the auxiliary (**'d**) after pronouns (**I**, **you**, **he** etc):
- We**'d been waiting** for hours for the bus.

In very informal speech we use the contracted form after names and nouns as well:
- She said my sister**'d been sleeping** all morning!

In formal contexts and writing we use the full form **had** + *past participle* + **ing** *form*.

It is possible to use the same auxiliary with more than one **ing** *form* if the subject of the verbs remains the same:
- We had been **singing**, **dancing**, and **laughing** all evening.

❷ questions and negatives

To make the question form, we reverse the first auxiliary (**had**) and the <u>subject</u>:
- **Had** <u>the cake</u> **been cooking** for long enough when you took it out?

To make the negative we can use **had not**, **hadn't**, or **'d not**:
- Simon **hadn't been talking** very loudly so I didn't hear him.
- When Stephen took his exam he**'d not been studying** very long.
  NOT ~~... he'dn't ...~~

We often reply to a past perfect continuous question with a short **yes** / **no** *answer* using the auxiliary **had** or **hadn't**:
- '**Had** Graham **been talking** all through the meeting?' 'Yes, he **had**.'

❸ use

We use the past perfect continuous to talk about *an activity or situation which began before the time we are talking about in the past*:

- When you arrived, I'**d been watching** TV since 7 o'clock.
- It was lunchtime and Tom **had been working** in the garage all that morning.

We also use this form to talk about *repeated events over a period up to a moment in the past*:

- The children **had been going** to school by bus for three months, when they cancelled the school bus service.

We often use the past perfect continuous in questions with **how long** to ask *how long something had been happening at a moment in the past*:

- **How long** had Michael been working in Brussels before he moved to Paris?

❹ in reported speech

We use the past perfect continuous when we say *what someone said or thought in the past*, when they used the present perfect continuous:

- Tom said he **had been talking** too much. (= Tom said '*I've been talking too much!*')

(For more on reporting speech, see units 60 and 61.)

❺ already and just

With the past perfect continuous we can use *just* and *already*:

- When Grace did her first concert, she **had already been learning** the flute for ten years.
- When I met David, he **had just been opening** a new bank account.

❻ since and for

We often use the past perfect continuous with **since** and **for**. We use **since** with a time (e.g. **6 o'clock**, **last week**) and **for** with a period of time (e.g. **three weeks**, **three hours**):

- When I got home, Paul had been waiting **since** nine o'clock.
- Miss Burn had only been working **for** about half an hour when she got up and left.

❼ past perfect continuous or simple

If we are talking about *a single event or a short action before a time in the past*, we usually use the simple form:

- We got to the station at 6.35 but the train **had** already gone. It **had left** at 6.30.
- We **had seen** the film before, so we didn't go to the cinema.

For *longer actions and situations before a time in the past* we usually use the continuous form:

- It **had been raining** all morning.
- We **had been talking** for a long time.

Some verbs, such as **be**, **have**, and **know**, are not often used in the continuous.
(For verbs which are not normally used in continuous forms, see unit 17.)

A Read the following sentences and decide what happened first. Write **1** in the brackets after the thing that happened first and **2** after the thing that happened second, or if the two things are at the same time write **S**.

0 Yesterday I got to work late (2) because I'd missed the train (1).

1 Miss French had made me some coffee ( ) but it was cold ( ).

2 At lunchtime I had to go to the bank ( ) but I'd left my wallet in my jacket pocket ( ).

3 When I got back to the office, ( ) Mr Dearlove had been waiting for me for about an hour ( ).

4 After we'd been talking for a few minutes, ( ) the phone rang and it was my wife ( ).

5 She asked me ( ) if I had managed to get some cash at lunch time ( ).

6 I said ( ) I had not been able to get any ( ).

7 I said ( ) that I had met Louise outside the bank ( ).

8 I realised ( ) that Mr Dearlove had been waiting patiently all the time I was talking to my wife ( ).

9 I had been telling her the story ( ) while he sat there listening ( ).

B Put the verbs in brackets in the past perfect continuous or simple in the gaps.

0 In the morning Kirsty got out of bed and looked out of the bedroom window. She saw that the sun was shining but that it _had been snowing_ (snow).

1 She .... (sleep) in the attic at the top of the house.

2 The noise of the postman's van .... (wake) her up.

3 She .... (arrive) the evening before in the dark.

4 When she arrived, her mother .... (wait) for her at the station.

5 She .... (forget) how lovely the view was from up there!

6 She could see some footprints in the snow and she hoped the postman .... (bring) something for her.

7 She could smell coffee and toast – someone .... (get up).

8 When she went into the kitchen, she saw that her mother .... (buy) a new cooker.

9 It was nice to be home! She .... (live) abroad for too long!

C Write sentences about what happened to Andrew, using the words in the brackets, and the past perfect simple or continuous.

0   When I phoned Andrew, he was very unhappy (because / something terrible / happen / the day before)
    because something terrible had happened the day before.

1   Last Monday, water started coming through Andrew's ceiling, (because the water tank / start / to leak)

2   He couldn't phone the plumber (because / he / lose / his phone number)

3   He went next door but his neighbours were not in (because / they / go / away on holiday)

4   Eventually he managed to contact a plumber but he was very anxious, (because / the water / drip / for hours)

5   When the plumber finally arrived, Andrew (wait / for three hours)

6   The plumber took a long time to come to Andrew's house (because / he / work / on another job)

7   An hour later Andrew had to call a builder as well, (because / the ceiling / collapse)

8   Andrew was very upset (because / the dirty water / ruin / his collection of football memorabilia)

9   He was sure he could get back some money (because / he / insure / everything)

10 The next week he received a season ticket from his local team, (because / the manager / hear / about Andrew's disaster)

11 He was very pleased and excited, especially (because / his heroes / invite / him / to meet them!)

Next week, Mark and Diego **are going** on tour with their ice-dance team. They **are going** to Australia and **travelling** right across the country, performing in all the big towns. Julie, their manager, is busy organising the tour. She has to get the team of eight safely all the way from Bournemouth to Brisbane and back in a month, a round trip of about 8,000 miles! They **are flying** from Heathrow airport on December 6th at 6.30 a.m. It is summer in Australia so they have to take all their summer clothes as well as their costumes for the show. Julie hopes it won't be too hot for them. They **arrive** in Perth on December 7th and **perform** there each night for the next three days, then they **fly** to Alice Springs in the heart of Australia and **stay** there for another three days. They **visit** Adelaide, Melbourne and Sydney, where they **are spending** Christmas day, if all the plans go well! They **are flying** to Brisbane after New Year and then **returning** to Britain on January 7th.

Diego is very excited about it. He has never been to Australia and he**'s going to try** to visit his Aunt Tracey in Canberra while he is there. Mark's girlfriend is also in the team and they **are thinking** of getting married in Sydney! They have heard it is a very romantic place for a wedding.

❶ future forms

There is no future tense form in English. Instead we use present tense forms, or **will**, to talk about the future. We choose a form to say whether an event is *planned*, *expected*, *intended*, or whether it is *dependent* on something else. We often have a choice of two or more different verb forms in a sentence about the future, with no significant difference in meaning. But sometimes there is only one correct form that we can use.

❷ present simple for future schedules and timetables

We use the ***present simple*** for *future schedules* or *timetables*, rather than personal plans:
- The Michigan ferry **leaves** at 4.30.
- The college term **starts** in October.

Note: We don't use the present simple with future meaning in main clauses when we are talking about ordinary, unscheduled events. We usually use the ***present continuous*** or **be going to** to talk about personal plans and ordinary, unscheduled events in the future:
- **Is** Harry **staying** for dinner this evening? NOT ~~Does Harry stay for dinner this evening?~~
- Jack**'s going** to phone you. NOT ~~Jack phones you.~~

❸ present simple for suggestions

If we want to *suggest an action in the future to someone*, we use **why** with a *present simple negative question*:

> ▪ **Why don't** you **stay** for dinner?
> ▪ **Why doesn't** Carl **come** over this evening?

To suggest *some action that we can do in the future with other people*, we use **Let's** + *infinitive* or **Why don't we** + *infinitive*:

> ▪ Come on! **Let's catch** this bus.
> ▪ **Why don't we stay** in Paris tomorrow night?

❹ present continuous for personal plans and arrangements

We use the **present continuous** to talk about *personal plans and arrangements*:

> ▪ Mr Jenkins **is coming** to Harlow for the wedding.
> ▪ Mr Parsons **is delivering** the papers this weekend.

There are some verbs which are not usually used in the continuous. We don't usually use verbs describing *states*, such as **be** and **see**, in the continuous with future meaning. In these cases we usually use **will** or **be going to**:

> ▪ They**'ll be** in Turkey on Thursday. NOT ~~They'll be being in Turkey…~~
> ▪ He**'s going to see** the Greek islands from the plane. NOT ~~He is seeing the Greek islands …~~

Note: **See** can be used in the continuous for future plans when it has the meaning of *meet*:

> ▪ I**'m seeing** John at six o'clock. (= *I'm meeting John at six.*)

(For more on verbs that are not often used in the continuous, see unit 17.)

❺ be going to for intentions and expectations

To say what *someone intends to do*, we usually use **be going to** + *infinitive*:

> ▪ Maria **is going to write** a report on the meeting.
> ▪ The staff **are going to work** very hard over the next two weeks.

We also use this form for *things which we expect to happen*:

> ▪ I really think it**'s going to** snow soon.
> ▪ Lucy**'s going to** win the cup, I'm sure.

❻ present simple with **when, as soon as**, and **I hope**

In a time clause with future meaning, beginning with **when** or **as soon as**, we use the present simple to talk about something happening in the future. The <u>main clause</u> uses **will** or **be going to**:

> ▪ **When** I **am** old, <u>I think I'll live by the sea</u>.
> ▪ <u>Mr Franks is going to come and see us</u> **as soon as** he **gets** here.

After **I hope** we can use the present simple (or **will**) to talk about future events or situations:

> ▪ I hope you **have** a lovely time in France. (= I hope you**'ll** have a lovely time …)
> ▪ I hope Frank **is**n't late! (= I hope Frank **won't** be late!)

future: present simple, present continuous, and be going to

A Read the following sentences and say whether the underlined words describe:
(a) a schedule or a timetabled event
(b) a suggestion
(c) a personal plan or arrangement
(d) a personal intention or an expectation

0 <u>Let's find out</u> something about Stephen's plans! ....*b*....

1 Stephen Cross <u>is studying</u> hard all summer. ....

2 It's <u>going to be</u> very hard work. ....

3 The first exam <u>is</u> on June 13th – a very unlucky day! ....

4 Stephen and his friends <u>aren't going to go</u> out much in June. ....

5 Stephen's flatmate Bob <u>is doing</u> the same exams… ....

6 …so they <u>are going to revise</u> together. ....

7 Stephen <u>is going</u> to Barbados to see his mother when the exams are finished. ....

8 When he gets home, he <u>is going to do</u> absolutely nothing for a month! ....

9 His girlfriend Sophie said '<u>Let's not see</u> each other in June.' ....

10 But she <u>is flying</u> to Barbados with him in July! ....

B Read the following email from Bob Markham to his friend Dean in California. Decide if the underlined verbs have present or future meaning.

Hi Dean,

How are you? [0]<u>I'm</u> fine. My news is that my cousin Paul [1]<u>is arriving</u> tomorrow. [2]<u>He's living</u> in Australia but [3]<u>he comes</u> to England every year, Dad says. This summer [4]<u>he's spending</u> a month in Cambridge. [5]<u>He's going to work</u> for a study centre here, doing some research or something. I think he's a scientist or economist – anyway, it's something boring. I think he [6]<u>lives</u> in Perth. [7]<u>He's arriving</u> at Heathrow airport at 7.30 a.m. and Dad says [8]<u>I'm going to have to</u> go to meet him. Then [9]<u>he's staying</u> at my house for a few days, in my room! Of course Phyllis won't let him have her room. It's a real nuisance! I hope he [10]<u>behaves</u> well! When [11]<u>he gets</u> here, [12]<u>I'll have to</u> spend a lot of time with him showing him around Cambridge. If he's boring, [13]<u>I'm thinking</u> of introducing him to my friend Gecks. He's the most boring person in the world!

[14]<u>I'm</u> in a hurry now, so – bye for now!

Bob

0 *present* ....
1 ....
2 ....
3 ....
4 ....
5 ....
6 ....
7 ....
8 ....
9 ....
10 ....
11 ....
12 ....
13 ....
14 ....

present continuous, and be going to

Look at the clues and the beginnings of the sentences, and write ten sentences about what is happening tomorrow. In each sentence use the correct form of the verb in brackets.

0 **F1 FORMULA 1** | SEA GA2 241 | BERNIE ECCLES PRESENTS FORMULA ONE RACING AT SILVERSTONE | 28.50 3.50 GRAND 32.00 PRIX SILVERSTONE | THE GRAND PRIX - JULY 11th | www.formula1.com
(see)

Keith *is going to see the Grand Prix at Silverstone.*

1 From: London | Departs: 7.30am
(leave / at)

The train ....

2 To: Northampton | Arrives: 8.45am
(get / to)

It ....

3 EUSTON STATION – CAFE | THANK YOU | COFFEE 1.20 | CROISSANT 1.10 | TOTAL 2.30 | CASH 2.50 | CHANGE 0.20
(have / breakfast)

He ....

4 -- | Great! | See you at Northampton Station at 9, | Imran | --
(meet)

Keith ....

5 FARE: SINGLE | FROM: NORTHAMPTON BR STN | TO: SILVERSTONE RACE TRK
(take the bus)

They ....

6 -- | Sorry, | I can't come. | Take lots of photos for me.
(come)

Bob ....

7 I can't come. | Take lots of photos for me, | Bob | --
(take)

Keith ....

8 THE COPSE GRANDSTAND B | Silverstone Formula 1 International World Championship, Grand Prix | THE COPSE GRANDSTAND B | Silverstone Formula 1 International World Championship, Grand Prix
(sit)

Keith and Imran ....

9 PROGRAMME: FIRST RACE: 10am
(begin / at)

The first race ....

10 Lunch Menu | The Priory Restaurant | Silverstone
(have / lunch)

They ....

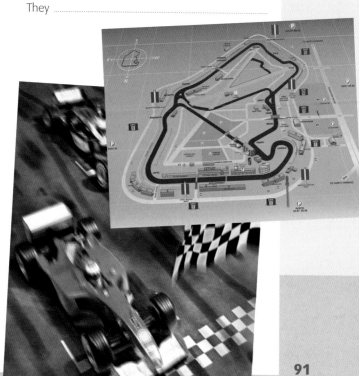

When you come back home, my darling,
with your knapsack on your shoulder,
we'll be waiting for you at the station,
with love in our hearts for my soldier.

The guns will stop soon, my love,
and the smoke will drift away,
and those who fought so bravely,
will wake from the nightmare one day.

Think of me each day, my darling,
and I won't be sad and blue.
Our love was made in heaven and
My Christmas present will be you!

❶ form

We can use **will** (or **'ll**) + *infinitive* to talk about the future. We usually use the contracted form (**'ll**) especially in conversation:

- She**'ll finish** the job next week.
- Things**'ll get** better soon.

We use **will not** (or **won't**) in the negative:

- The staff **won't like** the new plan.

We also sometimes use **shall**, with **I** and **we**, to talk about the future:

- I **shall phone** you tomorrow.
- We **shall see** what happens next.

The contracted form of the negative is **shan't**, though this is not very common now:

- I **shan't** see the beginning if I don't hurry!

We can also use **be going to** + *infinitive* to talk about the future. We often use the contracted form, **'m / 's / 're going to**, after the subject:

- **I'm going to** finish this essay later.
- That pan**'s going to** boil over!

We use the contracted form **'m / 's / 're not going to** or **isn't / aren't going to** in the negative:

- **I'm not going to** say anything to Elizabeth.
- We**'re not going** to buy anything in the market. = We **aren't going to** buy ...

❷ will and be going to for hopes, expectations, and intentions

We can use **will** or **be going to** to talk about *hopes* (things that we want to happen):

- I hope it **won't rain**.
- Dad hopes Jane **is going to be** happier in her new house.

We can use **will** or **be going to** for *expectations* (things that we think will happen):

- The drought in Africa **will end** soon. (= The drought **is going to end** soon.)
- Graham **won't like** your idea. (= Graham **isn't going to like** your idea.)

We often use **expect** or **think** in a first clause:

- I expect John **will be** late for the interview.
- Oil experts think the price of oil **is going to go** down soon.

When we can predict something because of some evidence, we often prefer to use **be going to**:

- It**'s going to be** slippery. It's been snowing all night! (OR It'll be slippery ...)
- We**'re going to have** to buy a new car. The gearbox is broken. (OR We'll have to buy ...)

We usually use **be going to** for *intentions* (things that we or someone else have decided to do):

- Dan's **going to post** the letter on the way home.

We can use **will** for *intentions* after **I think**:

- I think I**'ll visit** my mother this weekend.

❸ will for offering, promising, and requesting

We use **will** when we are *offering* or *promising to do something*:

- I**'ll come** and see you tomorrow. I**'ll see** you at 5.
- We**'ll practise** a lot before the next match, don't worry.

or, when we are *asking someone to do something*:

- **Will** you **pass** me that pen, please?
- **Will** the boy at the back **stop** talking, please.

❹ if, when, etc.

We use **will** in a future clause when there is a present or future condition in the <u>other clause</u> (**if** + *present simple*):

- I**'ll lend** you a pencil <u>if you need one</u>.
- <u>If you want a pencil</u>, I**'ll lend** you one.

We can use **will** or **be going to** in a clause when there is a future time described in the <u>other clause</u> beginning with **when** or **as soon as**:

- **When** <u>the sun comes out</u>, we**'ll go** for a swim. (= **When** the sun comes out, we**'re going to go** for a swim.)
- **As soon as** <u>we get the caravan</u>, I think we**'ll go** on holiday. (= **As soon as** we get the caravan, we**'re going to go** on holiday.)

(For more on conditional clauses, see units 28 and 29.)

❺ shall

Shall can be used in place of **will** in sentences with **I** and **we**, but it is quite formal and old-fashioned, and not very common now:

- We **shall** both need to sign the document. (= We will both need to …)
- I **shall** speak to the manager about this! (= I will speak to the manager …)

In questions that are *suggestions* or *offers*, we use **shall** with **I** and **we** (and not **will**):

- **Shall** we get tickets for the game? (*suggestion*)
- **Shall** I pay? (*offer*)

We don't usually use **shall** instead of **will** in other kinds of questions:

- **Will** we be able to see the rocket launch from here?

To make a *suggestion about something we can do in the future*, we often use **Why don't we +** *infinitive* or **Let's +** *infinitive*. **Why don't we** and **Let's** are more informal and relaxed than **Shall we**:

- **Why don't we** have lunch together on Saturday? (= *Shall we have lunch* …)
- **Let's** discuss the project. (*Shall we discuss the project?*)
- **Let's** meet at 3. (= *Shall we meet at 3 o'clock?*)

❻ use of adverbs

If we want to use an adverb (such as **probably** or **definitely**) with either **will** or **be going to**, it goes before the main verb or **going to**:

- The advanced students will **definitely** <u>pass</u> the exam.
- She's **probably** <u>going to</u> be late.
- Will Tom **definitely** <u>finish</u> the painting today?

A

Mike and his brother, Ben, are looking after a friend's house while he's away. The friend is coming back tomorrow. Read the cues in brackets and write what Mike says to Ben.

0 (Mike asks Ben to clean the carpet.)
   Will you clean the carpet?

0 (Mike offers to throw away the newspapers.)
   I'll throw away the newspapers.

1 (Mike suggests they buy a new dishwasher.)
   ....

2 (Mike asks Ben to do the washing-up.)
   ....

3 (Mike offers to take out the rubbish.)
   ....

4 (Mike asks Ben to try to find the cat.)
   ....

5 (Mike offers to water the plants.)
   ....

6 (Mike asks Ben to do the laundry.)
   ....

7 (Mike offers to polish the hall floor.)
   ....

8 (Mike suggests they both put away the clothes.)
   ....

9 (Mike offers to mow the lawn.)
   ....

10 (Mike suggests they get the window repaired.)
   ....

and **shall**

B Stephen and his girlfriend, Sophie, are talking about what they're going to do when they finish their exams. Put the phrases in the box in the appropriate gaps in the following text. Sometimes two options are equally good.

won't be	'll be able	~~'ll have~~	let's
are you going to	'll stay	'll be	'll have	will be
will make	'll love

STEPHEN: When I finish my exams, I think I (0) __'ll have__ a long holiday at home. My mother (1) .... happy to have me back at home for a while. What (2) .... do?

SOPHIE: I think I (3) .... in London for a few weeks and enjoy all the tourist attractions. I haven't had a chance to see anything yet. London is so fascinating. It (4) .... nice to have time to look around, and go to the theatre and the galleries and everything.

STEPHEN: That's a great idea! I might stay for a week and do the same. If the weather's good, we (5) .... to have a picnic in Hyde Park and behave like real tourists!

SOPHIE: You (6) .... to tell your mother first. She (7) .... very pleased!

STEPHEN: I tell you what (8) .... her happy! If you come with me to Barbados! Oh, go on! (9) .... go together! You (10) .... my island!

C Put the correct form of **will**, **shall**, or **be going to** in the gaps in this conversation. Use contracted forms wherever you can. Sometimes more than one answer is possible.

JUSTIN: Hi, Diana, I'm getting a bit desperate! If you help me, I (0) __'ll__ love you forever! I (1) .... give a talk at the College tomorrow evening about careers in the theatre, and I (2) .... need some visual aids – theatre programmes, posters, photographs, and that sort of thing. Have you got anything you could lend me?

DIANA: Yes, of course I (3) .... lend you whatever I can find. I have a big box of stuff from my days in the theatre. It (4) .... be nice to look at it all again.

JUSTIN: Oh that's wonderful! Thank you so much. (5) .... I come round to your place this evening?

DIANA: Yes, that would be lovely. (6) .... we have dinner together and then I (7) .... show you all the stuff I've got?

JUSTIN: Brilliant! I (8) .... (not) be finished at work until about 6.30. (9) .... I come round about 7?

DIANA: OK. I (10) .... see you then. Bye!

1 form and use

present simple
for *schedules and timetables*:
- We **land** in Alicante at 3.30.
- The university term **begins** in October.

after **when**, **as soon as**, and **I hope**:
- When they **arrive**, we'll go out and eat.
- I hope you **have** a good flight.

present continuous (**am / is / are** + **ing** *form*)
for *arrangements*:
- Mrs Dark **is teaching** the course next term.
for *personal plans*:
- Anna **is working** in New York next week.

be going to
for *intentions*:
- He**'s going to try** to catch that bus.
for *expectations*:
- I think I**'m going to lose** my job.
for *predictions based on evidence*:
- That ball **is going to break** the window.

will
for *hopes*:
- I hope you**'ll like** what I bought for you.
for *expectations*:
- Rachel thinks she**'ll be** a bit late.
after **think** for *intentions*:
- I **think** I'**ll go** for a walk with the dog now.
after an **if** *clause*:
- If we don't hurry, we**'ll be** late too.
after **I wonder if**:
- **I wonder if** Paul **will** ever **finish** that book.
for *offers*:
- I**'ll make** a cake for your birthday.
for *promises*:
- I**'ll send** you some of my home-made jam.
used to *ask someone to do something*:
- **Will** you **sign** Tom's card please?

shall with **I** and **we**
shall I / we ... ? in *requests for advice*:
- **Shall we** take the train or the bus?
shall I / we ... ? for *suggestions and offers*:
- **Shall I** help you with your homework?
used in formal, first person statements:
- **We shall** need a compass for this journey.

let's and **why don't**
let's and **why don't we** for *suggestions about things we can do*:
- Come on! **Let's** find a coffee bar.
- **Why don't we** sit and rest for a minute?
why don't you /doesn't he for *suggestions about things other people can do*:
- **Why don't you** give Helen a call?

(For more on these future forms, see units 23 and 24.)

future: review of present tenses, will and be going to

A Read the following text. Put in the correct form of the words in brackets, using the *present simple*, **will**, **be going to**, **shall**, or **Let's**. Use contracted forms. More than one form is sometimes possible.

ANNIE: I don't believe it! My computer has crashed again! I think I
(0) *'ll phone* (phone) the helpline.

JOSH: Yes, that's a good idea. Why (1) .... (you / try)
phoning them now? I think the helpline (2) ....
(be / open) at least until 5 o'clock.

ANNIE: OK. I really hope they (3) .... (be able to) tell
me how to fix it, or I (4) .... (not / get) my
essay finished in time. I hate technology!

JOSH: But the benefits are fantastic! Just think how great it (5) .... (be) when computers and
robots (6) .... (do) all our housework and boring jobs.

ANNIE: Oh no! I think people need to be in touch with the real world, if not, we (7) .... (forget)
the value of helping each other – and the earth.

JOSH: Rubbish! I wonder if you (8) .... (ever / grow up)? We're very lucky, but what about all
those people who have to spend their whole life working hard on the land or in factories? If we all have
computers and robots and things, we (9) .... (have) lots more time for hobbies and things.

ANNIE: There's nothing wrong with working on the land. In fact, I (10) .... (dig) the garden this
weekend! (11) .... (do) it together!

JOSH: Oh, you're just a romantic! Now, I (12) .... (make) a nice cup of coffee with my new
espresso machine and then I (13) .... (go) to the video shop. Kerry and Jim are coming to my
flat to watch a DVD this evening. Why (14) .... (you / come) along too? Or,
(15) .... (you / go) to the woods to write poetry this evening?

ANNIE: No, I'm not. You're horrible! Of course I (16) .... (come). (17) ....
(I / bring) some microwave popcorn?

B Read the following sentences about Diego and Mark's tour in
Australia and choose the best future form of the verb for each one.
Sometimes more than one form is possible.

0 Diego and Mark *leave / are leaving* (leave) Britain on December 6th.

1 They .... (fly) from Heathrow to Perth, Australia.

2 The flight .... (take) about nine hours.

3 They .... (perform) in their show in seven different cities
over the next month.

4 If everything goes according to plan, they .... (spend)
Christmas day near Sydney.

5 It .... (be) great having their Christmas dinner of
barbecued turkey on the beach!

6 Diego .... (try) to learn how to water ski while he's there.

7 He knows that water skiing can be dangerous and he does not want to
injure himself, so he .... (be) very careful.

8 The show wouldn't be able to go on without him as he
.... (be) the leading man in the show this year.

9 The last city they .... (visit) is Brisbane, where they
.... (stay) for three days, before flying back to London.

26

'I sometimes look at the first-year students in my class at the university and wonder about their lives. What **will** they **be doing** in ten years' time? **Will** they **be working**? In three years they **will have finished** their degree courses and **will be looking** for work. Some of them **will have returned** to the university to take another course, and some of them **will have changed** course and **will be studying** something completely different. When they started their electronics degree I'm sure all of them **were going to work** really hard, and **were going to get** first-grade degrees, and go and get really well-paid jobs; but I'm sure that lots of them **will have changed** their minds completely before the end of the first year. Many of them **will be doing** badly in their studies, and **not turning up** to lectures, and **staying** in bed all day.

And what about me? What **will** I **be doing** in ten years? I hope I **will have retired** and **bought** myself a Harley Davidson. I'd like to cruise down through the USA, just like I **was going to do** when I was a teenager ...'

❶ will be doing: form

This is also called the *future continuous*. It is formed by **will** + **be** + **ing** *form*:

singular	plural
I **will be working** (I'll be working)	we **will be working** (we'll be working)
you **will be working** (you'll be working)	you **will be working** (you'll be working)
he / she / it **will be working** (she'll be working)	they **will be working** (they'll be working)

We usually use the contracted form of **will** (**'ll**) in speech and in less formal writing:
  - We**'ll be taking** the train tomorrow.
  - Pete**'ll be having** his birthday party that day.

For the negative we use **will not / won't** + **be** + **ing** *form*:
  - We **won't be using** the computer this morning.

We make questions by reversing the <u>subject</u> and the first auxiliary (**will**):
  - **Will** <u>Sara</u> **be playing** tennis this afternoon?

If we use an adverb with this form, we usually put it after the first auxiliary:
  - I won't **always** be working here.

❷ will be doing: use

We use this form to talk about *an event, activity, or situation that is in progress at a time in the future*:
  - When I arrive in Singapore, Chen Min **will be waiting** for me.

We often use this form colloquially to talk about *plans for the future*. The meaning of **will be doing** is very similar to **be doing** (*present continuous* with future meaning):
  - Rob**'ll be staying** with us for two days next week. (= Rob's staying with us ...)

❸ will have done: form

This is also called the *future perfect*. It is formed by **will** + **have** + *past participle*:

singular	plural
I **will have earned** (I'll have earned)	we **will have earned** (we'll have earned)
you **will have earned**	you **will have earned**
he / she / it **will have earned**	they **will have earned**

We usually use the contracted form of **will** (**'ll**); and in speech we often contract **have** to **'ve**:
  - Jack: 'I**'ll've earned** enough money soon to buy a new boat.'
  - Sue: 'Bill **will've finished** mowing the lawn by lunchtime.'

To make the negative of this form, we use **will not** (**won't**) + **have** + *past participle*:

- I **will not have got up** if you phone at six o'clock tomorrow.
- The performance **won't have finished** by ten o'clock.

We make the question by reversing the <u>subject</u> and the first auxiliary (**will**):

- **Will** <u>Mark</u> **have left** by the time you get to his house?

If we use an adverb with this form, we usually put it after the first auxiliary:

- You'll **never** have seen anything like that film!

❹ will have done: use

We use this form to talk about *something which we think is going to happen before some time or another event in the future*:

- When Dave gets home, Cheung **will** already **have left**.

We also use this form to say that *something will be the case at some time in the future*:

- Next year we **will have lived** in this house for seven years.

We use this form colloquially to talk about *something which we think has probably happened before now*:

- I'm sure Paul**'ll have forgotten** my name. (= *It's likely that he has forgotten my name.*)
- You**'ll've seen** him on the telly. (= *It's likely that you have seen him on the TV.*)

We use the negative to say that *something probably hasn't happened*:

- Bill **won't've heard** the news yet. (= *It's likely that Bill has not heard the news yet.*)

❺ was going to do: form

This is also called the *future in the past*, and is formed with **was / were** + **going to** + *infinitive*:

singular	plural
I **was going to park**	we **were going to park**
you **were going to park**	you **were going to park**
he / she / it **was going to park**	they **were going to park**

To make the negative, we use **was not** (**wasn't**) / **were not** (**weren't**) + **going to** + *infinitive*:

- We **weren't going to take part** in the competition.
- Andrew **wasn't going to speak** at the meeting.

A question is made by reversing the <u>subject</u> and the first auxiliary (**was / were**):

- **Was** <u>Stephanie</u> **going to marry** John?
- **Weren't** <u>Kim and Yumi</u> **going to start** college today?

If we use an adverb with this form, we usually put it after the first auxiliary:

- Mary was **never** going to go back to her old job.

❻ was going to do: use

We use this form to talk about *something that we intended to happen in the past*; often it did not happen, or we don't know if it did or not:

- I **was going to come** and see you yesterday. (= *I intended to come and see you but I didn't.*)
- When I met you, you **were going to work** for the BBC. (= *You meant to work for the BBC but you may not have succeeded.*)

The negative form means that we *didn't intend to do something or that we didn't want to*, but usually we did it anyway, or it happened anyway:

- I **wasn't going to go** for a swim – but then the water looked so nice!

We often use the negative form in questions when we are *asking for information about someone's intentions*:

- **Weren't** you **going to lend** me your car?

A Rewrite the following sentences with the same meaning, using the verb forms in brackets.

0 Yumi wanted to be a secretary when she was younger. (was going to / be)
   Yumi was going to be a secretary when she was younger.

1 She was offered a place at a secretarial college in Tokyo. (was going to / study / at)
   ....
   ....

2 She did not intend to stay at home when she left school. (was going to / leave)
   ....
   ....

3 She stayed at home and started working in a restaurant eleven months ago. (will have / work)
   In a month's time ....
   ....

4 She and her friend Mitsuko have registered to start a nursing course this September. (will be / start)
   ....
   ....

5 The nursing college is in Kyoto. They want to live in Kyoto and are looking for a flat there. (will be / live)
   ....
   ....

6 She is saving money, and soon she will have enough money to pay for her course. (will have / earn)
   Soon ....
   ....

7 She doesn't want to work while she is studying. (will not be / work)
   ....
   ....

8 They wanted to share the flat with another girl … (were going to / share)
   ....
   ....

9 … but the other girl did not get a place at the college. (will not be / go / to)
   ....
   ....

10 They are leaving for Kyoto in September. (will be / go / to)
   ....
   ....

B Read the Archaeology Society newsletter and put the right form of the verb in brackets in the box at the bottom. Use **will be + ing** *form*, **will have + ** *past participle*, or **was / were going to + ** *infinitive*.

The Archaeology Society Newsletter

The Archaeology Society [0](meet) next Friday. We [1](use) the Education Room in the City Museum, but it is not available. Instead, we [2](meet) in the lecture theatre.

We [3](have) a talk by Professor Takemi, but he cannot come. We [4](learn) about Mayan civilisation in South America. Instead, Professor Highbury [5](speak) about Roman villas. By the end of the evening we [6](learn) all the new discoveries about Roman villas. Prof Highbury [7](take) us out to a Roman villa near the town, but the weatherman says it [8](rain) so we [9](stay) in the museum. I'm sure he [10](bring) a lot of fascinating things for us to see.

0 *will be meeting*
1 ....
2 ....
3 ....
4 ....
5 ....
6 ....
7 ....
8 ....
9 ....
10 ....

will have done, was going to do

C Read the text and choose the right phrase from the box to put in each gap.

> will be taking   will be starting   will not be eating   will all be getting up   will have learnt
> were going to offer   won't be opening   ~~will be handing~~   will have all found   were going to use

Delia is welcoming new guests who have arrived for a weekend course in T'ai Chi at 'The Inside Story' Health and Fitness Centre ...

'Good evening everyone. It's lovely to see you all! I'd like to tell you something about the course we're running this weekend, and I (0) *will be handing* out some general information about "The Inside Story" Health and Fitness Centre at the end.

By the end of the weekend, we hope you (1) _____ a little about the ancient art of T'ai Chi, and about physical and mental balance. You (2) _____ at 6.30 a.m. and the teacher (3) _____ the first class at 7.00. You (4) _____ anything before the class, but you may have a cup of tea or juice. The class is two hours and breakfast is served at 9.30.

In the afternoon, we (5) _____ you the chance of a swim in "The Inside Story" pool, but unfortunately we have had a problem with the filter and I'm afraid it (6) _____ at all this weekend. If the weather is good, we (7) _____ you outside into the Japanese garden to do the afternoon class.

Our teacher is the eminent T'ai Chi master Yeung Ma-Li, who is coming in the place of the teacher we (8) _____ this time, who is unfortunately ill at the moment.

You (9) _____ your rooms by now and I hope you're all comfortable.

Dinner is at 8.00 – and it's all vegetarian, of course!'

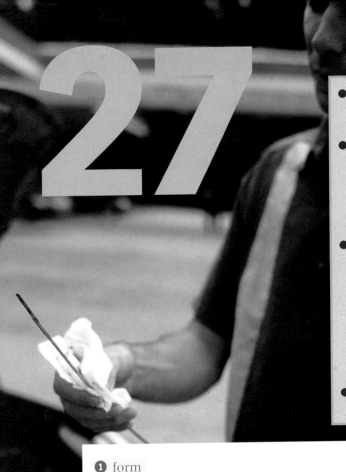

- All engines consume a certain amount of oil during normal use. **Check** the oil regularly, and particularly before long journeys.

- **Park** the vehicle on a flat, level surface, with the engine at the normal running temperature. **Do not leave** the engine running! **Wait** for a few minutes to allow the oil to return to the oil pan to get an accurate measurement.

- **Remove** the dipstick and **wipe** it with a clean cloth. **Put** the dipstick in as far as it will go. **Take** the dipstick out again and **look** at the oil level. This should always be within the range shown on the figure. If the oil is below the limit, **remove** the filler cap and add oil. Then **check** the level again. When you are sure that the level of the oil is right, **put** the filler cap back, making sure that it is tightly closed.

- **Use** only the recommended oils. **See** page 176 for the right oil to use.

❶ form

The *imperative* has no subject, as the meaning is always *you must*. It has the same form as the *infinitive* of the verb. We often use an exclamation mark (!) after an imperative:

- **Go** away!
- **Stop** it!
- **Give** that to me!

The negative is formed with the auxiliary **don't** + *infinitive*:

- **Don't smoke** in the sitting room.
- **Don't eat** all the biscuits!

When we use an adverb like **always**, **ever**, or **never**, it goes before the imperative:

- **Always close** the door of the fridge.
- **Never light** a match when there is a gas leak.
- **Don't ever light** a match when there is a gas leak.

❷ use

We use the imperative to *tell someone to do something* or *not to do something*.
It can be used as a *command*:

- **Come** here immediately!
- **Stand** up straight!

The imperative is often used for *instructions* for making or doing something:

- **Put** the lid on the pan.
- **Drill** four holes in the board.

We also use the imperative for *advice*:

- If a bull attacks you, **don't run** away.
- If you go to a yoga lesson, **wear** comfortable clothes.

It is often used for the *rules* of an organisation or institution:

- **Carry** your key with you at all times.
- **Wear** your uniform while you are in the building.

As an alternative to the imperative, written notices use **no** + **ing** *form* for *rules* and *laws*:

> ■ **No parking** (= Don't park.)
> ■ **No fishing** (= Don't fish.)

But an exception to this is the common sign :

> ■ No entry NOT ~~No entering~~

When we are talking about *rules* and *laws*, we often use **there's** with **no** + **ing** *form*:

> ■ **There's no smoking** in this cinema.
> ■ **There's no parking** in the playground.

When we want to *encourage someone to do something*, we use **Do** or **Please** with the imperative:

> ■ **Please have** some tea.
> ■ **Do read** this novel. It's wonderful.
>
> and when we want to *encourage someone not to do something*, we use **Please don't**:
>
> ■ **Please don't** leave without paying!
> ■ **Please don't** be angry!

There are other ways of giving an imperative which are more polite, using phrases such as **you must / you should / it is important that you / it is essential to** + *infinitive*:

> ■ **You must always read** the instructions before you begin.
> ■ **It is essential to wear** gloves and a mask.

❸ reporting an imperative

When we are *reporting someone using an imperative*, we use **told** + *object* + **to** + *infinitive*:

> ■ The teacher **told me to bring** in my essay today. (= *She said 'Bring your essay …'*)
> ■ She **told Petra to finish** the work at home. (= *She said 'Finish your work …'*)

When we *report someone using a negative imperative*, we use **told** + *object* + **not to** + *infinitive*:

> ■ He **told us not to light** a match in case there was a gas leak.

Remember: When we report what someone said, we often have to change pronouns (**me** etc) and possessives (**my** etc); so, for example, when we report this sentence:

> ■ John: 'Please give **me** back all **my** mini-disks.'
>
> we say:
>
> ■ John told me to give **him** back all **his** mini-disks.

(For more on reporting speech, see units 60 and 61.)

imperative (stop, don't move)

A Look at the signs and match them with the instruction.

0  1 2 3 4 5

6 7 8 9 10

A Don't go faster than 30 miles an hour.
B Be careful of deer on the road.
C Put your rubbish in the bin.
D Be careful of old people crossing the road.
E Drive slowly! School children crossing.

F No smoking.
G Don't drink the water.
H No entry.
I No overtaking.
J Don't light fires.
K Don't use your mobile phone.

B Read the following dialogue and choose the right word or words from the box to put in each gap.

> answer   ~~make~~   to finish   come   turn
>
> say   don't be   change   tell   give   leave

0 NABILA: I want a cup of tea! _Make_ me a cup of tea.

1 IMRAN: I don't want any tea. .... so lazy!

2 NABILA: The phone's ringing! .... the phone!

3 IMRAN: It's Jake! .... and speak to him.

4 NABILA: I'm not here! .... to him that I'm out!

5 IMRAN: Sorry, Jake, she's out. Bye. ... Now, ... up the volume on the TV. I can't hear the music.

6 NABILA: I hate this band. .... the channel.

7 IMRAN: No, I think they're cool. .... me the controller.

8 NABILA: No, I want to watch the news. .... me alone!

9 IMRAN: I'm going out. .... Mum that I'll be back at 11.

10 NABILA: You're not allowed to go out. Mum told you .... your homework.

(stop, don't move)

C Phyllis has been arguing with her brother, Bob. She is telling Jasmine about it. Read what Phyllis says to Jasmine. Look at the underlined words and rewrite them, using the word in brackets and an *imperative*.

"⁰Oh Jasmine, Bob's so horrible! He said I had been in his room! He said ⁰'You must not leave my room in such a mess!' I hadn't been in his stupid room, but he didn't believe me. He said ¹'You must help me tidy up!' And then he said ²'You have to get a rubbish bag for all your things!' There was hardly anything of mine in there! I said ³'You should stop being such a bully!' Then he said ⁴'You must not smoke in my bedroom.' 'But I never smoke'. And then he said ⁵'You must not use my CD player.' As if I would use his rubbish CD player! Mine's much better. And he said ⁶'You must give me back all my CDs', and he called me a thief! I said to him ⁷'You shouldn't talk to me like that.' So he said ⁸'You must let me look in your room!' So he marched into my room, and I said ⁹'Please get out immediately!'

He's so horrible, Jasmine, ¹⁰I advise you not to speak to my brother again!"

0 (don't) *Don't leave my room in such a mess.*
1 (please) ....
2 (get) ....
3 (stop) ....
4 (don't) ....
5 (don't) ....
6 (give) ....
7 (don't) ....
8 (let) ....
9 (get) ....
10 (ever) ....

14 (he / me / his) ....
....

15 (he / me / his) ....
....

16 (he / me / him / his) ....
....

17 (I / him / me) ....
....

18 (he / me / him / my) ....
....

19 (I / him) ....
....

Now report what Phyllis and Bob said, using told, the underlined words above, and the words in brackets.

0 (Bob / me / his)
   Bob told me not to leave his room in such a mess.
11 (he / me / him) ....
....

12 (he / me / my) ....
....

13 (I / him) ....
....

And this is what Phyllis said to Bob the next day:
20 (I / Jasmine / you) ....
....

THE INSIDE STORY

Are you feeling tired and lacking in energy? Are you a little overweight? Is your hair dull and lifeless? **If your answer is** 'Yes' to any of these questions, then you need us!

If you fill in this questionnaire today, you will have the opportunity of spending a trial weekend at 'The Inside Story' for only £300!!

When you take up this offer, we will extend you a warm welcome. **As soon as you arrive**, you will be introduced to the other guests and shown around our elegant premises. You will enjoy a busy and fun weekend with good and healthy organic food, lots of exercise, and you will be able to take advantage of relaxing massage and aromatherapy sessions. And you will meet lots of interesting people.

If you don't take advantage of this offer, you are going to regret it for ever! So come on, give us a try!

❶ zero (or *general*) conditional: form

To make the *general* conditional, we use the **present tense** in both the condition (or **if**) clause and in the consequence clause:

condition clause	consequence clause
■ **If** you **invest** in the stock market,	you **are risking** a lot.
■ **If** the water **is** warm enough,	we **swim** every day.
■ **If** you **press** the switch,	the light **comes** on.

The consequence clause can come <u>first</u> in the sentence:

consequence clause	condition clause
■ You **are risking** a lot	**if** you **invest** in the stock market.
■ We **swim** every day	**if** the water **is** warm enough.
■ The light **comes** on	**if** you **press** the switch.

Note: We don't usually write a comma (,) before **if**.

There may be a sequence of events, or consequences, after the condition clause. They all use the same present tense:

■ If there is warm weather in the spring, the snow **melts**, the river **bursts** its banks, and the village **is** flooded.

Sometimes we use another word or phrase in the condition clause, such as **when** or **as soon as**, when the meaning is very similar to **if**:

■ **When** water gets into the mechanism, it stops working. (= *If water gets into the mechanism, it always stops working.*)

■ **As soon as** the sun comes out, the flowers open. (= *If the sun comes out, the flowers open immediately.*)

❷ zero (or *general*) conditional: use

We use the *general* conditional when we want to talk about *a predictable sequence of events*, and not about a particular event or situation and its consequence. We use it to say that something is always followed by something else – when this happens, that happens:

■ If it rains in April, the crop is good.

■ If you are polite to Mr Thomas, he is usually very helpful.

It can also mean that *two things always happen at the same time* – if one thing happens then the other must be happening:

- If Ricardo comes home late, he's always noisy.
- If you smell smoke, it's my toast burning.

❸ first (or *particular*) conditional: form

To make a *particular* conditional, we use the **present tense** in the condition clause and a **future form** in the consequence clause:

condition clause	consequence clause
If the sun **comes** out,	this room **will get** hot.
If the floor **is** wet,	it**'s going to be** very slippery.
If the program **is downloading**,	we**'ll be able** to read the file.
If she **can afford** the flight,	Donna**'s coming** to Perth.

We can use the present simple or present continuous in the condition clause:

- If the cat **is** lost, the children will be very sad.
- If Hugh **is playing** the piano, we'll sit and listen.

The consequence clause can come first:

consequence clause	condition clause
We**'ll be able** to read the file	if the program **is downloading**.
Donna**'s coming** to Perth	if she **can afford** the flight.

The **future form** in the consequence clause is usually **will** + *infinitive*:

- If Tom arrives in time, we**'ll give** him some lunch.

or, it can be the **going to** + *infinitive* form:

- If I have time, I**'m going to get** her a present.
- When Jack goes shopping, he's **going to buy** some more eggs.
- As soon as I find my screwdriver, I**'m going to mend** that door handle.

We can also use **present continuous** (**be** + **ing** *form*) for personal plans and intentions in the consequence clause:

- If the meeting is boring, I**'m going** home!

or, the future continuous (**will be** + **ing** *form*):

- Francis **will be arriving** at seven, if the bus is on time.

There can be two or more consequence clauses connected to the condition clause. All of them need to use a future form:

- If you don't study now, you **won't pass** your exam, you **aren't going to be able** to go to college, you **won't get** a good job, and you **won't earn** much money!

❹ first (or *particular*) conditional: use

We use this form when we are talking about *something which may or may not happen*, but if it does, something else will definitely follow; it is like the general conditional, but it refers only to a *particular situation* in the present or future and not to a general truth:

- Be careful! If you open the door, that dog **will escape**!
- My wife **is going to go** to Africa, if she gets her visa.
- If the sun comes out, the snow **is going to melt**.
- The President **will be** very happy if he is re-elected.

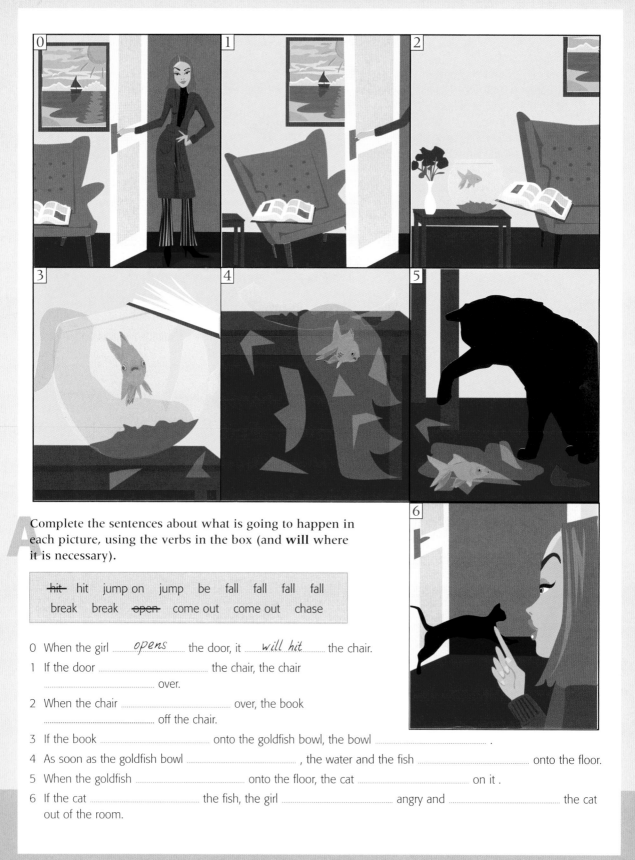

A Complete the sentences about what is going to happen in each picture, using the verbs in the box (and **will** where it is necessary).

~~hit~~ hit jump on jump be fall fall fall fall
break break ~~open~~ come out come out chase

0 When the girl ____*opens*____ the door, it ____*will hit*____ the chair.

1 If the door _____ the chair, the chair _____ over.

2 When the chair _____ over, the book _____ off the chair.

3 If the book _____ onto the goldfish bowl, the bowl _____ .

4 As soon as the goldfish bowl _____ , the water and the fish _____ onto the floor.

5 When the goldfish _____ onto the floor, the cat _____ on it .

6 If the cat _____ the fish, the girl _____ angry and _____ the cat out of the room.

B Match the following clauses to make sentences.

0 If Sam gets up soon,

1 As soon as he gets dressed,

2 If he is late for school again,

3 He tries to find his school clothes

4 If he doesn't get up soon,

5 His Mum makes him a snack to eat in the bus

6 When he leaves the house today,

7 When he gets to school,

A ...when he gets up.

B ...he often falls asleep at his desk.

C ...he won't have time for breakfast.

D ...he's going to have to leave the house.

E ...his teacher will be very angry.

F ...he won't be late for school.

G ...if he doesn't have time for breakfast.

H ...he is going to meet his friend Ben at the bus stop.

0	F	3	......	6	......
1	......	4	......	7	......
2	......	5	......		

C Put the verb, either in the present simple or the will form, in the following sentences. Circle the correct letter to indicate if the meaning is *general* (G) or *particular* (P).

0 If his computer isn't plugged in, it ....*won't work*..... (not / work)   G (P)

1 When that kind of kettle is boiling, it .... (whistle)   G P

2 Don't worry! As soon as the conductor raises his baton, the audience .... (stop) making so much noise.   G P

3 Shut the freezer! I bought some ice cream today and it .... (melt) if you leave the freezer door open.   G P

4 If you don't buy a paper today, you .... (not / see) my picture on the front page!   G P

5 Whenever your mother comes to visit, you .... (tidy up) the house.   G P

6 Help me! When the guests arrive, we .... (serve) the drinks.   G P

7 In the game of musical bumps, as soon as the music starts, the children .... (start) dancing.   G P

8 We always .... (eat) fish on Fridays, when we can get some.   G P

D Read the following information and choose the best verb from the box to fill the gaps; put it in the right tense and form.

put	~~not grow~~	not feed	not be
produce	develop	be	become

Gardenias are beautiful flowers but quite hard to grow successfully. If you don't feed them with the right nutrients, they (0) ....*don't grow*.... very big. They are sensitive to lime in the soil; but if you (1) .... the right balance of nutrients on them at the right time of year, they (2) .... into very big plants and (3) .... beautiful, bright flowers. If you (4) .... them enough, they produce very small flowers. If there (5) .... enough sunlight, the stems (6) .... long and pale, and the flowers (7) .... quite small.

Gerald Compton is planning a 40th birthday party for his wife, Margaret. He and the children are making a list of people to invite.

DAD: ...Well, **if we invited** Auntie Daphne, we would have to invite Uncle George, and that's a bit of a problem.

JAMES: Oh, he's not so bad – as long as we don't have any rock music. Do you remember how he danced at Frank's wedding ...!

ANNA: I wasn't there. I **wish I had seen** it!

SAM: He was wild! I think we should invite them both. Auntie Daphne would be so upset **if you didn't invite** her.

DAD: OK. ... Auntie Daphne and Uncle George ... and what about the neighbours? I think the Thompsons are going to be in America in June, but they wouldn't be very happy **if we didn't tell** them. And the Chens, shall we invite them?

JAMES: Yes, of course! And **if you asked** them, you would have to invite their daughter, Mei Ling ... oh, and their son, of course.

DAD: Right ... Mr and Mrs Chen, Mei Ling, and Jia Sheng.

ANNA: Do you think Mum knows about the party?

DAD: I don't know. It's hard to keep secrets from her!

SAM: I know. How about **if we pretended** to be organising a family dinner for her 40th birthday, then she'd never guess!

DAD: That's a brilliant idea! I'll ask her which restaurant she wants to go to...

❶ second (or *imaginary*) conditional: form

To make the *imaginary* conditional, we use the **past simple** in the **if** clause (the condition clause), and **would + infinitive** in the consequence clause:

condition clause	consequence clause
■ If Graham **won** first prize,	he **would be** very proud.
■ If they **built** a skating rink,	they **would make** a lot of money.

Note: We often contract **would** to **'d**:

■ If Graham won the competition,	**I'd** be delighted.

The consequence clause can come first:

consequence clause	condition clause
■ The children **would be** disappointed	if we **didn't take** them to the cinema.
■ I **wouldn't worry**	if Sophie **was** late.

We used to use the past subjunctive form of the verb **be** (**were**) in place of the past simple (**was**) in the condition clause (e.g. **If I were Prime Minister** ...), but this is not common now. It only remains in certain idioms, and in very formal English:

■ **If I were you**, I'd be careful. (= *If I was you, ...*)
■ **If it were possible**, I would retire tomorrow. (= *If it was possible, ...*)

❷ second (or *imaginary*) conditional: use

We use this form when we are thinking about the consequences of *something we can imagine in the present, but which is not the case*:

■ If I was better at golf, I would play more often. (= *I'm not very good at golf, so I don't play much.*)
■ Maria would play chess with you if you had a chess set. (= *You don't have a chess set so she doesn't play with you, at the moment.*)

We also use this form to talk about the consequences of *something that might happen in the future*:

■ We would have fresh basil in June if we planted some soon.
■ If it rained, the plants would grow bigger.

We can use other modals (e.g. **could**, **might**) in the consequence clause, in the place of **would**:

  ■ If I did that computer course, I **could** get a better job. (= ... *I would be able to get* ...)
  ■ If Geri worked a bit harder, she **could** be very successful.

We use the form of the imaginary condition clause with sentences beginning **I wish** when we regret that *something is not the case now*:

  ■ I wish I **did** more exercise. (... *but I don't do much exercise.*)
  ■ I wish **I had** more free time for hobbies and reading. (... *but I don't have much free time.*)

❸ third (or *imagined*) conditional: form

To make the *imagined* conditional, we use the ***past perfect*** in the condition clause and ***would + have + past participle*** in the consequence clause:

condition clause	consequence clause
■ If we **had tried** sooner,	we **would have got** seats for the concert.
■ If Renzo **hadn't met** Kim,	he **wouldn't have gone** to Hong Kong.

We can also put the consequence clause before the condition clause:

consequence clause	condition clause
■ Jack **would have passed** his driving test	if he **had practised** parking.
■ Tim **wouldn't have got** the tickets	if he **had known** how bad the film was.

We can use other modals (e.g. **could**, **might**) in the consequence clause, in the place of **would**:

  ■ If Elsie had wanted to, she **could** have come with us.
  ■ If the tree hadn't been cut down, it **might** have fallen on the house.

❹ third (or *imagined*) conditional: use

We use this form when we are *imagining the consequences of an imagined situation or event in the past –* if history had been different:

  ■ If Andrew **had got** the job at Princeton, he **would have left** England. (*He didn't get the job at Princeton so he is still in England.*)
  ■ Phyllis **would have bought** that handbag if she **had had** enough money. (*She didn't have enough money so she didn't buy it.*)
  ■ If I **hadn't looked** in that cupboard, I **wouldn't have found** my screwdriver. (*I did look in that cupboard and so I have found my screwdriver.*)

We use this past form of the condition clause with sentences beginning **I wish** when we want to say that *we regret that something happened, or didn't happen*:

  ■ I wish John **had asked** me to marry him! (... *he didn't!*)
  ■ I wish John and Carmen **had never met**! (... *but they did!*)

❺ mixed conditionals

We often use a mixture of the imagined and the imaginary conditionals when we want to talk about the *present consequences* of *something that might have happened in the past, but didn't*:

  ■ If Helen **had left** earlier, she **would be** on the train now. (... *but she isn't on the train because she didn't leave in time.*)
  ■ Jake **would be** on the committee if he**'d been** more confident. (... *but he isn't on the committee.*)

A Phyllis and Jasmine are talking about getting fit. Write what they say to each other, using the clues in brackets and the *second conditional*.

0 (Jasmine says they could get fit quickly by going to aerobics classes.)

JASMINE: We would *get fit quickly if we went to an aerobics class.*

1 (Phyllis says she would love to go, but only if Jasmine comes too.)

PHYLLIS: If you ....

....

2 (Jasmine says she might come too, but she doesn't have any exercise clothes.)

JASMINE: I'd come ....

....

3 (Phyllis says she would buy some new exercise clothes if she joined a class.)

PHYLLIS: I could ....

....

4 (Jasmine says she really wants to buy some clothes but she isn't sure she has enough money.)

JASMINE: I'd love ....

....

5 (Jasmine says they could do dancing classes to get fit.)

JASMINE: If we did dancing classes, ...

....

6 (Phyllis says they are very unfit. They are lazy.)

PHYLLIS: We wouldn't ....

....

7 (Phyllis says she regrets that she doesn't go to dancing classes.)

PHYLLIS: I wish ....

....

8 (Jasmine says she used to wear a size 10, but she doesn't do enough exercise.)

JASMINE: I would still ....

....

9 (Phyllis says she would go swimming, but there isn't a nice pool nearby.)

PHYLLIS: I would ....

....

10 (Jasmine says she will try to find a good dance class and asks Phyllis to enroll too.)

JASMINE: If I ....

....

B Finish these sentences with a *consequence clause*. Use the beginning of the next sentence to complete the previous sentence.

I'll tell you a story about how a bicycle bell made Joe the happiest man in the world.

If someone hadn't rung a bicycle bell,⁰ *the dog wouldn't have started barking.*

If the dog hadn't started barking,¹ ....

....

If the cat hadn't jumped onto the table,² ....

....

If the teapot hadn't got broken,³ ....

....

If the tea hadn't spilt all over our letters,⁴ ....

....

If we'd been able to read our letters,⁵ ....

....

If we had found out about Joe's millions,⁶ ....

....

If he hadn't gone backpacking to Morocco that day,⁷ ...

....

If Joe hadn't met Fatima,⁸ ....

....

If he hadn't married Fatima,⁹ ....

....

If she hadn't come to Britain,¹⁰ ....

....

Now he's the happiest man in the world.

C Read the following pairs of sentences and make them into one sentence, using a condition clause with **if ... not** and a consequence clause. Sometimes you need to use a *mixed conditional*.

0 DAVE: It was your fault! – You forgot the map. We got lost.

If you hadn't forgotten the map, we wouldn't have got lost.

1 TOM: You wore the wrong shoes. You have got horrible blisters on your feet.

2 DAVE: The water bottle broke. We have very little water left.

3 TOM: The sun is so hot. We feel so tired.

4 DAVE: I forgot the insect repellant. Mosquitoes have bitten us all over.

5 TOM: We brought very little food. I'm so hungry!

6 DAVE: We chose to have this holiday in August. It's too hot.

7 TOM: My mobile phone has run out of power. We can't phone anyone.

8 DAVE: We walked across that field. That bull chased us.

9 TOM: You fell down that hole in the bank. Your back hurts.

10 DAVE: We are in the countryside. We are tired and miserable.

D Choose the best form of the verbs in the passage, and write it underneath.

Josh has just had an interview. He wanted to work as a games software developer for Gargantuan Games. He is talking about the interview ...

It was terrible! I did almost everything wrong! It [0]<u>would have been / was</u> fine if they [1]<u>asked / had asked</u> me about computer programming. I'm really good at that. But they just asked me about games! I [2]<u>didn't mind / wouldn't have minded</u> if they [3]<u>had asked / asked</u> me about their own games, but they asked me about other types I knew nothing about. It [4]<u>was / would have been</u> a good idea if I [5]<u>did / had done</u> some research on games before I went. I'm so stupid! And another thing – if I [6]<u>knew / had known</u> all the other staff dressed casually, I [7]<u>wouldn't have / wouldn't</u> worn a formal suit. I tell you – even if they [8]<u>would ask / asked</u> me back for another interview, I [9]<u>wouldn't go / wouldn't have gone</u>!

0 *would have been*
1 ....
2 ....
3 ....
4 ....
5 ....
6 ....
7 ....
8 ....
9 ....

30

Travel chaos this weekend

A £100m engineering programme means that sections of three of the busiest lines **will be closed** over the August bank holiday weekend.

All trains between Reading and London **have been cancelled** until 0500 BST on Tuesday. Extra trains **have been scheduled** from Waterloo. Services between London and Stansted Airport **will be disrupted** on Sunday, while trains from London to Birmingham New Street **will be diverted** around Coventry and Birmingham International on Saturday and Sunday.

The head of the rail company said, 'The choice **has to be made** when to do the work, and I recognise that some people **are going to be inconvenienced** this weekend.'

'The bank holidays are three-day weekends and when major works **are being done** it gives us the opportunity to do these efficiently and at a reduced cost.'

A representative of the Rail Passengers Council said that passengers **had not been informed** of the plans. He told our reporter that increased disruption **could be accepted** if people thought it **was being planned** efficiently.

❶ uses of the passive

In a passive sentence the important thing is what happens, not who or what does something (the *agent*):

> ■ Screws and nails **are kept** in different boxes. (*It isn't important who does it.*)
> ■ The bridge **was constructed** in 1864. (*We don't know who constructed the bridge.*)

We often use the passive form with **by** when the action is more important than the *agent*:
> ■ Leila's favourite vase **was broken by** <u>Imran</u> yesterday.

The agent of a passive sentence is the subject of the active sentence:
> ■ Imran broke Leila's favourite vase yesterday.

We also use the passive form when there is a lot of information about the *agent*, and it is easier to understand when this is at the end of the sentence than at the beginning:
> ■ The Honda was bought by **the man with the smart suit and the moustache**.

When there is no agent specified in the passive, we use **someone** or **something**, or the impersonal **they**, in the active form:

passive	active
■ Linda's horse **was sold**.	= { **Someone** sold Linda's horse. / **They** sold Linda's horse.
■ Mrs Khan's roses **were damaged**.	= **Something** damaged Mrs Khan's roses.

(For more on *impersonal pronouns*, see units 6 and 31.)

❷ passive forms: present and past

The passive is made with a form of the auxiliary **be** in the appropriate tense (**am / are/ is**, **was**, **have been**, **was being** etc) and the *past participle* of the main verb. Here are examples of present and past forms in the passive:

> ■ *present simple passive*: Stamps **are sold** in supermarkets now.
> ■ *present continuous passive*: Jacob's car **is being repaired** at the moment.
> ■ *present perfect passive*: The managing director **has been fired**!
> ■ *past simple passive*: My brother **was** last **seen** in Montenegro.
> ■ *past continuous passive*: The cat **was being chased**.
> ■ *past perfect passive*: The collapse of the mine **had been caused** by flooding.

The negative of passives is made by adding **not** or **n't** after the first auxiliary:
> ■ The key **was not** put in the usual place.
> ■ This paper **hasn't** been recycled.

Questions are made by putting the *auxiliary* first, then the <u>subject</u>, then the *main verb*:
    ■ **Was** <u>Peter's father</u> irritated by what she said?
If we use a question word, the auxiliary comes after it:
    ■ Where **are** <u>the pans</u> stored?

If we want to use more than one passive verb, we only need to use the auxiliary once:
    ■ Candidates **are selected** and **notified** by post, and **invited** to an interview.

If we use an adverb (**always**, **often** etc) in a passive sentence, it comes after the first auxiliary:
    ■ The steak **is** always overcooked in this restaurant.

❸ passive forms: future and modal

We can use these present tense forms in the passive to talk about the future:
    ■ *present simple passive*: Paul **is presented** with the certificate this afternoon.
    ■ *present continuous passive*: Helen **is being interviewed** tomorrow afternoon.

We also use **be going to** and **will** with a passive infinitive (**be** + *past participle*) to talk about the future:
    ■ *passive with* **be going to**: The prisoner **is going to be watched** at all times.
    ■ *passive with* **will**: You **will be told** when to turn on the engine.
(For more on future forms, see units 23–25.)
Modal passives are made in the same way, with a passive infinitive:
    ■ *passive with* **can**: Any problem **can be solved** in the end.
    ■ *passive with* **could**: Tom **couldn't be persuaded** to come out with us.
    ■ *passive with* **have to**: A decision **has to be made** soon.

❹ passive forms with **by** or other prepositions

If we want to say *who or what did the action*, we use **by** after the passive verb:
    ■ Many beautiful churches **were destroyed by** Cromwell.
    ■ Jenny's clothes **are** all **bought by** her mother.

When we use a past participle in a passive structure like an adjective, we can use a different preposition (such as **with**, **at**, **in**, or **of**) after the verb:
    ■ Tom **was shocked at** the price of the meal.
(For more on verbs with prepositions, see unit 66.)

❺ passive phrases with two objects

We often use verbs with two <u>objects</u>:
    ■ The shop sold <u>the last customer</u> <u>a faulty bicycle</u>.
In the passive voice we can make the phrase in two ways; with the first object at the beginning of the sentence and the other after the verb, or the reverse:
    ■ <u>The last customer</u> was sold <u>a faulty bicycle</u> by the shop.
    ■ OR <u>A faulty bicycle</u> was sold **to** <u>the last customer</u> by the shop.
Note: We put the agent (e.g. **by the shop**) at the end of the sentence.

❻ verbs not usually used in the passive

We also do not usually use *state verbs* (such as those describing *feelings* or *states*) in the passive:
    ■ Phil really **likes** Beethoven. NOT ~~Beethoven is really liked by Phil~~.
    ■ These shoes don't **fit** me. NOT ~~I am not fitted by these shoes~~.
(For more on state verbs, see unit 17.)

A Read the following passage and change each underlined active verb phrase into a passive phrase.

0 On Wednesday evening there was a talk about China. <u>About 100 people attended the talk in the village hall</u>.
The talk *was attended by about 100 people in the village hall.*

1 <u>Bob Michaels gave the talk</u> – he was a young traveller who had recently returned from a cycling trip in Gansu province in China.
The talk ....

2 <u>The local paper had published an article about him</u> and his travelling companions.
An article about him ....

3 <u>He said the experience had amazed him</u>, and he wanted to share his excitement with us.
He said he ....

4 His favourite place was the Mogao caves, where <u>people had painted hundreds of pictures on the walls</u>.
Hundreds of pictures ....

5 He also talked about the enormous nature reserves, where <u>people looked after giant pandas in the forests</u>.
Giant pandas ....

6 The local people were very friendly, he said, and <u>welcomed them wherever they went</u>.
They ....

7 <u>The buildings and decorations fascinated him</u>.
He ....

8 <u>He showed us some amazing photographs</u> of villages in the mountains and the desert.
We ....

9 Before he left, <u>they offered us a tiny cup of green tea</u> and a delicious sweet cake.
We ....

10 <u>His talk really inspired me</u>, and I plan to go to China as soon as I can afford to!
I ....

B Read the text and write the form of the verb in brackets which is best, either active or passive.

Caviar (0) ..*is*.. (be) a great delicacy, especially in Russia, and it (1) .... (often / eat) as an hors d'oeuvre. It (2) .... (consist) of the eggs of the sturgeon, which (3) .... (know) as roe. To make caviar, the eggs (4) .... (salt) and thoroughly (5) .... (wash). The sturgeon is a large bony fish, similar to a shark;. It (6) .... (lay) its eggs in fresh water. There are 24 known species, and the largest can (7) .... (be) up to 8.4 metres long. The Beluga is the largest member of the sturgeon family and it (8) .... (find) in the Caspian Sea, the Black Sea, and the river Volga in Russia. It produces more eggs than any other type of sturgeon. The roe of the Beluga sturgeon (9) .... (consider) the best, but caviar can (10) .... (obtain) from other types of sturgeon. Real caviar is very expensive, but a substitute can (11) .... (make) from lump fish roe, which is not as expensive.

C Look at the picture and complete the sentences using passives to describe the picture. All the verbs should be in the *present continuous* or in the *present perfect*.

0 A baby *is being carried* (carry) by his mother.

0 An ambulance *has been parked* (park) outside the entrance.

1 A woman .... (examine) by a doctor.

2 The old woman .... (help) by the nurse.

3 Another woman .... (take) into the lift.

4 The young men .... (offer) a cup of tea.

5 A cup of coffee .... (spill) on the floor.

6 The girl's leg .... (bandage).

7 The floor .... (sweep).

8 The two women .... (show) an x-ray.

D Look at what people are saying about Delia's party. Rewrite the following sentences changing the underlined words to passive forms.

0 'Delia has invited me to a dinner party.'
  I have been invited by Delia to a dinner party.

1 'They are holding the party at the health club where she works.'
  ....

2 'Delia is celebrating because her boss has promoted her.'
  ....

3 'Do you think they will expect us to dress formally?'
  ....

4 'I don't know what guests usually wear at these kind of things.'
  ....

5 'I don't know. No one has ever invited me to a party at a health club!'
  ....

6 'Has anyone asked Mr Drayton to come to the party too?'
  ....

7 'I don't think anyone has ever introduced Delia to Mr Drayton.'
  ....

8 'Maybe they will serve us lettuce leaves and carrot juice!'
  ....

9 'I hope we won't offend them if we refuse.'
  ....

117

The Reverend Richard Meux Benson **had** the Church of St Mary and St John **built** on land he owned in East Oxford. He was vicar of the parish from 1870–86, and the design of the church **was based** on traditions of the Oxford movement. The church **was designed** by A. Mardon Mowbray, and **was built** of Charlbury stone in early decorated style. The foundation stone **was laid** in 1875. Construction of the church took a long time, because they did not have enough money to finish it for many years. The original plans included a spire, but this **was** never **built**. Much of the design for the interior **was** never **completed**, either. People **must have been** very disappointed by its plainness. However, they continued adding details to the church until 1912, when it **was completed**. Now, it **is thought** to be a very lovely building.

❶ formal use of the passive

When we are writing technical, scientific, or academic text we prefer to use the passive. This helps to focus on essential elements of information:

- The Eiffel Tower **was built** in 1889. (*In this sentence it is not important who built it.*)
- DNA **was identified** in 1953. (*In this sentence the discovery is most important and the date, not who made the discovery.*)

Using the passive form can make what we are saying seem more serious and formal. For this reason it is frequently used in legal documents and other official documents, such as regulations:

- Members **are expected** to display their membership card at all times.
- Smoking **is not permitted**.

❷ modals with passive verbs

If we want to use a passive structure with modal verbs (**will**, **must**, **should** etc), we use the *passive infinitive* form **be** + *past participle*. We use this form to talk about something in the present or future:

- We **should be allowed** to have more time to finish the essay. (*present*)
- Tomorrow we **will be given** the keys to the new house. (*future*)

We use the passive infinitive form **have been** + *past participle* to talk about something in the past:

- The parcel **must have been lost** by the courier company. (= *The courier company must have lost the parcel.*)
- The exams **should have been marked** last week!
- Frank **would have been missed** if he hadn't come to the meeting.

❸ impersonal subject pronouns in place of passives

In informal language we don't often use the passive. Instead we often use the *impersonal pronoun* **they** with an active verb. **They** can be singular or plural. If *we don't know the gender of the person*, we often use **they**:

- The new secretary – **they** will do the filing. = The filing **will be done** by the new secretary. (**They** *is singular here, but we don't know if the subject will be a man or a woman.*)

118

- **They** are building the whole shopping centre in a year. = The whole shopping centre **is being built** in a year. (**They** *refers to a group of builders and takes a plural verb*.)
- **They** had recently painted the walls blue. = The walls **had** recently **been painted** blue.

If we are talking about *one person, and we don't know who it is,* we can also use **someone** or **somebody**:
- **Someone** left the door open. = The door **was left** open.
- **Someone** had left the door open. = The door **had been left** open.

If we are talking about *everyone,* or *many people,* we say **people** with an active verb:
- **People** buy flowers on Mother's Day. = Flowers **are bought** on Mother's Day.

❹ generalisations using passives

We often use the passive form with a *state verb* when we are talking about *a feeling which most people have about something*:
- Ghandi **was respected** by everyone who met him.
- Rock music **is enjoyed** by most people under 40.

It is said and **It is thought** are passive idioms sometimes found in formal written English when referring to *something that a lot of people believe*:
- **It is thought** that the earthquake killed over 3,000 people.
- The village was buried under the lava, **it is said**.

❺ passives using **get** and **have**

We can use a form of **get**, in the place of **be**, in a very informal and idiomatic type of passive when we want to talk about *something happening to someone or to something*:
- I **got hit** by a cricket ball. = I **was hit** by a cricket ball.
- A lot of parcels **get damaged** in the post. = A lot of parcels **are damaged** in the post.

Notice that we add **do** or **did** in questions and negatives when we use **get** in a passive:
- **Do** you **get given** such nice presents every day? = **Are** you **given** such nice presents every day? (= *Do people give you presents like that every day?*)
- I **don't get given** presents like that every day! = I'**m not given** presents like that every day. (= *People don't give me presents like that every day.*)

❻ have / get something done

We can use a passive form to talk about *jobs that people do for us*:
- My house **is being painted** next week.
- Sylvia's hair **is cut** every three weeks.

In informal speech and writing we can also use **have something done** or **get something done** to say the same thing:
- I'**m having** my house **painted** next week. = I'**m getting** my house **painted** next week. (= *I have arranged for someone to paint my house.*)
- Sylvia **has** her hair **cut** every three weeks. = Sylvia **gets** her hair **cut** every three weeks. (= *Sylvia pays someone to cut her hair every three weeks.*)
- I **had** my car **repaired** last week. = I **got** my car **repaired** last week. (= *I paid someone to mend my car last week.*)

Both **have something done** and **get something done** are informal usages, but **get** is more informal than **have**.

A

Choose the correct verb from the brackets and write it in the gap in the correct passive infinitive form.

wash	inhale	use	pierce	avoid	expose
~~keep~~	spray	protect	follow		

X Clearitall X
drain clearing product

Warning! This product must (0) _be kept_ out of the reach of children.

The product must (1) .... only as directed.

Contact with the skin must (2) .... by wearing gloves and covering the arms.

If contact with the skin occurs, the skin must (3) .... in plenty of warm water.

If contact with the eyes occurs, a doctor's advice must (4) .... immediately.

The product must not (5) .... through the mouth or nose.

The container must (6) .... from strong sunlight and not (7) .... to temperatures above 50 degrees.

The tin must not (8) .... or burnt even after use. It must not (9) .... near a naked flame or on any hot material.

B

Rewrite the underlined phrases in this report using the passive.

When we got home, we saw that [0]someone had left the door open. It was soon clear that [1]someone had burgled our house. [2]They had stolen all the electrical equipment from the living room, and [3]they must have dragged it into the garden. [4]They had crushed the flowers in the flower beds and [5]they had trodden mud into the hall carpet. [6]The sight of my bedroom shocked me. [7]They had thrown all my clothes on the floor and [8]opened all my drawers. [9]They had taken all my jewellery and my favourite silver clock. I really hope that [10]the police catch the criminals and [11]the courts punish them soon.

0 _the door had been left open_
1 ....
2 ....
3 ....
4 ....
5 ....
6 ....
7 ....
8 ....
9 ....
10 ....
11 ....

C Read the following sentences and rewrite each one in a more informal style, using the word in brackets:

0   The big house in the village has always been lived in.
    (someone) *Someone has always lived in the big house in the village.*

1   The walls in the hall had been painted pale blue.
    (they) ....

2   The garden had been planted with roses and honeysuckle and lots of traditional British plants.
    (people) ....

3   The kitchen has recently been modernised.
    (they) ....

4   The carpets have been taken out, and the floorboards have been polished.
    (they) ....

5   The last owners paid for someone to build some wardrobes.
    (get) ....

6   Now the new owners are having the roof repaired.
    (get) ....

7   They are arranging for someone to clear the garden.
    (get) ....

8   It's very sad, but graffiti has been written on the front door.
    (someone) ....

9   People's names have been scratched into the paint.
    (they / their) ....

10 The owners have arranged for someone to repaint the door next week.
    (get) ....

The Grantsfield Hotel

Schedule for chamber maids: Isobel
Special responsibility: Floor 4

6.00 a.m: **Make** tea for the staff.
6.30 a.m: **Do** the shoes for the guests on your floor.
7.00 a.m: Prepare the breakfast trays for the guests on your floor. (See the list on the noticeboard in the staff kitchen.)
8.00 a.m: **Do** the ironing for guests. (See the list on the noticeboard in the laundry.)
8.30 a.m: **Do** the stairs between your floor and the floor below, and clean the corridors and landings on your floor.
9.30 a.m.–12 a.m: **Do** the rooms (400–412):
  ● **make** the beds
  ● dust, polish, and tidy the rooms
  ● clean the bathrooms and replace shampoo etc. (See the inventory list.)
  ● replace tea, coffee, milk, and sugar
  ● check the contents of the minibar and replace any missing items.
    Don't forget to write the items used on the form provided.

General comment: **Don't** *disturb the clients unnecessarily. If the room is occupied, leave it and come back later!*

❶ make and **do**: meaning and use

Make is used to talk about:

construction: ■ Carpenters **make** tables. *production*: ■ I'm **making** lunch / a cup of tea.
creation: ■ Cinecittà **makes** films. *obligation*: ■ I **made** Joe give me his last sweet.

Do is used for:

general activity: ■ What **are** you **doing**?
work, jobs, and activities: ■ I've **done** the washing-up. She's **doing** her make-up.
work activities (with an **ing** *form*): ■ She's **doing** some **painting**.
completing or finishing (with a **past form**): ■ Hazel **has done** her homework. Tom **did** the crossword.

We also use **do**:

as an *auxiliary verb* in questions and negatives: ■ '**Does** Liam **work** here?' 'No he **doesn't**.'
in *negative imperatives*: ■ **Don't walk** on the grass.
as a substitute for other verbs where there is no auxiliary: ■ 'I love this music!' 'So **do** I!'
to emphasise something: ■ Maria really **does** speak English well.

❷ common phrases with **make**

make + preposition

make out something = *see something with difficulty*:
■ It's very dark, but I can just **make out** the number of the house.
make it out = *understand something*:
■ I think she's speaking Japanese. Can you **make it out**?
make something up = *invent something*:
■ I didn't know the answer to question 3 so **I made something up**.
make up your mind = *decide something*:
■ I can't **make up my mind** whether to go to the theatre or the cinema.

make + noun phrase

make the bed = *tidy the bed*:
■ I **made the bed** and went out to work.
make a mistake = *do something wrong*:
■ Karen **made a mistake** in her calculations.
make (such) a fuss = *complain and argue*:

- I don't know why my boss **makes such a fuss** when I'm late!

make a nuisance of yourself / itself / etc. = *irritate or upset other people*:
- That dog is really **making a nuisance** of itself.

make friends (with) = *develop a friendship with someone*:
- I'd like to **make friends with** Sue, but she's not very friendly.

make a fool of myself / yourself / ourselves etc. = *behave stupidly*:
- Sue **made a fool of herself** dancing the tango at the disco.

make fun of someone = *to laugh at*:
- Jack hates people **making fun of him**.

make your / her / his / etc. **way to** = *go somewhere*:
- You must **make your way to** the exit at once!

make a difference = *influence something, make something or someone change*:
- This charity really **makes a difference** to children.

make no difference or **not make any difference** = *not influence or change anything or anyone*:
- You can talk to Sam if you like, but it **won't make any difference**.

make something work = *succeed in using*:
- I can't **make** this coffee machine **work**.

compounds with **make**

makeover = *a big improvement in someone's appearance* (US):
- Jenny is looking so scruffy. I think she needs a complete **makeover**!

make-up = *cosmetics, colours for the face and skin*:
- I've finished my purple mascara. Where is the **make-up** counter?

❸ common phrases with **do**

do + preposition

do something up = *close or fasten*, or *decorate or mend*:
- Can you **do up** your shoes?
- I've **done up** my bedroom. It's lovely now!

have (got) something / nothing to do with someone (or **something**) = *to be about, connected with*, or *relevant to something*:
- The book **has something to do with** Mexican history.
- The film **had nothing to do with** the Civil War.

do without (someone or **something)** = *manage without*:
- I don't think Delia can **do without** her mobile phone!

do in verb phrases

something (or **someone**) **will do** = *be sufficient* or *adequate*:
- How much will the shopping cost? I think £50 **will do**.

do some good = *help someone* or *something*:
- Collecting money for charity **does some good** for society.

other idiomatic uses of **do**

do (some) business with someone = *arrange a financial or business deal*:
- We **have been doing business with** Carlton Enterprises for many years.

do your / our / her best = *try as hard as possible*:
- We **must do our best** to keep calm during the test.

Well done! = *Congratulations! Very good!*
- You've passed your driving test! **Well done!**

That will do! = *that is sufficient or enough*:
- You can stop writing now. **That'll do!**

well done = *cooked a lot*:
- I prefer my steak **well done**.

123

A

Read the dialogue and choose the right form of either **make** or **do**, and write it in the gaps.

HARRY: We really should tidy up the flat! My mum's coming for lunch today, remember?

PETRA: Today! I'd completely forgotten. What are we going to (0) ...*do*...? It's such a mess!

HARRY: Oh, it'll be alright. She doesn't expect it to be perfect. We'll (1) .... our best.

PETRA: OK, I'll (2) .... the vacuuming. If we clean and tidy up the place a bit, that will (3) .... Where is the vacuum, by the way?

HARRY: That might be a problem. I couldn't (4) .... it work last time I tried.

PETRA: Gosh, Harry, you (5) .... such a mess with your hobbies! Why can't you (6) .... your model-making in the garden shed? There's sawdust all over the carpet. And if the vacuum (7) .... not work, I'm not brushing the carpet! You'll have to (8) .... it.

HARRY: I don't understand why you (9) .... such a fuss! My mother won't mind a bit of sawdust.

PETRA: OK, if you say so. What about lunch – what are you going to (10) .... for her lunch?

HARRY: I've already (11) .... the lunch. There's a quiche and some salads in the fridge. Oh, and I (12) .... a fruit trifle.

PETRA: Wow! Sounds great! I think you're right Harry, the sawdust won't (13) .... any difference. After all, she's coming to see you, not to inspect a clean flat!

B

Read the passage and circle the correct underlined word.

It was 5 a.m. Detective Inspector Annie Stevens was (0) making / doing her make-up. She had a hard day ahead of her and was (1) doing / making her best not to think about it. She had (2) made / done a lot of mistakes, but she had also (3) made / done some good in the world. A lot of criminals were behind bars who had (4) made / done a nuisance of themselves. She had (5) made / done a difference. She liked to (6) make / do a nuisance of herself in the criminal world. Smiling to herself, she quickly (7) did / made her bed and (8) did / made the washing-up from the previous night – one plate and one glass doesn't take long to wash – and then she left her flat.

Suddenly the lights in the corridor went out. She could just (9) make / do out the window at the end of the landing. She (10) made / did her way to the lift door and pushed the button, but it didn't open. She couldn't (11) make / do it out. Why wasn't the emergency electricity supply working? 'It's just a coincidence,' she thought, 'this has got nothing to (12) make / do with me – I mustn't (13) do / make a fool of myself – nobody's going to try to (14) do / make me in – that would be crazy! They would be (15) making / doing a bad mistake! Come on Annie – that will (16) make / do!'

She turned quickly and went back into the flat. It was time to leave the police force, or maybe she just needed a break. They would have to (17) make / do without her for a while at the station. She (18) made / did herself a cup of tea and picked up the phone …

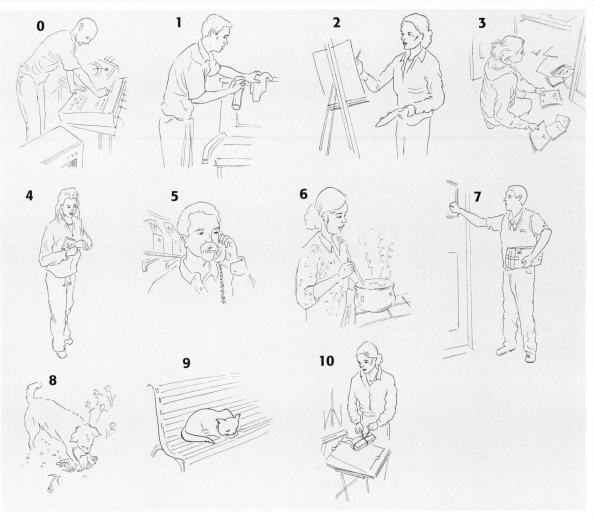

Rewrite the following sentences using make or do and the given words.

What are the Khan family doing today?

0 Imran is constructing a new sound system in the sitting room.

   He is making a new sound system.

1 Ahmed is in the studio cleaning the piano.

   .... the cleaning.

2 Anisha is not here. She is in Dorset on a course studying painting.

   .... a painting course in Dorset.

3 Nabila is in her bedroom throwing her books and magazines on the floor.

   .... a mess.

4 Nabila's friend, Jenny, is laughing at her because she hasn't got the new 'Slur' album.

   .... fun of Nabila.

5 Qasim is on the telephone with a colleague discussing a business deal.

   .... some business on the phone.

6 Auntie Bunty is cooking some delicious lentil stew.

   .... some cooking.

7 The postman is knocking very loudly on the front door.

   .... a lot of noise.

8 The dog, Bobo, is digging up the flowers in the garden.

   .... a nuisance of himself.

9 The cat, Snowy, is sleeping on a bench in the garden.

   .... absolutely nothing.

10 Anisha is closing up her paintbox, ready to go home.

   .... up her paintbox.

MRS COMPTON: **Get up**! Come on, James, I **haven't got** time to keep on calling you. I've **got** to **get** to work myself! **Get out of** bed now!

JAMES: Oh Mum! I don't need to **get up** so early. I didn't **get home** till nearly 11 o'clock last night! If I **don't get** enough sleep, I won't be able to **get through** the day.

MRS COMPTON: You won't be able to **get away with** turning up at college late every day! How can I **get through to** you? If you **don't get off** that bed and into the bathroom and out of that door in half an hour, I'll **get** a bucket of water and throw it over you!

JAMES: Mum, I just don't **get it**! Why do you **get** so grumpy these days? OK, I'll **get up**, just to **get you off my back**!

MRS COMPTON: Good! That's better. Now I can **get off** to work.

❶ common uses of **get**

Get is a very common verb in English. We use it in many different ways:

get + *adjective* = *become*:
- I don't want to go out in the snow and **get cold**.

get to + *noun* = *arrive at*:
- The bride **got to the church** at half past three.

get here / there = *arrive*:
- My uncle **got there** before three.

get + *noun* = *obtain or receive*:
- Sarah **got three CDs** for her birthday.
- Did you **get any money** from the cashpoint?

get to do something = *have the opportunity to do something*:
- He **got to meet** the Prime Minister!

get someone to do something = *persuade someone to do something*:
- The teacher **got John to answer** the question in German.

get something done = *pay someone to do something*:
- I often **get my hair cut** at Sylvester's.

❷ uses of **have got**

We use **have got** (and **has got**, **had got**) to mean *possess*; in informal British English **have got** is used more often than **have**:
- **Have** you **got** any milk? (= *Have you any milk? / Do you have any milk?*)
- Sam **had got** some money in his pocket. (= *Sam had some money.*)

We use **have got to do something** to talk about *obligation* or *necessity*:
- I**'ve got to meet** my mother this afternoon. (= *I must meet my mother…*)
- You**'ve got to wear** a suit. (= *You have to wear a suit.*)

❸ multi-word verbs with **get**

Multi-word verbs are verbs made up of two or more words. Many multi-word verbs with **get** describe *motion*.

We can use **get** with a ***place preposition*** (**in / into / on / onto / off / under / over / through / down**) to talk about *movement in relation to something*:
- **Get into** the car! We're late.
- The pony **got over** the gate and escaped.

We can also use **get** with an *adverb* (**back** / **away** / **up** / **down**) to talk about *movement*:

> **get back** = *return*:
> - Jacky **got back** in time for tea.
>
> **get away** = *escape* or *go*:
> - It's time to **get away**.
>
> **get up** = *get out of bed or stand up*:
> - I always **get up** before dawn.

We can also use **get** + *adverb* (**away** /**out**) + *preposition* (**of** / **from**) to talk about *movement in relation to something*:

> - Orlando needs to **get away from** the office for a while.
> - We **got out of** the sea and dried ourselves.

(For more on multi-world verbs, see units 66 and 67.)

❹ idioms with **get**

Get is used in a large number of idioms:

> **get off someone's back** = *stop annoying someone*:
> - You really should **get off** Sam's **back**!
>
> **get someone off someone's back** = *persuade someone to stop bothering someone*:
> - Thanks for **getting** Tanya **off** my **back**.
>
> **be getting on** = *getting old*:
> - My granddad's really **getting on**! He's 86 this year!
>
> **get a lot out of something** = *benefit a lot from something*:
> - Yvonne **got a lot out of** the philosophy course.
>
> **get something together** = *organise something successfully*:
> - Lucy was very depressed but now she**'s getting** her life **together**.
>
> **get it** = *understand something*:
> - This homework is really hard, Dad! I just don't **get it**!
>
> **get away with something** = *avoid punishment for something bad*:
> - Peter **got away with** parking on the double yellow line.
>
> OR = *convince people of something untrue*:
> - Tim **got away with** pretending he had a degree in economics and they gave him the job.
>
> **get by** = *just manage (usually financially)*:
> - No, they're not rich, but they**'re getting by** on her salary.
>
> **get into something** = *become interested in something*:
> - Andy**'s getting into** football.
>
> **get on** (**well** or **badly**) = *do something well or badly*:
> - I think I **got on well** in the test this morning.
>
> **get on** (**well**) **with someone** = *be friendly with someone*:
> - Frank really **gets on** well with Imran.
>
> **get out of something** = *avoid doing something you don't want to*:
> - Hannah **got out of** cleaning the stairs yesterday. I did it for her.
>
> **get over something** = *recover from something*:
> - Jan had flu, but she's **getting over** it now.
>
> **get through something** = *finish something*:
> - I can't **get through** this Russian novel!
>
> **get through to someone** = *make contact with someone (often by telephone)*:
> - Lauren **got through to** Paul at last.
>
> OR = *communicate with someone*:
> - I'd like to be friends with Donna, but I can't **get through to** her.
>
> **get together** = *meet someone (usually socially)*:
> - Give me your phone number. I'd love to **get together** some time.

A Read the conversation between Mrs Compton and James. Underline all the phrases with **get** or **got**, and write them next to the correct meaning in the box below.

JAMES: Mum! When I <u>got up</u> this morning I couldn't get into the bathroom for ages. I really needed to use it because I had to get ready for my interview today. I told Anna to get out of the bathroom, but I just couldn't get through to her! She's too young to be getting into make-up and clothes.

MRS COMPTON: It's not true. She's getting quite mature now. Anyway, how did you get on at your interview?

JAMES: Oh, not too bad. I got there on time, and I got on with the man who interviewed me.

MRS COMPTON: I'm really glad you got your hair cut before you went. Do you think you've got the job?

JAMES: I don't know. I didn't know very much about computers, but I think I got away with pretending that I did. I won't get the result until next week.

leave	
have been given	
manage or succeed	
made them believe	
becoming interested in	
someone cut your hair	
becoming adult	
was friendly with	
prepare	
communicate with	
receive	
got out of bed	*got up*
enter	
arrived	

B Read the following sentences. Use the words in brackets to write the correct expression with **get**, from the box, in each gap.

> gets by   get through   getting into   get
> ~~get to~~   gets on well   get out of   get to
> get together   has got to   is getting

0 Diego and Mark usually ....*get to*........ (arrive at) the ice-rink at 6 a.m.

1 They often .... (meet) in the evening as well.

2 At the moment they are .... (becoming interested in) dancing.

3 Mark only works part time, but he .... (manages financially) as he still lives with his parents.

4 Lucy, Mark's girlfriend, ... (is good friends) with Diego.

5 She is training as a dancer and .... (is becoming) very fit and strong.

6 Mark didn't .... (have the opportunity to) see her performance at the end of term because he was in a competition that day.

7 She says that next time he .... (must) come and support her.

8 She hates the written exams and only wants to .... (finish) them.

9 'I don't .... (understand) it! I know everything, but I get so stressed!' she says.

10 'I don't know how I can .... (avoid) doing any more exams.'

Read the following conversation between Phyllis and her Dad, and look at the underlined **get** phrases. Write the correct meaning from the box for each **get** phrase.

---

didn't have   becomes   becoming   becoming enthusiastic about   ~~entered the room~~

persuade   have become   returning   don't have   meet   has   became   benefit a lot from

organise my life   must   is progressing

PHYLLIS: I went for a job interview today. I had only just ⁰<u>got through the door</u>, when they told me they ¹<u>hadn't got</u> enough time to interview me today. I ²<u>got</u> really annoyed!

ANDREW: I think I am ³<u>getting old</u>. Things ⁴<u>have got</u> much harder in the world of work. People ⁵<u>haven't got</u> any respect for each other any more …

PHYLLIS: I'm ⁶<u>getting into</u> the idea of working for myself – running my own business. Maybe I could ⁷<u>get</u> Bob to be my partner. I think I'd ⁸<u>get a lot out of it</u>.

ANDREW: Bob is studying to be a vet – and ⁹<u>he's getting on</u> really well. I don't think that he would be interested in starting a business.

PHYLLIS: What time is he ¹⁰<u>getting back</u> today? I haven't talked to him for ages. We really should ¹¹<u>get together</u>. I need to talk to him, as I really need to ¹²<u>get my life together</u>.

ANDREW: ¹³You<u>'ve got to</u> sort it out for yourself, Phyllis. Don't try and get Bob involved in your plan. ¹⁴He<u>'s got</u> enough problems keeping up with his course. It ¹⁵<u>gets</u> harder each year.

0 *entered the room*   6 ....   12 ....
1 ....   7 ....   13 ....
2 ....   8 ....   14 ....
3 ....   9 ....   15 ....
4 ....   10 ....
5 ....   11 ....

*… and I **asked** the courier, Kevin, to give me a seat at the front of the coach. I **told him** I suffered from travel sickness, but Kevin wouldn't listen! He **told me** to sit at the back and try to sleep! I **asked him if** he had brought any bags, or a bucket, or tissues or anything, and he **said** that he was sure there were some in the bus. When I began to feel bad, I **asked** the driver where the equipment was and he said there wasn't any! I **asked** Kevin to stop the coach so I could get some fresh air, but he **said** that we had to get to Vancouver before dark as the icy roads were dangerous in the dark. I **won't tell you** what happened! It was a horrible journey. When I got back home, I **told** my wife I would never go by coach again. The trouble is, I get airsick too! I guess I'll have to travel by train – **they say** no one gets sick in trains!*

❶ reporting speech

When we want to tell someone what someone else has said or is saying, we use reported speech. There are two ways to do this:

We can use **direct speech**, where we repeat exactly what the person said; we use speech marks (' '), also called **inverted commas**, around the direct speech:
- David said, 'Let's go to the zoo!'

Or, we can use **indirect speech** when we report the content of what someone says:
- David said we should go to the zoo.

In **indirect speech**, if the information we are quoting is about the present or the past, we change the verb in the <u>second clause</u> to a *more past* tense:
- 'I**'m** really tired,' said Peter. = Peter said that <u>he **was really tired**</u>.
- 'I **didn't lie**,' said the Prime Minister. = The Prime Minister said <u>he **had not lied**</u>.

If the information is about the future, we use **would** + **infinitive**, or **was / were going to**:
- 'We**'re going to do** our homework,' said the children. = The children said that <u>they **would do** their homework</u>.
- 'I **will** soon **finish** it,' said Tom. = Tom said <u>he **would** soon **finish** it</u>.

(For more on reporting speech, see units 60 and 61.)

❷ say

We can use **say / said** with **direct speech** (reporting exactly what someone says):
- Mary **says**, 'I've got enough butter.'

When we say who is speaking after the inverted commas, we often reverse the <u>name</u> and **say**:
- 'It's nice to see you,' **said** <u>David</u>.

Note: We don't usually reverse a pronoun (e.g. **he**, **she**) and **say**:
- NOT 'It's nice to see you,' ~~said he~~.

We can also use **say / said** with **indirect speech** (reporting what someone says, without speech marks). We often add **that** before the second clause, but we can also leave out **that**:
- David **said that** it was really nice to see us. = David **said** it was really nice to see us.

We use **say** at the beginning of a sentence if we are describing what *kind of thing* was said:
- Paul **says** what he thinks, but Jake **says** nothing.

We use **they say** when we are talking about *a general opinion*:
- **They say** that the man is innocent.

In more formal language we also use **It is said** to report *a general opinion*:
- **It is said** that the rainforests are under threat.

We also use the phrase **say so**, and **say not**, when we want to say *whose opinion we are reporting*:

- Italy's very lovely. Leo **says so**. (= *Leo says that Italy is very lovely.*)
- I thought France was cheaper, but Leo **says not**. (= *Leo says France isn't cheaper.*)

❸ tell

We use **tell / told** when we talk about giving some information *to someone*; we don't use **to** before the person spoken to:

- 'I'm in a hurry,' Mary **told David**. NOT ~~I'm in a hurry,' Mary told to David~~.

With *indirect speech* we often use **that** before the second clause:

- Mary told David **that** she was in a hurry. NOT ~~Mary told to David …~~

We use **tell + someone + what** to talk about *what someone says or thinks*:

- Yvonne **told** Rachel **what** the problem was.

We use **tell** with a *wh phrase* to give information about *time*, *place*, or *reason* etc:

- The receptionist will **tell** you **where** your rooms are.
- Please **tell** Tanya **why** she didn't get the job.

When we are *reporting someone giving instructions*, we use **tell someone to** + *infinitive* or **tell someone not to** + *infinitive*:

- The policeman **is telling** the girl **not to cycle** on the pavement.
- Robin **told** Elsie **to clear** the table.

We use **can tell** to mean *recognise* or *understand* something:

- I **can tell** you're not enjoying the film.

We use **can't tell if**, often with **or not**, to say we *can't guess* or *can't understand* something:

- The examiner **can't tell if** Sarah is a good student **or not**.

We use **tell** in the following expressions:

tell a story:
- Daddy **told** Debra **a story** as they drove along.

tell a lie/the truth:
- William wouldn't **tell** me **a lie**! I'm sure he'll **tell** me **the truth**.

tell the time (= *read the time from a clock or watch*):
- Sam is learning to **tell the time**.

❹ ask

We use **ask** to report *someone asking something* in *direct speech*, when we do not specify *who* is asked:

- 'What time is it?' Tom **asked**.
- 'Shall we buy some postcards?' **asked** Karen.

When we report *someone asking someone else a question* in *indirect speech*, we use **ask + if / whether**:

- We **asked if** we could see the pictures.
- She **asked whether** I had packed the bags myself.

We also use **ask** when we say *who the question was said to*:

- Mary **asked** me **if** I could speak French.

Note: We do not say **ask to someone**:

- NOT ~~Mary asked to me if I could speak French~~.

We use **ask + someone + to + infinitive** when we *want someone to do something*:

- I'm **going to ask** the DJ **to play** this song.

We can use **ask** with a *question word phrase*:

- Paula **asked** Frank **where** the museum was.
- People often **ask how** this engine works.

say, tell, and ask

131

A Add the correct form of the verbs **ask**, **say**, or **tell** in the gaps in the following text.

Demeter, the goddess of motherhood and fertility, had a daughter called Persephone. One day Persephone didn't come home and her mother was very frightened. She (0) ....*asked*.... everyone she met if they had seen Persephone. The goddess Hecate (1) .... that she had heard Persephone screaming, but she couldn't (2) .... Demeter where Persephone went. Together, they went to talk to the sun god and (3) .... him where she was. He (4) .... them that Hades, the god of the underworld, had taken Persephone to his dark underground kingdom. Demeter was so angry and sad to lose her daughter that she (5) .... the other gods that she wouldn't join them on Mount Olympus, and she (6) .... she would stop any plants growing on earth until she got her daughter back. The world became dry and cold, and nothing would grow.

In the end Zeus had to (7) .... Hermes, the messenger of the gods, to go down into Hades' kingdom and to (8) .... him to let Persephone come back to see her mother. Hermes immediately went to talk to Hades and (9) .... 'If you don't let her return, everyone on earth will die!' And eventually Hades (10) .... he would let Persephone go up to the surface for nine months of each year.

B Choose the correct underlined word and write it below.

Then Professor Arkwright showed the students a slide of Demeter, and [0]<u>says / said / told</u>, 'When Persephone returned to her mother in Hermes' golden chariot, her mother was very happy and allowed the flowers and grain to grow again.' Then he [1]<u>say / said / asked</u> the students to [2]<u>told / asked / tell</u> him what the story symbolised. Katya [3]<u>said / asked / told</u> that she thought it was about how bad men are, and how women must stay away from them. The professor laughed and [4]<u>said / told / ask</u> 'You may be right. But I think there is a metaphorical meaning.' Then he [5]<u>ask / tell / asked</u> what happened when Persephone came back. 'Plants started growing again,' [6]<u>told / said / tells</u> Karen. 'Exactly,' [7]<u>told / tells / said</u> the professor. 'And what does that make you think of?' he [8]<u>told / said / asked</u>. 'Oh, I see!' [9]<u>tells / said / asked</u> Franka. 'It's Spring! Of course. She is under the earth for three months during the winter, when nothing grows, and she is up in the sunshine during spring and summer! That's lovely!'

'But it also [10]<u>said / asks / says</u> that women are in control!' added Katya.

0 *said*

1 ....

2 ....

3 ....

4 ....

5 ....

6 ....

7 ....

8 ....

9 ....

10 ....

C Read the report of the conversation between Police Constable Corrigan and Mrs Hoskins. In each sentence there is a mistake. Cross out the wrong verb and write the correct word at the bottom.

0 P.C. Corrigan thanked Mrs Hoskins for coming to the police station and ~~tells~~ her if she saw the accident.

1 Mrs Hoskins told, yes, she saw everything.

2 'The bike came out of Green Road,' she asks P.C. Corrigan.

3 She say that it wasn't going very fast.

4 P.C. Corrigan said if the van was going quite fast.

5 She told, 'The van driver didn't notice the bike!'

6 Then he says her when the driver braked.

7 'He braked when he heard the crash' she asks him.

8 He tells he thought that both of them were to blame.

9 Mrs Hoskins told if the cyclist was badly hurt.

10 The policeman said her that he wasn't badly injured.

0 *asked*   6 ....

1 ....   7 ....

2 ....   8 ....

3 ....   9 ....

4 ....   10 ....

5 ....

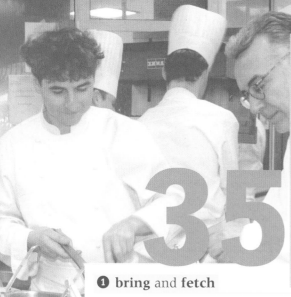

CHEF: How many ducks do we need? **Fetch** me the order again; I can't remember it.

SOUS-CHEF: Just a minute, I'm doing the sauce. I'll **bring** it in a minute.

CHEF: **Take** that pan off the heat! The chicken breast is burning! Did you **take** the steak to the customer?

WAITER: Yes, I **took** the rare steak to table six.

CHEF: Oh no! Go and **bring** it **back**! I hadn't put any vegetables on it!

WAITER: If the customer doesn't complain, we can leave it. Maybe he doesn't like vegetables.

SOUS-CHEF: Chef, shall I **fetch** some more duck from the fridge? I think we need another three portions.

CHEF: Yes, **bring** three more, and the single cream. I need to make some more bechamel sauce … Oh, and waiter, **take** the soup to table four, and **fetch** me the new orders.

❶ bring and fetch

Bring is an irregular verb. The past participle and past simple form is **brought**.

Bring is used to talk about carrying something *from somewhere else to here*. We can use it with **me** or **us**:

 ▪ Could you please **bring** me a phone. I need to call my lawyer.

We can also use it with a name or another personal pronoun (**you**, **him**, **her** etc) when we are talking about carrying *something to someone else* who is close to us:

 ▪ **Bring** the gentleman a size 11 in this style. (*I am helping a customer try on these shoes.*)

If the direct object (often a thing) goes immediately after the verb, we must use **to** or **for** before the indirect object (often a person):

 ▪ Graham **brought** a sandwich **to** Sally. (= *Graham brought Sally a sandwich.*)
 ▪ Sarah always **brings** a lovely present **for** the hostess. (= *Sarah always brings the hostess a lovely present.*)

We sometimes use **bring** to mean that *something usually carries something with it*:

 ▪ April often **brings** high winds.

Bring and **fetch** are very similar in meaning, but **fetch** always involves *going somewhere to get something*; **bring** is used when we carry something *from where we already are*:

 ▪ When you come back from Switzerland, **bring** me some chocolate. (*You are there now.*)
 ▪ I'll **fetch** you some aspirin if you lie still. (*I'll go and get some.*)

We can also use **go and fetch** to say that someone *goes to get something*:

 ▪ Could you **go and fetch** me another cushion?

Note: In US English, speakers often leave out **and** in these sentences:

 ▪ **Go fetch** the newspaper, and **go fetch** your father his tea, please.

(For more on American English usage, see page 292.)

❷ multi-word verbs with bring

Common multi-word verbs with **bring** are:

bring (something) back = *return to its original place*:
 ▪ Please **bring back** the CD you borrowed.

bring up = *say* or *mention*:
 ▪ I didn't **bring up** the fact that he owed me £200. I said nothing.

bring (someone) up = *look after a child until he or she is adult*:
 ▪ Great Aunt Jemima **brought** Greta **up**.

bring together = *unite*:
 ▪ I think music **brings** people **together**.

bring in or **bring something into** = *bring from outside into the building or room*:
 ▪ It's raining! **Bring in** the washing! OR **Bring** the washing **into** the house.

❸ take

Take is an irregular verb. The past participle is **taken** and the past simple form is **took**.

We use **take** when we want to talk about carrying something *from one place to somewhere else*:
- My father **took** me to the station on his motorbike.

We also use it to say that someone *obtains and keeps something*. It doesn't matter *where* the thing is:
- Has Yumi **taken** my clean socks? (= *She might have my socks now.*)

We can use **take** to mean *need* or *use* when we are talking about *time*:
- Dan **takes a long time** to wake up in the morning.

We can also use the empty subject **it**, with **take**, to talk about *time*:
- **It took** three hours to read the article.

We often use a name or an object pronoun (**me**, **him**, **her** etc) after **it** + **take**:
- **It took Jane** three years to learn Russian. OR It took **her** three years …

We also use **it** + **take** with *other quantities*:
- It takes **three eggs** to make that cake.
- It took **all my patience** to finish the job.

❹ multi-word verbs with **take**

Common multi-word verbs with **take** are:

take (something) in = *listen to and understand*:
- I'm afraid I didn't really **take** the lecture **in**. It was too boring.

take someone out = *pay for and accompany someone somewhere*:
- Jack is **taking** Rachel **out** to the theatre.

take (something) out = *carry something outside the house*:
- Don't forget to **take** the rubbish **out**.

take (something) off = *remove clothing or any other covering*:
- Delia **took** the tablecloth **off** the table.

take off = *leave the ground*:
- The plane should **take off** at about 2 p.m.

take up = *start something new*:
- Andrew is **taking up** motorcycle racing.

❺ idioms with **take**

There are several idioms with **take** where it carries another meaning:

take a train / bus = *use a form of public transport*:
- Rupert usually **takes the bus** to the supermarket.

take a bath / shower = *wash* (more common in US English):
- Chi-Nan **takes a shower** every morning.

take + some medicine / milk in your coffee / sugar in your tea etc. = *choose to consume*:
- Do you **take sugar** in your coffee?

take an exam / test = *write or do*:
- Dora's **taking** her driving **test** on Tuesday.

take care = *be careful*:
- I hope you will **take care** not to fall off the cliff.

take responsibility for = *accept responsibility for*:
- Mr Tanako **took responsibility** for the company's problems.

take part in = *be involved in*:
- I wanted to **take part in** the May Day parade.

A Read the following text and put in the appropriate verb, **bring**, **take** or **fetch**, in the appropriate form in each gap.

The parents are setting up the tables for the school fair.

0 Mr Franks asks Tim to .....*fetch*..... some more cloths to cover the tables, so he goes into the kitchen to get them.

1 Mrs Parsons gives him a big pile of tablecloths and he .... them into the hall.

2 Patrick's mum has .... lots of sausage rolls. They are all in two big tins in the kitchen.

3 She said it has .... six pounds of pastry to make them.

4 Halima and Greta go to .... some plates to put them on.

5 Mr Franks .... up the fact that lots of the families are vegetarian.

6 Patrick's mum says she has .... the trouble to make two kinds of sausage rolls, meat and vegetarian.

7 Mrs Parsons suddenly remembers she has forgotten to .... any milk.

8 She asks Helen if she would mind .... three litres of milk from the shop.

9 Helen .... a big basket and goes to the shop on the corner.

10 Mr Franks likes school fairs because they .... parents and teachers together.

11 It's good to .... the families into the school sometimes …

12 … but it does .... a lot of hard work!

B Read about Lucy's day and correct the underlined verbs if they are wrong. If they are correct, write a tick (✔).

Lucy usually [0]<u>brings</u> a shower before work if she has time, and then [1]<u>takes</u> the underground to work. It [2]<u>fetches</u> about half an hour. She has to go and [3]<u>take</u> the mail from the mail room and [4]<u>fetch</u> it to the office manager. Then she often [5]<u>brings</u> a coffee break at about 10.30. It is hard to remember which of her colleagues [6]<u>fetches</u> milk in their coffee. Nobody [7]<u>takes</u> sugar nowadays! If they have a meeting she has to [8]<u>take</u> the projector from the store room and set it up in the conference room. She also has to collect all the filing from the central office and [9]<u>fetch</u> it to the right filing cabinets. She has to [10]<u>bring</u> care to file all the invoices in the right places. She has to [11]<u>bring</u> her son from the child minder at 5.30.

0	*takes*	6	....
1	....	7	....
2	....	8	....
3	....	9	....
4	....	10	....
5	....	11	....

Read the following phone conversation between Kerry and his brother Steve. Choose the best phrase from the box to fill the gaps.

> took my   ~~took me~~   take up   take it in   brought up   taken over
> brought you up   taken in   brought us back   fetched   took off
> taking part   took her   take responsibility

KERRY: Hi, Steve. Where are you?

STEVE: I'm in Lima! It's fantastic. But it (0) _took me_ three days to get here!

KERRY: Well, what on earth happened?

STEVE: The plane (1) .... from Melbourne, and then after half an hour there was a problem and it (2) .... to Australia. I was so scared! Then we had to stay overnight and fly the next day.

KERRY: It's great to hear from you! When I (3) .... Mum from work yesterday, I accidentally (4) .... the fact that you had left the country. She was really worried! It (5) .... some time to (6) .... when I told her you were on your way to Peru! She said she must have (7) .... all wrong! I'm so glad you (8) .... advice and went there. I thought you hadn't (9) .... what I said to you about South America.

STEVE: Oh yes, it was the best advice ever. Now I'm here, I'm (10) .... in a music festival. We've (11) .... the whole central square! I have to (12) .... for the technical side – the sound system and the lighting. It's so cool!

KERRY: Brilliant! It's a good thing you decided to (13) .... electronic engineering, and not archaeology!

137

STEPHEN: Phew! That was a difficult lecture! **Can you understand** genetics?
HARRY: No, not really. I **can't remember** the rules. It's really complicated, and I haven't got a book about it.
STEPHEN: I've got a book about it but I still **can't follow** it.
HARRY: **Can** you **lend** it to me?
STEPHEN: I **can photocopy** the pages you need.
HARRY: No, you **can't**! That's illegal!
STEPHEN: No, you **can photocopy** some pages from books. You **can't photocopy** more than 5% a book – I think that's the law ...
HARRY: That's great! I hope you're right. Thanks. Now, **can I get** you another coffee?

❶ form

Can is a modal verb and is used like an auxiliary verb before a main verb:

- Graham **can repair** his motorbike engine.
- You **can come** to lunch on Friday, if you want.

Questions with **can** are made like questions with auxiliaries; we use **can** + _subject_ + _infinitive_:

- **Can** <u>we</u> **leave** now?
- **Can** <u>John</u> **see** the screen from there?

The negative form of **can** is **cannot** or **can't**:

- I **cannot** find the photocopier.
- Helen **can't** remember his name.

Note: **Can't** is more common in spoken English. It is rare to use **cannot** in speech, but we use it sometimes in _academic_ and _formal contexts_, especially in writing:

- The management **cannot** refund any money.
- Deposits **cannot** be made after 10 p.m.

Short **yes** / **no** _answers_ to questions with **can** and **can't** repeat the modal, not the main verb:

- 'Can you see me?' 'Yes, I **can**.'
- 'Can Paula speak German?' 'No, she **can't**.'

❷ can for skill and ability

We use **can** in statements to say that someone or something _has a particular skill or ability_:

- George **can play** football really well.
- My brother **can speak** a bit of German.

We use **can** in questions to _ask if someone has a particular skill or ability_:

- **Can** Jane **read** Braille?
- **Can** you **use** the scanner?

We use **can't** and **cannot** to say that the someone or something _does not have a particular skill or ability_:

- Keith **can't run** very fast.
- Most fish **cannot fly**.

❸ can for possibility

We use **can**, and often **you can**, to say that _something is possible_:

- We have an indoor pool, so we **can swim** every day.
- You **can buy** nice fruit at the market.

We use **can**, often with **you**, to ask _if something is possible_:

- **Can** they **see** the sea from their flat?
- **Can** you **buy** apples in the market?

We use **can't**, often with **you**, to say that _something is not possible_:

- You **can't send** such big files by email.
- You **can't teach** an old dog new tricks.
- She **can't be** cross – she's smiling. (= _It's not possible that she is cross._)

138

❹ **can** for permission

We use **can** to say that *something is permitted*, or to *give permission to someone*:
- The children **can sit** in the front row.
- Go on, you **can have** the last slice of cake.

We use **can** in questions to *ask for permission to do something*:
- **Can** I **drive** the car today, Dad?
- **Can** we **open** another bottle?

We use **can't** to say that *something is not permitted*:
- Tom **can't get** a day off work this week. His boss won't allow it.
- Sorry, you **can't borrow** the car today. I need it myself.

We often use the impersonal form **you can** when we want to say that *something is generally permitted*:
- **You can take** photographs in the museum.
- **You can walk** on the path, but not on the grass.

We use **can** with the impersonal **you** to *ask if something is generally permitted*:
- **Can you use** a credit card in that shop?
- **Can you pay** in Euros?

We often use the impersonal **you can't** to say that *something is generally not permitted*:
- **You can't smoke** in any restaurant in this city.
- **You can't park** in Oxford Street.

❺ **can** for requests and offers

We use **can** to *ask for something*. It is more polite than using **I want** or the *imperative*:
- **Can** I **have** a cup of coffee, please?
- **Can** you **shut** the window, please?

We also use **can I** or **can we** to *offer something to someone*:
- **Can** I **get** you a coffee?
- **Can** I **carry** that for you?

❻ expressions with **can** and **cannot**

We use **can** with a sense verb (**see**, **hear**, **smell**, **feel** etc) to mean *able to and do*:
- Sarah **can hear** the bells ringing across the valley. (= *Sarah hears the bells …*)
- I **can taste** the additives in this fizzy drink. (= *I taste the additives …*)

We use **can't** and **cannot** when we want to say that we think *something should not be the case*:
- William **can't go on** arriving late every day. (= *He shouldn't arrive late …*)

We often use it in this way with **you** *to give advice*:
- You **can't let** Gavin win every time! (= *You ought not to let him win …*)

We also use **can't** and **cannot** to say that it is *difficult to believe that something is the case*:
- You **can't be** 40! (= *It's difficult to believe that you are 40.*)
- Gloria **cannot be** engaged to Sean! (= *It's difficult to believe that Gloria is engaged to Sean.*)

❼ **can't have done** for the past

We use **can't have** + *past participle* to say that *we think that something has not happened in the past*, often because of some present evidence:
- Tom **can't have been** to the shops – there's still no food in the fridge.
- Mary **can't have gone** to work – her car keys are still on the hall table.

139

A Ask the teacher for permission to do the following things.

0 (have a new notebook)
Can I have a new notebook please?

1 (open the window)
....

2 (get a glass of water)
....

3 (move to another table)
....

4 (hand in your homework tomorrow)
....

5 (leave the lesson early)
....

Now give people permission to do the following things.

0 (come in now)
You can come in now.

6 (finish the work later)
....

7 (talk to each other)
....

8 (find the word in the dictionary)
....

9 (all change groups)
....

10 (go to your next lesson)
....

B Read the text and look at the questions below.

Diego and Mark both love ice-skating. Every Friday evening they go to the ice rink and meet their friends for a skating session. Mark has a serious skating lesson on Saturday morning, but Friday is just for fun. At the ice rink you can hire skates but Mark and Diego take their own. There is lots of loud music and usually the rink is very busy. You can get coffee and burgers and things in the café. Diego is very good at skating but he isn't having lessons now. He is learning jazz dance, as he's already a very experienced ballroom dancer. A lot of the techniques of dance are very similar to skating. Mark used to do ballroom dancing and jazz dance, but his friends don't think it's very cool! Mark has a skating partner called Lucy and they do competitions together. They won the silver cup for ice dance last year. They are both very fit. On Sunday they don't go to the ice rink because it is closed.

Underline the right reply to each question.

0 Can Diego dance?
<u>Yes, he can.</u> / No, he can't.

1 Can Mark ice-skate?
Yes, he can. / No, he can't.

2 Can you get anything to eat at the ice rink?
Yes, you can. / No, you can't.

3 Can Diego do ballroom dancing?
Yes, he can. / No, he can't.

4 Can Mark dance with a partner?
Yes, he can. / No, he can't.

5 Can you use your own skates at the rink?
Yes, you can. / No, you can't.

6 Can they go skating on Sundays?
Yes, they can. / No, they can't.

7 Can Lucy skate?
Yes, she can. / No, she can't.

8 Can Mark do ballroom and jazz dance?
Yes, he can. / No, he can't.

9 Can you listen to music while you skate?
Yes, you can. / No, you can't.

10 Can you take skating lessons at the rink?
Yes, you can. / No, you can't.

C

Now ask questions to get the following information, using **can** or **can't**.

0 Ask if people are allowed to park in the street: *Can you park in the street?*

1 Ask if Helen has learnt to play the trumpet: ....

2 Ask if Mr and Mrs Long know how to do the tango: ....

3 Ask if people can buy tickets online: ....

4 Ask if it is possible to order flowers on the phone: ....

5 Ask if your son, James, is permitted to have a week away from school: ....

6 Ask if we are allowed to sit in this row of seats: ....

7 Ask if you are experienced in using the Internet: ....

8 Ask if you will allow me to pick these flowers: ....

9 Ask if it is possible to get money from the bank after 5 p.m: ....

10 Ask if Jane does T'ai Chi well: ....

D

Read the following speech by Harland Green, the director of a small English language college, to the staff in his college. Look at the underlined phrases with **can**, and then list them in the correct column of the table below.

<u>Can I have</u> your attention, please? Last night I was tidying up the staff room and I found an examination essay under the big table, with no name on it. I'm sure <u>you can imagine</u> how worried I was. We have just sent the exam papers off to be marked, and I'm afraid we left that one out of the parcel. <u>I can't understand</u> how it happened. I was sure we had checked all the papers and the list of candidates. To be honest, it wasn't a very good essay – in fact the student <u>can't have been</u> very proud of it, or they would have written their name on it. Now, <u>we can do</u> one of two things: <u>we can ask</u> each student if they recognise the essay, or <u>we can put</u> the essay on the noticeboard to see if any student recognises it. <u>You can't send</u> papers to the examining board late, but <u>we can ask</u> the examining board to cancel that person's application and enter them next term, instead. I'm sure <u>this student can do</u> better next time. <u>Can anyone tell me</u> who left that paper under the table? I know <u>you can't have done</u> it deliberately. <u>You can tell me</u> in private, if you don't want to admit it in public.

1 present possibility or ability	2 present impossibility or inability	3 permitted or not permitted	4 request	5 past impossibility
			Can I have	

'**Could** you **lend** me your car this afternoon, Dad?' Phyllis asked her father.
'I'm afraid not. But you **could borrow** Bob's,' he replied.
Phyllis grumbled, 'Oh no. It's too small and old. And the colour! … I **couldn't go** into town in that!'
Bob laughed. 'Hey, don't be so rude! I like it. Anyway, **couldn't** you **get** your own car?' he said.
'Oh, you know I **couldn't afford** to run it. I tried to find a job but I **couldn't**,' Phyllis said. Bob **could hear**
    the self-pity in her voice. Oh dear! This **could** be nasty. When Phyllis started using that tone of voice …
'I tell you what,' said Bob, 'I'll give you a lift into town and pick you up later. That way you won't have to
    actually drive my car. How's that?'
Phyllis beamed. She **couldn't believe** her ears! 'Oh Bob, I **couldn't have** a better brother! Thank you so
    much! **Could** you be ready at 6, OK?' and Phyllis skipped out of the room.
'Humph!' grunted Dad from behind his newspaper.

❶ form

Could is a modal verb and is used like an auxiliary verb before a main verb:
> ▪ We **could go** out for a picnic today.

Questions with **could** are made like questions with auxiliaries; we use **could** + *subject* + *infinitive*:
> ▪ **Could** <u>Sandra</u> **take** the dog for a walk?

The negative form of **could** is **could not** or **couldn't**:
> ▪ Peter **couldn't** see the street sign.
> ▪ I **could not** remember what David had said.

Note: **Couldn't** is more common in spoken English. We usually use **could not** in formal written
English or when we want to stress impossibility:
> ▪ Joe **could not** understand why John had said that.

❷ could for possibility

Could + *infinitive* is often used to say that *something is possible now* or *in the future*:
> ▪ Tom isn't in his office – he **could be** in a meeting.

With action verbs we usually use the ***continuous infinitive*** (**be** + **ing form**) to talk about
something that is possibly happening now or in the future:
> ▪ Tom is not in his office – he **could be having** lunch in the canteen.

(For more on action verbs and state verbs, see unit 17.)

When we stress **could**, we mean that *we think something is possible* but there is some doubt. There
is an implied BUT clause:
> ▪ James **COULD** be at the dentist (but I thought his appointment was yesterday).

We use **could not** (**couldn't**) to indicate that *something is impossible now and in the future*:
> ▪ Helen **couldn't bear** to touch a spider (even a very small one).

❸ could for suggestions

Could + *infinitive* is often used for making a *suggestion* about what someone should do in the future:
> ▪ You **could take** the exam in April. (= *Why don't you take the exam in April?*)

We also use **couldn't** in questions to make a *stronger suggestion*:

■ **Couldn't** the children **tidy up** their bedrooms once a week?

❹ could for requests

Could can be used in questions as a polite form of *request*:

■ **Could** you **pass** me the butter, please? (= *Will you pass me the butter, please?*)

The most polite way of requesting something is to use **couldn't** in the first clause, and **could** in the *tag question*:

■ You **couldn't** possibly **lend** me your umbrella, **could** you?

(For more on tag questions, see unit 59.)

If you use **couldn't** in the interrogative, it is *a strong request* and is not as polite as **could**:

■ **Couldn't** you **clean** the bath when you've finished?

❺ could in conditionals

Could is used as the conditional form of **can** to mean *would be able to*. There is often an **if** *clause*, either stated or implied:

■ John **could play** the trombone in the orchestra if he practised a lot.

■ I **could stay** at home tonight and make the dinner (if you wanted me to).

(For more on conditionals, see units 28 and 29.)

❻ could for the past

Could can be used as the past tense of **can** or **be able to** when we are talking about *an ability someone had* or *something that was permitted*:

■ When Jeannette was four, she **could** already **read**. (= … *she was already able to read*.)

■ The boys **could** only **use** the small plates. (= *They were only permitted to use* …)

We can use **could** for ability in the past, but we do not use it for a *particular achievement in the past*. For this we use **managed to**, or **succeeded in**, or **was able to**:

■ Enrico **managed to** explain the problem to Sandra. NOT ~~Enrico could explain~~ …

■ Tom **succeeded in** beating all his opponents. NOT ~~Tom could beat~~ ….

■ Graham **was able to** wear his old motorcycle suit. NOT ~~Graham could wear~~ …

We use **could** with a sense verb (**see, hear, smell, feel** etc) to mean *was able to and did*:

■ He **could hear** the sound of horses' hooves in the distance. (= *He heard the hooves* …)

■ Petra **could feel** the heat from the sun on her back. (= *she felt the sun's heat* …)

The negative of the past of **could** is **couldn't**:

■ John **couldn't find** his book this morning. (= *He was not able to find* …)

■ You **couldn't walk** on the grass. (= *You were not allowed to walk* …)

❼ could have done for the past

We use **could have** (**could've**) + *past participle* to indicate *something that was possible in the past but didn't happen, or was unlikely*:

■ Stephen **could have gone** home at Easter (*but he didn't*).

■ Edward **could've won** the tennis match (*but I'm not sure if he did*).

We use **couldn't have** + *past participle* to say that *something was impossible at a time in the past*:

■ Ian **couldn't have come** to France with us as he didn't have any money.

A Rewrite the underlined phrases with a phrase using **could** or **couldn't**.

[0]<u>Bob Markham would be able to do</u> a higher degree in veterinary studies if he wanted to, as he is doing very well in his undergraduate course. [1]<u>He would be able to choose</u> another course at university, such as medicine, but he wants to work with animals. After his degree [2]<u>it is possible that he will go</u> to work in Africa for a couple of years, as he is specialising in exotic animals. He says [3]<u>he would not able to bear working</u> in a zoo because he doesn't like to see animals in captivity, even if the animals have large enclosures. He thinks that [4]<u>it is possible that zoos are</u> necessary, as so many animals are in danger of extinction now, and breeding programmes in zoos [5]<u>might be</u> the only way to save them. But he says he [6]<u>would be able to work</u> in a zoo only if the animals were able to live in a natural environment.

[7]<u>'Why don't you stay on</u> at university and become a teacher like me,' says his Dad.

'No, Dad,' says Bob. 'I really want to work with real animals in the real world. And [8]<u>I wouldn't be able to teach</u>. Anyway, unless I do some work, I won't even get my degree! [9]<u>Will you help me</u> with some revision? I have an exam on virology and I've forgotten everything!'

'Yes of course,' says Dad, [10]<u>'Will you wait</u> five minutes while I finish my sandwich?'

'Sure. Thanks, Dad.'

0 *Bob Markham could do* ....

1 ....

2 ....

3 ....

4 ....

5 ....

6 ....

7 ....

8 ....

9 ....

10 ....

B Read the following text and write in the phrases with **could** from the box in the correct gaps in the text.

> couldn't get   couldn't have hoped
> couldn't do anything   could come
> ~~could never have imagined~~   couldn't get into
> could join   couldn't you try   could leave
> could achieve

Janet Coogan (0) *could never have imagined* that her son Paul would be such a big success as he is now. When he was at school, he (1) .... very well. He was not very good at sports and he (2) .... the football team. She used to say to him, (3) '.. a bit harder? If you got some qualifications, you (4) .... something in your life.'

When he was older he (5) .... a job, so he spent all his time playing football in the park. One day the manager of Harrington Harriers football team saw Paul playing football in the park with his friends and asked Paul if he (6) .... to London for a trial for Harrington Harriers. Paul asked his Mum, and she said he (7) .... straightaway. He did the trial and they said he (8) .... the team the next week. And now he's a millionaire. 'Well,' says Mrs Coogan, 'I (9) .... for anything better!'

C Write **could** or **couldn't** in the gaps in the following story.

'Excuse me! (0) ....*could*.......... you tell me where the station is?' the small man in the dark coat asked me.

He was smiling, but I (1) .... hear the anxiety in his voice. I was in a hurry, and I (2) .... have walked on, but the man sounded so worried I (3) .... ignore him.

'Yes, but it's a long way from here,' I said. 'You (4) .... take a bus.'

I noticed that the man had two big suitcases. He obviously (5) .... walk very far with those bags.

'There is a bus stop on the corner,' I explained. 'I don't take buses any more, but I think you (6) .... get to the station on the number 45.'

'Oh dear, I've just come from there,' he replied, 'and I (7) .... find a timetable. I (8) .... understand the map.' His voice was getting more and more stressed and he could hardly speak.

'(9) .... you call a taxi?' I asked.

'No, I (10) .... afford that. I'm afraid I'm going to have to walk … and I know I'll miss my train.'

I (11) .... let him walk off like that, so I said, 'I suppose I (12) .... give you a lift … my car's parked over there.'

'Oh, I (13) .... ask you to do that!' he said, his eyes shining.

'Come on, in you get,' I said. And he did.

It **may be** possible one day for men to live on the planet Mars. Mars **may have had** a climate very like ours many millions of years ago, and the inhabitants **may have ruined** it with pollution, just as we **may be doing** to our own. If we succeed in setting up a colony there, we **might be able** to grow plants and trees in an artificial atmosphere, until it creates its own ecosystem, and gradually a new atmosphere **might be created** around the dead planet. Astronomers have found evidence of a liquid under the surface that **may be** water, and if there is water, it is very possible that there **might** once **have been** some form of life on the planet. The temperature on Mars is very low and the only life form that **might have survived** is bacteria. But the discovery of water on Mars **may be** important in ways that we don't even know yet.

❶ form

May and **might** are modal verbs and are used like auxiliary verbs. They are followed by an *infinitive*, or the *continuous infinitive* (**be** + **ing** *form*), of the main verb:

- Ken **may have** the flu.
- Gary **might be leaving** this morning.

We can use **may** in questions, to ask for *permission*; we use **may** + <u>subject</u> + *infinitive*:

- **May** <u>I</u> **take** your order now, madam?
- **May** <u>we</u> **speak** to the manager, please?

We don't usually use **might** as an auxiliary in a question. We do use **might** after **Do you think** to ask about *future possibility*:

- **Do you think** you **might** buy a new coat this autumn?
- **Do you think** Graham **might** finish the project on time?

The negative is **may not** or **might not** or **mightn't**; we don't use **n't** after **may**:

- You **mightn't** recognise Pauline.
- We **may not** have time for lunch.

❷ **may** and **might** for possibility

May / **might** + *infinitive* is used to mean that *some action or event is possible in the future*. There is no real difference between **may** and **might** in this use:

- We **may go out** for dinner tonight, or we **might get** a takeaway.

When talking about possible events in the future, we can also use the *continuous infinitive* of action verbs, with more or less the same meaning as the *infinitive*:

- We **may be going out** for dinner tonight, or we **might be getting** a takeaway.

We can also use **be going to** to talk about *plans and intentions*:

- Dana **may be going to come** and live in Harrow. (= *She intends to come …*)

We can use **may** / **might** to say *that something is possibly happening at the moment*. In this meaning, we use the *infinitive* of state verbs:

- Helen **may seem** cross and upset but she isn't really.

and the *continuous infinitive* of action verbs:

- Gordon **might be working** in the factory today.

(For more on action verbs and state verbs, see unit 17.)

We use **may** / **might** + **not** when we are saying that *something is possibly not the case*:

- France **might not be** the richest country in Europe. (= *It is possible that it is not the richest, but it might be.*)

■ Dr Thompson **may not have** much patience today. (= *It is possible that he will not have much patience.*)

Note: We can also use **can** and **could** for *possibility*. (For more on **can** and **could**, see units 36 and 37.)

❸ **may** for permission and requests

We also use **may** + *infinitive* when we are *giving permission to someone to do something*, but this is more formal than **can**, and less common now:

■ You **may use** the bathroom now. (= *You can use the bathroom now.*)
■ Rupert **may have** the morning off. (= *Rupert can have the morning off.*)

Note: We don't use **might** with this meaning.

We use **may** to *ask for permission to have or do something*; this is more polite than using **can**:

■ **May** we **have** some more time to finish the paper?
■ **May** I **see** that letter, please?
■ **May** I **read** the letter to you?

We use **may not** to say that *something is not permitted*, particularly when we are being polite:

■ You **may not smoke** in the restaurant.

We use **may not** in short answers when we *refuse permission*:

■ 'May I come in?' 'No, you **may not**!'

We use **may I / we + have** when we are *asking for something*, or *ordering something* in a polite way:

■ **May I have** some mayonnaise with my sandwich?

❹ **might** for suggestions

We use **might** + **try** when we are making *a formal suggestion of an action*:

■ You **might try** Ibiza this year.
■ She **might try** telephoning the manufacturer.

We use **might as well** to talk about *a choice of action (when there seems to be no real alternative)*:

■ You **might as well** take the bus. It's too far to walk.
■ We **might as well** stay in this evening. I haven't got any money.

Note: We also use **may as well** in this way, though it is less common.

❺ **may / might + have done** for the past

We can use **may have / might have** + *past participle* to say that *we think something was possible in the past*:

■ Ian **may have been** in the army. (= *I think he was in the army.*)
■ Sun-Chi **may have failed** her exam!

We use **might have** + *past participle* when we want to say that *someone should have behaved differently in the past*:

■ I didn't know you'd lost the key. You **might have told** me! (= *I wish you had told me.*)
■ Tom's essay was really short. He **might have tried** harder. (= *He should have tried harder.*)

❻ **might** in reported speech

When someone said or thought something using **may** or **might**, we use **might** to report it:

■ Gina thought Jane **might get** here late. (= *Gina thought 'Jane may get here late.'*)
■ Larry said he **might have left** his wallet on the bus. (= *Larry said: 'I might have left my wallet on the bus.'*)

A Lucy and her boyfriend, Mark, are having dinner in a Chinese restaurant.
Read their conversation and put in the missing phrases with **may** and **might** from the box.

May we have	might as well	might be
I might try	~~may have given~~	May I take
I might get	might give	you may not
	May I show you	May I see

MARK: We're a bit late. They (0) *may have given* our table to someone else!

LUCY: I hope not! This is a lovely place. They (1) .... us another table.

WAITER: Good evening, sir. Good evening, madam. (2) .... to your table?

MARK: Oh, thank you very much.

WAITER: (3) .... your coats?

LUCY: Thank you very much, but I think I'll keep mine. (4) .... cold.

WAITER: Oh, I do hope not, madam! Oh, and I'm afraid (5) .... smoke in the restaurant.

MARK: That's fine. (6) .... a jug of water, please?

LUCY: It (7) .... a bit warmer in here!

MARK: Never mind. Just keep your coat on. Let's order. (8) .... the menu?

LUCY: Hmm … I think (9) .... the chicken chow mein.

MARK: Yes. I (10) .... have the same.

B Read the following sentences and complete the gaps with phrases using **may** or **might**. There is often more than one possible answer.

0 Diego is in a skating competition in Hamburg. He is doing very well. In fact, ...*he might*...... win!

1 Suddenly Diego trips and loses his balance as he is spinning in the compulsory dance! .... fall.

2 He is very disappointed and wants to stop, but he doesn't. He still has a chance to come second in the competition, so he thinks he .... finish.

3 Mark is very impressed with the way he continues. He says he thought that Diego .... walk away in the middle of his dance.

4 Diego asks the judges if he can do his dance again. He says to them, '.................................... again?'

5 The judge says it is not permitted. 'No, ...!'

6 After the competition Diego says he thinks the judges were wrong. 'They .... let me do it again!'

7 He is not sure why he tripped but he thinks it was possibly because of the lace of his skating boot. 'It .... the lace of my skate that made me trip.'

8 Now it is Mark's turn to do the compulsory dance. He is afraid of falling. He thinks .... lose points in the same way as Diego.

9 They are waiting for the results. They think they still .... in the top three in the competition.

10 Diego suggests that he and Mark should try roller-skating! '.................................... roller-skating instead of ice-skating,' he laughs.

C Look at the picture below and, using the words in the clue, make complete sentences with **may** or **might**. Some sentences are about the future and some are about the past.

0 the policeman and the thief (catch)
The policeman may / might catch the thief.

1 the thief and the handbag (steal)
....

2 the driver and the lamp-post (hit)
....

3 the dog and the road (run across)
....

4 the girls and the shoes (buy)
....

5 the man and the café (be in)
....

6 the woman with the baby and this bus (catch)
....

7 the children and the film (see)
....

8 the young man, the flowers, and the girl (give)
....

9 the young man, the flowers, and the flower stall (buy)
....

10 the older woman and the eggs (break)
....

D Read the situation and write what you would say in each situation. You must use **may** or **might**. Sometimes both are possible.

0 You are outside a café and you offer your friend a cup of coffee: '*May I get you a cup of coffee?*'

1 You and your friend want to sit at a table where a woman is already sitting. You ask her if you can sit here. '...'

2 You want to open the window. You ask the woman if you can. '...'

3 You want two cups of coffee and a Danish pastry. You ask at the counter.
'...'

4 Your friend can't decide what to eat. You suggest a Danish pastry.
'...'

5 Your friend orders one, but it is very expensive. He thinks you should have told him it was so expensive.
'...'

6 You ask permission to pay for it.
'...'

7 He says he possibly does not have enough money.
'...'

8 You think you haven't got enough and you will have to go to the cash machine.
'...'

9 He suggests that you pay on a credit card.
'...'

10 You ask the waiter if you can pay with a card.
'...'

39

DELIA: Yes, of course, Mr Heinrich. Just a minute, I'**ll have** a look …
Yes, we have a booking in your name from tomorrow evening. You
are booked for reflexology, aromatherapy, yoga, and you would
prefer a vegetarian diet …

MR HEINRICH: Good, that's right. I am flying to Heathrow. **Will** there **be**
someone to meet me at the airport?

DELIA: Yes of course. What time is your flight?

MR HEINRICH: It leaves Cape Town at 7.30 a.m. and, if there aren't any
delays, it'**ll land** around … umm …

DELIA: 7 p.m. Don't worry, I'**ll phone** the airport to check before I
leave to collect you.

MR HEINRICH: So you'**ll be meeting** me personally?

DELIA: Yes, and I'**ll be carrying** a card with our 'Inside Story' logo and
your name on it. What **will** you **be wearing**?

MR HEINRICH: OK. I am 45, a bit freckly, average build … oh, and I'**ll
be wearing** a beige suit and brown shoes. **Shall** I **carry** a 'Times'
newspaper?

DELIA: No, that's alright. We'**ll find** each other. I hope your flight goes
smoothly!

❶ will: form

Will is a modal verb and is used like an auxiliary verb before the **_infinitive_** of the main verb:
- Jack **will answer** when you knock on the door.
- You **will see** Dan at the ice rink.

We usually use the contracted form **'ll** after a **_pronoun_** (**I**, **you** etc) in speech and informal writing:
- **They'll** come and visit you in the hospital.

We often use **'ll** after other types of words when we are speaking, but not in writing:
- I'm afraid the **house'll** be too expensive for us.

Questions with **will** are made like questions with auxiliaries; we use **will** + _subject_ + **_infinitive_**:
- **Will** you **buy** some more olives?

Negatives with **will** are made by adding **not** or by using **won't**:
- Helen **will not** stay for dinner.
- I **won't** forget what you said to me.

In speech, we usually use **won't** because **will not** usually means that _we refuse to do something_:
- I **will NOT** pay for such bad quality goods! (= _I refuse to pay_ …)

But we use **will not** in _formal_ and _academic contexts_, especially in writing:
- The management **will not** refund any money.

When we use an adverb (e.g. **still**, **never**) with **will**, the adverb goes before the infinitive:
- Philip will **never** leave Italy

❷ will: for the future

We use **will** + **_infinitive_** to talk about _something that we expect to happen_:
- Rachel **will love** her present.

We often use **will** with **I think**, **I hope**, **I'm sure** etc, or a word like **probably**, **definitely**:
- Do you think she'**ll be** here by seven?
- She **will** probably bring **Joel**.

(For more on future forms, see units 23–26.)

❸ **will** with conditionals and time expressions

We use **will** + *infinitive* when there is some form of <u>condition</u>, either stated or implied:

  ■ **I'll** get a discount <u>if I pay in cash</u>.

(For more on conditionals, see units 28 and 29.)

When we want to say that *one future event follows another*, we use **will** + *infinitive* and a <u>time expression</u> with **when**, **before**, **after**, or **as soon as**:

  ■ You**'ll be** much happier <u>when you start your new job</u>!
  ■ Gordon **will prepare** the salad <u>an hour before the guests arrive</u>.

The **will** clause can follow the time expression:

  ■ <u>As soon as the test is finished</u>, the teachers **will mark** the papers.

❹ **will** as offer, promise, or request

We use **will** + *infinitive* when we are *offering or promising something*:

  ■ **We'll have** a game of chess after dinner.
  ■ Don't worry, **we'll be** there in plenty of time.

We use **will** in questions when we are *asking someone to do something*:

  ■ **Will** you **sit** over there, please?

❺ **will** + **be** + **ing** form

We sometimes use the ***continuous infinitive*** (**be** + **ing** *form*) after **will**, to say that we believe *something will be in progress <u>at a certain time</u> in the future*:

  ■ **I'll be thinking** of you <u>during your exam tomorrow</u>!

and we use this form to talk about *something in the future which is part of a plan*:

  ■ The coach **will be leaving** as soon as the passengers are on board.

❻ **will** + **have done**

We use **will have** + *past participle* to indicate that *something happens before something else in the future*; this is known as the ***future perfect***:

  ■ Phone me in half an hour. I **will have finished** my homework by then.

❼ **shall**

We can use **shall** with ***first person pronouns*** (**I** and **we**) in statements about the future, but it is not very common now in everyday speech. We usually use **will** or **'ll**:

  ■ I **shall** have dinner on the train. (= I *will have dinner on the train*.)

We use **shall** in questions with **I** or **we** when we are *making a suggestion* or *offering to do something*. We don't use **will** in this way:

  ■ **Shall** we **pack** our suitcases this evening?
  ■ **Shall I** help you with the washing up?

We do <u>not</u> use **shall** in short answers to **shall** *questions*:

  in reply to suggestions with **shall we**, we use **let's** or **let's not**:
  ■ '**Shall** we leave now?' 'Yes, **let's**.'
  ■ '**Shall** we have a rest now?' 'No, **let's not**.'
  in reply to suggestions or offers with **shall I**, we use **go on** or **do / don't**:
  ■ '**Shall** I phone the cinema?' 'Yes, **go on**.'
  ■ '**Shall** I invite Charlie tomorrow?' 'No, **don't**.'

A Read the sentences. Each one is an example of one of the explanations of uses listed in the box. Write the letter of the explanation each one exemplifies.

A **will** for what we expect to happen in the future	E **shall I / we** for suggestions and offers
B **shall** for what we expect to happen in the future	F **will + have done** for one future event before another
C **will** with a conditional	
D **will** for offers and promises	G **will + be doing** for part of a plan

0 Nabila will have to look after the family next week. ......*A*......

1 Nabila's mother, Anisha, is going into hospital on Tuesday and she will be having a small operation on Wednesday. ....

2 'I shall probably have to stay in the hospital for a few days,' she tells Nabila. ....

3 Auntie Bunty says, 'I'll come and help while Anisha is in hospital.' ....

4 Anisha will be very tired when she comes home. ....

5 She will have slept very little in the hospital when she comes home. ....

6 'If Bunty looks after the cooking, we'll be able to manage the rest,' Nabila says. ....

7 'Ahmed will be starting his new job on Monday,' says his dad. ....

8 'He won't be able to help very much,' Qasim says. ....

9 'Shall I take some time off work?' asks Ahmed. ....

10 'No, I'm sure we'll manage perfectly well, thank you,' Nabila says. ....

B There are ten errors in this text. Read the text and underline the errors, then correct them.

Stephen is going home for Christmas. He <u>is being</u> very tired after his exams. According to his itinerary, if he wants to be sure not to miss his flight, Stephen is having to arrive at Heathrow airport at least an hour before the flight is due to leave. Then he is checking in and make his way to the departure gate. When he lands in Barbados, his mother will waiting for him at the airport. I'm sure she is very excited to see him after all this time. He told her not to bother to go to the airport but she said 'I am not sitting at home worrying about your plane crashing. If I don't have something to do, I am going crazy!' He is leaving on December 18th and he has been sitting exams all that week so he shall probably be very tired. He is very excited to be going home and he is sure he is having a wonderful time with all his family. He has quite a big family and they are all being at his mother's house for Christmas dinner.

0 ....*will be*....	4	8 ....
1	5	9 ....
2	6	10 ....
3	7	

Use the correct form of the verb in brackets, with **will** or **shall**, in each gap. Use the contracted form (**'ll**) if you can.

BARBARA: I think I (0 go) on a diet!

STEPH: Oh dear! (1 you / still / eat) your meals with me?

BARBARA: (2 we / both / try) to lose some weight together? It would be much easier.

STEPH: OK! That's a good idea. So we (3 not / have) chips for dinner tonight!

BARBARA: No way! If we don't eat too much fat, we (4 definitely / lose) some weight.

STEPH: It's a great idea! When I have lost a few kilos, I (5 be able to) buy some nice new clothes!

BARBARA: Yes, and just think what we (6 do) in August!

STEPH: Yes! Instead of hiding away, we (7 wear) our cool, new, summer clothes.

BARBARA: Great! But what shall we have for dinner, then? (8 we / have) salad?

STEPH: Yes, let's have salad, oh, and (9 you / buy) some cottage cheese when you go to the shop?

BARBARA: But I hate cottage cheese! I (10 get) some white fish. That's low fat, isn't it!

STEPH: Yes, but you know what goes really well with fish?

BARBARA: Yes …

BARBARA and STEPH: CHIPS!

0   *'ll go*
1   ....
2   ....
3   ....
4   ....
5   ....
6   ....
7   ....
8   ....
9   ....
10 ....

40

Dear Gaby,

I'd like some advice on a very serious problem. Last week my sister Melissa asked me if I would lend her my favourite, silver, high-heeled shoes. She said she would look after them very carefully, but I wouldn't let her borrow them. The next morning I found them all scratched and dirty, but she wouldn't admit that she had taken them! My mum said she would give me the money to buy a new pair, but that wouldn't be fair to mum! Do you think it would be fair if I ruined Melissa's favourite shoes? She's got some lovely, pink ones with bows on the front ...

Yours angrily,

Susanna

❶ **would** in conditional sentences

Conditional sentences have two clauses: a condition clause (with **if**) and a consequence clause. After a condition clause with **if** + *past simple*, we use **would** + *infinitive* in the consequence clause; this is called the **second** (or **imaginary**) **conditional** and we use it to talk about a *possible event or situation* and its imagined consequence:

condition clause	consequence clause
▪ If Stephen phoned her this evening,	she **would be** pleased.
▪ If I lived near the sea,	I **would learn** how to sail.

We usually use the contracted form of **would** (**'d**), especially after pronouns:

▪ If I lived near the sea	I**'d** learn how to sail.

The consequence clause can come first in the sentence:

consequence clause	condition clause
▪ She **would be** pleased,	if Stephen phoned her.

Note: If the condition is *something we expect to happen* we use the **first** (or **particular**) **conditional**: **if** + *present* in the condition clause and **will** in the consequence clause.

If the verb in the condition clause is in the past perfect, the second verb is **would have** + *past participle*. This is called the **third** (or **imagined**) **conditional**. It means that the *condition did not happen*, but if it had, the consequence would have been this:

▪ If I **had got** to the stadium in time, I **would have seen** the whole match.
   (*I didn't get to the stadium in time*.)
▪ If I **had drunk** coffee all evening, I **wouldn't have been** able to sleep.

Would can be used in a consequence clause without the condition clause if it is obvious what the condition is:

▪ Come for dinner. My wife **would be** really pleased to see you! (*if you came* is understood.)
▪ Vindaloo is very hot. You **wouldn't like** it. (*if you tried it* is understood.)

(For more on conditionals, see units 28 and 29.)

❷ **would** used in polite conversation

Would (or the contracted form **'d**) is often used before **like** / **prefer** / **love** (+ **to** + *infinitive*) or with **rather** (+ *infinitive*) to say *what we want* in a polite way:

▪ I**'d like** 300 grams of cheese, please.
▪ I**'d love to come** for dinner. Thank you!
▪ Annie **would rather stay** at home this evening.

We use **would like** in questions when we are *offering* or *suggesting something to someone*:

- **Would** you **like** another glass of orange juice?
- **Would** Sabina **like** to come with us?

We use **would you mind if**... to ask someone for *permission for something*:

- **Would you mind if** Garry stayed for a couple of days?
- **Would you mind if** I left early?

We use **would you mind + -ing form** to ask someone *to do something*:

- **Would you mind lending** me your catalogue?
- **Would you mind not talking** during the play?

We use **would** to communicate respect and humility. This is not very common now as conversation is less formal than it used to be:

- **Would** this seat **be** free? (= *Is this seat free?*)
- Sorry, I don't think that**'d be** possible. (= *That isn't possible.*)

❸ **would** as past habit

We use **would + infinitive** to indicate *something that often or habitually happened* in the past, in a similar way to **used to + infinitive**:

- When Louise was a girl she **would** often **play** in the park after school.
  (= *... she regularly played in the park.*)

Note: this use of **would** is rather formal and old-fashioned.

When we stress **would**, the effect is a *criticism of a persistent past action*:

- David **WOULD keep** on singing, even though they told him to stop.

❹ **would** and **wouldn't** as past willingness and refusal

We use **would + infinitive** to say that *someone was willing to do something*, often in contrast with something they were not willing to do:

- William **would iron** his shirts, but he wouldn't iron his trousers.

We use **wouldn't + infinitive** to mean *refused to do something*:

- James **wouldn't help** me when I wanted help.
- The car **wouldn't start** this morning.

❺ **would** for advice

We often use **would/wouldn't** with **if I were you** to *give advice*. Sometimes we leave out the **if I were you** clause:

- I **wouldn't speak** to him again (if I were you).

We can also *ask for advice* with **would**:

- What do you think? **Would** you **take** the underground or the bus?

❻ **would** for what someone said, thought, or felt

We often use **would** as the past of **will** in the second clause when the first clause is about *what someone said* or *thought*, or *how they felt*:

- Peter said he **would** leave at 6 p.m. (= *Peter said 'I'll leave at 6 p.m.'*)
- I hoped they **wouldn't** forget the tickets. (= *I thought 'I hope they won't forget the tickets.'*)
- Martin was afraid that the paper **wouldn't** publish his article.
  (= *Martin thought 'I'm afraid they won't publish it.'*)

(For more on reporting speech, see units 60 and 61.)

A Read the following conversation and write, in the gaps, the correct form of the verb in the brackets using **would** or **wouldn't**. Use the contracted form (**'d**) if you can.

SHOP ASSISTANT: Good morning, sir. Can I help you?

MR HALL: Yes, thank you. It's this suit. I bought it from you and it's too small. I (0) ___'d like___ (like) my money back, please.

S.A: If you have the receipt, I (1) _____ (be) happy to give you a refund. Let me see … ah! I'm afraid the date on this receipt is June of last year.

MR H: Oh, was it that long ago? If you hadn't told me that, I (2) _____ (have / believe) it. Doesn't time fly!

S.A: I'm afraid I can't refund your money. I (3) _____ (like) to help, but you bought it over a year ago. If you had come back then I (4) _____ (change) it.

MR H: But (5) _____ (you / refund) the money if I could prove that the suit had shrunk?

S.A: I don't think that (6) _____ (be / possible).

MR H: Oh! It's so depressing! When I was young, I (7) _____ (wear) the same suit to every event, year after year, but then I put on a little weight, and my brother (8) _____ (not / lend) me his suit. The trouble was that people (9) _____ (invite) me to dinners and I couldn't resist a good meal.

S.A: I have an idea, sir. (10) _____ (you / mind) trying it on, and I'll see if it (11) _____ (be) possible for us to alter the suit. We could probably let out the seams a little here, and here.

MR H: Well, if I saved some money that way, that (12) _____ (be) great.

S.A: If I were you, I (13) _____ (give) it a try. Please come this way, sir.

B There is one mistake in each of the following sentences. Underline the mistake and then rewrite it correctly underneath.

0 Nabila Khan would <u>practised</u> the violin every evening when she was a child.

 Nabila Khan would practise the violin every evening when she was a child.

1 Her brother Imran told her to shut up, but she wouldn't stopped.

 ....

2 He said, 'I'd like having some peace to do my homework!'

 ....

3 She said that she would never passed her music exam if she didn't practise.

 ....

4 Her father said, 'It had been better to practise in the afternoon.'

 ....

5 Nabila wouldn't agreeing.

 ....

6 Imran said, 'Will you like to take up the piano instead? I prefer the piano.'

 ....

7 If her father had bought her a piano, she would to learn to play it.

 ....

8 But she would not to give up the violin. She wanted to play both!

 ....

9 She is sorry now. 'I didn't like to have a sister like me!' she says.

 ....

C

Read the following sentences and make an appropriate second sentence from the jumbled words.

0 DELIA: Look at that beautiful wristwatch! / it / I / get / for Mum / 'd / to / love /.

   I'd love to get it for Mum.

1 CHRIS: 400 euros for a watch? / pay / I / much / wouldn't / that /.

2 DELIA: We could share the cost. / you / would / mind / 200 Euros / paying/?

3 CHRIS: They are cheaper in America. If I were you, / I / it / would / there / buy /.

4 DELIA: It's not the same! / I / like / 'd / something European / buy / for Mum / to /.

5 CHRIS: OK. When she went abroad, when we were children, / us / bring / she / lovely things / would always /.

6 DELIA: It's nearly one o'clock. / to / you / would / like / have / lunch/?

7 CHRIS: Oh yes, I didn't have any breakfast. / to / what / you / eat / would / like / ?

8 DELIA: I don't know how you manage! If I didn't have breakfast, / feel / I / all morning / tired / 'd /.

9 CHRIS: I haven't got any cash, or / buy / a / I / sandwich / would / you /.

10 DELIA: That's alright. I'll get it. But I have to hurry. I have to get back to work as / give / my manager / the afternoon off work /me / wouldn't /.

D

Read the following story and make sentences using **would** or **wouldn't**.

0 You have got into a crowded train. One seat has a bag on it. You ask the woman sitting beside it if the seat is free.

   'Would *that seat be free?* '

1 You ask the woman if she minds moving her bag.

   'Would you mind .... '

2 The woman moves her bag and you sit down in the seat. The train is very hot. You want to open the window but you don't know if the other passengers want the window open. You ask them:

   'Would you mind .... '

3 The man beside you is eating some grapes. He offers you some. He says:

   'Would .... '

4 The woman advises you not to eat them. She says:

   'I .... '

5 She advises washing them. She says:

   'If .... '

6 The man is offended because the woman thinks he is offering dirty grapes. He says:

   'I .... '

7 You say you want to eat some of his grapes.

   'I .... '

8 The woman says that when she was a child she always went to St Ives by train for her holiday

   'I .... '

9 The man comes with the refreshments cart. You ask for a cup of coffee and a pastry.

   'I .... '

Joel is telling Sylvia about his interview for a job in a car showroom ...

'The manager said that employees **have to wear** clean, smart clothes while they are at work. They **mustn't wear** jeans or trainers! They **mustn't smoke** or **drink** in any part of the building, and they **have to eat** all their meals in the canteen. They **mustn't have** anything but coffee, tea, or soft drinks at their workstations.

They **have to keep** their hair clean and neat, and tied back if it's longer than the shoulder. All the men **must be** clean-shaven, and the women **mustn't wear** too much make-up, but they **needn't avoid** it altogether.

Employees **must be** polite and courteous to the public, but they **need not tolerate** abuse. He said if they find themselves in a difficult situation, they **must** immediately **call** a manager to deal with it. I didn't like the sound of it! I don't think I'll take the job.'

❶ must: form

Must is a modal verb and is used like an auxiliary before the *infinitive* of the main verb:
- I **must finish** this job soon.

We don't add an auxiliary in questions and negatives:
- **Must** they **make** so much noise?
- You **mustn't be** late!

Must is used to talk about the present or the future; to talk about the past, we usually use **had to** (see below).

Must can be used with *simple*, *continuous*, and *perfect infinitives*:
- *simple*: The cherries **must cost** more than the grapes.
- *continuous*: Harry **must be walking** to work today.
- *perfect*: Caroline **must have arrived** before us.

We often use the pronouns **you** and **they**, with modals, meaning *everyone* or *someone*:
- If you want to be healthy, **you must do** some exercise every day. (= *everyone*)
- **They must have closed** the shop this afternoon. (= *someone*)

(For more on impersonal pronouns, see unit 6.)
We also use the empty subjects **it** and **there** with **must**:
- **It must be** really difficult to be patient with your children.
- **There must have been** twenty people in the audience.

(For more on empty subjects, see unit 10.)

❷ have to, need to, have got to: form

Have to and **need to** are *semi-modals*, which means they have the same meanings as modals, but they need auxiliaries for the question and negative forms:
- **Do** I **need to bring** a sleeping bag?
- That man **doesn't have to talk** so loudly.

Need to in the negative can be used like a modal verb; it does not need an auxiliary or **to**:
- You **need not run**. / You **needn't run**. (= You **don't need** to run.)

We can use **have to** and **need to** in any tense:

- Mike **had to run** to catch the bus.
- Jane **has been needing to sneeze** for hours.
- I**'ll have to** go to school soon.

Have got to is more idiomatic and is usually used only in the present simple:

- We**'ve got to be** quick!
- Paul**'s got to leave** now.

Note: We don't usually use this form for questions, negatives, or other tenses. We usually use **have to** for these forms.

❸ **must** and **can't** for assumption

We use **must** when we are *assuming that something is the case*:

- Imran **must be** a very good musician. (= *I assume he is a good musician.*)
- You **must have got** there terribly late! (= *I think you got there very late.*)

When we make a *negative assumption* we do not use **mustn't**, we use **can't**:

- The petrol tank **can't be** empty – I filled it up this morning. NOT ... ~~mustn't be~~ ...
- We **can't have finished** all the biscuits! NOT ~~We mustn't have finished~~ ...

(For more on **can** and **can't**, see unit 36.)

❹ necessary and obligatory

To say that something is *necessary* we usually use **need to**, though we also sometimes use **must**:

- **I need to buy** some more milk. (= *I **must buy** some more milk.*)
- My dog **needs to go** for a walk every day. (= *My dog **must go** for a walk every day.*)

To say that something is *obligatory* because of *a law or rule*, or because *another person obliges us*, we use **have to**, or **have got to**:

- Sarah **has to get** to work by 7.30.
- She**'s got to wear** a blue uniform.

Must is more formal than **have to** or **have got to**. We usually use **must** in sets of rules:

- Employees **must wear** their name badges and carry identification at all times.

❺ not necessary

To say that *something is not necessary*, we use **need not**, **don't need to**, or **don't have to**:

- You **need not fill** in the form today.
- We **don't have to use** black ink.
- Lauren **didn't need to** phone me.

❻ not obligatory

To say *something is not obligatory because there is no rule or law about it*, we usually use **not have to**:

- You **don't have to have** a visa to go there.
- Harry **doesn't have to come** for an interview.

❼ forbidden

If we want to say that *something is forbidden or is a very bad idea*, we use **must not** (**mustn't**):

- You **must not bring** dogs into the restaurant.
- Teachers **mustn't shout** at the students!

Note: **Must not** is more formal than **mustn't**.

Do you want to cycle to school?

○ If you do, you must get a safety certificate, and you can only get one from the free training course we are running every Thursday afternoon after school.

○ Even if you haven't got a bike, you can come along and get your certificate using one of our bikes.

○ You must have a helmet, and you have to wear it!

○ You need to have a bicycle lock, and you must remember to lock your bicycle securely outside the school.

○ You must not leave your bicycle by the fence. Always put it in the bicycle sheds.

○ You must always use lights at the front and back of your bike when you are cycling at night, and remember – never ride on the pavement!

Look at this letter about a cycle training course and then read the following sentences. Choose and underline the best modal for each one.

0 If you want to cycle to school, you **must** / **need** have a safety certificate.

1 You **mustn't** / **have got to** do the training course to get a certificate.

2 The children **don't have to** / **must** have a bicycle to do the training course.

3 Children **must** / **need** wear helmets when they ride bicycles.

4 Bicycles **must** / **need** be locked securely when left outside the school.

5 You **mustn't** / **don't have to** leave your bike by the fence.

6 If you have got a bike, you **have got** / **need** to know the Highway Code.

7 You **must** / **needn't** use the cycle lane on busy roads.

8 You **don't have to** / **mustn't** pay anything for the course!

9 They **needn't** / **mustn't** ride on the pavement.

10 You **'ve got to** / **needn't** have lights on your bike when you cycle at night.

B

Andrew and Phyllis are trying to put together a desk from a pack.

Make sentences which mean the same as the following, using the correct form of the modal in the brackets. Use contracted forms where you can.

0 The instructions say, 'Mark the position of the screws.' (have got to)

You *'ve got to mark the position of the screws.*

1 The instructions say, 'Lay out the pieces on the floor.' (have got to)

You ....

....

2 It is important that we check that all the pieces are there. (must)

We ....

....

3 The instructions say, 'Start with sections 1, 2, and 3.' (have to)

You ....

....

4 Don't glue the pieces together before you are sure that they are in the right position. (must not)

You ....

....

5 It's impossible to make the desk without having another person to help you. (need)

You ....

....

6 It is necessary to hold the glued pieces together for 30 seconds. (need)

You ....

....

7 Do the instructions say I should put this section here? (have got to)

Have I ....

8 Is it necessary to glue the back on before the front? (have got to)

Have you ....

....

9 There's a piece missing! Must I phone the manufacturer and complain? (have to)

Do ....

....

10 Having a cup of tea would help us to work better! (need)

We ....

....

C

Read the following text and look at the words in the box. Choose which word or phrase goes in each gap.

> have to do   must have been   mustn't forget
> need to choose   has to do   needn't come
> ~~must be~~   have to show   must wear
> have to go   need to change   must be
> got to wait   have to do

JAKE: My audition is tomorrow. I'm so scared! You (0) *must be* really happy your audition is over! Tell me what you (1) .... in the audition.

RUPERT: Well, when you arrive you (2) .... your letter of invitation for the audition, and then you (3) .... to the reception desk and fill out a form. If you (4) .... your clothes, they send you to a dressing room on the second floor.

JAKE: Yes, the letter says, 'All candidates (5) .... loose, comfortable clothing and soft shoes.'

RUPERT: That's right! You (6) .... to take some soft shoes. The first thing you (7) .... is move around the room to some music, and the panel sits around the edge making notes.

JAKE: Oh, that (8) .... really embarrassing!

RUPERT: No, because you all do it together, it's OK. Then you (9) .... a partner to do some improvised acting. That's worse! And have you prepared a speech?

JAKE: Yes. Everyone (10) .... that. Then you've just (11) .... in the waiting room, and if they don't call out your name after that, you (12) .... back in the afternoon!

RUPERT: I know. That's exactly what happened to me!

JAKE: Oh I'm sorry. That (13) .... horrible!

42

Starting your own business?

Here are some helpful tips from George Stanton …

1 Make a plan: You **should start** by making a business plan, with advice from a Small Business Advice Centre. Your adviser **should be able to** help you work out how much money you will need to set up the business and how much you **should expect** to make in the first few years.

2 Do your research: Get the facts! You **should make sure** you know everything you can about the competition. If someone else is already doing what you want to do, you **should find** out how much they charge for their goods or services and how successful they are. If no one else is doing what you want to do, you **ought to think** about why not!

3 Don't neglect design: The way a product looks tells people what they are buying. If you are going to sell a product, you **should invest** in a good designer for the product and the packaging. If you are offering a service, advertising **should be** a significant part of your budget. You **should hire** an experienced website designer, as advertising on the Internet is essential nowadays.

4 Plan your working environment: If you are going to employ other people, you **ought to have** a pleasant place for them to work. You **should** always **take** a lot of care with decoration and lighting, so you and your employees enjoy working there.

5 Do what you like and like what you do: The most important thing in business is that you believe in your product or service. You **should think** about the environmental impact, and any other ethical implications, of what you are planning to do. Then, if you are happy, just enjoy the adventure! You **should be** a huge success!

❶ should and ought to: form

Should and **ought to** are modal verbs and are used like auxiliary verbs. For the present and future they are followed by an *infinitive*, or the *continuous infinitive* (**be** + **ing** *form*), of the main verb:

- Gary **should go** to the dentist.
- The assistant **ought to be keeping** the shelves tidy.

To make questions with **should**, we use **should** + <u>*subject*</u> + *infinitive*:
- **Should** <u>Paul</u> **book** the restaurant?

We can use **ought** in the same way, but it is more common to use **should** in questions:
- **Ought** <u>we</u> **to answer** the phone? (= **Should** we **answer** the phone?)

The negative is **should not** or **shouldn't**. We usually use **shouldn't** in speech, and **should not** in writing and formal contexts:
- Graham **shouldn't** go the motorbike rally.
- Clients **should not** leave their bags in the waiting room.

We can use **ought** in the same way, but it is more common to use **should** in the negative:
- You **oughtn't to** be so rude to her. (= You **shouldn't be** so rude to her.)

For the past we use **should have / ought to have** + *past participle*:
- We **ought to have bought** some more paper.
- Ulrich **should have** worked harder last term.

❷ should and **ought to** for choice and advice

We use **should** or **ought to** + *infinitive* to *say what we think is the best action* or to *give advice*:
   ■ I think I **should tidy** my room!
   ■ You **ought to be patient** with the children.
To *say what we think is the best thing for someone to be doing now*, we use the **continuous infinitive** of action verbs:
   ■ You **should be tidying** your room now, and not watching television.

We use **should not** or **ought not to** when we want to *advise someone not to do something*:
   ■ Jerry **shouldn't eat** so much sugar.
   ■ You **oughtn't to drive** so fast.

We often use **should** and **ought to** in questions to *ask for advice*:
   ■ Do you think I **should take** the job?
   ■ **Ought** I **to start** cooking dinner now?

We use **should have** or **ought to have** + *past participle* to *say that something was wrong in the past, and something else would have been better*:
   ■ The shop **should have opened** at 9 a.m., not at 10!
   ■ He **ought to have been arrested** and not allowed to go free!

❸ should and **ought to** for expectation

When we *expect something to be the case now or in the future*, we often use **should** or **ought to** + *infinitive*:
   ■ There **should be** lots of information on adventure holidays on the Internet.
   ■ Sandy **ought to arrive** any minute!
We often use the **continuous infinitive** of action verbs after **should** and **ought to**; the meaning is the same as with the *infinitive*:
   ■ My uncle **should be sending** me some money soon. (= My uncle **should send** me some money soon.)

When we are talking about *something we expect to have happened*, we use **should have** or **ought to have** + *past participle*:
   ■ Tom **should have left** for work by now.
We also use this form for *something that we expected to happen, but it did not*:
   ■ Annie's flight **should have left** by now, but it's still on the runway.
We use **shouldn't have** to talk about *something that we didn't expect to happen that did happen*:
   ■ The handle **shouldn't have come** off. (*It looked very strong.*)

❹ had better and **it's time** for advice

We use **had better** + *infinitive* to *strongly recommend some action or behaviour* (*because of the possible consequences of not doing it*). It is idiomatic and can only be used about future events or situations. We often use the contracted form **'d better**, especially after a **personal pronoun**:
   ■ We**'d better order** some more photocopying paper.

We use **had better not** to *strongly recommend not doing something*:
   ■ You**'d better not forget** your husband's birthday!

When we want to say that *we think someone should do something now* we use **it's time to** + *infinitive*:
   ■ **It's time to take** your medicine.
We also use **it's time** + *subject* + *past simple* (**It's time someone did something**) with a present meaning:
   ■ **It's time** John **gave up** smoking. (= *John should give up smoking.*)

163

A Lucy's niece, Jamila, has come to stay with her for the weekend. Look at the picture, and then give Lucy some advice on how to make her kitchen safe for a three-year-old. Use the words and phrases to make sentences.

0 dangerous chemicals / she / keep / out of reach of / should / children /
  She should keep dangerous chemicals out of reach of children.

1 ought / store / sharp knives safely / she / to /

....

2 leave / shouldn't / electric cables hanging down / she /

....

3 hot pan handles / she / ought / away from the edge of the cooker / to / keep /

....

4 she / shouldn't / on / let / children climb / the kitchen furniture /

....

5 on / allow / she / the kitchen surfaces / oughtn't / animals / to /

....

6 the ironing board / on / she / shouldn't / a hot iron / leave /

....

7 oughtn't / too many plugs / she / put / in one socket / to

....

8 on / put / child locks / ought to / the cupboard doors / she /

....

9 clean up / should / on the floor / she / anything spilt /

....

10 she / her kitchen / clean and tidy / keep / should /

....

and **had better**

B Read the following conversation between Imran and Anisha Khan. Choose the correct option of the two underlined in each sentence, and write it underneath.

ANISHA: Imran, ⁰isn't it time / shouldn't you were thinking about your future? You can't spend the rest of your life playing rock music!

IMRAN: Why not? I ¹ought / should be able to earn a good living with my music.

ANISHA: Yes, you ²ought to / shouldn't be able to, but are you? You really ³time to / should go and get a good degree in something useful.

IMRAN: What ⁴ought / should I study? I don't want to do anything else except play with my band and compose music.

ANISHA: Well then, obviously you ⁵ought / 'd better to do a music degree.

IMRAN: But then they make you study classical music. Why ⁶is it time / should I have to study Mozart and Bach and stuff?

ANISHA: There ⁷oughtn't / should be lots of courses now that teach modern music. Have you looked?

IMRAN: No, I haven't. Do you think I ⁸shouldn't / should?

ANISHA: Yes, of course. ⁹You'd better / It's time you took responsibility for your life …

0 *isn't it time*
1 ....
2 ....
3 ....
4 ....
5 ....
6 ....
7 ....
8 ....
9 ....
10 ....

C Make sentences with the same meaning as the following, using the words in brackets.

0 Imran ought to listen to his mother. (should)
   Imran should listen to his mother.

1 Imran should go to college next year. (ought to)
   ....

2 Imran will probably be a success with his band. (should)
   ....

3 Why does he need to get a degree? (should)
   ....

4 There are probably lots of contemporary music courses available. (should)
   ....

5 It's time he did a degree in music. (ought to)
   ....

6 Ought he to study Bach and Mozart? (should)
   ....

7 Should he give up his band now? (it's time)
   ....

8 He ought to be planning his future. (should)
   ....

9 He needs to find some information about courses soon. (had better)
   ....

10 His mother ought not to tell him what to do. (should)
   ....

Lucy had an audition for a part in a stage show recently. She's just heard from the dance company. She is talking to her friend, Karen, on the phone …

'No, of course I didn't get a part! I **couldn't have got** one. … Oh, it was so horrible! I **shouldn't have gone** to the audition in the first place! I **ought to have found out** more about the company. Oh Karen, they **must have been** amazed when I started dancing. They really **should have told** me before I made a fool of myself! How **could** I **have been** such an idiot? And then, when I found out the audition was for children up to the age of 12, I really **should have left** immediately. … I **may have ruined** my entire career!!!'

❶ perfect modals: form

We can use modals to talk about the past and completed actions, like this: *modal* + **have** + *past participle*:

- We **might have lost** our place in the queue.
- Stefano **should have come** first in the competition.

We make questions using perfect modals like this: *modal* + <u>subject</u> + **have** + *past participle*:

- **Would** <u>Paul</u> **have seen** your text message?

The negative is made by adding **not** or **n't** after the modal verb:

- We **shouldn't have eaten** so many chocolates.
- The bus **might not have** come yet.

Ought has **to** before the auxiliary **have**:

- I **ought to have used** more sugar in the cake.

We usually use the contracted form of **have** (**'ve**) after all the modals when we are speaking:

- The wheel **could've** come off.
- Paolo **must've** earned a lot of money!

But in writing we only use the contracted form (**'ve**) in informal writing. We usually don't write **'ve** in questions or negatives, nor after **to**:

- We shouldn't **have** paid so much for them. NOT ~~We shouldn't've paid~~ …
- I ought **to have** asked Kim to come. NOT ~~I ought to've asked~~ …

❷ what has possibly happened (**may** / **might** / **could**)

When we want to say that *it is possible that something has happened*, we use the modals **may**, **might**, or **could** + **have**. There is no real difference in meaning:

- Graham **might have done** the shopping.
- Graham **may have done** the shopping.
- Graham **could have done** the shopping.

(= *It is possible that Graham did the shopping but I don't know if he did.*)

We use the negative **might** / **may** + **not have** to mean *it is possible something has not happened*:

- We **might not have missed** the last train.
- We **may not have missed** the last train.

(= *It is possible we haven't missed the train.*)

Note: We don't use **could have** in this way. (See section 3, on the next page.)

❸ what we think happened (should / must / will; could / can + not)

If we want to say that *something almost certainly happened*, we use **should**, **must**, or **will** + **have**:

    ▪ Enrico **should have got** home by now.   } (= *I am almost sure that he got*
    ▪ Enrico **must have got** home by now.   } *home by now.*)
    ▪ Enrico **will have got** home by now.

We use **couldn't** or **can't** + **have** to mean *it is <u>not</u> possible that something happened*:

    ▪ Frank **can't have been** at the cinema.   } (= *It is not possible that he was at*
    ▪ Frank **couldn't have been** at the cinema. } *the cinema.*)

❹ past in the future (will have)

We use **will have** to talk about *things that we think will happen before a time in the future*:

    ▪ When Olga arrives, Frank **will have finished** the housework.
    ▪ Mei Ling **will have done** all her homework by six o'clock.

❺ with an if clause (would / wouldn't + have)

We use **would have** when we want to say that *something depended on something else* happening in the past, often with an **if** clause:

    ▪ If I had seen Olivia, I **would have told** her the news. (= *I didn't see Olivia, so I didn't tell her the news.*)

We can use **wouldn't have** + *past participle* when we want to say that *something <u>not</u> happening depended on something else*:

    ▪ If we had taken a taxi, we **wouldn't have been** so late. (= *We didn't take a taxi, so we were late.*)
    ▪ If Peter hadn't met Gail, he **wouldn't have left** England. (= *Peter did meet Gail, so he did leave England.*)

❻ imagining a better past (should / ought to + have)

If we want to talk about *something that happened in the past which was not right or good and we imagine something better*, we use **should** or **ought to** + **have** + *past participle*:

    ▪ I think we really **should have bought** that car. } (= *It's a pity we didn't buy*
    ▪ We really **ought to have bought** that car. } *that car.*)

❼ criticism for not doing something (should / might / could + have)

To *complain that someone did not do something*, we use **should**, **ought to**, **could**, or **might** + **have**:

    ▪ They **should have checked** the contract more carefully, before they signed it.
    ▪ You **might have told** me there was no more bread!
    ▪ The boss **could have given** us a bit more time to finish the job.

❽ things that were not necessary (need not + have)

We use **didn't need to have** or **need not have** to say *that something happened that was not necessary*:

    ▪ You **didn't need to have bought** so much milk. } (= *It was not necessary*
    ▪ You **need not have bought** so much milk.   } *to buy so much milk.*)

A Read the dialogue and choose the best modal of the two in the brackets to fill the gaps.

Paul and Steve have finished making the chest of drawers. It hasn't gone very well …

PAUL: When you try to open the drawer, it sticks. Do you think I (0) ......*should*...... (should / may) have put it together differently?

STEVE: Oh … that may be because of glue. I (1) .... (must / ought) have spilt some glue on the runner. I obviously didn't clean it off well enough …

PAUL: And these two legs, they look different from the other two.

STEVE: We (2) .... (would / might) have put them on backwards.

PAUL: What? I thought so! I really (3) .... (couldn't / ought) to have checked them before I put the sides on.

STEVE: I must say the instructions (4) .... (will / might) have been a bit clearer.

PAUL: Well, I can't stay now. I've got to meet Karen at 6. I told you that we (5) .... (should / may) have started earlier.

STEVE: I thought this would only take us a couple of hours. It (6) .... (will / need) have taken us a whole day!

PAUL: You (7) .... (oughtn't / needn't) have varnished it all first! We (8) .... (should / may) have done that after it was put together!

STEVE: But you didn't say anything at the time. You (9) .... (could / would) have told me!

PAUL: There wasn't any point in talking to you. You (10) .... (wouldn't / shouldn't) have listened if I had told you!

B Margaret Compton is in a bad mood. She is talking to Sam. Write what she says, using the words in brackets.

0 Oh Sam! Your room is an awful mess. (should / have / tidy)
   You should have tidied your room.

1 I don't know if you did the washing up last week. (might / have / do)

2 It was your turn to do the vacuuming today and you didn't. (ought to / have / do)

3 George did the dusting, but it was not necessary. (need / n't / have / do)

4 It was possible for you to pass your Maths exam. (could / have / pass)

5 You stayed out late at night. You failed your exam. (if / stay / would / have / pass)

6 Anna had to do her homework and she had plenty of time while 'Friends' was on the TV. (could / have / do / while / was watching)

7 I wanted to make a nice meal for us. I didn't because there were so many other jobs to do. (would / have / make / if / there / not / be)

8 I wish you had told me there was no milk left. (you / might / have / tell)

....

9 I wish you had not drunk a big glass of milk! (should not / have / drink)

....

10 I'm going out. You will vacuum the carpet before I get home. (you / will / have / vacuum / by the time)

....

C Mei Ling and James are revising for an exam together. Read their conversation. Cross out the wrong words and write the correct word at the end of each speech. Sometimes more than one correct version is possible, so write them all down.

JAMES: Let's study chapter six in the book this afternoon; then, when we have done that, we'll ~~be~~ revised everything for tomorrow's exam. (0) ...._have_.........

MEI LING: OK – I think I understand about the Hundred Years War now. I really would have read that chapter from the book before now. (1) ....

JAMES: Yes – I think I must have missed that lesson. I needn't have forgotten everything! (2) ....

MEI LING: I mustn't have remembered if you hadn't lent me your notes. They were really useful. (3) ....

JAMES: I'm still not very sure about the dates of the war. I can have learnt them by now. (4) ....

MEI LING: I think it was from 1335 – or it ought have been from 1337 till 1453. I know it wasn't exactly a hundred years. (5) ....

JAMES: It can have started in 1337. And wasn't Joan of Arc alive at that time? (6) ....

MEI LING: Oh yes – she's one of my favourite historical characters! She drove the English out of Northern France. She could have been an amazing girl! She was only about 16, or something. (7) ....

JAMES: She won't have been only 16! How did she get the army to follow her? (8) ....

MEI LING: It must to be her religious passion that convinced people. She believed God was telling her to fight the English, and to help Charles to become the King of France. (9) ....

JAMES: And what happened to her in the end?

MEI LING: They burnt her – at the stake – in 1431. Horrible! She ought to have been very brave and clever – but a bit crazy! (10) ....

JAMES: Do you think there will be a question on the Hundred Years War in the exam? They could not have put a question on it in the exam; if they haven't, then I'll be really disappointed! (11) ....

SUSAN: **Can** you **tell** me what I **should do** to get fit?

DELIA: You **ought to book** an appointment with a personal trainer. Also, you **ought to lose** a few pounds and that **should help** improve your fitness. You **should go** to the gym three times a week.

SUSAN: Good, OK. But how much **will** it **cost? Will I have to buy** any special equipment?

DELIA: Here is the price list. You **had better get** some good quality shoes, but you **won't need** any other gear – just loose comfortable clothes.

SUSAN: What about my diet?

DELIA: Yes, well, you **needn't cut out** all your favourite foods, but you **must eat** a sensible and balanced diet. While you are exercising, you **should avoid** getting too tired or hungry.

SUSAN: That all sounds great.

DELIA: Excellent! **Would** you **like** to make an appointment with one of our personal trainers?

SUSAN: Well, I'm not sure. My husband thinks that I **shouldn't spend** time at the gym ...

❶ modal verbs: uses

Modal verbs (e.g. **can**, **may**, **might**) are used like auxiliary verbs before the *infinitive* of the main verb; they add to the meaning of the main verb:

- The ship **will leave** tomorrow. (= *The ship definitely leaves tomorrow.*)
- The ship **may leave** tomorrow. (= *It is possible that the ship leaves tomorrow.*)

We mainly use modals to:

talk about *skill* and *ability* – **can**, **could** (for the past):
- I **could run** 100 metres in 10 seconds when I was younger.

talk about *permission* – **can**, **may**:
- **Can** I **borrow** your video camera for a few days?

make *requests* – **can**, **could**, **will**, **would**:
- **Could** you **mend** my bike?
- **Would** you **mind mending** my bike?

make *offers* – **can**, **would like**:
- **Can** I **give** you a lift in the car to your rehearsal?
- **Would** you **like** a cup of tea and a scone?

make *suggestions* – **could**, **might**:
- You **could shut** down the computer and see if that solves the problem.
- You **might try shutting** down the computer ...

give *advice* – **should**, **ought to**:
- Mary **should**n't **be** so quick to criticise other people.

talk about *possibility* – **can**, **could**, **may**, **might**:
- The management **might** really **like** our new plan.
- You **could**n't **meet** a nicer person than Howard.

talk about *probability* and *expectations* – **will**, **shall**, **must**, **should**, **ought to**:
- You **must be** exhausted after running all that way.
- Jane**'ll be** in Mexico now. She **should have arrived** there yesterday.

talk about *intentions* and to make *promises*: **will**, **shall**:
- I**'ll phone** you when I am about to leave the office.

talk about *obligation* or *necessity* – **must**:
- Jean, you **must eat** more or you'll get too thin.

(For more on the use of these modals, see units 36–42.)

We often use the impersonal **you** with modals to talk about *anyone* or *everyone*:

- A few years ago, **you couldn't get** a decent cup of coffee in England.

We can use any modal, except **would**, in the consequence clause of a *particular* (or *first*) *conditional*; the modal that we choose depends on the meaning we want to give:

- If I see Janet, I **can ask** her for her advice.
- If I see Janet, I **may ask** for her advice.

In the consequence clause of an *imaginary* (or *second*) or *imagined* (or *third*) *conditional* we can only use **would**, **could**, or **might**:

- If I saw Janet, I **would ask** her for her advice.
- If I had seen Janet, I **could have asked** her for her advice.

(For more on conditional sentences, see units 28 and 29.)

❷ modal verbs: form

Modal verbs (e.g. **can**, **may**, **must**) have the same form with all persons: I / you / he / she / we / they **must**.
Modal verbs have no infinitive form: NOT ~~I will must~~ NOR ~~I do must~~ NOR ~~I don't must~~
Modal verbs don't have a participle form: NOT ~~I have must~~

We don't add an auxiliary to make a question or a negative with a modal. We use the modal as the auxiliary in questions, negatives, and in short answers:
- '**Must** you **send** him a birthday card?' (NOT ~~Do you must~~) 'Yes, I **must**.'
- 'Sam **shouldn't eat** sweets all day.' (NOT ~~Sam don't should~~) 'No, he **shouldn't**.'

❸ modal verbs: time

We can use modals with different kinds of infinitive to talk about *the past*, *the present*, and *the future*. To talk about an event or situation in the present or future, we can use either an *infinitive* (**do**) or, with action verbs, a *continuous infinitive* (**be doing**):
- Harry **may be** in his room, or he **may be working** in the library.
- Harry **may leave** his job next week, and he **may be giving** a speech at the party.

We can also use **be going to** for a future event:
- Harry **may be going to visit** John this afternoon.

To talk about an event or situation in the past, we use a *perfect infinitive* (**have done**) or a *perfect continuous infinitive* (**have been doing**):
- Harry **may have been** in Madrid yesterday, and he **may have been staying** at the hotel.

❹ semi-modal verbs

There are a few verbs, called *semi-modal verbs*, that have the same meanings as modals but which we use differently in questions and negatives from ordinary modals:

have to, **need to**, and **used to** must have an auxiliary in the question and negative forms:
- **Does** Jake **need to** buy some new shoes?
- Kenneth **doesn't have to** work very hard.
- **Did** Kate always **use to** work so hard?

the negative of **had better** is **had better not**:
- You**'d better not** say anything to Jeremy.

be able to, **be supposed to**, and **have got to** already contain an auxiliary:
- **Have** you **got to** get back to work soon?
- Jenny **isn't supposed to** use the computer for personal correspondence.

Note: In the negative, **need** can be used like a modal verb; we don't need an auxiliary or **to**:
- Sandy **needn't** tell him the answer. (= Sandy **doesn't need to** tell him the answer.)

Unlike modal verbs, we can use **have to**, **need to**, **be able to**, and **supposed to** in the past tense:
- Stephen **had to** leave home at dawn to catch his flight.
- Tom **wasn't able to** fix the tap.

Note: **Used to** is only used in the past tense.

We can't use two modals together, but we can use a semi-modal after another modal (or semi-modal):
- We **might need to** clean up the garden.
- I think I**'m supposed to be able to** dance the tango.

44 EXERCISES   modal verbs: review

A   Read the following conversation and look at the verbs in brackets. Some of the modals should be negative and some of them should be positive. Put them in the correct form in the gaps.

BOB: I (0) ......*can't believe*...... (can / believe) how horrible the weather is! It's the middle of summer and it

(1) .... (should) be wet and cold!

STEVE: And you (2) .... (be supposed to) be going on an adventure holiday in Wales next

week. Oh dear! The weather (3) .... (could / get) better next week. If it doesn't, I'm afraid

your holiday (4) .... (may / be) a great success.

BOB: Oh I don't know; even if the weather is bad, it (5) .... (could / be) wonderful, staying in

round stone huts in the mountains, with no electricity and just open wood fires at night.

STEVE: Do you think you (6) .... (might / have to) cook over an open fire? It

(7) .... (would / be) great fun if the weather was good, but I wouldn't like to try and fry an

egg in the rain!

BOB: Do you think I (8) .... (should / cancel) the booking if the weather goes on like this?

STEVE: No, I think it (9) .... (might / be) nice anyway. Well, maybe not nice, but at least it

(10) .... (will / be) boring.

BOB: You (11) .... (ought to / come) along too!

STEVE: Oh, no thanks! I (12) .... (have to / stay) here and work. Also, I (13) ....

(need to / save) some money for my holiday in Ibiza!

B   Now read this conversation between Bob and Steve two weeks later. Bob has come back from his holiday. Complete the gaps with the correct forms, positive or negative, of the words in brackets.

STEVE: How was your holiday in Wales?

BOB: It was great. I (14) .... (could) believe how wonderful the weather was. My holiday

(15) .... (could / be) a bigger success. I'm glad that I didn't cancel the booking.

STEVE: (16) .... (you / have to) cook over an open fire?

BOB: Yes, I did. But I burnt my fingers a bit.

STEVE: You (17) .... (should / be) more careful; you (18) .... (could / hurt)

yourself quite badly.

BOB: Oh, it was nothing serious. Anyway, what have you been doing?

STEVE: Oh, nothing much, except saving money. But I got a big pay rise last week, so I (19) ....

(need to / try) to save money.

BOB: You (20) .... (should / come) to Wales and enjoyed the sunshine!

B

Read the following text and choose which modal or semi-modal is best in each gap.

0   You ....*could*........ (could / have to) not hope to meet a nicer man than Rev. Michael Baldry, the chaplain of Witherton United football team.

1   If he had lived, he .... (may / would) have been 80 this week.

2   He was very popular with the players, as you .... (can / able to) see from all the condolence cards here.

3   'I don't think I .... (ought / may) to tell anyone what to do, but just listen to them,' he .... (need / used to) say.

4   He .... (might / used) to come along to all the home matches and the team and the fans .... (will / be able) miss him a lot.

5   James Thompson, the goalie, says every team .... (ought / should) to have someone like him.

6   Footballers sometimes .... (need / must) to talk to someone, just like anyone else.

7   You .... (supposed to / should) have seen him when we lost to Riverton Rovers in the final last year!

8   He was so upset but he .... (had / was able to) support us and help us.

9   His family say he .... (ought / may) be in the great football club in the sky.

C

Read the following information about healthy food and make the questions, using the clues in brackets, and then answer them using the short form.

> Iron is very important in the diet. It helps children grow and increases resistance to disease. It is particularly important for young women, pregnant women, and old people. We all need a lot of iron in our diet. A lack of iron makes people anaemic and causes fatigue and depression. Good sources of iron are liver, lentils, whole grains, green leafy vegetables, egg yolk, and molasses. When you are planning meals for someone who is ill or who has a bad cold, you should try to include some foods with iron in them.

0   (we / need to) include iron in our diet?
    Do we need to include iron in our diet? -
    Yes we do.

1   (men / need to) have more iron than women?
    ....

2   (we / can) survive without iron?
    ....

3   If we are very tired and low, (it / might) be a lack of iron in our diet?
    ....

4   (vegetarians / can) get enough iron?
    ....

5   (anaemia / might) be caused by a lack of iron?
    ....

6   (a cheese omelette / would) be high in iron?
    ....

7   (we / could) survive without iron in our diet?
    ....

8   (children / can) grow strong and healthy with no iron?
    ....

9   (we / supposed to) give green, leafy vegetables to someone with a bad cold?
    ....

The **cold**, **winter** wind whistled around them as Susie and Frank stood shivering in the **imposing** doorway of the **strange** house. Although they were **lost**, **tired** and **hungry**, Frank hesitated a moment before pulling the **rusty**, **old** bell-pull. The house was quite **dark** and **silent**. From inside the house they heard the **distant** clang of a **large** bell and saw a **dim** light approaching through the **dirty**, stained-glass window above the door. They could hear many **large**, **heavy** bolts being drawn back, one by one, and then the **thick**, **oak** door began to creak open ...

❶ ways of using adjectives

An adjective is a word which describes things or people. It can go before a <u>noun</u>:

- There's a **black** <u>cat</u>.
- John was a **clever** <u>man</u> with an **amazing** <u>ability</u> to make money.

Or, it goes after **something**, **everything**, **someone**, **anyone**, **anything**, **somewhere** etc:

- Sharon is hoping to meet **someone new**.
- I'd like to have **something warm** to drink.

An adjective can also go after **be** or a *sense verb* (**seem**, **feel**, **look** etc):

- The sun **is hot**.
- You **look** very **tired**.
- This house **seems** very **dark**.

(For more on state verbs, see unit 17.)

❷ adjective phrases after verbs

When we use an adjective after a verb, we can use an adjective phrase.
Some adjectives (e.g. **ready**, **willing**, **happy**, **sorry**) can go before an *infinitive with* **to**; we often use this form to describe *a person's attitude to something*:

- We're **ready to leave**.
- Phoebe is really **happy to see** so many people here.

Some adjectives (e.g. **interested**, **pleased**, **angry**, **cross**) can go before a *preposition + noun* or a *preposition +* **ing** *form* to describe *people's feelings about something*:

- They are **interested** <u>in quantum physics</u>.
- Bob is **angry** <u>with his younger brother</u>.
- Tim is feeling **cross** <u>about losing the match</u>.

Some adjectives (e.g. **bored**, **happy**, **cross**) can go before an **ing** *form* when they describe *how an action makes us feel*:

- Sue and I often get **bored lying** on the beach.
- We are **happy playing** volleyball.

174

❸ adjective sequence before nouns

When we want to give more information about something, we can add several adjectives. They are used in a particular sequence which depends on their meaning:

number: how many?	**three** boxes
size / dimension: what size?	three **small** boxes
age: how old?	three small, **old** boxes
colour / shade: what colour?	three small, old, **red** boxes
origin: where from?	three small, old, red, **Italian** boxes
material: made of what?	three small, old, red, Italian, **wooden** boxes
type: what type?	three small, old, red, Italian, wooden, **jewellery** boxes

Note: we usually use commas between adjectives, but not after the last adjective in the sequence. We do not usually use commas after numbers.

Adjectives describing *temperature*, *weight*, *shape*, or *beauty / ugliness* usually come after an adjective describing *size or dimension*, but before other adjectives:

- We've had a <u>long</u>, **cold** winter.
- I need a <u>small</u>, **light** tent for my holiday.
- A <u>tall</u>, **handsome** waiter served us.

Adjectives describing *what we think about something* (e.g. **wonderful**, **awful**, **gorgeous**, **strange**) usually come after a number but before other adjectives:

- We went to a **wonderful**, <u>little</u> museum.

Other types of adjectives do not have a particular sequence. We can choose the order:

- I walked down the **empty**, **dirty**, and **dark** hall. OR … the **dirty**, **empty**, and **dark** hall. OR … the **dark**, **dirty**, and **empty** hall.

If the adjectives come after the verb, we can use them in any order but we often follow the rules described above; we need to use **and** before the last adjective:

- The house was small, warm, **and** friendly.
- The little girl looked tired, cross, **and** hungry
- This road is busy **and** noisy during the rush hour.

❹ other words used as adjectives

Nouns can be used like adjectives before other nouns; some need hyphens, and some are joined to the noun:

- My father is a **brain** surgeon.
- There's a **shoe**-repairer in the High Street.
- Gary loves **house**work.

We can use **ing** *forms* like adjectives, if they describe either a *sport*, an *art*, or an *activity*:

- They're building a **swimming** pool.
- Hester bought some **dancing** shoes.

We also use **ing** *forms* to describe *the effect of something on someone*:

- Pete was reading a **fascinating** article. (= *The article fascinated Pete.*)
- The film was really **interesting**. (= *The film interested me.*)

We can also use **ed** *forms* (past participles) as adjectives to describe *what was done to something or someone*:

- The pirate dug up the **buried** treasure. (*the treasure was buried*)
- The **injured** man waited for an ambulance. (*the man was injured*)
- That plate is **hand-painted**. (*someone painted the plate by hand*)

A Some adjectives are missing from this story. Put the adjectives in brackets with the right nouns to expand the sentences. Sometimes you will need to change **a** to **an**.

0 Susie and Frank, a couple, were standing outside a castle. (young / huge)
Susie and Frank, a young couple, were standing outside a huge castle.

1 Their car was stuck in a hole in front of the gates. (new / muddy / impressive)

2 After a wait, a man in a suit answered the door. (long / tall / black)

3 He had a watch on a chain in his pocket. (old-fashioned / thick / gold / waistcoat)

4 Frank didn't think any person still dressed in that way. (normal / weird)

5 He was carrying a candle, and spoke in a strange voice, 'Can I help you?' (dripping / deep)

6 'Evening,' said Susie, 'can you help us? The river is flooded and we can't get through. We need somewhere to sleep tonight.' (good / warm)

7 The man turned and went into the entrance hall, pointing with one finger. (silent / dark / white)

8 They followed him into the house, and the door slammed shut behind them. (cold / heavy)

9 The house had a smell, and there was a silence. (damp / unholy)

10 Suddenly the silence was broken by a scream followed by laughter. (terrifying / mad)

11 Susie and Frank turned and ran out of the house and got into their car. (awful / safe)

12 'I've seen a lot of films that started like that,' said Frank. 'I'm not such a fool!' (horror / stupid)

B

The story continues …
When Susie got back to Australia she wrote to her brother telling him about the experience. Some adjectives are missing from the letter. Choose the right one from the box.

freezing	weak	fantastic	horror	late
expensive	smoked	motorway	cool	
100 years old	flooded	~~terrible~~	mouldy	
	hot	fresh	lost	narrow

Hi Jake,

Our holiday in Britain was (0) *terrible* . It was very (1) .... (in fact, we spent all our money!) and the weather was (2) .... We hired a sports car which looked (3) .... but it didn't go very fast. We were driving along this (4) .... road when we came to this bridge. The river was (5) .... so we had to go back, but we got (6) .... After driving for hours we got to this castle. Honestly, it looked like something out of a (7) .... film! The man who answered the door had a suit that was about (8) ...., with holes at the elbows. When he said 'The master is waiting for you!', we knew it was time to leave! When we found a hotel, they said that we were too (9) .... for dinner, and they wouldn't give us anything (10) .... to eat or drink – not even a cup of tea! The room was damp and the sheets smelled (11) .... I don't think anyone had slept there for years! For breakfast they gave us kippers, which are a kind of salty, (12) .... fish! Yuch!!! And they didn't have coffee, only some tea which was really (13) .... and tasteless. We had breakfast later in a (14) .... service station. I couldn't wait for a nice cappuccino and a (15) .... croissant!

If you ever go to Britain, I recommend staying in London! It's (16) ....!

Love Susie

C

Look at the picture and write a description of each item in the sale using the clues in brackets. Remember – the sequence of adjectives is:
(1) number (2) size (3) age (4) colour / shade
(5) place of origin (6) material (7) type / style

0 a pot (eighteenth century / coffee / silver / small)
   a small, eighteenth century, silver coffee pot

1 a clock (British, grandfather, tall, oak)
   ....

2 teaspoons (modern, eight, silver, Italian)
   a set of ....

3 cloths (Dutch, four, large, white, table, lace)
   ....

4 children's books (illustrated, six, Victorian)
   ....

5 a paperweight (small, red and blue, glass, Venetian)
   ....

6 a bowl (fruit, 25 cm, china, blue and white)
   ....

7 boots (nineteenth century, riding, black, leather)
   a pair of ....

8 a painting (large, oil, Portuguese, modern)
   ....

9 ties (large, patterned, silk, four, 1960's)
   ....

10 cards (faded, ten, post, 1940's, funny)
   a set of ....

Turlingtons Auctioneers
Sale Room 3
Monday 24 January

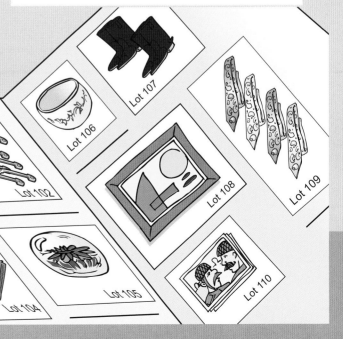

Lot 100
Lot 101
Lot 102
Lot 103
Lot 104
Lot 105
Lot 106
Lot 107
Lot 108
Lot 109
Lot 110

William the Conqueror won the Battle of Hastings in October 1066. It was the last time a foreign army **successfully** conquered England. The inhabitants of northern France and central England were both **originally** Danish, but they had fought **bitterly** for centuries. The two royal families were **directly** linked by blood but, for more than five centuries, they had both tried **desperately** to gain parts of each others' territory. The King in Britain at the time was Harold. He was also being attacked from the North, at the same time, by Harald, the King of Norway. When William of Normandy **suddenly** landed in Kent, Harold had to gather his men **quickly** and march down to defend southern England. Harold's army consisted of about 9,000 men, and most of them were inexperienced peasants who did not fight very **expertly** nor, perhaps, **willingly**. Many of Harold's experienced fighters had been killed at Stamford Bridge, and those remaining were **probably very** tired. The Norman invaders fought **bravely** and **expertly**. The battle was long and cruel and many men were **tragically** killed on both sides. Harold, himself, was killed and **eventually** the Normans **triumphantly** broke through the English lines and claimed the victory.

William the Conqueror became the Norman King of England and had to fight **forcefully** and **constantly** to maintain and expand his nation until his death, near Rouen in France, in 1087.

❶ what are adverbs?

Adverbs can be one word, or a phrase, called an *adverb phrase*. Adverbs can give us several different types of information. They can:

- make adjectives or other adverbs more or less strong (*modifiers*: **very**, **quite**, **awfully**)
- say when or how frequently something happens (*time*: **soon**, **tomorrow**, **often**)
- say where it happens, or in what direction (*place*: **at school**, **somewhere**, **away**)
- say the way it happens (*manner*: **blindly**, **happily**, **fast**)
- indicate which part of the sentence is the important part (*focus*: **only**, **just**, **even**)
- indicate how likely something is (*probability*: **certainly**, **possibly**, **definitely**)

❷ adverbs: form

We can make adverbs by adding **ly** to an adjective. These are mostly manner adverbs, which say how something happened:

> kind → **kindly**   quiet → **quietly**   successful → **successfully**

If the adjective ends in *consonant* + **y** we change it to **i** + **ly**:

> pretty → **prettily**   happy → **happily**

Note that there are some adverbs which are irregular in some way. The adjective **good** has the adverb **well**. Some adverbs have the same form as an *adjective* + **ly** but the meaning is different:

adjective	adverb
real = *true*	**really** = *very*
fair = *just* or *light (hair / skin)*	**fairly** = *quite* or *rather*
near = *close*	**nearly** = *almost*

The adverb **fast** has the same form as the adjective:

- That's a **fast** car. (adjective)
- The car went very **fast**. (adverb)

❸ adverbs as modifiers

Intensifiers (e.g. **very**, **extremely**, **really**, **so**) make the meaning of an adjective stronger:

- Mr Dean was **extremely annoyed**.

Diminishers (e.g **not very**, **fairly**, **quite**, **rather**) make the meaning of an adjective weaker:

- Mrs Dean was**n't very happy** about the party.

(For more on modifiers, see unit 48.)

We use adverbs like **horribly**, **awfully**, **wonderfully** to say *what we feel about something*:
  - Eliza was **amazingly clever**. (*Her cleverness amazed me.*)
  - My brother has a **horribly tidy** house. (*The tidiness is horrible.*)

We can use **really** + *verb* to intensify the meaning of thinking and feeling verbs (e.g. **want**, **enjoy**):
  - I **really wanted** to see Hamid before he left.

❹ time adverbs

Time adverbs can describe *a definite time* (**yesterday**, **now**, **tomorrow**, **on Thursday**) or *an indefinite time* (**soon**, **sometime**). Adverbs describing *a definite time* usually go at the end of the sentence:
  - I went to Grantham **yesterday**.

Adverbs describing *an indefinite time* or *frequency* (**usually**, **often**, **always**, **just**, **already**, **ever**, **never**) usually go before the <u>main verb</u>:
  - Steve's **just** <u>got</u> back from Peru.
Soon, **late** and **early** usually go after the main part of the sentence:
  - Harry's coming to stay **soon**.
Late and **early** can be modified with a time phrase (e.g. *an hour, three days*):
  - Lucy usually arrives **an hour early**.

❺ place and manner adverbs

We use place adverbs and adverb phrases to talk about *where something happens* or *in what direction*. They usually go after the main verb:
  - We got **there** quite late.
  - Mr Davis went **out** into the snow.

Manner adverbs tell us *how something happens* or *what the situation is like*. These usually go after the main part of the sentence:
  - The choir sang **beautifully**.
  - Mary's work is going **well**.
But we often use them before the verb if there is a following phrase or clause:
  - He **calmly** explained the problems he'd been having with the computer.

We use manner adverbs, such as **badly**, **well**, **carefully**, before **ed** *forms* used as adjectives:
  - The walls were **badly plastered**.
We also use some manner adverbs (e.g. **historically**, **politically**, **morally**) before adjectives.

❻ probability adverbs

Probability adverbs (**probably**, **certainly**, **definitely**) tell us *how likely something is*. These usually go before the main verb:
  - Stephen will **definitely** go to Barbados this summer.
But if **be** is the main verb, they go after **be** / **is** / **was** etc:
  - Dan is **probably** Swedish.
In negative sentences the adverb goes before the auxiliary (**isn't**, **doesn't**, **won't** etc):
  - They **certainly** won't order the snails! NOT ~~They won't **certainly** order the snails!~~

❼ focus adverbs (**only, just, even**)

We use adverbs (e.g. **only**, **just**, **even**, **fortunately**) to focus meaning on a part of a sentence. They go before the phrase we want to stress. The important word is usually stressed when we speak:
  - We **only** picked the best strawberries. (*We didn't pick the bad strawberries.*)
  - There are **even** more students than last year. (*Last year there were a lot.*)

A Read the following story and put each adverb or phrase in brackets in the right places. Sometimes there is more than one possible place. Write one or more arrows where the adverb can go.

0 Paul had an interview for a new job. (yesterday)

1 He didn't do very well in the interview. (probably)

2 His friend Steve phoned him. (in the evening)

3 'Did you want the job?' Steve asked him. (really)

4 'Yes. I'm bored at the office … (very)

5 … and the pay is terrible,' he said. (really)

6 'I say stupid things at interviews. (always)

7 I was late for the interview … (half-an-hour)

8 and I forgot the name of the company! (even)

9 They told me they would phone me.' (tomorrow)

10 Steve said, 'Never mind. Let's go for a pizza and forget it!' (out)

B Read the letter from Mark to Lucy. Look at the adverbs or adverb phrases in the box and choose the best one to go in each gap.

well	very	only	last night	here	all over the ice	usually
~~really~~	already	probably	in my room	unfortunately		

Hotel Excelsior
369 Dawson Street
Toronto
Ontario, Canada

Dear Lucy,

I'm (0) __really__ sorry I haven't written for so long. We have been (1) .... busy since we arrived (2) ...., and this is the first time I have had an afternoon free to relax (3) .... The show is going (4) ...., and the audiences are lovely. (5) .... we had to do four curtain calls, and they threw flowers (6) ....! It's (7) .... because it's such a cold country that everyone here seems to understand so much about skating. Toronto is a fascinating city, and the lake is lovely, but we can (8) .... stay here for four days. (9) ...., we have to go on to Winnipeg tomorrow. When we go on tours, we (10) .... stay in each place for at least a week, but this time it's a bit more rushed.

I'll write when I have some more free time,

Lots of love,

I'm (11) .... missing you!

Mark

C Look at the adverbs, in blue, in the following passage and write which of the six types of adverb they are.

Either:

A *modifier*: very, quite, awfully
B *time or frequency*: soon, tomorrow, often
C *place*: at school, somewhere, away
D *manner*: happily, fast
E *probability*: certainly, possibly, definitely
F *focus*: just, only, even

The Bayeux tapestry was almost ⁰certainly made for the Bishop of Bayeux, ¹probably to go ²round the walls of the nave of Bayeux Cathedral. We think it was made ³in England, ⁴shortly after 1066. It shows ⁵beautifully embroidered scenes from the invasion of Britain by the Norman army of William the Conqueror. Some of the scenes are ⁶just not ⁷historically accurate. Although it is ⁸incredibly detailed, and has taught us a lot about early-Norman life, it is ⁹definitely told from the Norman point of view, and is not ¹⁰completely accurate. Even though it is ¹¹very carefully made, you can see that the eight sections were made by different people and ¹²possibly at different times. The border is ¹³differently spaced and the Normans and Saxons look different.

The panel which shows a knight at the battle of Hastings dying ¹⁴in agony with an arrow through his eye is ¹⁵really famous. No one knows if this ¹⁶definitely was Harold, the King, or not.

It is kept inside a glass case in a museum that was ¹⁷specially built for it at Bayeux in northern France. It is ¹⁸very fragile and the environment is ¹⁹carefully monitored so that it will not fade or fall apart.

0 E	7	14
1	8	15
2	9	16
3	10	17
4	11	18
5	12	19
6	13	

D Read this review of a play from 'The Tilehurst News'. There is a choice of adverbs to put in each gap. Write in the correct one.

Last night The Tilehurst Players (0) ...... *bravely* ...... (bravely / rather) put on a production of 'The Importance of Being Earnest' by Oscar Wilde. It is a (1) .... (brilliantly / partly) witty play and the dialogue and characters are (2) .... (tremendously / usually) an absolute joy for both the actors and the audience.

The production, by director Damian Smythe, was (3) .... (daringly / often) unusual. For some reason the director had decided to set the play in the Stone Age, with Algernon and the rest of the cast (4) .... (soon / minimally) dressed in animal skins.

Lady Bracknell, Algernon's elderly and (5) .... (often / extremely) large aunt, was (6) .... (very / happily) brave to appear in something that looked like a small, and (7) .... (brilliantly / rather) bald, badger skin. The set was the simplest I have (8) .... (absolutely / ever) seen, consisting of a couple of rocks which were made of (9) .... (extremely / badly) painted polystyrene.

The audience seemed to (10) .... (really / daringly) enjoy the performance. I have (11) .... (quite / never) heard an audience laugh so much!

Hi Mum,
I have arrived safely here in England. It is much colder than it is back home and I have to wear much thicker clothes. My room here is smaller than mine at home, but it is painted the brightest orange you have ever seen! It is going to be more expensive to live here, as I have to pay for the heating. I started college yesterday and found the course harder than I thought it would be. But the teacher is the nicest person I have met yet.
I'm sorry I didn't write sooner, but I'm busier than the other students as I have to work in the evenings as well.
Love, Stephen

❶ what are comparatives and superlatives?

We can compare one thing with another by using a *comparative* adjective or adverb. This tells us that something has *more of a particular quality*:
■ This house is old but that house is **older**.

We often use **than** after a comparative:
■ Gary is **fitter than** Pedro.

If we want to say that something has *the most of a particular quality*, we use a **superlative**:
■ The oak tree is **the biggest** in the park. (*The other trees are all smaller.*)

❷ adjectives and adverbs with one syllable

To make comparatives or superlatives, we mostly add **er** or **est** to the adjective or adverb:
tall, tall**er**, (the) tall**est**   fast, fast**er**, (the) fast**est**
If the adjective ends in one *consonant*, we double it and add **er** or **est**:
big, big**ger**, (the) big**gest**   sad, sad**der**, (the) sad**dest**
If the adjective or adverb ends in **e**, we add **r** or **st**:
safe, safe**r**, (the) safe**st**   brave, brave**r**, (the) brave**st**

The following frequently used adjectives have irregular forms of comparatives and superlatives:
good, **better**, (the) **best**   bad, **worse**, (the) **worst**
far, **further**, (the) **furthest**

If the adjective ends with *consonant* + **y**, we change the **y** to **i** and add **er** or **est**:
dry, dr**ier**, (the) dr**iest**   happy, happ**ier**, (the) happ**iest**

If the adjective is a *past participle*, we use **more** and (the) **most**:
bent, **more** bent, (the) **most** bent   torn, **more** torn, (the) **most** torn

❸ adjectives and adverbs with two or more syllables

If a two-syllable adjective or adverb ends in a *consonant*, we usually use **more** or (**the**) **most**:
modern, **more** modern, (the) **most** modern   foolish, **more** foolish, (the) **most** foolish

If a two-syllable adjective or adverb ends in a *vowel* sound, including **y** and **w**, we often use **er** or **est**:
yellow, yellow**er**, the yellow**est**   rusty, rust**ier**, the rust**iest**

But if an adverb is made of an *adjective* + **ly**, we use **more** or (**the**) **most**:

> quick**ly**, **more** quickly, (**the**) **most** quick**ly**

If the adjective has more than two syllables, we use **more** or (**the**) **most**:

> beautiful, **more** beautiful, (**the**) **most** beautiful
> delicious, **more** delicious, (**the**) **most** delicious

If the adjective ends in a *suffix*, such as **ful** or **less** or **like**, we only use **more** or (**the**) **most**:

> harmless, **more** harmless, (**the**) **most** harmless
> childlike, **more** childlike, (**the**) **most** childlike

Note: These rules are based on what sounds better and is easier to say. There are many exceptions to these rules. For example, we would usually say:

> ▣ Sam is **more friendly** than John.

But we would also say:

> ▣ He is **the friendliest** boy in the class.

❹ **the** with superlatives

We usually use **the** before superlative adjectives:

> ▣ 'Moby Dick' is **the most popular** American book ever.
> ▣ Grazia's daughter was **the naughtiest** girl in the class.

We often leave out **the** when the superlative is at the end of a sentence:

> ▣ The blue one is **heaviest**. (= The blue one is **the heaviest**.)
> ▣ Which book is **best**? (= Which book is **the best**?)

We don't use **the** with *superlative adverbs* when we are *comparing the same person or thing in different situations*:

> ▣ Harriet types **quickest** on a laptop.
> ▣ People work **hardest** when they are interested in their job.

❺ other ways of comparing things

If we want to *compare something in a negative way*, we use **less** or **the least**:

> ▣ Strawberry is **less popular than** vanilla ice cream.
> ▣ Pistachio is **the least popular**.

We also use the form **not as … as** to *compare negatively*:

> ▣ Diesel is **not as** expensive **as** petrol. (= *Diesel is less expensive than petrol.*)

And if *two things are equal*, we use **as … as …**:

> ▣ Diesel is **as** toxic **as** petrol.

When we want to say that *something is increasing or decreasing*, we can use the comparative twice, or say **more and more** or **less and less** with the adjective or adverb:

> ▣ Travel is getting **safer and safer**.
> ▣ Flying is **less and less** expensive.
> ▣ Aeroplanes are flying **more and more quietly**.

Note: Some adjectives don't usually have a comparative or a superlative form because the meaning of the word is absolute. Examples of these are:

> full / empty   freezing / boiling   correct / incorrect   right / wrong

We can use **any** after comparatives, and **ever** or **yet** after superlatives:

> ▣ She's **lazier** than **any** other member of staff.
> ▣ Lianne is the **worst** receptionist **ever**!

A Look at the two pictures and make two statements about each of them, comparing them. Use the words in brackets.

0 (small, old) *Ivy cottage is smaller and older than the Morgan building.*

1 (tall, modern) ....

2 (peaceful, beautiful) ....

(busy, crowded) ....

3 (old, smart) ....

(young, short) ....

4 (new, expensive) ....

(rusty, not fast) ....

B Read the following passage and underline any errors. There are ten errors in the passage. Then write the passage again correctly.

Some people think alternative medicine is <u>more good</u> than normal medicine. Alternative medicine treats people with naturaler things, such as plants and herbs, and the patients often feel more safe. Of course, it is expensiver, but I think it is more nice to pay for individual treatment. My homoeopath is the most kind and helpfullest doctor I have ever met. Alternative treatments are getting popularer and popularer as people realise that drugs are not always the most idealest cure. Even the British royal family are interesteder in alternative medicine now!

Some people think alternative medicine is better than
....
....
....
....
....
....
....
....

adjectives and adverbs

C Choose which is the right form and circle it.

Mrs Kumar likes to buy ⁰(the freshest)/ the most fresh fruit and vegetables she can get, so she goes to the market ¹most near / nearest to her home. It isn't ²as expensive as / so expensive than the corner shop, and it's ³enjoyabler / more enjoyable. Some stalls are ⁴more bad / worse than others, and their vegetables are ⁵older / more old. The market is ⁶busier / more busy and ⁷more noisy / noisier than the corner shop but it's ⁸more friendly / friendlier and ⁹interestinger / more interesting.

D Write a sentence which says the same thing as the two sentences.

0 Gail's picture is colourful. Martin's is not.
Gail's picture is more colourful than Martin's.

1 Martin's statue is tall. Halima's statue is taller.
Martin's ....

2 Gail's photograph is strange. Martin's photograph is ordinary.
Gail's ....

3 Keith's sculpture is amazing! None of the other works of art are so amazing.
Keith's ....

4 Halima's picture is very small. Martin's is quite big.
Halima's ....

5 Gail's picture is expensive. Halima's is not very expensive.
Gail's ....

6 Gail's sculpture is lovely. Martin's is ugly.
Gail's ....

7 Martin's picture is very dark. Gail's is light.
Martin's ....

8 Halima's statue is old-fashioned. Martin's statue is modern.
Halima's ....

9 Keith's sculpture is shocking. The others are not.
Keith's ....

10 Martin is very happy. The others are not.
Martin ....

E Choose the right answer (a, b, or c).

0 The Taj Mahal is ...*a*.... than the Empire State Building.
(a) more beautiful (b) bigger (c) less famous

1 Sean Connery is .... James Bond.
(a) well-known (b) the most famous (c) a more famous

2 China is .... country in the world.
(a) as big as (b) the most large (c) the biggest

3 'Titanic' was .... film of the decade.
(a) the richest (b) as much money as (c) the most profitable

4 The Euro is .... currency.
(a) the most new (b) the newest (c) as newer as

5 White whales are .... mammal on earth.
(a) the largest (b) the less large (c) the most big

6 .... runner is the cheetah.
(a) A fastest (b) The fastest (c) The most faster

7 Zebras are much .... than horses.
(a) more stupid (b) as stupid (c) stupid

8 Playing tennis is .... as jogging.
(a) good for you (b) as good for you (c) better for you

9 .... mountain in Europe is Mont Blanc.
(a) The highest (b) The most high (c) Highest

DELIA: Hello, you must be Doctor Franchini. I'm **really pleased** to meet you. I hear you've had a **very bad** flight. What happened?

DR FRANCHINI: It was **absolutely awful**! I'm **so lucky** to have got here alive!

DELIA: What on earth happened? You look **utterly exhausted**!

DR FRANCHINI: Well, it started out **quite well**. The weather was **really lovely** in Rome, but then the security checks at the airport took a **very long** time – but that's OK because I know they are **totally necessary** now. The problem was that, when we finally took off, a thunderstorm started.

DELIA: Oh my goodness! That must have been **pretty frightening**!

DR FRANCHINI: Oh yes, it was. I'm **quite a nervous** passenger, but the flight to England is**n't very long** so I wasn't **too worried** – until the thunder started crashing around the plane. I was **absolutely terrified** we were going to be hit by lightning.

DELIA: What did you do?

DR FRANCHINI: I asked the steward if we were going to turn back to Rome, but he said everything was **just fine**! Anyway, we got here safely in the end, but I think it's an absolute miracle!

DELIA: Well Doctor, now that you're here, would you like to go to your room and make yourself more comfortable? We've given you a **very pleasant** room with an **absolutely beautiful** view over the lake!

DR FRANCHINI: Oh, thank you so much. I'd love to go and lie down for a while.

❶ modifying adjectives

When we want to *describe something* we can use an adjective There are two kinds: those that are *gradable* and those that are *absolute* or *ungradable*.

Most adjectives are *gradable*, meaning *there can be more or less of the quality they describe*:

> bad, good, lucky, rich, long, lovely, nervous, painful, worried, pleased, generous, expensive

Ungradable adjectives are those that describe something *total*:

> perfect, ideal, amazing, impossible, exhausted, right, wrong, sure, enormous, beautiful

We use a kind of *adverb*, called a *modifier*, before an adjective to say *how much*. Read the conversation above to see how frequently we use *modifiers* (such as **very**, **really**, **absolutely**) in ordinary speech. But note that there are some modifiers that we can only use with ungradable adjectives and other modifiers that we can only use with gradable adjectives.

❷ intensifiers (**very**, **incredibly**, **quite**, **too**)

Adverbs that we use to make the meaning stronger are called *intensifiers*. **Very** is the most common intensifier, and is only used with *gradable* adjectives:

- Steve is a **very nice** young man.
- That coffee is **very strong**.

If we want to intensify the meaning of an *ungradable* adjective, we use **absolutely**, **totally**, **perfectly**, **completely**, or **quite**:

- Paul is **absolutely brilliant** at chess!
- All the flowers were **completely dead**.
- You're **quite right**. (= *absolutely right*)

There are some casual, informal ways of intensifying the meaning of both *gradable* and *ungradable* adjectives. Here are some commonly used intensifiers:

> **so**, **really**, **awfully**, **amazingly**, **terribly**:

- I'm **so sorry** I can't come to the party.
- Jack was **terribly late** for the meeting!
- The film was **amazingly realistic**.

Thoroughly can be used in this way, but usually only for *physical and not abstract things*:
- They're all **thoroughly dirty**! NOT ~~They're all thoroughly intelligent~~.

We also sometimes say the same *intensifier* twice to emphasise the meaning:
- It's a **very**, **very** long way to Acapulco.
- The rain was **really**, **really** heavy.

We use **too** before an adjective to mean *excessively*, often followed by *to + infinitive*. We can use **much** to intensify **too**:
- Paul's bag was **much too heavy** to carry.

❸ such, such a, and so

We use the intensifier **such** (**a**) before gradable and ungradable adjectives, but only before a noun. We use **such a** with singular nouns and **such** with plural nouns:
- Harry bought **such a huge** ice cream. NOT ~~The ice cream was such a huge~~.
- There were **such big**, **black** clouds in the sky. NOT ~~The clouds were such big~~.

We use **so** to intensify the adjective after the verb **be** or a sense verb (**look**, **seem**, **smell**, **taste** etc):
- The house looked **so welcoming**. NOT ~~It looked a so welcoming house~~.

❹ diminishers (not very, slightly, fairly, not enough etc)

We can use modifying adverbs to say that something has *less of a particular quality*. These are called *diminishers*. We usually use diminishers with *gradable* adjectives. The most common is **not very**:
- The roses are **not very successful** this year.
- The staff were **not very happy** about their pay rise.

Other common diminishers are **slightly**, **pretty**, **fairly**, **reasonably**:
- Although the road was **slightly muddy**, we had a **pretty nice** walk.
- Phil said that the exam had been **fairly easy** and he was **reasonably happy** about it.

We use **a bit** as a diminisher after **be** and perception verbs, but only with negative qualities:
- Stephen's room looks **a bit** untidy. (= *not very untidy*)

We use **not** + *adjective* + **enough** to mean *not sufficiently*, often followed by *to + infinitive*:
- The curtains were **not long enough** to reach the floor.

Quite and **rather** are often used as diminishers before *gradable* adjectives:
- The chocolate mousse tasted **quite** nice, but I preferred the profiteroles.
- That cashmere scarf is **rather** expensive.

Note: This meaning of **quite** is different from **quite** before an *ungradable* adjective:
quite nice (= *fairly nice*) BUT quite right (= *absolutely right*)

We can use **quite** and **rather** as diminishers with **a / an** + *adjective* + *singular noun*:
- That was **rather a** good meal, but there was **quite a** big bill!

❺ modifiers with adverbs

Most modifiers can be used with adverbs in the same way they are used with adjectives. They come before the adverb:
- The band was playing **rather** softly. (= *fairly quietly*)

When we use **not very** with an adverb, we use **not** before the *main verb* and **very** after it:
- Ron was**n't** working **very hard**.
- Mrs Drayton did**n't** speak **very enthusiastically** about her class.

A Choose the more appropriate modifier in each sentence and circle it.

Phyllis went shopping in the winter sales ...

0 She spent <u>a quite</u> / <u>an absolutely</u> enormous amount of money.

1 She went with a <u>really</u> / <u>totally</u> good friend called Jasmine.

2 Jasmine isn't <u>very</u> / <u>a bit</u> rich, but she is <u>completely</u> / <u>very, very</u> generous.

3 They went to all the <u>really</u>/ <u>quite</u> expensive shops in town.

4 She bought some <u>absolutely</u> / <u>very, very</u> amazing presents for her family and friends.

5 Phyllis bought lots of <u>a bit</u> / <u>quite</u> expensive things for herself.

6 She's <u>too</u> / <u>fairly</u> lazy to search the shops for bargains.

7 She bought some boots which are <u>rather</u> / <u>completely</u> uncomfortable.

8 She put them on, and as the day went on her feet got <u>completely</u> / <u>really, really</u> painful.

9 By the time the shops shut, she was <u>such</u> / <u>quite</u> exhausted.

10 They went and had a lovely meal in a <u>terribly</u> / <u>such</u> expensive restaurant.

B Read the situations and then circle which of the following two alternatives you would prefer.

0 You are sitting on the beach alone. Do you want: a really good book OR quite a good book?

1 You are going to a concert. Do you want to hear: an utterly brilliant singer OR a fairly good singer?

2 It is freezing cold outside. Do you want: a fairly warm sweater OR a very warm sweater?

3 You have to choose a painting for an art prize. Do you choose: quite an original painting OR a really original painting?

4 Your grandfather leaves you a choice of houses in his will. Which do you choose? a thoroughly ugly house OR a rather ugly house

5 You are entering the Grand Prix. Which do you need? an amazingly powerful car OR quite a powerful car

6 You have to choose a new football coach for your team. Do you want: a football coach who is a bit aggressive OR a football coach who is terribly aggressive?

7 You want to invite a friend to invest in your business. Do you ask: a very rich friend OR a pretty rich friend?

8 In order to succeed in your business, do you think you need: a very new idea OR a fairly new idea?

9 You want to relax in the evening but you are quite tired. Do you choose: an awfully long video OR quite a long video?

10 You really need to get high marks in your English exam. Which must you write? an absolutely correct answer OR quite a correct answer?

C Look at the picture and choose the right adjective from the box for each of the gaps in the following sentences.

tiny   delicious   old   ~~beautiful~~   lazy
peaceful   long   untidy   brightly coloured
rotten   hot

That's an absolutely (0) ..... *beautiful* ..... garden!

It looks as if the weather is a bit too (1) ....

Oh look! There's a really (2) .... kitten under the table!

That gardener must be utterly (3) ....

That flower bed is a bit (4) ....

There's a girl with quite (5) .... hair sitting on a very (6) .... garden seat.

The fence is almost completely (7) ....

There are some really (8) .... butterflies on the roses.

That looks like an absolutely (9) .... picnic!

Oh, I wish I could be there! It looks so (10) ....

QUASIM: Now, let me see ... notebooks – umm – how **many** small notebooks are there?
AHMED: Hardly any. We need to order **some**.
QUASIM: What about those children's exercise books with the bright covers? Are there **any of** those left?
AHMED: Yes, we've still got **loads**. I don't think they're displayed properly ...
QUASIM: And the pen and pencil sets for children?
AHMED: Yes, we've **hardly** sold **any** of them. I think we should display them at the front ...
QUASIM: All right, all right, I haven't got time to think about display now!
AHMED: Yes, but Dad ... if we don't think about these things, we'll never sell **more** goods!
QUASIM: I know ... Just write down **all** your ideas as we go, but don't waste my time!
AHMED: Right. There are **none of** those large drawing books, but we've still got quite **a lot of** the smaller ones.
QUASIM: Good. And pens and pencils? How **many** are left?
AHMED: There are **a couple of** boxes of HB pencils, and **lots of** ball pens. People seem to prefer the gel pens now.
QUASIM: Shall I order **a dozen** boxes of them, then?
AHMED: Yes, I think we need **a few** boxes of each colour.

❶ using number quantifiers

Number quantifiers are words which we use to talk about *how many* there are of something. We usually use number quantifiers with *plural* nouns:

a few grapes   **some** people   **a couple of** kids

But there are some quantifiers, **no** and **each**, that we can use with *singular countable* nouns.

We can use most quantifiers without a following noun when *it is clear what we are talking about*:
■ 'Have we got any grapes?'   'No we need to buy **some**.'

We can use most quantifiers with **of + the** / **these** / **my** / etc. + *plural noun* when we are talking about *something specific*:

a few of the grapes   **some of the** people   **a couple of the** kids

We use **of** with a pronoun (**them**, **these** etc) when *it is clear who or what we are talking about*:
■ Most of the kids wanted to go on the trip but **a couple of them** didn't want to.

❷ meaning and use

No means *not one*:
■ There are **no** oranges left. (= *There is not one orange left.*)
In formal English we can use **no** with a *singular countable* noun at the beginning of the sentence:
■ Warning: **No** child can use this equipment. (= *No children can use ...*)
Note: We don't use **no** with **of**, or without a following noun; we have to use **none**:
■ NOT ~~There are **no** (of them) left.~~ BUT There are **none** (**of them**) left.

None of means *not one of something specific*, usually before **the** or **these** etc:
■ **None of the** students passed the exam.
Not any means *not one of something general*:
■ There are**n't any** Greek students in the college this year.

Hardly any means *almost none*:
■ There were **hardly any** people in the sea.

Enough means *a sufficient amount*:
■ We had **enough** 50p coins in the till.

A few means *some, but not many*:

■ There are **a few** grapes in the bowl. Harriet ate **a few of** the grapes.

Note: **Quite a few** means *many*, and is more informal:

■ **Quite a few** painters live in the south of France.

Few means *not very many*, and is used in formal English, and usually only at the beginning of the sentence:

■ **Few** flowers smell as sweet as the rose.

Some means *a number of, usually not very big*:

■ There were **some** children in the park. **Some of** them were playing football.

When we want to ask a question about quantity, we usually use **any**:

■ Are there **any** third-year students in the library?

Several means *more than two or three*:

■ There are **several** French people in the class.

Lots of / a lot of is colloquial and means *many* or *a large number*:

■ **Lots of** people like strawberries.

In more casual colloquial use, we can also use **loads of** with the same meaning:

■ I bought **loads of** cartons of orange juice for Jo.

A lot of is often used with **quite** in informal English:

■ **Quite a lot of** people eat them with cream.

Many means a *large number*, and is more formal than **a lot of**:

■ There are **many** different types of cheese in France.

Not many means *a few*:

■ There are**n't many** biscuits left. Who's eaten so many of them?

Most means *almost all of something*:

■ **Most** houses didn't have central heating in the 1950s.

All means *every*. We use **all of the** or **all the** before a plural noun:

■ The policeman arrested **all the** suspects. (= *all of the suspects*)

Note: We don't usually use **all** without a following noun; we use **everything / everyone** instead:

■ NOT ~~All in the queue were cross~~. BUT **Everyone** in the queue was cross.

But we can use **all** on its own when it refers back to the subject:

■ <u>The people</u> had **all** left. (= *All the people had left*.)

All can be used after a *pronoun*:

■ He bought tickets for **us all**. (= *all of us*)

Every is used to mean *all the individual examples of something*, but we use it with *singular* nouns:

■ Jane picked **every** flower from the rose bush. (= *all the flowers …*)

Each means *every individual one*. Without **of**, we use a *singular countable* noun:

■ **Each** guest had a name tag. (= *Each of the guests …*)

When we use **of**, we use a plural noun or pronoun:

■ I gave **each of** the customers a free gift. (= *I gave each customer …*)

Both means *each of two*:

■ **Both** doors were locked. I tried to unlock **both** of them.

A couple of means *about two*:

■ There are **a couple of** kids playing ball in the garden.

A dozen means *twelve*:

■ Malcolm sent Julia **a dozen** red roses.

Kilo / pint / ounce of are examples of quantifiers which are *specific measures*:

■ I'd like three **kilos of** apples, please.

A Look at the picture and choose the right word from the box to fill in the gaps in the sentences. Notice if the words start with a capital letter or not.

| few   no   None   many   some   ~~lots of~~ |
| couple   All   Both   Most |

CAKE STALL

plain
coconut
cake 50p
biscuits 10p
muffins 50p
scones 50p
sponge cakes £2.50p
fruit cakes 30p
iced buns 50p
chocolate chip 30p

0 There are ..... *lots of* ..... muffins on the plate.

1 .... of the slices of cake have been sold.

2 There aren't .... chocolate chip cookies left.

3 The girl wants a .... scones and the cookies.

4 There are .... chocolate eclairs at all.

5 .... the buns are iced.

6 The man is putting .... biscuits into a bag.

7 There are a .... of fruit cakes.

8 .... of the biscuits are coconut flavour.

9 .... of the customers are children.

B Simon is writing about the school fair. Some of the quantity words are wrong. Underline the wrong words and write the wrong word in brackets and then the correct word. Sometimes more than one quantifier is possible.

On Saturday I went to the fair with my friend Sarah. We went to the cake stall and there were <u>few of</u> lovely things to buy. I wanted to buy <u>any</u> iced buns and <u>enough of</u> chocolate chip cookies, but the cookies had <u>every</u> gone. Sarah was in front of me in the queue and bought a <u>couple</u> scones for her Mum, and <u>dozen of</u> cookies. There were <u>any</u> left for me. I didn't have <u>some of</u> money to buy a fruit cake, so I had to have <u>few of</u> slices of sponge cake instead. I was really cross with Sarah because she had bought <u>most</u> the best things from the stall, so she shared <u>each</u> her cookies with me. I gave her a <u>loads of</u> my iced buns and she gave me a <u>few</u> her chocolate chip cookies, and then I was happy. The fair was great. I also won a coconut.

0 (few of) lots of
1 ....
2 ....
3 ....
4 ....
5 ....
6 ....
7 ....
8 ....
9 ....
10 ....
11 ....
12 ....

C Read the following conversation and choose the quantifier from the box that means the same as the word in brackets. Write it in the gap.

a dozen	no	any	~~a lot of~~	some	each	a couple of	all	lots of
	a few	enough	hardly any	both of	n't many			

JOSH: Well … we need some more characters in this game. So far we've only got ⁰(many) *a lot of* Martians. It's a bit boring.

TIM: You're right. Shall we create ¹(two) .... swamp monsters?

JOSH: All right. Do you want ²(each of two) .... them to look the same?

TIM: No. I think it would be nice if ³(both) .... of them was a different colour.

JOSH: Fine. And how about ⁴(a small number of) .... creatures that fly? That would make it more interesting.

TIM: OK. I'll start drawing ⁵(more than one) .... flying monsters and two swamp monsters.

JOSH: Do you think we've got ⁶(sufficient) .... different scenes?

TIM: Oh, we've got about ⁷(twelve) .... backgrounds. Maybe I should design a few more.

JOSH: Hmm. We've got ⁸(almost none) .... water scenes. Have we got ⁹(some) .... swamps for the swamp monsters?

TIM: I don't think so. There are ¹⁰(many) .... rocky desert scenes, but ¹¹(not any) .... swamps.

JOSH: And we have ¹²(not a lot of) .... different types of plants. How about a man-eating cactus?

TIM: Great! I'll have a meeting with ¹³(every) .... the other members of the team and we'll get to work …

Foxcomb Farm
*Come and visit our farm shop and try **some** of our fresh organic produce!*
*We sell only healthy, organic food, **all of** which is grown here at the farm.*
*Because we take a pride in the quality of **all** our produce, we don't use any*
chemicals or pesticides. As well as selling a large selection of fruit and
*vegetables we also sell **a lot of** dairy produce. Our animals are all fed on a*
*natural, healthy diet. We always have **plenty of** organic milk in stock; **most of***
*the milk is sold but we also use **a lot of** it to make yoghurt, butter, and cream.*
*If we have **too much** milk, we sometimes give **some** to the local cheesemaker.*
*Occasionally, we also stock **a little of** his delicious cheese in our shop.*
For anyone who is thinking of placing a regular order, we offer a sample box
*which contains **a little bit of** each dairy product and **enough** fruit and*
vegetables for one person for a week.
We look forward to welcoming you to our shop!
Mary and Peter Ross

❶ using amount quantifiers

Amount quantifiers are words which we use to talk about *how much* there is of something. We use this kind of quantifier with **uncountable** nouns:

> **some** water   **a little** sugar   **plenty of** time

(For more on uncountable nouns, see unit 1.)

We can use most quantifiers without a following noun when *it is clear what we are talking about*:

> ▨ 'Have we got any paper?'   'No, we need to buy **some**.'

We don't use **no**, **much**, **most**, and **all** in this way, except with **much** in questions and negatives and with **too much**:

> ▨ I have**n't** got **much**.   ▨ I've eaten **too much**.

We can use most quantifiers with **of** + **the** / **this** / **my** / etc. + *noun* when we are talking about *something specific*:

> **most of the** light   **a bit of this** earth   **some of my** soup

We can also use **of** with a pronoun (**it**, **them**, **these** etc) when *it is clear what we are talking about*:

> ▨ Most of the milk was spilt on the floor but **some of it** was left in the glass.

We can use an **ing *form*** as an **uncountable** noun:

> ▨ We did **lots of** <u>shopping</u> while we were on holiday.
> ▨ Karen likes to do **a bit of** <u>swimming</u> each week.

❷ meaning and use

No is used with positive verbs to talk about *the lack of something*:

> ▨ **No** news is good news.   ▨ Barbara's got **no** money.

Any is used after negative verbs:

> ▨ There was**n't any** milk in the fridge. (= *There was **no** milk* …)
> ▨ We did**n't** have **any** honey left. (= *We had **no** honey* …)

Any is also used in questions:

> ▨ Did Diane take **any** toothpaste with her?

We use **none of** + **the** / **this** / **my** etc. to mean *not any*:

> ▨ **None of the** luggage was damaged.

A little means *a small amount of something*:

> ▨ My grandfather has **a little** money in the bank.

A little is quite formal; we usually use **a bit of** or **some** in spoken English.
We often use **so little** to mean *a surprisingly small amount*:

> ▨ There is **so little** kindness in the world.

We use **too little** to mean *not enough*:

> ▨ **Too little** free time is bad for you.

Some means *any quantity*:
> ▨ He says he's got **some** information about the robbery.

Some is often used with **more** to mean *an added amount*:
> ▨ We need to buy **some more** coal.

A bit of is used in casual English and means *a small quantity*:
> ▨ There was **a bit of** trouble at the station last night.

It is often used with **little**:
> ▨ I had **a little bit of** jam with my croissant.

Enough means *an adequate quantity*:
> ▨ Have you got **enough** suntan lotion?

A lot of means *a large quantity*, and is very common in conversation:
> ▨ There is **a lot of** salt in this bread.

We also use **lots of** or **loads of** in less formal conversation:
> ▨ Karen has got **loads of** talent.

Plenty of is idiomatic and means *a sufficient quantity, more than enough*:
> ▨ The skiing was good as there was **plenty of** snow.

It is not used in negatives:
> ▨ NOT ~~There hasn't been **plenty of** rain~~. BUT There hasn't been **a lot of** / **much** rain.

Much means *a certain quantity*, and is mostly used in questions and negatives, often with **very**, meaning (**not**) **a lot of**:
> ▨ 'Have you got **much** free time this term?' 'No, I have**n't** got **very much** time at all.'

Too much means *an excess*:
> ▨ There's **too much** milk in this tea.

We also use it in the question **How much ... ?**:
> ▨ **How much** did the ticket cost?

Much in positive statements is more formal than **a lot of**, and is not often used now, except with **so** meaning *a surprising amount*:
> ▨ Paul made **so much** noise we had to shut the door.

Most means *almost all*:
> ▨ **Most** tea is grown in China.   ▨ **Most of the** rush hour traffic uses the ring road.

---

❸ uses of **all**

All with an uncountable noun means *every example of something*:
> ▨ **All** chocolate is high in calories. (= *Every kind of chocolate* …)

We use **all the** / **my** / **our** etc. to talk about *a specific thing*. We don't usually use **all of the** / **my** / **our** etc. with uncountable nouns:
> ▨ **All the** rainwater ran down the gutter.

We don't usually use **all** without a following noun; we use **it all** or **all of it** instead:
> ▨ NOT ~~Sue has used **all**~~. BUT Sue has used **all of it**.
> ▨ NOT ~~The shop has sold **all**~~. BUT The shop has sold **it all**.

All is used in several idiomatic expressions:
> **all over the place** = *everywhere*:
> ▨ After the explosion there was dust and rubble **all over the place**.
> **all gone** = *none remaining*:
> ▨ You can't have any coffee as it's **all gone**.

all dirty / **broken** / **sweaty** etc. = *very dirty etc*:
> ▨ The clothes are **all dirty**!

195

A Mark and Diego are preparing a special dessert. Put the quantifiers in the box in the correct gaps in their conversation. Sometimes more than one answer is possible, but be careful to use all the words in the box.

lot	any	~~much~~	all	a bit	some	many	some	lots	a lot
	plenty	some	much	all	lot	any			

MARK: OK, we've got the flour, the milk, and the sugar. Now, how (0) ....*much*........ flour do we need?

DIEGO: Err, let's see … we need 250 gms. Wow, that's a (1) ....! I don't know if we have enough.

MARK: Yes, we have plenty; we've got (2) .... in that cupboard. Do we need self-raising or plain flour?

DIEGO: Plain. It says we need (3) .... dried fruit. Have we got (4) ....?

MARK: I think so. I'm not sure if there's enough. I wouldn't be surprised if it was (5) .... gone. I know my new flatmate Sofia eats (6) .... of it in her breakfast cereal. Do you have enough butter?

DIEGO: Yep, there's (7) .... of butter. I think we both bought (8) .... yesterday. How (9) .... eggs do we need?

MARK: Err, I think there are quite a (10) .... in this recipe ... wait a minute ... yes, six.

DIEGO: Oh. We've only got six left. That means we won't have (11) .... left. Do you think that's OK?

MARK: Yes, I don't mind. OK, now we need a lemon, and (12) .... sugar.

DIEGO: Don't put too (13) .... sugar in it! It's not good for you.

MARK: No, but you have to follow the recipe. We can put in (14) .... of sugar, can't we?

DIEGO: All right. ... Good, now, you have to mix it (15) .... together with the whisk ...

(no, a little, a lot of etc)

B The Compton family are at the beach having a picnic. Read their conversation and choose and circle the correct quantifier.

MARGARET: Where shall we sit? Do you want ⁰**some** / **enough** shade, or shall we sit in the sun?

GERALD: There isn't ¹**most** / **much** shade, except by the wall.

JAMES: Let's sit by the wall. It's a bit windy today, so we need ²**a bit** / **plenty** of shelter. There's ³**much** / **plenty** of space.

MARGARET: Why don't you kids go and have ⁴**some** / **a bit** fun in the water? We'll get the picnic ready.

SAM: OK. I'll put ⁵**most** / **all** our clothes in the big bag.

MARGARET: Be careful! You'll get the picnic ⁶**all** / **much** sandy!

GERALD: Ahh, this is nice! I really needed ⁷**some** / **plenty** peace and quiet. Can I have a drink?

MARGARET: There's ⁸**a bit** / **some** orange juice in that bottle, and a couple of bottles of water. The children always drink ⁹**a lot** / **much** at the beach.

GERALD: Is there ¹⁰**most of** / **any** tea or coffee?

MARGARET: No, I didn't have ¹¹**some** / **enough** time to make hot drinks.

ANNA: Mum, did you bring ¹²**any** / **much of** sun cream? My shoulders are beginning to burn already!

MARGARET: Oh, I'm glad you reminded me! But don't use ¹³**too much** / **all**! The others will need ¹⁴**a bit of** / **quite a lot** too.

GERALD: Where's my hat? I get badly burnt if I get ¹⁵**plenty of** / **too much** direct sun.

SAM: I'm really hungry, Mum! Did you bring ¹⁶**most** / **much** food?

MARGARET: You can't be hungry already! Oh, go on then. There's ¹⁷**lots of** / **plenty** to eat. Have ¹⁸**enough of** / **some** fruit.

C Read the following text and look at the underlined phrases. There is a mistake in each one. Rewrite them correctly underneath.

Kevin only likes skiing when there's ⁰<u>plenty snow</u>. He once had a holiday in Bulgaria in January when there was ¹<u>hardly any it</u>. He stayed with some friends in a little wooden chalet in a forest, which was really beautiful, but there was ²<u>not many choice</u> of food in the nearest restaurant. They went to the supermarket in the ski resort and bought ³<u>some of local bread</u> and cheese and sausage, but there wasn't ⁴<u>enough of choice</u> of vegetables. The weather was gorgeous but the snow was gradually melting and, in some places, you could see ⁵<u>some of grass</u> under the snow. They had paid ⁶<u>quite a lot money</u> for skiing tuition, and the teacher was having ⁷<u>a lots of difficulty</u> teaching beginners in those conditions. The ground was very slippery and they fell over ⁸<u>all time</u>. They spent ⁹<u>most the time</u> sitting in the wet snow! They had ¹⁰<u>loads fun</u> in the evenings and enjoyed ¹¹<u>all of local culture</u>. The people were very friendly and kind.

0 *plenty of snow*
1 ....
2 ....
3 ....
4 ....
5 ....
6 ....
7 ....
8 ....
9 ....
10 ....
11 ....

197

Almost all British children have played games with horse chestnuts, or 'conkers', at some time in their life. There are **several** traditional games which **every** child used to learn at school, and **each** region has its own traditions. Children collected as **many** conkers as they could in order to find the largest and strongest conker. **A lot of** children, especially boys, still take the game extremely seriously, and **many of** them prepare their conkers using **some** secret ingredients, such as vinegar.

Over the last **few** years, **some** horse chestnut trees have been attacked. The attacker is the larva of the leaf-mining moth. **A few** years ago there weren't **any** leaf-mining moths in Britain, but because the temperature is rising in northern Europe the pest is spreading further north **each** year. So far there has not been **too much** damage to British trees, but quite **a lot of** individual cases are being found. Fortunately not **every** tree is in danger. This moth only likes to eat horse chestnut leaves, so **all** the other trees are safe.

It would be tragic if the British horse chestnut tree disappeared, as we would lose an important part of our cultural heritage.

❶ using quantifiers with countable and uncountable nouns

Some quantifiers can be used with both *countable* nouns (e.g. **pens**) and *uncountable* nouns (e.g. **ink**):

some **pens**   some **ink**

Quantifiers which refer to a *number* can only be used with *countable* nouns:

several **pens**   every **day**

Quantifiers which refer to an *amount* can only be used with *uncountable* nouns:

too much **salt**   a bit of **lemon juice**

We can use **ing** *forms* as uncountable nouns:

▪ I did a bit of **shopping** in town today.

(For more on countable and uncountable nouns, see unit 1.)

❷ form and use

Here is a summary of which quantifiers can be used with countable and uncountable nouns:

number quantifiers (used with *countable* nouns)	amount quantifiers (used with *uncountable* nouns)
each, every, all ▪ **Each / Every** person received a gift. ▪ **All the** trees in the wood are oaks.	**all** ▪ He's spent **all** his money. ▪ You gave it **all** to me.
most ▪ **Most** children don't like olives. ▪ I've read **most** of these books.	**most** ▪ **Most** music is relaxing. ▪ Sarah feels tired **most of** the time.

(too / not) many
- There were **too many** customers in the shop.
- **Too many** of the windows are broken.
- There are**n't many** people in the pool.

(too / not) much
- There's **too much** salt in the sauce.
- **Too much** of the sea is polluted.
- I do**n't** have **much** patience with telephone sales people.

a lot of
- **A lot of** our clients come back again.
- He's made some friends, but not **a lot**.

a lot of
- There's **a lot of** water on the floor.
- We have some food, but not **a lot**.

lots of, several
- Frank bought **lots of** new clothes.
- **Several** people complained.

lots of
- Madeleine has **lots of** sugar in her tea.
- **Lots of** their furniture is antique.

plenty of
- There are **plenty of** nice shops in Brighton.
- The children ate **plenty of** the sandwiches.

plenty of
- We need **plenty of** time to do the homework.
- We've still got **plenty of** the milk we bought this morning.

enough
- Have you got **enough** plates for us all?
- We've got **enough** of the 6 cm nails.

enough
- There isn't **enough** rice for six people.
- There isn't **enough** of the blue paint left.

some
- Jake owns **some** nice paintings
- **Some** of the children are sick today.

some
- Would you like **some** fruit?
- The waiter forgot **some** of our food.

a few, not many
- Gina bought **a few** magazines.
- **A few** footballers came to the party.
- **Not many** students pass the final exam.

a little, a bit of, not much
- There's **a little** time left.
- Would you like **a bit of** cake?
- I do**n't** need **much** money.

few
- **Few** foreigners have visited the village.
- **Few** of the people he met spoke Russian.

little
- I'm afraid there's very **little** hope.
- **Little** fruit is available in February.

no, not any, hardly any
- There are **no** tomatoes left for the salad.
- There are**n't any** oysters in the shop.
- I've got **hardly any** exercises to do.

no, not any, hardly any
- There's **no** paper in the printer.
- We do**n't** have **any** furniture in the living room.
- **Hardly any** of the staff came to work today.

grams, kilos, tons etc.
- How much is **a kilo of** almonds?
- The lorry carries 500 **tons of** coal.

grams, kilos, litres, tons etc.
- A **kilo of** flour costs about £1.00.
- The tank holds sixty **litres of** petrol.

❸ specific number quantifiers

We have some words which mean *a specific number*. These can only be used with countable nouns:

dozen (12), **half-dozen** (6), **couple** (2), **both** (each of 2), **a pair of** (2) etc:
- I ordered a **dozen** duck eggs.
- There are a **couple of** people at the bus stop.
- **Both** my hands are freezing.
- Yvette needs a new **pair of** shoes.

(For more on quantifiers, see units 49 and 50.)

A Marianne is doing a weekend painting course in Sardinia. She is talking to Gustav as they paint. Read their conversation and choose which of the quantifiers in brackets is best in each gap.

MARIANNE: I love these courses. I come (0) (all / every) ......*every*...... summer for a week or two. Have you been here before?

GUSTAV: Yes, I've been here (1) (several / lots) .... times. Last time I came at Easter and there weren't (2) (some / many) .... other people. It was very quiet and I got (3) (many / lots of) .... work done. When there are (4) (too much / too many) .... people I find it hard to concentrate. People just talk (5) (most / all) .... the time.

MARIANNE: Oh, I know! Some people only come here to make friends. It's really so annoying! I have (6) (so little / too few) .... time back in England to paint, I really want to take advantage of the opportunity while I'm here.

GUSTAV: Have you got any more Prussian Blue paint? I haven't got (7) (a few / any) .... left …

MARIANNE: Oh yes, I've got (8) (a lot of / plenty) .... here. I find I use more cobalt here. Of course, it depends when you work. If you work late into the evening, the sky changes colour. It changes to (9) (lots of / few) .... different shades of blue …

GUSTAV: I prefer to stick to one shade and mix it with (10) (a bit / a few) .... other colours – (11) (a few / a little bit) .... of black, or (12) (some / much) .... white, a spot of red … you know.

MARIANNE: Oh gosh! I haven't got (13) (every / enough) .... confidence to do that yet. I'd love to see how you do it. I suppose you get through (14) (litres / dozens) .... of paint!

GUSTAV: I get through (15) (many / lots of) .... paper, too. Yes, it does take (16) (much / lots and lots) .... of practice, but it's my hobby so I don't mind at all.

MARIANNE: I'm afraid I do hardly (17) (some / any) .... practice at home. I do a life-drawing class just once a week, and (18) (a few / a little) .... sketching at the weekends. I'm never going to learn how to use colour that way, am I!

GUSTAV: No you're not. You have to be brave and try (19) (lots of / too much) .... different techniques. I'll give you (20) (plenty / a few) .... tips, if you like. Now, for example, the blue you are using here is much too bright. … You really should mix it with (21) (a bit of / most) .... white … like this.

MARIANNE: Oh you're so kind! I can see that I still have (22) (plenty / many) .... of things to learn about painting.

B Read the phrases in each column and see if you can put together the two halves to make sentences about Marianne and Gustav. Use the information that you learnt about them in the previous exercise.

0	Gustav has had lots	A	time to get to know each other.
1	Marianne hasn't got	B	few tips.
2	Gustav prefers not to paint with too	C	all his Prussian blue paint.
3	She uses lots	D	of paper and paint.
4	Marianne hasn't done	E	every week.
5	He uses a lot	F	of different types of blue.
6	Marianne does a drawing class	G	of practice at painting in Sardinia.
7	Gustav is going to give Marianne a	H	many people around.
8	He has finished	I	very much painting in the past.
9	They have plenty of	J	much confidence in her art.

0 *G*   2 ....   4 ....   6 ....   8 ....
1 ....   3 ....   5 ....   7 ....   9 ....

C These are the pictures that Gustav and Marianne painted. Read the comments the teacher and the other students made about them. Write an answer to the comment, saying what you think, using the words in brackets.

0 There isn't much detail in Marianne's picture. (lots of)
Yes, there is. *There's lots of detail.*

1 Marianne has obviously had lots of experience of using colour. (very little)
No, she hasn't. ....

2 She has done a lot of painting before. (very much)
No, she hasn't. ....

3 Gustav didn't have enough different paints. (plenty of)
Yes, he did. ....

4 They both do lots of painting at home. (Marianne / hardly any)
No, they don't. ....

5 In Gustav's painting you can see a few trees and some houses. (any / or)
No, you can't. ....

6 You can't see any recognisable things in Marianne's painting. (lots of)
Yes, you can. ....

7 Marianne's painting doesn't have any birds in it. (a few)
Yes, it does. ....

8 Marianne has lots of self-confidence. (not / enough)
No, she doesn't. ....

9 They both use a lot of cobalt blue. (Marianne / not / much)
No, they don't. ....

10 How much would you pay for Gustav's painting?
....

A Stephen is going to meet his mother. She has arrived **from** Barbados. She is just coming **out of** the gate.

B Mr and Mrs Khan are waiting **at** the departure gate. They are going to Pakistan. Imran is standing **beside** Nabila.

C Keith is standing **on** the observation platform. He is carrying his binoculars **round** his neck. He is writing **in** a little book.

D Delia is waiting **in front of** the exit for her client to arrive. She is holding **up** a board with his name **on** it.

E An aeroplane is flying **over** the airport. It is going to land **on** the runway **behind** the building.

F Two security guards are running **into** the building with a dog. They are hurrying **towards** the luggage reclaim. A man is hiding **underneath** a pile of suitcases.

5
2

❶ what are space prepositions?

Space prepositions are words and phrases which tell us about:

the *position* of something or someone in space:

▪ The supermarket is **near** the cinema.

the *direction* of something or someone:

▪ We were walking **towards** the supermarket, when Ken said 'Let's not go shopping; let's go **to** the cinema, instead.'

❷ position and direction prepositions

position prepositions	direction prepositions
next to / beside / by / near ▪ Imran was standing **beside** Nabila. ▪ Nabila wants to stay **next to** her mother. ▪ The restaurant is **near** the beach.	**towards / to** ▪ They are hurrying **towards** the luggage reclaim. ▪ They are walking **to** the exit.
at ▪ They are waiting **at** the departure gate.	**at** ▪ Stephen is smiling **at** his mother.
in / inside ▪ Keith is writing **in** a little book.	**in / into** ▪ The guards are running **into** the building.

off ▦ The plane is **off** the ground.	**off** ▦ A suitcase is falling **off** the trolley.
on / on top of ▦ My coat is hanging **on** the hook. ▦ The cat is sitting **on top of** the TV.	**on / onto** ▦ The parachute landed **on** the ground. ▦ The suitcases have fallen **onto** him.
outside ▦ The taxis are waiting **outside** the terminal.	**out of** ▦ Stephen's mother is coming **out of** the gate.
from ▦ Mrs Khan is **from** Pakistan.	**(away) from** ▦ Mrs Cross has flown in **from** Barbados. ▦ Delia is walking **away from** the entrance.
underneath / under ▦ A man is hiding **underneath** the suitcases.	**underneath / under** ▦ The dog is disappearing **under** the trolley.
at the bottom ▦ Stephen is standing **at the bottom** of the stairs.	**down** ▦ An Airbus is taxiing **down** the runway.
at the top ▦ A flag is flying **at the top** of the mast.	**up** ▦ The guards ran **up** the stairs.
in front of ▦ There is a kiosk **in front of** the building.	**forward** ▦ The crowd is pushing **forward**.
in the middle of ▦ Stephen is standing **in the middle of** the crowd.	**through** ▦ Mrs Cross is coming **through** the gate.
across ▦ There is a walkway **across** the road.	**across** ▦ The people are walking **across** the road.
behind ▦ Mrs Gold is standing **behind** her husband in the queue.	**behind** ▦ The taxi drove **behind** the terminal.
above ▦ A big sign hangs **above** the entrance.	**over** ▦ An Airbus is flying **over** the runway.
round / around ▦ The passengers are sitting **around** the table in the waiting room.	**round / around** ▦ A little boy is running **round** the room.

❸ movement verbs without a preposition

We need a preposition and a noun phrase after most verbs to talk about *position* and *direction*:

▦ The teacher sat **on** the table.
▦ A large bag is lying **under** the chair.
▦ She walked **into** the river.
▦ The policeman dived **under** the water.

But some verbs, such as **reach** and **enter**, tell us about the *place* or *direction* of the event; in these cases we don't need to use a preposition:

▦ Mr Barker **attended** the staff meeting. (= *Mr Barker **was at** the staff meeting.*)
▦ Stephen **reached** the Arrivals gate. (= *Stephen **arrived at** the Arrivals gate.*)
▦ She **entered** the airport lounge. (= *She **went into** the airport lounge.*)
▦ The aeroplane **rose**. (= *The aeroplane **went up**.*)

A Answer the questions using the words in brackets and a preposition.

0   What is Imran doing? (looking)   *He's looking at the rocket ride.*

1   What's Auntie Bunty doing? (walking) ....

2   Where is Nabila? (sitting / a dodgem car) ....

3   What's Qasim doing? (sitting / a giraffe) ....

4   Where is Anisha? (going) ....

5   What's Ahmed doing? (climbing / the stairs) ....

6   Where is the mermaid? (swimming / a tank) ....

7   What is the parrot doing? (flying) ....

8   Where is Auntie Bunty's hat? (lying / the ground) ....

9   What's the clown doing? (riding / a unicycle) ....

10   Where is the dog? (coming) ....

B Put the prepositions in the box into the correct gaps in the text.

around	on	above	~~in~~	on	above	in	beside	into	at	up	from	under	into

(0) ....*In*.... the dining room, six people sat (1) .... a big table and waited. A big, brown dog lay (2) ....
the table (3) .... the carpet. The clock hanging (4) .... the wall (5) .... the mantelpiece ticked.
(6) .... the clock, there was a photograph of a happy, smiling couple. The maid came (7) .... the room
carrying a tray of tea. Mrs Dalloway poured tea (8) .... the cups and then picked (9) .... a sugar cube.
'Would you like sugar (10) .... your tea? she asked, smiling politely (11) .... the man on her left. He had
a big white scar (12) .... his left eyebrow. Suddenly they heard a loud scream coming (13) .... the
street ...

C Choose a preposition that will go in each space. Sometimes two prepositions are possible.

An assault course:

First, you have to crawl (0) _under_ the netting, (1) .... the mud. After that you have to climb
(2) .... the wall and (3) .... the top. Then you have to jump (4) .... the other side and
run as fast as you can (5) .... the trees. Then you have to swing (6) .... the ropes which are
hanging (7) .... the river and jump (8) .... them, landing (9) .... the finishing mark.

D Choose the correct preposition in brackets to complete each sentence. One is a *direction preposition* and
one is a *place preposition*.

0 My cousin has moved _out of_ New York. (out of / outside)

1 She used to live .... Manhattan. (into / in)

2 The windows of her apartment looked .... Central Park. (towards / in)

3 Now she lives in the country .... a river. (beside / towards)

4 There is a bridge .... the river. (above / across)

5 When it is hot the children jump .... the bridge into the water. (off / away)

6 Then they climb .... the bank and dry themselves in the sun. (on / onto)

7 .... her house, there is a pine forest. (behind / through)

8 Her children go to the school .... the village. (into / in)

9 Now, they don't want to go .... New York, even for a visit! (at / to)

205

Freddie Mercury was born Farrokh Bulsara **on** September 5th 1946 in Zanzibar. The family lived there **until** 1947, when they moved to India. While he was at boarding school in Panchgani, just outside Bombay, he began having piano lessons. **By** the time he was 16, the family had decided to move to England with his younger sister Kashmira.

They moved to London and Freddie went to Isleworth School **for** two years; then he went to Ealing College of Art to study Graphic Illustration. He left college **in** 1969 with a Diploma in Graphic Art and Design. **During** his time at art school he played and sang in several bands. Freddie joined his first serious band **in** 1969. They were called 'IBEX'. They were not a great success, and **after** a couple of years he joined another band called 'Smile'. He soon took control of the band, and decided to change the name to 'Queen'. Very quickly 'Queen' became a huge success, and **by** 1975 they were one of the top bands in the world.

He tragically died of Aids **in** 1991 **at** the age of 45, but his fame has lived on, and he will always be regarded as one of the greatest rock musicians of the twentieth century.

❶ what are time prepositions?

Time prepositions are words at the beginning of phrases which tell us *when* something happens or *for how long*:

> **at** six o'clock   **in** 2005   **by** midday   **before** noon   **for** a long time

❷ in

We use **in** with specific periods of time to say that something happens *within a period of time*:
- ▪ Ian is coming to visit us **in** the summer.

We also use **in** in time expressions which mean that *something happens at the end of a period of time*:
- ▪ I'll be home **in** twenty minutes.

There are some idiomatic expressions using **in**:
> **in time** = *a moment before it is too late*:
- ▪ The vet operated **in time** to save the cat's life.
> **in plenty of time for** = *a long time before something*:
- ▪ Sonia got to the cinema **in plenty of time for** the film.

❸ on

We use **on** with time expressions to say that something happens *during a particular day or date*:
- ▪ Stephen's graduation ceremony is **on** Tuesday, September 14th.

❹ at

We use **at** in expressions which mean something happens *exactly at a particular time*:
- ▪ The shop closes **at** half-past five.

We also use **at** to talk about something that happens during **the night** or **the weekend**:
- ▪ It gets very cold **at night** in the desert.
- ▪ We always go to the beach **at the weekend**.

Note: In US English people say **on the weekend**.

There are some idiomatic expressions which use **at**, such as:
> **at the moment** = *during this period of time*:
- ▪ Keith is studying electronic engineering **at the moment**.

❺ before, after, and during

We use **before** and **after** to talk about *a sequence of events*, and we use **after** with *periods of time*:
- Cinderella had to get home **before** midnight.
- **After** a couple of months Paul got a job as a translator.

We use **during** for something that continued *through a specific period of time*:
- **During** 1998 Franco was working in Thailand.

We also use **during** when we are talking about something happening *within a period of time*:
- We ate popcorn **during** the film.

❻ by

We use **by** to talk about something which happens *before a particular time or date*:
- We'll finish the meeting **by** four o'clock.

❼ for

In time expressions we use **for** in phrases which mean *how much time something continues*:
- The sailors were in the lifeboat **for** two weeks.

We use **for** in certain expressions:

forever / **for ever** = *without an end*:
- Writing a book takes **forever**!

for now = *just in the present, perhaps not in the future*:
- Helga is living here **for now**.

❽ since

We use **since** in time expressions to say *something started at a particular time*. We often use the present perfect continuous with **since**:
- Imran has been practising the guitar **since** three o'clock.

❾ from – till / until / to

If we want to talk about *something that started at a moment in the past and continued until a later time*, we use **from** for the start time and **till**, **until**, or **to** for the finish time:
- The pool is closed **from** 9 a.m. **until** 3 p.m.

There are some common idioms using **from**:

from time to time = *occasionally, sometimes*:
- I see Jane **from time to time** in the office.

from now on = *starting now and continuing into the future*:
- **From now on** Tom is going to the gym three times a week.

❿ other uses of time words

We use **ago** to say *how much time it is since something happened*. We put **ago** after the time. We only use it to talk about time *up to now*:
- Delia came to work at The Inside Story five years **ago**.

We can also use **before**, **after**, **until**, and **since** as conjunctions between two clauses:
- Ahmed arrived three months **before** Elsa met him.
- You've been working really hard **since** you got here.

A Read the following passage and put the correct word from the box in each gap. You must use some of them more than once.

for	on	ago	since	at
from	till	before	in	

Delia has decided to take up yoga. She has had backache (0) ....*for*.... some time, and (1) .... last week she has had to take painkillers every day. She takes one (2) .... 9 a.m. before she starts work, and then again (3) .... lunch-time. She has to stand up (4) .... most of the day, and she realises she has got to do something about it (5) .... it's too late!

The beginners yoga class is (6) .... 6.30 (7) .... Monday, and lasts (8) .... an hour. There is another one in the morning on Wednesday, (9) .... 9.30 (10) .... 10.30, but she can't do that one as she is always busy (11) .... the morning. She went to a yoga class a couple of years (12) ...., but she didn't like it much. It seemed to go on (13) .... ever! But now she is determined to try again.

B Five students are doing a weekend course at 'The Inside Story' fitness centre. Look at their training schedule for Saturday, and then answer the questions using the words in brackets.

Saturday May 18th							
Please note: the personal trainers are not available on Sunday. Make sure you see yours today!							
Name of student	9–10.30	10.30–11	11–12.30	1–2	2–3.30	3.30–4	4–5.30
Pam Styles	gym	break	swimming	lunch	personal trainer	tea break	sauna
Kofi Mbusa	swimming	break	gym	lunch	massage	tea break	personal trainer
Kieran McBain	yoga	break	personal trainer	lunch	swimming	tea break	massage
Terry King	gym	break	yoga	lunch	personal trainer	tea break	massage
Julie Huang	yoga	break	personal trainer	lunch	swimming	tea break	sauna

0 When does Pam go swimming? (from, till) *She goes swimming from 11 till 12.30.*

1 What time is Julie's appointment with the personal trainer? (at) ....

2 What time do they have lunch? (from, till) ....

3 What time of day do they have their massages? (in) ....

4 What does Kieran do in the first afternoon session? (during) ....

5 What time do they all finish their day's training? (at) ....

6 When do they do the hardest work? (in) ....

7 What day do they all see their personal trainers? (on) ....

8 When does Terry have his massage? (from, till) ....

9 When do Kieran and Julie go swimming? (at, in) ....

10 At lunch-time, how long have they been exercising? (since) ....

C Margaret Compton is talking to her friend Alison on the phone. Match the beginnings and endings of what Margaret and Alison say. Put in the name of who says each sentence, and write out their conversation.

0 Hello Alison. What are you doing

1 I'm tidying Tom's room. I've been doing it

2 I decided not to tidy James's room ever again

3 Oh, I don't think I could stand a really messy room

4 I just keep the door shut, and I make him tidy it

5 You're very brave! Now, what are you doing

6 I don't know yet. We never manage to book

7 We can't book anything, either, at least

8 A new job? But you've worked for the Post Office

9 Yes. It's in a small stationery shop. My interview is

10 Shall we meet after your interview

A in the evening?

B for very long.

C from time to time.

D at the moment?

E during the summer?

F on Wednesday afternoon.

G in time to choose what we want.

H not until I know about my new job.

I during this year, and I haven't!

J since I've known you.

K since 9 o'clock this morning.

Margaret: Hello Alison. What are you doing at the moment?

54

The men were **in trouble**. They had set off up the mountain without enough food, water, and cooking gas to last the climb. **In fact** they were so badly prepared that they had run out of food after the third day. And then Paul slipped on the glacier and broke his leg. He just sat there, **surrounded by** snow, almost in tears. Dave was not very comforting.

'You've got to keep moving **in spite of** the pain. We can't melt the snow to drink when the gas runs out, and there isn't much water left **at all**, so we have to keep moving. **In any case**, we can't just stay here.'

'OK, why don't you leave me here **by myself**. **At least** one of us will get down safely.'

'We must tie up your leg in some way, and I'll lower you down on a rope,' Dave said.

They tied his leg straight **by means of** a sleeping bag and some rope. **In** order to make the rope long enough he had to tie lengths of it **end to end**. It took a very long time, but **at last** Dave was ready. **Little by little** he began to lower Paul over the edge of the ridge of ice ...

❶ uses of at

At can be used as a space preposition and as a time preposition:

- There's a big oak tree **at the end of the path**.
- Jack usually gets home **at 6 o'clock**.

At can also be used in expressions with other meanings:

at least = *that many (or that much) and possibly more*:
- There were **at least** ten big beetles under the table!

at all? (in questions and negatives) = *even a small amount*:
- Have you got any money **at all?**

(not) at all (in negative sentences) = *absolutely not*:
- Rowena does**n't** like chocolate **at all**.

at last = *finally, after a long wait*:
- I'm so happy you're home **at last**!

at once = *immediately, straight away*:
- When the teacher came in the children stopped talking **at once**.

be at it = *doing a particular thing*:
- Could you give me some more coffee, while you**'re at it**?

❷ uses of in

In can be used as a space preposition and as a time preposition:

- The cat is shut **in** the wardrobe.
- Let's meet Keith **in** the morning.

In can also be used in expressions with other meanings:

in (good) time = *not late*:
- I always like to get to the theatre **in good time** for the performance.

in fact = *to add some information supporting what I say*:
- I was late getting to the station. **In fact**, I missed the train.

in case = *if this is the situation, OR to be ready for a situation*:
- There are some matches **in case** the fire goes out.

in spite of = *not stopped or prevented by*:
- **In spite of** the rain, it was quite warm.

in any case = *whatever the situation or circumstances*:
- The coat was too big, and, **in any case**, it was too expensive.

be in trouble = *have problems*:
- Imran **is in trouble** with his Dad for staying out all night.

in order to = *for a particular purpose*:
- We took a picnic **in order to** save some money!

in person = *really, personally*:
- I'd like to meet Nelson Mandela **in person**.

in particular = *specifically, particularly*:
- Are you looking for anything **in particular**?

in love (**with**) = *love romantically*:
- I really think Diego is **in love with** Rachel.

in tears = *crying*:
- Poor Rachel was **in tears**.

❸ uses of **by**

By is used as a space preposition to mean *beside*, or as a time preposition to mean *before*:
- The house was built **by** the river.
- We must get home **by** seven o'clock as it will be dark.

By is also used to mean *through* or *by means of*:
- They left **by** the back door.
- We got there **by** train.

We often use **by** after a <u>passive verb</u> to talk about:

the *relationship* between two things:
- Lightning is often <u>followed</u> **by** thunder.
- The cottage <u>was surrounded</u> **by** flowers.

the *cause* of something:
- Rachel <u>was worried</u> **by** the bright flash.

the *agent* of an action:
- My favourite poem <u>was written</u> **by** Ted Hughes.
- My cat Jasper <u>was bitten</u> **by** a dog.

By can also be used in some idiomatic expressions with other meanings:

one by one = *singly, one followed by one*:
- The dancers came onto the stage **one by one**.

by myself / yourself / himself etc. = *alone, without help*:
- It's better if you do the homework **by yourself**.

by the way = *this is on another subject*:
- I'm really hungry. **By the way**, where is Jim?

little by little / bit by bit = *a small amount, and then another, and another…*:
- The audience began to clap **little by little**, until they were all applauding.

by means of = *using*:
- Mr Dean climbed over the wall **by means of** a long ladder.

❹ uses of **to**

To is often used as a space preposition, and as a particle before an ***infinitive***:
- I want to go **to** the beach.
- I want **to** <u>go</u> to work.

To can also be used in some idiomatic expressions with other meanings:

be up to something = *doing something, possibly bad*:
- Keith is definitely **up to** something! There's a terrible noise coming from his room.

face to face = *personally, looking directly at each other*:
- Enemies should talk to each other **face to face**.

end to end = *place or attach more than one thing in a line*:
- The teacher put the tables **end to end**.

enough / too … to = *enough / too much for a particular purpose*:
- We have **enough** petrol **to** get home.
- It's **too** far **to** walk to the next village.

A Read the text and add the correct preposition (either **at, in, by, to**) in the gaps.

0 You must all get out of the building ....*at*.... once!

1 There is a fire in the basement and we should leave soon .... case the fire gets worse;
we'll really be .... trouble if it does get bad.

2 Go down the stairs, one .... one.

3 You must leave .... the back door of the building.

4 I'm sure we can see enough .... spite of the smoke.

5 .... order to stop the fire spreading, we must keep the doors closed.

6 I think there will be enough air .... breathe in the hall.

7 Don't be frightened .... any loud noises.

8 The firemen have already put out .... least half the fire.

9 .... the way, is anyone here a doctor?

10 I'm not worried .... all. .... fact, this is quite exciting!

B Choose the best phrase from the box to put in the following sentences.

at all	worried by	in love	in case	at once	~~up to~~	in fact
	face to face	written by	at last	too shy to		

PHYLLIS: Hello Mei Ling. What are you (0) .*up to*.? You're looking guilty.

MEI LING: I was looking for you. I'm a bit (1) .... this letter! Do you think it was
(2) .... James?

PHYLLIS: Let me see it. Oh, yes, of course it was. (3) ...., I think he's the person who sent you
the flowers too.

MEI LING: Do you? I thought he was (4) .... talk to me.

PHYLLIS: He is! But he's getting braver, (5) ....! I really think James is (6) ....
with you!

MEI LING: Oh don't be stupid! He doesn't really know me (7) ....!

PHYLLIS: Well, you could go and ask him (8) ....

MEI LING: Oh, I couldn't do that (9) .... it wasn't him!

PHYLLIS: Well I can find out for you! I'm going to phone him (10) ....!

MEI LING: No, Phyllis, you mustn't, please!

C Match the questions and answers.

0 When are you leaving?
1 Have you ever met a famous actor?
2 Have you read 'The Beach'?
3 How many mistakes did you make in the test?
4 What's wrong with Sam?
5 What do you want for your birthday?
6 Is it cold outside?
7 What time shall we leave?
8 How much coffee have we got?
9 Shall we take the lift?
10 Do you like Gary?

A No, who was it written by?
B I don't know, but he was in tears.
C At once! I have to go now.
D No, but I'm going to take a coat in case it gets cold later.
E If we leave at three, we should be in time for the game.
F I don't think we have any at all.
G Yes, I once met Kenneth Brannagh in person.
H No, let's go down by the stairs.
I Yes, I like him in spite of the way he behaves.
J I can't think of anything that I want in particular.
K Oh, I don't know. At least ten!

D Anna Compton and her mum are talking about what to do at the weekend. Circle the phrase in brackets that goes best in the gap.

0 MUM: Let's have a trip to the coast tomorrow! We could go .... car. (by / by means of the)

1 ANNA: Oh yes! But we should take our beach umbrella .... it rains. (in any case / in case)

2 MUM: Where shall we go? Is there any beach .... that you prefer? (at least / in particular)

3 ANNA: Let's go to Widecombe Bay, or is it .... far .... drive? (too … to / enough … to)

4 MUM: It is a bit far, and Sam doesn't like long car rides .... (at all / at once)

5 ANNA: OK. Let's go to Lulworth Cove! .... , did you get any petrol yesterday? (In fact / By the way)

6 MUM: Yes, but the petrol tank was completely empty! I don't know what Dad's been ....! (up to / in to)

7 ANNA: We'll have to leave early if we want to get there .... (in the time / in good time)

8 MUM: We could make a picnic – or we should .... take something to drink. (at last / at least)

9 ANNA: .... , I could go to the shop now and buy some things for the picnic! (In case / In fact)

10 MUM: That would be great! Oh, and while you're .... you could get some sun cream. (up to it / at it)

Sir Terry Frost, the famous artist **from** Cornwall, died recently. He discovered his **talent for** painting when he was a prisoner of war in Stalag 383. Later, he studied in London, but he moved **away from** London to St Ives in Cornwall in 1950. The boats in St Ives harbour and the flat stones on the beach were **inspiration for** the abstract shapes and soft colours he chose for his paintings at this time. Fashions change and Pop Art **took over from** abstract art, but Frost's work continued to be popular. His colours got hotter and hotter but the abstraction never cooled. His work was always full of life and optimism. His funeral was attended by local fishermen as well as famous people **from** the art world. West Cornwall will remember him **for a long time**.

❶ uses of **for** with nouns

We often use **for** with the present or past perfect to describe *how long something is, or was, the case*:
- Our neighbours have been living in their house **for 40 years**.

We use **for** after some nouns:
      reason / cheque / inspiration etc. **for** something:
- There is a **reason for** his bad behaviour.   I gave him a **cheque for** £200.

      ticket / train / bus for a place:
- The **ticket for** Milan was £185.

      have **a talent for** something:
- Steve has **a talent for** cookery.

We can use **for**, or the possessive **'s** ending on the noun, when we are talking about *something that can be used by someone*:
- They don't sell **gloves for men**. = They don't sell **men's gloves**.

We use **for** before a noun in some expressions:
      for example:
- I really like river fish – trout, **for example**.

      for ever / forever:
- Lucy wanted the summer to last **forever**.

❷ **for** after adjectives

We use **for** after some adjectives:
      famous / sorry for something or someone:
- What is Amsterdam **famous for**?   The landlord was **sorry for** the poor girl.

      meant / intended for:
- The letter was **meant for** my neighbour.

❸ **for** after verbs

We use **for** with some verbs to talk about an *intention, purpose*, or *goal*:
      look for something / someone:
- Steve is **looking for** a new flat.

      apply for something (usually a job):
- Leonie is **applying for** Michael's job.

      ask (someone) **for** something:
- They **asked** the waitress **for** some more coffee.

      leave for somewhere:

- Phil is **leaving for** Paris tomorrow.

blame someone / something **for** something:
- The team **blamed** the manager **for** their failure.

thank someone **for** something:
- The class **thanked** Miss Howard **for** teaching them so well.

forgive someone **for** something:
- She **forgave** the class **for** having behaved so badly.

work for someone (or an organisation):
- Ruth **worked for** the Social Services.

❹ from after adverbs and adjectives

We use **from** after adverbs such as **away**, **up**, **in**, **back** to talk about *movement away from something*:
- The boat pulled **away from** the shore.   ▪ Helen jumped **up from** her seat.
- When Dad gets **back from** work, we can eat.

Note: **Out** usually goes with **of**, and not **from**:
- The cat's jumped **out of** the basket.

We use **from** after some adjectives, such as **different** and **distinct**:
- Mark's brother is very **different from** him.

❺ from with nouns

If we are talking about *someone who was born in, or is living in, a particular place,* we use **from**:
- Jane met a girl **from Cologne**. NOT ... a girl of Cologne.

When we talk about things *bought from* or *made in a particular place,* we use **from**:
- Alice bought a woollen **scarf from Skye**.
- The **cheese** we had at dinner was **from France**.

❻ from after verbs

The most common use of **from** is to talk about moving **from** one place **to** another place:
- The class ran **from** the sports field **to** the changing rooms.

We use **from** after certain verbs:

come from somewhere:
- Lucy **comes from** near Inverness.

suffer from something:
- Harriet's aunt is **suffering from** anorexia.

protect someone / something **from** something:
- We should always **protect** children **from** cruelty.

escape from something / someone / somewhere:
- The soldiers **escaped from** the camp.

hide from someone / something:
- They were **hiding from** the police for weeks.

take over from someone = *take the place of someone*:
- Janet **took over from** David when he went to work in the Japanese office.

❼ for and from in questions

When we make questions using a question word and a phrase with **for** or **from**, we usually put the preposition at the end of the question:
- What is Ibiza famous **for**?   ▪ Where does Raoul come **from**?

A Read this article about Sylvia Johnson. The prepositions **for** and **from** are missing. Choose which one should go in each gap.

Sylvia Johnson is (0) ..*from*.. County Durham, in the north of England. When she was a child, she suffered (1) .... asthma; this meant that when the other children did sport, she was given a piece of clay, instead, and told to make something with the clay. She forgives her teacher (2) .... it, and she says she can thank asthma and bad teachers (3) .... her success in life!

She moved away (4) .... her home town when she left school and applied (5) .... a job working (6) .... a publishing company. She started an evening class in pottery, and discovered that she had a talent (7) .... making pots. Every evening when she got home (8) .... work, she worked on her pots. When she had worked (9) .... three years, she decided to escape (10) .... publishing and look (11) .... a part-time job so she could do a degree in ceramics at university.

Now Sylvia works as a full-time potter and is very successful. She is famous (12) .... the tiny, delicate patterns on her pots. 'I feel really sorry (13) .... people who don't know the joy of making something beautiful with their hands. It's what hands were meant (14) ....! My life is completely different (15) .... how it used to be, but I couldn't ask (16) .... anything more!'

B

Michel and Stavros are sitting in a waiting room at Waterloo Station.

Make Stavros' questions from the following cues, using **for** or **from**. Michel's answers are given.

0 STAVROS: (how long / waiting here / ?)
How long have you been waiting here for?
MICHEL: About half an hour. I'm really tired.

1 STAVROS: (Where / come / ?)

....

MICHEL: Paris. I arrived this morning.

2 STAVROS: (What / come to London / ?)

....

MICHEL: I've come here to visit my cousin.

3 STAVROS: (Where / be / your ticket / ?)

....

MICHEL: Manchester. It cost me £38.50.

4 STAVROS: (How long / travelling / ?)

....

MICHEL: Six hours. I left at 4 a.m.

5 STAVROS: (What / run away / ?)

....

MICHEL: I'm not running away!

6 STAVROS: (Who / hide / ?)

....

MICHEL: OK! It's true. Someone is chasing me. You must help me!

7 STAVROS: (What / I / protect you / ?)

....

MICHEL: I can't tell you what the danger is.

8 STAVROS: (Who / work / ?)

....

MICHEL: I haven't got a job. I am a student. Oh!

A bullet flies past them!

9 STAVROS: (Who / meant / ?)

....

MICHEL: That was aimed at me! Thank you and goodbye!

10 STAVROS: (What / thank / me / ?)

....

MICHEL: Absolutely nothing!

C

Put the two halves of the following sentences together, and then write out the sentences underneath.

0 I found a ticket
1 When I came in, Susan jumped up
2 'I'm applying
3 'You can take over my job
4 I walked away
5 'When will you get back
6 'I don't know. I might stay there
7 'I don't blame you
8 'Can you ever forgive me
9 'That's alright,' I said. 'I forgive you
10 And she said 'I want to thank you

A forever,' she said.
B from Italy?' I asked her.
C for being so understanding.'
D for a job in Italy!' she said.
E for everything,' I said.
F for leaving so suddenly?' she asked.
G from the window.
H for wanting to go.'
I from me, if you want,' I said.
J for Milan on the table.
K from her chair.

0 *I found a ticket for Milan on the table.*
1 ....
2 ....
3 ....
4 ....
5 ....
6 ....
7 ....
8 ....
9 ....
10 ....

Sir Terry Frost, who died on 1st September 2003, was **the last of** the leading artists from the St Ives Group **of** artists. They were at the **head of** the abstract art movement in Britain from the 1930s to the 1950s, and lived and worked in or near St Ives in Cornwall.

Cornwall has always been **full of** inspiration for painters. In the nineteenth-century Turner, Whistler, and Sickert all came to Cornwall in **search of** the special light and, by the 1930s, the artists Ben Nicholson and Barbara Hepworth had chosen to live near St Ives. Other artists soon followed them.

The **influence of** Mondrian and Arp are clear in their work, as well as the **inspiration of** the surrounding landscape. They formed the Penrith Society of Arts in 1949 and writers, collectors, and artists such as Mark Rothko made the long journey down to the south west **corner of** Britain to visit their studios.

❶ of after nouns

We use **of** with nouns to say what something *contains*:

> a book **of poems**   the pot **of jam**   a handful **of dust**

But if we want to say what a thing is *made of* or *consists of* or *is used for*, we don't use **of**; instead we put the defining noun before the main noun, like an adjective:

> ▪ A **clay figure** stands on the piano. NOT A~~figure of clay~~ ...

Note: There are some archaic expressions which still use **of** to mean *with the quality of* or *made from*, such as **a man of iron, a child of our time, cloth of gold** etc, but this is not common now.

We use **of** after certain nouns:

> *abstract* nouns – **danger, risk, fear, hope, inspiration, influence, search** etc:
> ▪ He said there was a **risk of** fire. We didn't have a **hope of** getting a prize.
> *senses* nouns – **taste, smell, sound, feel** etc:
> ▪ Delia woke up to the **sound of** the postman and the **smell of** toast.
> *possibility* nouns – **chance, opportunity, possibility, certainty** etc:
> ▪ Ulrika had the **possibility of** starting a new life, but with no **certainty of** success.
> *position* nouns – **middle, edge, end, corner, top** etc:
> ▪ We ran to the **end of** the road.

To talk about *something well-known which is connected with a place*, we use **of** + *place name*:

> the Giant Redwoods **of** America   the Leaning Tower **of** Pisa

To say *which area something originated from*, we don't use **of**; we put the place name before the noun:

> <u>Brighton</u> Rock   <u>Kendall</u> mint cake   <u>Cheddar</u> cheese

If we are referring to a *country*, we use the nationality adjective (**Canadian, Spanish, French** etc):

> the Italian Alps   Spanish flamenco   British folk dance

❷ of in titles and professional roles

We often use **of** when we are talking about *jobs* or *positions*:

> the head **of** marketing   the Director **of** Studies   the manager **of** the Swindon office

---

When we are talking about *roles* in *government, royalty, or religious offices*, we use **of**:

> the Minister **of** Education   the King **of** Denmark   the Bishop **of** Sydney

❸ of after adjectives

We use **of** after certain adjectives, such as **full, tired, aware, afraid, typical, sure**:

> ▪ The cat was **afraid of** the thunder.

❹ of after superlative adjectives

We often use **of** after superlatives (including **last** and **first**) when we compare one person or thing with other people or things:

> ▪ **The first of** the runners finished the race in under three minutes.

We can use the idiom *superlative* + **of** (**them**) **all** to mean *more than anything / anyone*:

> ▪ Priam, who was **the bravest of them all**, sat on the throne.

❺ of after verbs

We use **of** after certain verbs, such as **approve**, **take care**, **die**, **consist**, **think**:

> ▪ Tina's parents didn't **approve of** her husband.

Note: We can also say **die from** and **think about** with the same meanings.

After **accuse** and **warn**, we use an *object* and then **of**:

> ▪ They **accused** <u>him</u> **of** taking the camera, without paying.

We use **be made** + **of** to talk about the material used in something:

> ▪ Is this suit **made of** linen?

❻ of after quantifiers (**a lot**, **some**, **all** etc)

After some quantifiers (such as **lots**, **a lot**, **none**) we usually use **of**:

> ▪ **Lots** and **lots** of people are afraid of spiders.

After other quantifiers (e.g. **some**, **most**, **each**) we use **of** if we are talking about *something specific*:

> ▪ **Some of the** guests were late.
> ▪ She's made a cup of tea for **each of** us.

With **all** and **both** we can leave out **of** when talking about *something specific*:

> ▪ We gave **both the** CDs back to Jack. = *We gave **both of the** CDs back to Jack.*

With **either** and **neither** we usually use **of** when talking about *something specific*:

> ▪ We didn't like **either of the** CDs that Jack gave us.

But if we are offering an alternative with **either ... or** or **neither ... nor**, we don't use **of**:

> ▪ I'll give Stephanie **either** the book **or** the CD.

With *units of measurement* (e.g. **metre**, **gram**, **acre**) we use **of**:

> ▪ I bought **a metre of** cable.

After a *precise number* we don't usually use **of**:

> ▪ There are 25 cows in his herd. NOT There are ~~25 of cows~~ in his herd.

But we do use **of** if we are talking about *a number, or a part, of a group*:

> ▪ One **of his** cows is ill.

Also, if we are talking about a large *estimated number* (**millions**, **hundreds**, **dozens** etc) we use **of**:

> ▪ There were **millions of** stars in the sky.

❼ the double possessive: of + possessive

We sometimes use the double possessive, **of** + **noun** + **'s** or **of** + *possessive pronoun*, to talk about *one of something that belongs to someone*:

> ▪ I borrowed some socks **of Kate's**. (= *I borrowed some of Kate's socks.*)
> ▪ John is a friend **of hers**. (= *John is one of her friends.*)

A

Read the following text and rewrite the phrases that need of. The number in brackets shows how many ofs are missing in each case.

0   Lord John Fortescue Wilkes Rigby Smythe-Bartleby used to be the Seventeenth Earl Ashbury. (1)
    the Seventeenth Earl of Ashbury.

1   But now he's just plain 'John Bartleby'. He is not the richest British aristocrat, but he is one the happiest aristocrats! (1)

2   When he left school, his father gave him a large house with 200 acres land, and a stable full racehorses. (2)

3   He tried to be a good landlord and was aware the responsibility that his father had given him, but he soon became tired living in the country – and he had always been afraid racehorses! (3)

4   One his brothers, Harvey, was much more interested in racing than him, so he asked him if he would take care the business for him. (2)

5   At 23 he went to the University East Anglia to study Environmental Science. (1)

6   He met Mandy Green at a barbecue at one his friends' houses and he fell in love with her immediately. (1)

7   His parents didn't approve her, and accused her trying to get his money, but he decided to give up his money and title, and marry her. (2)

8   Some his friends warned him the danger marrying a girl from a different background, but he said he was aware the dangers and happy to take the risk. (4)

9   Now they are joint directors research at the Alternative Energy Centre in Lyme Regis. (1)

B

Choose the right word to write in the gaps in this text. In each case decide whether or not to use of.

miles	aware	bottle	risk	each	~~neither~~
afraid	check	some	take care	thought	

Andrew and his neighbour Sally are going rock climbing together. It's his new hobby.

'Don't your kids want to come too?' she asked him.

'Oh no! (0) *Neither of* them is interested in climbing. They're too lazy!'

'Are you (1) .... the dangers?' she asked him.

'I think so. There's the (2) .... falling, obviously. But if you (3) .... your equipment and check everything regularly, it's no more dangerous than – driving a car, for example.'

'Yes, that's true. And are you (4) .... heights?'

'No. I've never (5) .... about that. I've never experienced vertigo.'

'That's lucky! Where's your equipment?'

'I put it all in the garage. Shall we (6) .... it? I've got (7) .... rope! I can't believe we'll need that much!'

'I've got crampons, harnesses, and belays for (8) .... us. And some Kendall mint cake. It's good for quick energy.'

'Great. And I've got a (9) .... water, and (10) .... those high protein bars.'

'Ok! Lets go!'

C Write down the recipe and method for making brown bread in correct sentences using the clues in the brackets, and **of** where necessary.

(wholemeal flour / 500 gm)	0	*Five hundred grams of wholemeal flour.*
(warm water / half a pint)	1	
(salt / 1 teaspoon)	2	
(sugar / 2 teaspoons)	3	
(butter / 50 gm)	4	
(quick dried yeast / 1 packet)	5	
(the ingredients / mix / all / together)	6	

D Read the following sentences. Some of the phrases are wrong. Circle the mistake and write the correct phrase on the line, with or without **of**.

LUCY: Well, this is lovely, isn't it? What shall we order? What about a (pot tea?) *pot of tea*

JAMILA: I don't like tea. Can I have a milk glass? (1)

LUCY: Yes, sure. What do you think at the cakes on the counter? (2)

JAMILA: Most them look horrible. I want chips. (3)

LUCY: You can't have chips! What about scones of Devonshire or a rock cake? (4)

JAMILA: Yeuch! I don't like either them. (5)

LUCY: I think the chocolate gateau looks the best at all! I'm going to have that! (6)

JAMILA: Oh, all right, but I wonder what it's made by? (7)

LUCY: I'm sure it's got lots and lots chocolate in it! (8)

JAMILA: Are you sure at that? They often use horrible chocolate! (9)

LUCY: Oh Jamila, I'm tired by this. Let's just have a drink and go. (10)

Is Phyllis a shopaholic?

1 Shopping is one of our favourite hobbies in the UK, **but** it is becoming an expensive obsession **as** shoppers are getting huge credit card bills **and** facing deeper and deeper debt than ever before.

2 **Although** 'retail therapy' can make you feel better for a while, consumer spending is increasing all the time, **and** it is estimated that nearly one in five people has a problem with their shopping habits.

3 Psychologists say an addiction to shopping hides a lot of pain and insecurity **and** compulsive shoppers feel they lack love, **and** they are looking for objects to replace it, **but** this creates a destructive cycle.

4 At first there is a feeling of exhilaration, **but** then dismay and self-hatred set in **and** the whole cycle starts all over again.

5 Phyllis certainly loves shopping **but** I don't think she is a true compulsive shopper **as** she always stops when her credit card says 'No!'

❶ what are clauses?

Clauses are sentences or parts of sentences that contain complete bits of information. Clauses usually contain a subject and a verb. Some sentences have only one clause:

- Keith rang.
- Lynne answered.

Some sentences are made up of more than one clause, each one adding another bit of information. They are often connected to other clauses with a comma, or a conjunction (e.g. **and**, **but**), or other linking word:

        clause 1   clause 2   clause 3

- While Keith was talking on the phone, the door opened and Alice came into the room.

❷ clauses which add information

Some clauses give *added information*; these begin with **and**:

- It was raining hard **and** the river was flooding.
- The water filled the street **and** cars were floating down the road.

Other clauses give *contrasting information*, and begin with **but**:

- It was a lovely morning **but** Tom felt depressed.
- He went to work as usual **but** he didn't work very hard.

❸ explanation clauses

Explanation clauses *answer the question 'why?'*, They begin with **because** and **as**:

- Francis doesn't take the car to work **because** walking is healthier than driving.
- Kevin is feeling tired **as** his training is very hard work.

❹ result clauses

These clauses describe the *consequence of something*. They usually begin with **so**:
- The roads were very busy, **so** Carol took the subway.
- It had been raining, **so** the ground was muddy.

❺ time clauses

Some clauses *answer the question 'when?'*. They may begin with **when**, **after**, **before**, **as soon as** etc:
- Peter went out **when** the rain stopped.
- **After** the Rabbi left, Susan left, too.

Many clauses indicate *a sequence of events*, linked with words such as **then**, **next**, and **finally**:

| 1 | 2 | 3 | 4 |

- Joan arrived, **then** Andrew walked in, **next** Gareth sat down, and **finally** Tamara ran in.

Some clauses describe how *one thing happens at the same time as something else*. These begin with **as** or **while**:
- Mr Grant drank a cup of coffee **while** he read his emails.
- **As** the snow fell, the footprints disappeared.

❻ clauses without a subject

When we use a sequence of clauses with the same subject, we often don't repeat the <u>*subject*</u>. We use a comma before each new clause; we use **and** before the last clause:
- When he stayed in Greece <u>he</u> visited the Parthenon, went snorkelling, danced with the local people, **and** bought lots of presents.

When we use a sequence of clauses with the same subject and verb, we usually don't repeat the <u>*subject*</u> and <u>*verb*</u>. It is clear what we mean because of the context:
- When David goes on holiday <u>he likes</u> swimming in the sea, walking in the mountains, **and** taking his wife to quiet little restaurants.

If we give an alternative, we use **or**:
- He wants to try sky-diving **or** to try parachute jumping.

Some **ing** *form* verb clauses are *time clauses* which say that *two things happen almost at the same time*:
- **Slamming on the brakes**, he stopped the car. (= *He slammed on the brakes and he stopped the car.*)
- **Running round the corner**, Diane tripped over the dog. (= *Diane ran round the corner and tripped over the dog.*)

Some clauses *answer the question 'how?'* and start with **by** and an **ing** *form* verb:
- Sharks stay alive **by moving** their bodies constantly. (= *Sharks move their bodies constantly and that's how they stay alive.*)

When we have two **by** clauses together, we can leave out the second **by**:
- We saved a lot of money **by cooking** our own food and (**by**) **not eating** in restaurants. (= *We cooked our own food and we didn't eat in restaurants, and that's how we saved a lot of money.*)

A Look at the text at the top of page 222 and write each clause as a sentence. Take out the underlined words and make new sentences of each clause.

0   *Shopping is one of our favourite hobbies in the U.K.*

1   ....

2   ....

3   ....

4   ....

5   ....

6   ....

7   ....

8   ....

9   ....

10   ....

11   ....

12   ....

13   ....

14   ....

15   ....

16   ....

B Read the following sentences and add a word or a comma in the gaps to make complete sentences.

Phyllis goes into town each weekend (0) ......*and*...... joins the millions of other British people hurrying up and down the high streets (1) .... window-shopping in the malls.

The biggest problem most people face is finding somewhere to park, (2) .... keeping calm in the middle of the crowds, (3) .... for others the love of the boutique can lead to very serious problems. People who spend a lot can become very depressed (4) .... lose their houses, (5) .... even become homeless.

Many famous people suffer from this obsession, (6) .... even the richest pop star or model can run out of money (7) .... find themselves in debt once the addiction gets hold of them.

One problem is that this illness is not taken seriously (8) .... most people think that it is a problem only for rich, middle-aged women, (9) .... they don't have much sympathy with the sufferers.

This isn't true, (10) .... it can ruin the lives of women and men of all ages, and from all economic brackets.

Advertising is a serious problem (11) .... it tempts people to buy useless things (12) .... telling them they really need that dress or handbag or even that new car.

Apparently, Internet shopping is not such a danger (13) .... people like the excitement of the crowds (14) .... they need to actually see and feel the things that they buy.

C Read the following sentences. Draw a line where the clauses begin and circle the linking words or punctuation.

0 Do you think you could be more successful | (and) enjoy a better lifestyle | (but) don't know how to improve things?

1 Find out what you want from life by making a list of all the good things you've done in your life and thinking about what they say about you.

2 Then you must make goals for yourself, but remember the goals you pick are for you, not for your parents, or your partner, or your boss, and you must try to forget what other people want you to do or be.

3 Before you start making your list, you may need to get away on your own for a while so you can take a step back and see things clearly.

4 Next, take a look at the way you live by looking around your home, then think about the impression it gives of you.

5 This doesn't mean that you have to have a spotless, tidy home, but it should be well-organised so you can focus on what you really want to do in your home.

6 Putting jobs off till tomorrow will make them seem much harder, so you should always do things immediately.

7 Exercise is really important and beginning the day with a bit of exercise will give you a lot more energy and enthusiasm for the rest of the day.

8 Finally, decide on one short-term goal and one long-term goal, write them both down on a big piece of paper, stick it up in a place where you will often see it, and now your new, successful life can begin!

Answer all the questions below. Write clearly in black ink. Sign the form at the bottom. Hand the form back to the officer when it is complete. It is important that you give accurate information.

	Client details – Confidential
What is your full name?	Catherine Ramsey
What is your permanent address?	19 Bletchley Avenue London NE 16
What is your date of birth?	26/10/82
Have you filled in this form before? If yes, when?	Yes /(No)
How long have you lived at your present address?	11 months
How many other people live at this address?	3
Do you share the cost of heating/lighting/telephone etc?	Yes /(No)
How much do you pay for these expenses and rent each month?	About £400
Why did you move there?	It's near to my family.
Would you agree to move to another address in the area?	(Yes)/ No
Have you ever been in trouble with the police? If yes, please give details.	Yes /(No)
Will you still be living at this address in six months? If not, where will you be living?	I don't know.

❶ present tense questions

When we make a question in the present simple with the verb **be**, we put the <u>subject</u> after the verb:

- Annette is tired. → Is <u>Annette</u> tired?
- Her house is at the end of the lane. → Is <u>her house</u> at the end of the lane?

When we make a question in the present simple with other verbs, we add the auxiliary **do** / **does** before the subject and the main verb (in the infinitive):

- Sanjit likes Hip hop. → **Does** <u>Sanjit</u> like hip hop?
- Ahmed and Miriam go to college in London. → **Do** <u>they</u> go to college in London?

If we are using an auxiliary or modal verb (**will**, **have**, **should**, **can** etc) in a question, we put the subject after the auxiliary or modal:

- Stephen is studying medicine → **Is** <u>Stephen</u> studying medicine?
- His mother can paint well. → **Can** <u>his mother</u> paint well?

❷ past and perfect questions

When we make a question with **be** in the past simple, we use **was** / **were** before the subject:

- **You were** late this morning. → **Were** <u>you</u> late this morning?
- **Jonathan wasn't** happy in his job. → **Wasn't** <u>Jonathan</u> happy in his job?

With other verbs we add the auxiliary **did** before the subject and the main verb (in the infinitive):

- Tamsin **found** her cat. → **Did** Tamsin **find** her cat?
- The cat **ran away** again. → **Did** the cat **run** away again?

If there is an auxiliary verb, we put the subject after the auxiliary; we don't need to add **did**:

- We **have** made some new friends. → **Have** <u>we</u> made some new friends?
- Keith **had** broken the record. → **Had** <u>Keith</u> broken the record?

If there are more than one auxiliary or modal in the question, we put the <u>*subject*</u> after the first auxiliary:

- Paul **had been** working all morning. → **Had** <u>Paul</u> **been** working all morning?
- She **could have** waited in the car. → **Could** <u>she</u> **have** waited in the car?

❸ questions with question words

Who, **what**, **which** (+ *noun*), and **whose** (+ *noun*) are question words. When they are the *subject* of the verb, we put them before the verb; we don't add an auxiliary:

- '**Who** knocked at the door?' 'The postman did.'
- '**What** is the prize?' 'It's a trip to Paris.'
- '**What** is making that noise?' 'The water heater is.'
- '**Which** is the best song on the album?' '"Honey" is the best song on the album.'
- '**Whose key** was left on the table?' 'Jane's key was.'

When we use **who**, **whose** (+ *noun*), **what**, and **which** (+ *noun*) as the *object* of the verb, we put the <u>*subject*</u> after the auxiliary or modal:

- '**Who** was <u>he</u> talking to yesterday?' 'He was talking to William.'
- '**What** was <u>he</u> hoping to see in London?' 'He was hoping to see the Tate Modern.'
- '**Which song** do <u>you</u> like best?' 'I like "Honey" best.'
- '**Whose cup of coffee** is <u>she</u> drinking?' 'She's drinking my cup of coffee.'

When we want an *explanation of something*, we use **why**, **when**, **where**, or **how**. We use the question form of the sentence after these words:

- '**Why** is <u>the door</u> open?' 'The door is open **to let in some fresh air**.'
- '**When** was <u>he</u> speaking to Mary?' 'He was speaking to Mary **this morning**.'
- '**Where** is <u>John</u> living at the moment?' 'John is living **in Oldham**.'
- '**How** did <u>she</u> know the answer?' 'She knew the answer **because she had read the book**.'

❹ tag questions

We can make a question from a statement by adding a *tag question*. The tag question uses the same auxiliary, modal, or **be** verb as the statement, but in the negative form:

- It's late, **isn't it**?
- These grapes are really delicious, **aren't they**?

To make a tag question after a statement using a verb without an auxiliary (i.e. in the present or past simple) we use **do** or **did** in the tag:

- Sarah dances very well, **doesn't she**?
- That boy just fell off his bike, **didn't he**?

If we want to make a question out of a negative statement, we add a tag question using the same auxiliary, modal, or **be** verb, in the positive form:

- Susanna isn't here at the moment, **is she**?
- Mr Godfrey hasn't been at work for a while, **has he**?

To make a command more polite, we add a tag question with **can**, **could**, **will**, or **would**:

- Bring me the Wilson file, **would / could you**?
- Sandy, stop kicking my chair, **will / can** you?

(For more on tag questions, see unit 59.)

58 EXERCISES — questions

A Read the following interview with the actor Scott Cranstone and ask the questions the interviewer might have asked him.

0 INTERVIEWER: *Are you happy about your career?*

SCOTT CRANSTONE: Yes, I'm very happy about my career. I've been incredibly lucky.

1 INTERVIEWER: ....

SCOTT: Yes, I've won an Oscar. I won it for 'best supporting actor' last year.

2 INTERVIEWER: ....

SCOTT: No, it wasn't for my film 'Strange Attractions'. It was for my role in the film 'Shame' with Jane Truman.

3 INTERVIEWER: ....

SCOTT: Oh yes, I really enjoyed working with her, and all the cast.

4 INTERVIEWER: ....

SCOTT: No, it's not true that we are getting married! She's very nice, but we are just good friends …

5 INTERVIEWER: ....

SCOTT: No, I haven't got a girlfriend at the moment. I'm too busy.

6 INTERVIEWER: ....

SCOTT: Yes, I'm working on a new film. It's a movie about Alaska. We're in rehearsal just now.

7 INTERVIEWER: ....

SCOTT: I've never been to Alaska. It's going to be very interesting.

8 INTERVIEWER: ....

SCOTT: No, Jane is not in this movie. My co-star is Heddy Gervais; she's Swedish.

9 INTERVIEWER: ....

SCOTT: Yes, that's right, I trained in London originally, then I went to the Actor's Studio in New York.

10 INTERVIEWER: ....

SCOTT: No, I'm not planning on coming to Britain at the moment, but I would love to come and work there again one day; so if anyone is thinking of offering me a part …!

B Read the passage and then make questions from the words in brackets.

Garden design

Good design is timeless. It is about proportion, form, and balance. This garden, designed by Camilla Arden, illustrates all of these qualities; it also has built-in furniture as an integral part of the design. It is composed of a number of different elements, but notice how the simple fence makes a straight line with the concrete block wall. The raised pool is attractive, while the timber seat cleverly runs around the pool, drawing the whole composition together. It is possible to have running water even in a garden without a pool. You can position a water tank underneath a fountain and the water can be pumped up through a pipe and fall back again into the tank. The sound of water can add a charming peaceful atmosphere. Using an arrangement of loose stones, plants, gravel and brick around your water feature can be very effective.

0 (good design / a question of fashion?)
Is good design a question of fashion?

1 (what / you need in a garden?)

2 (where / the water tank in this garden?)

3 (the fence and the brick wall make a straight line?)

4 (the wooden seat / is cleverly designed?)

5 (you / can have a water fountain without a pool?)

6 (how / the water fall back into the tank?)

7 (the sound of water / irritating?)

8 (the designer / has used several different elements in this garden design?)

9 (you / think this is a nice garden?)

10 (you / have a garden?)

228

C

Phyllis and Jasmine are taking part in a tennis tournament. They are at the court, looking at the list of matches. Read the conversation and add tag questions to the sentences.

0 PHYLLIS: Oh no! We're playing against Kerry! She's really good at tennis, *isn't she?*

1 JASMINE: You beat her last time, ...?

2 PHYLLIS: No! I lost badly. You remember, ...?

3 JASMINE: You're better now. And you've got a new tennis racket, ...?

4 PHYLLIS: Which court are we on? The courts are very full, ...?

5 JASMINE: Phew! It's too hot to play tennis, ...?

6 PHYLLIS: I know. You can't enjoy it when it's too hot, ...?

7 JASMINE: Ah, there she is. She's looking very smart, ...?

8 PHYLLIS: Wow! And look who she's with! It's not that Australian girl, ...?

9 JASMINE: Yes, what's her name? She was called Jennifer, ...?

10 PHYLLIS: We haven't got a chance of winning! They were the champions last year, ...?

D

After the match the journalist from the local newspaper interviews Jasmine. Write the questions she asks her.

0 JOURNALIST: Congratulations! You and Phyllis are the new women's doubles champions of the Hartley Tennis Club. *Are you pleased?* ....

JASMINE: Yes, of course we're really pleased.

1 JOURNALIST: ....

JASMINE: No! We never thought that we could win!

2 JOURNALIST: ....?

JASMINE: The hardest match? Oh, I think the match against Jenny and Kerry was the hardest.

3 JOURNALIST: ....?

JASMINE: The final score at the end was 2 sets to 1.

4 JOURNALIST: ....?

JASMINE: For me, the second set was the most difficult. I thought we were going to lose the match!

5 JOURNALIST: ....?

JASMINE: Oh yes! I love playing with Phyllis because she doesn't take it too seriously!

6 JOURNALIST: ....?

JASMINE: No! We never argue about tennis. If we lose, we just try harder next time.

7 JOURNALIST: ....?

JASMINE: No. I'm not going to play in the county championship. I prefer to just enjoy tennis. It's just a game for me.

8 JOURNALIST: ....?

JASMINE: Yes, it really is just a game for Phyllis, too. She just loves the sport.

9 JOURNALIST: ....?

JASMINE: I don't even know what the prize is! I don't play for prizes.

10 JOURNALIST: ....?

JASMINE: Well, this evening I'm going to have a hot bath and go to bed early! I'm exhausted!

HARTLEY TENNIS CLUB

"Hello?
Yes? … Oh, was Mr Grant very
angry with me? … No, I thought it would be
all right if I left her in the box under my desk. …. **Yes,
I did**, and I left a note explaining. … Oh, don't you think so?
… Yes, I left at about 2.30. … I know, but I'd finished what he
had given me to do. … **Yes, I had** – and the accounts too.
Harriet said she thought it would be all right. … I know, but
she's only a small boa constrictor,   and she's not poisonous. …
Because my flatmate is afraid of snakes and told me to get
rid of it. … **No, I couldn't!** … I don't understand it! You only
have to give it baby mice. … **No, of course not** live mice! Frozen
ones. You buy them from the pet shop. … **Well, I don't know**.
I think she's beautiful. She's called Aphrodite. … Why did
you say 'was' – what did he do? … **Did he?** Oh no!
How awful! … Oh no, you can't be serious! …
No thank you. I don't want a snakeskin
bag! …"

❶ short answers

A simple **yes** / **no** answer can sound too short or impolite. We can add emphasis to a yes / no answer, or make it more polite, by adding a subject and repeating the auxiliary verb, or **be**, from the question:

- '**Has** John read the book?' 'No, **he hasn't**.'
- '**Are you** ready?' 'Yes, **I am**.'
- '**Did** Lucy leave her purse in the shop?' 'Yes, **she did**.'

If the question has a *modal*, we repeat the modal in the short answer:

- '**Would you** like to see this film?' 'Yes, **I would**.'
- '**Can I** sit here, please?' 'No, **you can't**.'

If there is more than one auxiliary in the question, we just use the first one in the short answer:

- '**Will** Gordon **be** going to France soon?' 'Yes, **he will**.'
- '**Has** Ellen **been** doing a test?' 'No, **she hasn't**.'

If there is no auxiliary in the question, we use the auxiliary **do** / **does** / **did** in the answer:

- '**David plays** chess very well.' 'Yes, **he does**.'
- '**He won** every time.' 'No, **he didn't**.'

If we want to make the meaning of our answer stronger, we often add a word like **certainly**, **absolutely**, **really**:

- 'Do you like chocolate?' 'Yes, I **really** do!'
- 'Can Sarah speak German?' 'No, she **certainly** can't.'

There are other ways of answering with short **yes** answers. Here are some examples:

- Yes, I think so.
- Yes, of course.
- Certainly!
- I hope so.

Here are some examples of other short **no** answers:

- No, I don't think so.
- No, of course not.
- Not at all.
- I hope not.

❷ tag questions

In conversations we often use tag questions. They ask for a response from the other person and make the conversation more friendly.

After a *positive* statement we use **be** or an auxiliary in the *negative*, followed by a subject pronoun. We always use the contracted form in tag questions:

- Jordan**'s** getting much better at swimming, **isn't he**?
- Lorna **has** got very lovely hair, **hasn't she**?
- That play **won** a prize, **didn't it**?

After a negative statement we use **be** or the first auxiliary in the positive form, and the subject pronoun:

- **You haven't** got much paper, **have you**?   ■ **Tom didn't** buy anything, **did he**?

When the statement has an *empty subject* (**there** or **it**), we repeat it in the tag:

- **There's** lots of milk in the fridge, isn't **there**?
- **It's** too late to phone Harry, isn't **it**?

(For more on the empty subject, see unit 10.)

When the statement uses a modal verb (**can**, **ought to** etc), we repeat the modal in the tag question:

- Paul **can** speak French, **can't** he?
- We **ought to** see some whales from the boat, **oughtn't** we?

The exception to this is **may**, because we do not use **may not** in the short form. We usually use **might** instead:

- They **may** be a bit late, **mightn't** they?

Note: We say **aren't I** (NOT **amn't I**) in a negative **be** tag question with **I**:

- **I'm** too late, **aren't I**?

But when we use a positive tag question with **be**, we use **am**:

- **I'm not** trying very hard, **am I**?

If we are expressing a personal opinion or taste, we can use a short question asking for the other person's opinion or taste, using **do / don't** with **you**:

- I like lemon sorbet, **don't you**?   ■ I don't believe those lies, **do you**?

❸ answering tag questions

We usually reply to a tag question with a short answer.
If we *agree* with a negative statement, we reply with **No** and a *negative* phrase:

- '**You don't** take sugar, do you?' '**No, I don't**.' (= *I don't take sugar*.)

If we *disagree* with a negative statement, we reply with **Yes** and a *positive* phrase:

- '**It isn't** time for the class yet, is it?' '**Yes, it is**.' (= *It is time for the class now*.)
- '**You haven't** brought the book with you, have you?' '**Yes, I have**.' (= *I have brought the book with me*.)

If we *agree* with a positive statement, we reply with **Yes** and a *positive* phrase:

- '**Mary is** very lazy, isn't she?' '**Yes, she is**.' (= *She is very lazy*.)
- '**You have** forgotten the tickets, haven't you?' '**Yes, I have**.' (= *I have forgotten the tickets*.)

If we *disagree* with a positive statement, we use **No** with a *negative* phrase:

- '**We're late, aren't we**?' '**No, we're not**.'
- '**Your new bag was very expensive, wasn't it**?' '**No, it wasn't**.'

❹ other responses

When we are having a conversation, we often say things that are polite and pleasant and keep the conversation moving. Here are a few examples of positive things you can say when you *agree* with someone, or just want to encourage them to continue talking:

I know!   Exactly!   I see.   That's right.

Here are examples of polite negative things you can say when you *don't agree* with someone, or *are not sure*:

Really?   I'm not so sure.   Are you sure?   Do you really think so?

When you *strongly disagree*, you can say things like:

No, of course not!   Absolutely not!   No, not at all!

231

A A police detective is talking to a suspect. Make his statements into questions by adding tag questions.

0 You were arrested at six o'clock this evening, *weren't you?*

1 It was in the Cock and Bull pub, ...

2 You were carrying a sports bag, ...

3 The bag was full of mobile phones, ...

4 They were all stolen, ...

5 You didn't like the Officer who tried to arrest you, ...

6 In fact, you tried to hit him, ...

7 And then he had to put handcuffs on you, ...

8 Those phones weren't all stolen by you, ...

9 You will tell me the truth now, ...

10 Then the judge might be less severe, ...

B Now, reply to the policeman's questions using short answers and the cues in brackets.

0 You were arrested at six o'clock this evening? (yes)
Yes, I was.

1 It was in the Cock and Bull pub? (yes)
....

2 You were carrying a sports bag? (yes)
....

3 The bag was full of mobile phones? (no)
....

4 They were all stolen? (no)
....

5 You didn't like the Officer who tried to arrest you? (no) ....

6 In fact, you tried to hit him? (no)
....

7 And then he had to put handcuffs on you? (no)
....

8 Those phones weren't all stolen by you? (no)
....

9 You will tell me the truth now? (yes)
....

10 Then the judge might be less severe? (yes)
....

tag questions

Rewrite the following text as a conversation, adding tag questions and answers. The smiley faces (☺) mean Madeleine agrees, the sad faces (☹) mean she doesn't, and the question mark (?) means she doesn't know.

Madeleine and Megan are talking about fair rides.

0 MEGAN: We had a great time at the fair, *didn't we*?

   MADELEINE: ☺ *Yes, we did. / We certainly did!*

1 MEGAN: Zahrah was very brave on that last ride we went on, ...?

   MADELEINE: ☺ ....

2 MEGAN: Dee was too scared to go on it, ...?

   MADELEINE: ☹ ....

3 MEGAN: It was called The Twister, ...?

   MADELEINE: ☹ ....

4 MEGAN: I think it was. And it was really expensive, ...?

   MADELEINE: ? ....

5 MEGAN: Yes. All the rides cost a fortune, ...?

   MADELEINE: ☺ ....

6 MEGAN: But if you buy a day pass you can go on as many rides as you want all day, ...?

   MADELEINE: ? ....

7 MEGAN: Yes, but you'd be really tired if you went on all of them, ...?

   MADELEINE: ☺ ....

8 MEGAN: I really hate the ones that go upside down, ...?

   MADELEINE: ☺ ....

9 MEGAN: The candy floss was horrible, ...?

   MADELEINE: ☹ ....

10 MEGAN: I hope we can go again next summer, ...?

   MADELEINE: ☺ ....

CATHY: And then Steve **said** 'I don't want to see you ever again!'
JANICE: No! He didn't really say that?
CATHY: He did! He **said he'd had** enough of me wasting his time and money …
JANICE: Well! And what did you say?
CATHY: **I said I'd** never spent a penny of his money and I had plenty of my own.
JANICE: Quite right! Then what did he say?
CATHY: Well, he **said** 'You're a dirty little liar!' He shouted at me and I started to cry!
JANICE: I'm not surprised! Then what?
CATHY: **I said I wanted** him to go away and leave me in peace, and he **said he hoped** he never saw me again!
JANICE: No! But I **thought you were** getting married next week.
CATHY: Oh yes, we are. I'm afraid we do this kind of thing all the time. It doesn't mean anything.

❶ direct speech

When we want to say what we or someone else has said, or thought, we can do so in two ways. We can use *direct speech* or *indirect speech*.

In direct speech we say *exactly what was said or thought*, using verbs like **say**, **think**, **shout** etc. We usually use this form in writing and not very often in speaking. We use inverted commas (' ') to show what the person said:

- Paul **said** 'You're late!'
- Kelly **shouted** 'Get away from there!'
- I **thought** 'He doesn't really like me!'

We can write what the person said first or second. If it is first, we often use the verb before the name of the person speaking or thinking:

- 'Larry is my favourite actor,' **Tom said** / **said Tom**.
- 'I recognise that man,' **Andy thought** / **thought Andy**.

But if we are using a *pronoun* (**I**, **you**, **he**, **she**, **we**, **you**, **they**) we put it before the verb:

- 'I'm hungry,' he thought / ~~thought he~~.
- 'Don't worry!' she said / ~~said she~~.

We can use verbs that express the feeling of the speaker when we report what someone has said or thought. For example, we can use **hope**, **feel**, **be afraid**, **want**, **wish**:

- My sister **hopes** you can get tickets for the play.
- She **wants** to see the play tomorrow.
- She**'s afraid** you won't be able to get seats.

When we want to report what someone says to a particular person or people, we can use **say to** or **tell**:

- 'I'm leaving tomorrow,' Andy **said to** Lucy. OR 'I'm leaving tomorrow,' Andy **told** Lucy.

(For more on **say** and **tell**, see unit 34.)

❷ indirect speech: present and future

When we say or write *what we, or someone else, are saying or thinking at the moment*, we can use indirect speech with the present tense in both clauses, with or without **that**:

- Richard: 'I'm just leaving the station.' → Richard **says** that he**'s** just **leaving** the station.
- Dean: 'You mustn't worry about the cost.' → Dean **says** we **mustn't worry** about the cost.

We also use this form when we want to say *something that is always true*:

- Andy **says** he **doesn't like** drum and bass.

When we report *something that someone says about the future*, we use the same tense they used when they spoke:

■ Keith: 'I'm going to Boston next week.' → Keith says that he's going to Boston next week.

When we want to say *what someone is going to say*, we use an appropriate form for the future (**present continuous**, **going to**, **will**) with the same tense they will use:

■ This evening at the meeting Heather is **going to say** that she doesn't want the motorway to go ahead.
■ Annie French **will say** she's going to stop the development now.
■ Harold **is saying** that he supports the plans.

Note: If we are reporting *what we are thinking now*, we don't use the form **I think …**, **he thinks** etc. because **I think** means *I am not sure*:

■ I think I'll go to the bank. (= *I am **not sure** if I will go to the bank.*)
■ She thinks she is late. (= *She is **not sure** if she is late.*)

To report the thought *I am late*, we might say:

■ She **is thinking** that she is late.

❸ indirect speech: past

When we want to say *what someone said in the past*, we use the past tense in both parts of the sentence. We change the tense of the verb in what was said to the equivalent past tense:

present simple → past simple:
■ Keith: 'I **am** much too busy.' → He said he **was** much too busy.
■ Keith: 'I **don't have** time to chat.' → Keith said he **didn't have** time to chat.
present continuous → past continuous:
■ Sarah: 'I**'m working** very hard too.' → Sarah said she **was working** very hard too.
past simple → past simple or past perfect:
■ Mark: 'I **booked** the flight.' → Mark said he **booked** / **had booked** the flight.
present perfect → past perfect:
■ John: 'I**'ve lost** my wallet!' → John **said** he **had lost** his wallet.

When we report someone using **will**, **can**, or **may**, we say **would**, **could**, or **might**:

■ Paul: 'I **won't** have enough time!' → Paul **said** he **wouldn't** have enough time.
■ Moira: 'I **can't** stop to chat!' → Moira **said** she **couldn't** stop to chat.

Other modal verbs do not change in the past tense, so **should** and **might**, for example, are the same in past indirect speech:

■ Jack: 'We **might** see Liam this evening.' → Jack said we **might** see Liam this evening.

❹ pronouns and *place* and *time* phrases in indirect speech

When we are reporting what someone has said, we need to remember to change what is said, to have meaning from our point of view. We may need to change ***pronouns*** and ***possessives***:

■ Jenny: 'I gave Peter **my** keys.' → Jenny says **she** gave Peter **her** keys.
■ John: 'I**'ve found my** wallet.' → John said **he** had found **his** wallet.

But if we are using the impersonal pronoun **you** (= *anyone, everyone*), we don't change it when we report what was said:

■ Mrs Deely says **you** can't resist her chocolate cookies.
■ Anne said **you** should always check your mirror before driving off.

We may need to change the *time* or *place* reference, or even the verb, to reflect our point of view when we report what someone said:

■ Dilveer: 'I found the coffee **here**!' → Dilveer says she found the coffee **there**.
■ Tim: 'I'm **going** to **your** house **tomorrow morning**.' → Yesterday, Tim said he was **coming** to **my** house **this morning**.

A Rewrite the following things that people said as reported speech, using **said**.

0 'My old car has broken down.' (Paul)
   Paul said his old car had broken down.

1 'I need a new car.' (Paul)
   ....

2 'You don't have very much money.' (Gavin / to Paul)
   ....

3 'It's easy to get credit.' (Paul)
   ....

4 'It's stupid to get into debt.' (Gavin)
   ....

5 'I should get a second-hand car.' (Steve)
   ....

6 'You can't trust second-hand cars.' (Paul)
   ....

7 'You just have to get it checked by a mechanic.' (Steve)
   ....

8 'There is a really nice Honda for sale in Grants Garage.' (Gavin)
   ....

9 'I think I'll have a look at it.' (Paul)
   ....

10 'Japanese cars are very reliable and good value.' (Steve)
   ....

B Harry is on the phone to Janet. She is walking along the street in San Francisco. Harry is telling Ken everything she's saying. Write down what Harry says to Ken.

0 JANET: 'Hi, Harry! I'm here in San Francisco!'
   She says she's there in San Francisco.

1 JANET: 'It's great, and the weather's really beautiful.'
   ....

2 JANET: 'I've been staying in a great hotel.'
   ....

3 JANET: 'I think California is cool!'
   ....

4 JANET: 'I met a really nice man called Gary on the plane.'
   ....

5 JANET: 'I want to stay in San Francisco for an extra month.'
   ....

6 JANET: 'I hope it's OK to take some more time off work.'
   ....

7 JANET: 'I'm afraid they'll fire me if I don't come back soon.'
   ....

8 JANET: 'I really miss you all at the shop!'
   ....

9 JANET: 'Oh, and whatever you do, don't tell Ken about Gary!'
   ....

Read the conversation that happened this morning. Then read what happened when Sharon was called into her boss's office this afternoon; put in the correct form of the words in brackets.

This morning ...

MISS FRANKS: Hi Jeff! Have you got a parcel for me?

JEFF LEACH: Oh no! It's 9.35! I'm five minutes late! Will you sign the delivery slip here, quickly?

MISS FRANKS: Oh, it says 9.30. Shall I change that?

JEFF LEACH: No, don't change it. Leave it at 9.30.

MISS FRANKS: What? Do you mean you want me to cheat?

JEFF LEACH: Oh, go on. It's only five minutes! It means nothing to you, but if I deliver things late, they cut my pay and then they won't employ me any more. I really need this job!

MISS FRANKS: Oh don't be silly! I'm sure five minutes won't matter to them, either.

JEFF LEACH: You stupid, selfish girl! You just don't understand! It's all right for you, with your easy, relaxed job. You don't have to rush, and hurry, and risk your life on the road! You just don't understand how hard my job is!

MISS FRANKS: Well, it sounds to me as if you should quit your job and get an easier one! No one should have to live like that!

This afternoon ...

MR BAKER: Come in, Miss Franks. I'd like to ask you some questions about the events of this morning. Mr Leach came into your office. What time was that?

MISS FRANKS: It was 9.35 exactly. I know that because he was in a terrible state – out of breath and sweating – and he said he (0) ...._was_.... (be) five minutes late. He wanted me to sign the delivery slip and to say that he (1) .... (deliver) it five minutes earlier.

MR BAKER: So he wanted you to cheat. Why?

MISS FRANKS: He said that they (2) .... (pay) him to deliver things on time and that if he was late, they wouldn't pay him as much. He said he (3) .... (be afraid) they (4) .... (will / not / employ) him any more.

MR BAKER: And what did you say?

MISS FRANKS: I said that I (5) .... (not / think) it (6) .... (will / matter) being five minutes late.

MR BAKER: And what happened then?

MISS FRANKS: He got really angry. He said it (7) .... (be) all right for me with my job as I (8) .... (not / have to) rush and hurry, and that I (9) .... (can / not) understand how hard his job was.

MR BAKER: So what did you do?

MISS FRANKS: I said he (10) .... (should) quit his job and get an easier one!

James Cameron **invited** Lady Martha Brainstock, President of the Horticultural Society, to do an interview on the 9 o'clock news on TV6.

When she arrived, James **persuaded** her to let the make-up girl put some make-up on her face, and his assistant **asked** her **if** she wanted a drink before the interview. He **advised** her to have a drink of water so her throat would not be too dry during the interview, as the studio was very hot. When she was ready, James **asked** her to sit down in the chair and **told** her to relax and try not to look into the camera.

He **asked** her **if** she was happy about the growth in popularity of the organic movement. Lady Brainstock told him that she was delighted with the enormous increase in knowledge of ecology and in concern with environmental issues among the ordinary people in Europe. Then James **wanted to know if** she had always been interested in plants and **if** she had been a keen gardener as a child. Lady Brainstock said that she was afraid that she had come from a very rich family which had employed a gardener, so she had never been allowed to work in the garden and get her hands dirty. James **wondered why** she had chosen to go into horticulture. She laughed and explained that that was exactly why, because she had not been permitted to work with the earth when she was a girl, so it was what she wanted to do more than anything. She admitted that she liked flowers more than people!

After the interview James thanked her and said goodbye. Then he **asked** his assistant to be sure to find a spare pair of shoes for Lady Brainstock next time she was invited for an interview!

❶ reporting questions

When we want to report *someone asking for information now*, we use the present continuous form of **ask**, with **if** or **whether**, and with the rest of the sentence in the present tense. In a reported question we put the <u>*subject*</u> before the verb, and we don't use a question mark:

- Sheila: '**Are you** warm enough?' → Sheila is asking if **you are** warm enough.

We usually use **whether** when we are talking about *a choice of things*:

- Jonathan: 'Do you want coffee or tea?' → Jonathan is asking **whether** you want coffee or tea.

We also use **whether** when *a choice is implied* but not stated; sometimes we add **or not**:

- 'Do you take milk?' → He is asking **whether you take** milk (**or not**).

To report *someone asking for information now*, we can also use phrases such as **wants to know**, **would like to know**, or **wonders**. We use these phrases with **if** or **whether**:

- Paul: 'Has Maria finished the decorating?' → Paul **wonders if** Maria has finished the decorating.
  OR → Paul **wants to know whether** Maria has finished the decorating (**or not**).
  OR → Paul **would like to know if** Maria has finished the decorating.

We can use a question word (like **what**, **how**, or **why**) after **ask**, **wants to know** etc:

- Beryl is asking Christopher **what** he plans to do next.

If we want to report *a question someone asked in the past*, we use the past tense in both clauses:

- Jonathan **asked** whether we **wanted** coffee or tea.
- Paul **wondered** if Maria **had finished** the decorating.
- Dana **wanted to know** when the programme **started**.

To report *a question which someone will ask in the future*, we use a future form of **ask** with the rest in the same tense that the speaker will use:

- Mary **is going to ask** her mother **if** she **needs** any help on Sunday.

■ Imran **will ask** Jake **if** he **passed** his exam.

We don't use **wonder if** or **want to know** when *we report what someone is going to ask* in the future:

■ Fran is **going to ask if** she can leave work early. (NOT ~~Fran is going to wonder if she can leave work early~~.)

❷ reporting instructions, orders and requests

If we are reporting *a request*, we usually use the form **ask someone to do something**:

■ Tony **asked me to move** my chair.
■ The nurse **is asking the patients to wait** in the waiting room.

If we are reporting *a polite request*, we use **ask if** with **could** or **would**:

■ I **asked** Ahmed **if** he **could lend** me his pencil.
■ Dr Thomas **asked** Michael **if** he **would take off** his shirt.

When we give an *instruction*, we use **tell someone to do something**:

■ Anna **told me to move** out of her seat.
■ The doctor **is telling Mr Harris to take** his medicine.

To report *a negative instruction or request* we use **tell / ask someone not to do something**:

■ The teacher **told** us **not to** make so much noise.
■ We **asked** the people at the back **not to** push.

Note: We do not usually say **to not** after **tell** and **ask**:

■ We **asked** the people at the back **not to** push. (NOT ~~We asked the people at the back to not push~~.)

❸ other verbs used for reporting

There are other verbs which describe what someone says, such as **persuade**, **order**, and **advise**. These are used like **tell someone to do something** or **tell someone not to do something**:

■ Her boss **persuaded** Elena **to go** home.
■ The teacher **advised** Helen **to do** some extra revision.

We can also **invite someone to do something**:

■ Gordon **invited** Saffron **to dance** with him.

Other verbs, such as **agree**, **insist**, **admit**, and **suggest**, can be used in reporting speech. We use them like **said**, with or without **that**, and a new clause:

■ Gail **agreed** (that) it was time to leave.
■ Gail **insisted** (that) she should drive.
■ Gary **admitted** (that) he had stolen the car.

After **admit**, **suggest**, and **advise** we can use an **ing** *form* in place of the **that** *clause*:

■ John admitted that he had stolen the money. → John admitted **stealing** the money.
■ Mike suggested that they take the train. → Mike suggested **taking** the train.
■ The teacher advised **doing** some extra revision.

After **insist** we can use **on** + **ing** *form*:

■ Tim **insisted on bringing** his dog.

After **agree** we can use **to** + *infinitive*:

■ She **agreed to meet** us the next evening.

Note: We don't always use a verb after **ask** or **invite**, as they can both mean *ask someone to come*:

■ Madeleine **invited** Dawn (to come) **to** her party on Saturday.
■ She **asked** Karen **to** her party too.

A Rewrite the following as reported speech, using the verb in brackets. Here is an example:

0 Keith said 'Let's have a cup of coffee.' (suggest)

   Keith suggested we had a cup of coffee.

1 Felicity said to me 'Why don't you come and visit my friend Jane?' (invite)

   ....

   ....

2 Felicity said to me 'It's my birthday today.' (tell)

   ....

3 Keith said to her 'Can I come too?' (ask)

   ....

4 I said to him 'Do you know her?' (want to know)

   ....

   ....

5 He said 'I have never met her.' (admit that)

   ....

6 I said to him 'I don't think you should come.' (advise)

   ....

7 Felicity said to him 'Would you like to come and join us later?' (ask)

   ....

8 I said to him 'You must not come with us without a birthday present.' (tell)

   ....

   ....

9 Keith said to us 'You must let me come with you.' (persuade)

   ....

10 We said to him 'You can come with us.' (agree that)

   ....

   ....

questions and instructions

B The following sentences have errors in them. Underline the word or phrase that is wrong and then write the sentence correctly.

0 Lady Brainstock was <u>invited sit</u> in the black chair.
   Lady Brainstock was invited to sit in the black chair.

1 James Cameron wondered her if she had always loved flowers.

2 The interviewer asked how old was she when she started growing plants.

3 He told her to not look into the camera.

4 The assistant advised Lady Brainstock drinking some water.

5 James wondered if to ask her about her family or not.

6 She persuaded not to him make her wear red lipstick.

7 He wanted to know how had she become an expert in horticulture.

8 He asked her whether had she been to university.

9 She admitted her having studied at agricultural colleges in three different countries.

C Read the indirect speech in brackets and then write the things that Stefan and Delia are actually saying:

0 (Delia admits she doesn't like swimming.)
   'I'm afraid *I don't like swimming.*'

1 (Stefan suggests teaching her to swim better.)
   'I could _____'

2 (He says that he believes if she swims better, she will enjoy it more.)
   'I'm sure _____'

3 (Delia insists that she can swim very well.)
   'But _____'

4 (He suggests giving her a swimming lesson.)
   'I'll _____'

5 (She says she thinks he is very persistent.)
   'You're _____'

6 (Stefan persuades her to come to the pool tomorrow at 8.30.)
   'You really should _____'

7 (She wonders what he will be able to teach her.)
   'I wonder _____'

8 (He tells her to bring some goggles.)
   'Don't forget _____'

9 (Finally she agrees to meet him at the pool in the morning.)
   'OK! I'll _____'

The Internet

The Internet, **which links millions of computers through public and private telephone lines,** is an open, world-wide communications network. Although it is relatively young, it already links many millions of computers. No one owns the Internet, **which consists of networks run by governments, universities, and commercial and voluntary organisations**. There is an organisation called the Internet Society **that co-ordinates and sets standards for the Internet**.

The Internet grew out of a computer network **which was developed by the US government in the late 1960s**. In the next ten years it was extended to connect over 200 military and research establishments in the USA and other countries. 'Internetworking', **which was the term used at that time**, proved itself to be very useful. Some American universities started similar systems **that were used to help research projects**. Originally it was not set up for commercial dealing, but it has become a cheap and efficient way to advertise goods and services, **which most modern businesses now use**. An important part of the Internet is email, **which is used by millions of people all over the world**. In fact, most people **who own computers** now use email more than the postal service.

❶ relative clauses

When a sentence has two clauses, the second clause often gives us more information about someone or something in the first, or main, clause. Second clauses often begin with **which**, **that**, or **who**, and are called *relative clauses*. The relative clause usually tell us something more about the *object* of the main clause:

main clause	relative clause
▪ I collected <u>the package</u>	**that** I had ordered the day before.
▪ Kiera won <u>the game of chess</u>	**which** she was playing with Sofia.

Relative clauses that refer to *things* start with **that** or **which**. There is no significant difference between them:

- ▪ Janet often uses <u>the bicycle</u> **which** her mother gave her.
- ▪ They don't deliver <u>letters</u> **that** have no postcode.

Relative clauses that talk about *people* can start with **who** or **that**:

- ▪ Gary is <u>the African</u> **who** I met in the library.
- ▪ Paul met <u>the boy</u> **that** Ruth is going to marry.

We can use either **who** or **that** unless the relative clause is about *a named person*, in which case we must use **who**, and not **that**:

- ▪ I phoned Mrs French, **who** worked in the Health Centre.

We use **whose** to refer to *something owned by, or related to, someone*:

- ▪ Jack Gordon, **whose** car was a bit old, arrived last.
- ▪ Will invited Harry, **whose** sister was in his class at college.

We use **where** to talk about a place:

- ▪ That is the hospital **where** I was born.
- ▪ George and Ellie are visiting Exeter, **where** they were married.

Who, **which**, and **that** can be the *object* or the *subject* of the relative clause. Compare:

subject
- ▪ Anne bought a picture **that** came from Morocco. (***The picture*** *came from Morocco.*)

object
- ▪ The leg fell off the table **which** I had made. (*I had made **the table**.*)

Notes: When **who**, **which**, or **that** are the object, they are followed by a subject (e.g. **I**). We do not use a second object (NOT ... ~~which I had made it~~.)

There are two kinds of relative clause: *adding* clauses, which give additional information about something in the main clause, and *specifying* clauses, which define something in the main clause. For more on these, see below.

❷ *adding* clauses

Adding clauses, giving more information about things, usually begin with **which**. We usually use a comma before the relative clause:

- They have finished building the new library, **which** will open in June.
- Frank walked to the football pitch, **which** was about two miles away.

We can use **who** in *adding* relative clauses when we are talking about people:

- Paul had a meeting with his new boss, **who** he really liked.
- Peter's going out with Diane, **who** he hasn't been out with for years.

An *adding* relative clause can refer to *the whole of the first clause* and start with **which**:

- <u>Karen quit her job</u>, **which** was very stupid of her.
- <u>We went skiing in France last year</u>, **which** was quite expensive.

If the two clauses are *a sequence of events*, then we must use **who**, **which**, or **that** in the second clause and we do not need a comma:

- My mother knitted a sweater **that** she gave to my brother. (*She gave the sweater to my brother after she had knitted it*).
- I made them a sandwich **which** they ate very fast. (*They ate the sandwich after I had made it.*)

❸ *specifying* clauses

Specifying relative clauses give us information which defines something or someone in the main clause, and we don't use a comma before this kind of clause. They often begin with **that**, **which**, or **who**:

- The leg fell off the table **that** I had built. (**that I had built** specifies *which table*.)
- Helen posted the letter **which** Katherine had written. (**which Katherine had written** specifies *which letter*.)

We can omit the pronouns **that**, **which**, or **who** from this kind of sentence when they are not the <u>**subject**</u> of the relative clause:

- Pat borrowed the book (**that**) <u>you</u> liked so much.
- Shall we have the soup (**which**) <u>Tom</u> made yesterday?

But we don't ever omit **whose**:

- I saw the man **whose** daughter has been elected Chair.

We can also omit **where** in specifying clauses, but we must add the appropriate preposition after the verb:

- Helsinki is the city **where** my husband was born. OR Helsinki is the city my husband was born **in**.
- The Astoria is the cinema **where** we went last night. OR The Astoria is the cinema we went **to** last night.

❹ relative clauses inside main clauses (embedded clauses)

We can often put the relative clause in the middle of the main clause to talk about the object:

- We had that stew **that Gail didn't like** for dinner.

and to talk about the subject of the main clause:

- Mrs Hanson, **who lived in Wales for a few years**, has moved to France.

The same rules, about when we can leave out the pronouns **that**, **which**, or **who**, apply whether the clause is embedded or not. If the pronoun is not the subject of a *specifying* clause, we can leave it out:

- The house (**that**) **we wanted to buy** had just been sold.
- I found that perfume (**that**) **you like** in a little shop in town.

A Read the following text and see if you can find the ten relative clauses. Underline the relative clauses, the first one is done for you. Then circle the three embedded relative clauses.

Michael Anderson, <u>who you can see in the photograph opposite</u>, has been having an exciting time recently. He plays for the Southern Australian basketball team, which recently won the 'All Australia Cup'. He is 23, and started playing for the team when he was only 19. Last month a big American team offered him a job, which would have paid much more than South Australia could give him. He is a loyal Australian and was unhappy about leaving Australia, where he was born and has always lived. When our reporter interviewed him, he said that he had been over to the States to talk to the agent who had approached him. He said that when he arrived he had had a great time with the Americans, who were very welcoming. His wife Sandra, who he married last June, went with him. While they were there, she unfortunately began to feel ill and went to see the team doctor who told her that she was expecting a baby! They were very excited and returned to Australia immediately. He told our reporter he has decided to stay in Australia for the next year, at least. Sandra has had to give up her own sport, which was competition swimming, but she still swims for fun. She says it's very good for people who can't do strenuous exercise for some reason. We are very happy for the couple and very glad they decided to stay in Aussie!

B Add the correct pronoun (**which, that, who, whose,** or **where**) in the following sentences, if one is needed.

0 Stephen, ...*who*.... is studying medicine in London, is going on holiday.

1 His Aunt Anne has invited him to Epsom, ... she has been living for 20 years.

2 He is packing the bag .... he has just bought from the market.

3 His friend Paul, ... lives next door, has come to visit him.

4 The train .... he is going to catch leaves at 6 p.m.

5 Aunt Anne, ... house he is going to stay in, is a doctor too.

6 He has never been to her house, ... is in the countryside.

7 He gets out at Epsom station, ... she is waiting to collect him.

8 He really likes her new car, ... is a Seat.

9 Her children are very excited to meet their cousin .... they have never seen before.

You are showing your friend your holiday photos. Look at the pictures and use the clues to tell your friend about the pictures. Use relative clauses beginning with **that**, **who**, **where**, or **which**.

0 (apartment) (we stayed here)

This is the apartment where we stayed.

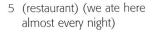

1 (view) (we saw it from our terrace)

This is ....

....

2 (Mrs Kallides) (she owned the building)

....

....

3 (family) (they lived next door)

....

....

4 (man) (he taught us scuba diving)

....

....

5 (restaurant) (we ate here almost every night)

....

....

6 (prize) (Greta won it at the talent competition)

....

....

7 (beach) (it was closest to our village)

....

....

8 (our friend Katie) (we met her on the beach)

....

....

9 (Steve) (I played tennis with him)

....

....

10 (big party) (the family gave for us the night before we left)

....

....

DELIA: I'm **hoping to take** a year away from 'The Inside Story'. It's not that I don't **like working** here, but I think I **deserve to have** a break.

CHRIS: But can you **afford to lose** your salary?

DELIA: I've got a bit of money saved, but it would **involve finding** another job somewhere, at least for part of the time. I am **aiming to travel** somewhere exotic, and **earn** some money while I'm there.

CHRIS: I think that's a great idea. I really **fancy seeing** some of the world while I'm still young.

DELIA: I've **decided to go** and talk to the owners and ask them if they could **arrange for someone to do** my job for a while, so I could have it back next year. I really **enjoy working** here, but ...

CHRIS: It's dangerous! You know you **risk losing** your job altogether!

DELIA: I know. But you can't go through life **avoiding taking** risks. I'm sure I'll **manage to find** some work as a fitness instructor in Australia or somewhere. Everyone is keen on fitness these days.

CHRIS: Well, I **wouldn't mind doing** your job for a year!

DELIA: Hey! Don't get any funny ideas! I still work here, remember!

---

❶ verb + **to** + infinitive

After some verbs which are about *the future* and *influencing the future*, we use **to** + *infinitive*:

- Tara is hoping **to start** university in October.
- We want **to have** a big party for your birthday.

Verbs used in this way are:

communication	future plans	thought and feeling
offer	aim	hope
agree	plan	forget
refuse	continue	learn
threaten	arrange	deserve
promise	fail	decide
	afford	want
	manage	expect
		would like / love / prefer / hate

We can also use **not** with **to** + *infinitive*:

- He promised **not to say** anything.

We can use an **ing** *form* after these verbs if it is used as a noun:

- We **hope smoking** will be banned. (The word **smoking** is used as a noun here, not as a verb.)
- The syllabus offered **swimming** as an option. (The word **swimming** is the name of an activity, not a verb.)

❷ verb + ing form

After verbs which are about *present activities and thoughts*, we use an **ing** *form*:

- Now Mr Harris has gone, the students **miss hearing** his jokes.
- They always try to **avoid answering** questions in class.

Verbs used in this way are:

negative words	thought and feeling words
finish	fancy (= *want to*)
delay	imagine
avoid	admit
deny	suggest
risk	miss (= *feel the lack of*)
	enjoy
	not mind (= *not object to*)

We can also use **not** before the **ing** *form*:

- He admitted **not having** read the email.

Some of these verbs can take an *object* before the **ing** *form*:

- Helen **misses** Peter **bringing her** tea in the morning.
- I can **imagine** the sea **washing** on the golden sands.

❸ verbs which can take both to + infinitive and ing form

After some verbs we can use an **ing** *form* or **to + infinitive** with no difference in the meaning:
continue:
- Nabila **continued playing** the piano. = Nabila **continued to play** the piano.

like / love / hate:
- Everyone **likes to listen** to music. = Everyone **likes listening to** music.
- Danny **hates to be** late for work. = Danny **hates being** late for work.

Some verbs can be used with an **ing** *form* and with **to + *infinitive*** but the meaning changes:
remember:
- I **remember seeing** Jane at the post office. (*I saw her before this moment.*)
- I must **remember to see** Mr Hewell at the bank. (*I must see him after this moment.*)

forget:
- Delia **forgot talking** to the manager. (*She talked to him before that moment.*)
- Delia **forgot to talk** to the manager. (*She didn't talk to him after that moment.*)

try:
- We **tried eating** soya mince. (*We tasted soya mince for the first time.*)
- We **tried to eat** soya mince. (*We attempted to eat soya mince.*)

stop:
- I want to **stop to have** some lunch. (*I'm going to have some lunch when I stop.*)
- I want to **stop having** lunch. (*I don't want to eat lunch again from now.*)

Some verbs can be used colloquially in both ways but with a different meaning:
mean:
- They **mean to buy** a new car. (*They intend to buy …*)
- It **means buying** a new car. (*It tells us that it is necessary to buy …*)

go on:
- The policeman **went on to explain** about the law. (*The next thing he did was to explain …*)
- The policeman **went on explaining** about the law. (*He continued explaining …*)

need:
- I **need to earn** more money. (*It is necessary for me to earn more.*)
- This coat **needs cleaning**. (*The coat needs to be cleaned.*)

verb + to + infinitive

STARFIGHTER

GARGANTUAN GAMES

A Read the following text and choose whether to use the **ing** *form* or **to** + *infinitive* of the verb in brackets.

Jim Patterson is hoping [0](develop) a new part of his company. He is trying [1](decide) what to invest in. His colleagues all suggest [2](move) in different directions. His games developers enjoy [3](work) with fantasy and visual art. Some of his employees think that he should aim [4](get) into the educational market, while others would prefer [5](get) involved in hardware production. His designer fancies [6](produce) a monthly magazine of games and cartoons. Jim wants to stop [7](waste) time with games which don't make much money, but he knows he would miss [8](play) games. He doesn't want to risk [9](lose) his place in the market, but he refuses [10](allow) the company to stand still!

0 *to develop* ....

1 ....

2 ....

3 ....

4 ....

5 ....

6 ....

7 ....

8 ....

9 ....

10 ....

B Anisha Khan is having trouble with her teenage children. They won't help in the house. Make sentences by drawing a line between the two halves.

0 Anisha's son, Imran, always avoids

1 He stays in his room and promises

2 Her husband, Qasim, manages to

3 Anisha never stops

4 To make Imran help, she has to threaten

5 Anisha's daughter, Nabila, sometimes offers

6 Anisha deserves

7 She doesn't mind

8 Qasim says they could afford

9 But Anisha refuses to

10 'I can't imagine

A working, either in the hospital or in her home.

B paying someone to do the jobs you boys should be doing,' she said.

C helping with the housework.

D have a stranger in the house.

E cooking, but she doesn't like cleaning.

F to employ someone to do their cleaning.

G to help later.

H to do the washing-up.

I to have a holiday.

J to stop his pocket money.

K stay out of the house most of the time.

(I hope to win) **and verb + ing form** (I enjoy winning)

C There are some verbs missing from the text. Choose the right one from the box to fill each gap.

to cut off	to have	arguing	to be	reading	having	to find
	sharing	to do	~~to help~~	cleaning	taking	

Dear Gaby,

I really need some advice! It's about my daughter, Phyllis. She is still living at home but she never offers (0) __to help__ in the house. I've tried to make her cooperate by threatening (1) _____ her allowance. She promises (2) _____ more jobs around the house, but then she always manages (3) _____ out when I am in, and she does nothing! It's driving me crazy! I work as a tutor in the university, and I don't expect (4) _____ the house in a total mess when I come home. But it usually is. I hate (5) _____, and I don't think it's fair that my son and I should have to do everything.

My son, Bob, is at college and, until he finishes (6) _____ his finals, I don't expect him to do much in the house. I used to really enjoy (7) _____ and listening to music in the evening, but now I am so tired every night that I just go to bed early. I really miss (8) _____ time to relax and enjoy (9) _____ my evenings with my family. Please can you tell me how to avoid (10) _____ with them! I think I deserve (11) _____ a bit more respect.

Yours exhaustedly,

Andrew.

D Here is Gaby's reply to Andrew. There are some mistakes in the use of the **ing** *form* or the **to** + *infinitive* form of the verb in this reply. Underline the mistakes and write the correct verb forms.

Dear Andrew,

I sympathise with you so much! We all deserve [0]not being treated like servants. But have you forgotten telling them how unhappy you are? I'm quite sure they love you and are not trying ruining your life! They are just spoilt and selfish! I'm afraid you must stop to look after everyone. If you don't, they will continue to do nothing. You must decide changing things, and arrange talking to them together one evening. Wait till you have finished to eat, then tell them the truth! I'm sure they will all agree doing lots of things – which they won't do! – but when they fail doing them, you must remind them! They will find it very difficult at first to remember doing their chores, and they will almost certainly avoid doing anything they don't want to do … but eventually you will win!

If you don't feel that you are winning, why not forget going to the supermarket!

Yours sympathetically,

Gaby

0	*not to be*
1	
2	
3	
4	
5	
6	
7	
8	
9	
10	

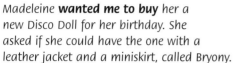

64

Madeleine **wanted me to buy** her a new Disco Doll for her birthday. She asked if she could have the one with a leather jacket and a miniskirt, called Bryony.

'I've got the whole set, apart from this one,' she told me, 'and I really need Bryony.'

I asked her why she needed so many dolls, and told her that when I was young I had just one baby doll and one teddy bear and that I played with bricks, and paper, and pencils. She said she **would hate to live** like that. All her friends had the whole set of dolls and she was the only one who didn't. She said she always got everything last. I **tried to persuade** her that there were more important things in life than being the same as everyone else, but she was not very encouraged by that!

'I**'d like you to grow up** understanding the real value of money, and to value the individual. We're all different, and all wonderful in our own ways,' I **tried to explain**.

'I **don't want to be** different and wonderful in my own way. I want a new Disco Doll!' she shouted. Then I got cross.

'You **won't force me to buy** you one. I**'d prefer to get** you something you can use and that will teach you something. Those dolls only **teach you to be obsessed** with clothes and make-up.'

'Well, then, I **want you to give** me money so I can learn about the value of money, and then I can choose what I buy for myself!' she said.

I give up!

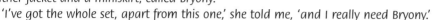

verb + (object) + **to** + infinitive

Verbs which take **to** + *infinitive* have a meaning connected with the future:

■ They **want to start** soon.

After some of these verbs we can also use an *object* + **to** + *infinitive*. These are verbs referring to *preference* or *taste*, and *how we influence* each other:

■ They **want** <u>us</u> to start soon.

preference	influence
want	ask
expect	tell
need	teach
(would) like	force
(would) love	encourage
(would) prefer	persuade
(would) hate	order
	help

Each of the *preference* verbs can take an *object* before **to**, but they don't have to have an object:

■ I **want** to go to Madrid. I **want** <u>Jane</u> to come with me.
■ Paul **expects** to finish the report tomorrow. He **expects** <u>us</u> to present it on Friday.
■ Mr Dawson **needs** to buy a new car. He **needs** <u>Jack</u> to help him to choose one.

The *influence* verbs, apart from **ask**, need an *object* before **to** + **infinitive**. **Ask** is the only influence verb that doesn't need an object:

■ Yolanda **asked** to have the day off. But Jenny **asked** <u>her</u> to come to work.
■ I **told** <u>Frank</u> to give Emma a lift.
■ Mrs Grant **teaches** <u>the children</u> to skate.
■ Paul **forced** <u>his brother</u> to share his chocolates.
■ David **encouraged** <u>me</u> not to give up, but to keep trying.

verb (+ object) + to + infinitive (she taught him to drive)

A In the following conversation a word is missing in each speech. Rewrite the phrase using the object, shown in brackets below, in the right place.

Trevor Thompson is going to do an article about 'Rizzible', Imran's band, for the local paper.

0 TREV: Hi Imran, would you like to interview you alone, or with the other boys from the band? (me)

.....would you like me to interview you.....

1 IZZY: The name's Izzy. You could interview me first, if you like, and I'll ask to come in afterwards. And don't forget Suse. We're not all boys, you know! (the others)

2 TREV: Sorry. I forgot you had a girl drummer. Cool. I'd like to sit at the drum kit, then I could photograph her, too. (her)

3 IZZY: I don't think I can persuade to be photographed. She hates being photographed. (her)

4 TREV: Well, I can't force to be photographed. But it would be great in the paper. (anyone)

5 IZZY: Well, I'll try, but I can't order to come in. She's quite ... umm ... independent! (her)

6 TREV: That's what people tell me! How did she start? Did someone teach to drum or did she teach herself? (her)

7 IZZY: I think she always wanted to be a drummer, and we always encourage to practise. (each other)

8 TREV: I really need to give me an interview. The readers will be interested in her. (her)

9 IZZY: OK, OK. I'll do my best. Is there anything you want to tell you about myself? (me)

10 TREV: Um, yes ... what's it like having a girl in the band? Would you prefer to sing in the band, instead of drumming? (Suse)

11 TREV: I expected to want to interview everyone, not just Suse! (you)

B Read the following information about Gloria Cross and her family. Rewrite the sentences using the verb in the brackets. Remember to use an *object* + **to** + *infinitive* in each sentence.

0 Gloria Cross says to her pupils: 'You should get a good education.' (encourage)

Gloria Cross encourages her pupils to get a good education.

1 She knows you can't make them stay at school if they want to leave. (force)

2 She always says that they should not give up. (persuade)

3 Parents should make their children value education. (teach)

4 She says that she would be happy if her son Stephen became a doctor … (would like)

5 … but she would not be happy if he did it because she wanted him to! (would hate)

6 Her daughter Therese came to Gloria for some advice. (ask)

7 She said she would be very happy if she became a teacher like her… (would love)

8 … but she would not use her power to make her do anything Therese didn't want to do. (force)

Gaby Rosenthal's thought for the day ...

Whether you like it or not, adults are examples to young people. If you are a teacher or a parent, it is really important to **congratulate your children on succeeding** in the things they do, however small. If they feel you are proud of them, they will **be proud of achieving** new things. If they **are keen on doing** something, however small or simple it is, it is important to show that you recognise it. If they **are bad at doing** something, they may feel embarrassed at failing, and you must **be prepared for them not succeeding** in everything. For example, my son is really bad at football, but I would not **dream of trying** to force him to practise. None of us **are good at doing** everything, and we must **forgive our children for not being** perfect, just as I hope we can forgive ourselves. Do not make them **apologise for letting** you down. You must, instead, **think about focusing** on their strong points and encourage them to **concentrate on working** on improving their performance in the things they enjoy. If you **suspect them of giving up** too easily, then gentle encouragement will help them to find the activities that make them feel good. Above all, remember it should be about <u>them</u>, and not about <u>you</u>.

6 5

❶ verb + preposition + **ing** form

To talk about *how we feel about something,* or *what we think about something,* we can use some verbs with a *preposition* (**of**, **to**, **at** etc) and an **ing** *form*:

- Lucy **dreams of going** to live in Australia.
- Jack is **looking forward to moving** house.

We also use a *preposition* + **ing** *form* after **be / seem / feel** etc. + *adjective*:

- The dog **is good** at chasing cats in the park.
- James **seems** <u>keen</u> on hearing the band.

With certain verbs we often put an *object* before the preposition:

- Margaret **suspected** <u>James</u> **of leaving** the front door open.
- The Ambassador **thanked** <u>the Prime Minister</u> **for inviting** him to the meeting.
- Dave **talked** <u>to the manager</u> **about employing** more staff.

❷ verb + **for** + **ing** form

The following verbs are used with **for** + **ing** *form*:

forgive someone for:
- Phil **forgave** Leo **for leaving** him to do all the work.

apologise for:
- Leo **apologised for being** so lazy.

❸ verb + **of** + **ing** form

The following verbs are used with **of** + **ing** *form*:

think of / about = *consider or have an opinion on*:
- The Comptons are **thinking of buying** a new car.
- What do you **think of test-driving** the new Audi?

suspect someone / something of:
- Margaret **suspects** her husband **of planning** a secret party.

dream of / about:
- I wouldn't **dream of lying** to you!

accuse someone of:
- The shop owner **accused** Sam **of stealing** a camera from his shop.

be proud of:
- We **are** really **proud of** Diego **winning** the competition.

be ashamed of:
- Tim **is** a bit **ashamed of getting** angry like that.

❹ verb + adjective + **at** + **ing** form

The following expressions are used with **at** + **ing** *form*:

be good at:
- My father **is** really **good at sailing**.

be bad at:
- Petra **was bad at speaking** French, though she could understand it.

be embarrassed at / about:
- You mustn't **be embarrassed at standing** up and speaking out.

❺ verb + **on** + **ing** form

The following verbs are used with **on** + **ing** *form*:

congratulate someone on:
- I want to **congratulate** you **on working** so hard this term.

insist on:
- George always **insists on me paying** for the meal when we go out.

be keen on:
- James **is** very **keen on surfing**.

❻ verb + other prepositions + **ing** form

The following verbs are used with other prepositions and an ing *form*:

in – succeed in:
- Karen never **succeeds in keeping** the car clean.

into – trick someone into = *dishonestly make someone do something*:
- The hypnotist **tricked** the audience **into dancing** around the theatre.

out of – talk someone into / out of = *persuade someone to do / not to do something*:
- The police woman managed to **talk** the man **out of jumping** off the roof.
- She **talked** him **into climbing** back into the room.

to – look forward to:
- Jack **is looking forward to having** a flat of his own.

from – prevent someone from:
- Mrs Khan **prevented** Imran **from shaving** his head.

about – talk about = *discuss, consider*:
- Imran used to **talk about leaving** the band.

like – feel like = *want to*:
- Phyllis always **feels like going** shopping.

against – warn someone against:
- The fire officer **warned** us **against leaving** the heater on.

A Read the following conversation and choose the best word from the box to put in each gap.

dream	~~succeeded~~	proud	embarrassed
accusing	forgive	trick	insist	feel
good	warned	keen	talk	think

Imran Khan's band 'Rizzible' is getting quite popular. An agent has offered them a recording contract. They are discussing their future …

IMRAN: Well, finally we've (0) _succeeded_ in making someone take us seriously! This is great!

DEN: Wait a minute! Who is this man, Johnny Grant? He might be trying to (1) .... us into signing this contract. I think we need a lawyer.

PHIL: I think we need to believe in ourselves. We could be really (2) .... at managing our careers. Lawyers are too expensive.

IMRAN: My dad (3) .... me against trusting people in the music business. I agree with Den.

ANGELO: Well, I think we should be more positive. I'm really (4) .... of getting this offer. I think we should take it.

DEN: Oh, you're so stupid! I (5) .... like phoning my Dad's lawyer right now.

IMRAN: Hold on! Who are you (6) .... of being stupid! Your Dad isn't going to pay for this – we are! I wouldn't (7) .... of doing anything until we've studied the contract.

PHIL: I agree. I'm not very (8) .... on throwing away my money. I don't want a lawyer to (9) .... us out of taking such a great opportunity.

DEN: I'd never (10) .... you for signing if it all went wrong.

ANGELO: Well, what do you (11) .... of having a meeting with our families? We shouldn't be (12) .... about asking for some help!

DEN: OK. If you all (13) .... on having this meeting, I suppose I'll have to accept it. But I think you're all crazy!

B Gargantuan Games has won a prize for their latest computer game. It is called 'Euphoria', and it is about trading between countries. Mr Patterson, the manager, is giving a speech to the employees. Here are his notes. Read them and then draw lines to match the two halves of his sentences.

- Congratulate everyone on success of 'Euphoria'.
- We thought it was too complicated.
- Thanks to Josh and Kim they made us test it first.
- Now we've beaten all the big games companies.
- I want to make different games from the other companies.

- I wasn't imaginative enough.
- I didn't think trade was a good subject for a game.
- I recognise talent.
- Josh and Kim understand the market.
- Is Kim going to Hong Kong?
- Offer them promotion!

(he's good at skating)

0 Well, guys, I want to congratulate all of you	A in beating all the bigger companies again this year.
1 I know some of us suspected this game	B of making a game about selling coffee and olives!
2 I am grateful to Josh and Kim for insisting	C on creating original and challenging games.
3 We have succeeded	D on testing it before we decided.
4 You know I'm really keen	E of being so unimaginative.
5 Now, I'm ashamed	F on making this new game such a huge success.
6 But I would never have thought	G at understanding the market.
7 I insist	H of being much too complicated.
8 Josh and Kim are very good	I on recognising talent.
9 I know some of you suspect Kim	J of looking for a job in Hong Kong.
10 But I want to tell you that I'm offering her and Josh a promotion, and I'm looking forward	K to working with them for many years!

C Read what Ralph is saying to his career adviser, and put in the missing words, using a word from the box.

of	like	on	of	from	in	~~about~~	to	of	on	of

RALPH: I'd like to talk to you (0) ...*about*...... taking a year out. I'm not sure I am as keen (1) ....

doing chemistry at university as I was. I'm not really looking forward (2) .... starting university, as

I've only just finished my exams. My father was really proud (3) .... me choosing to study

chemistry, but I'm not sure it's the right thing for me. He has always dreamed (4) .... me being

a successful scientist, and I feel a bit ashamed (5) .... disappointing him. I know he would never

insist (6) .... me doing something I really didn't want to, and I know he wouldn't prevent me

(7) .... changing my course. I was thinking (8) .... taking a gap year and travelling a bit.

I feel (9) .... seeing some more of the world. Do you think I might succeed (10) .... getting

a place to study astrophysics instead?

DELIA: I'm really sorry to **hear about** your bad back, Mr Demirel. You should have **spoken to** me about it straightaway.

ISMET: I know I should have **told** you **about** it, but it's an old problem ... I was just **waiting for** it to go away. I used to do a lot of sailing back in Turkey, and one day my yacht **collided with** another boat. I **fell into** the water, and I think I must have damaged my back. I can't **blame** it **on** anyone – it was my own fault.

DELIA: I'm sure we can work out an exercise routine that will help to make your back stronger. We really **believe in** the power of the body to protect itself. We have several specialists who **take care of** this kind of problem. What do you **think about** the idea of enrolling in our special Lower Back Treatment course? Just wait a minute while I **look for** the leaflet about it ...

ISMET: What does the course **consist of**? I already do quite a lot of exercise, and I'm healthy. I live on vegetables and fruit, really. I don't know what to **do about** it.

DELIA: Well, we **provide** you **with** a masseur, and an osteopath. And there is a choice of gentle exercise classes – yoga, t'ai chi, pilates etc. but we **concentrate on** lower back strength and flexibility ...

ISMET: Well, I don't know. I don't want to **spend** a lot of money **on** health clubs.

DELIA: I'm sure we can **provide** you **with** a reasonably priced course which will improve your life. You should **think** seriously **about** it.

6

❶ verb + at

The following verbs can take **at** before the object:

look at:
- Don't **look at** the sun! It will blind you.

shout (something) at:
- The man **shouted at** the dog, and it ran away.

Other verbs used with **at** are: **point (something) at**, **throw something at**, **smile at**, and **laugh at**.

❷ verb + with

The following verbs can take **with** before the object:

provide someone with = *give to someone*:
- The soldiers were all **provided with** a map of the area.

collide with = *meet violently*:
- He **collided with** a bus in the High Street.

Another verb used with **with** is: **charge someone with** = *formally accuse someone of*.

❸ verb + to

The following verbs can all take **to** before the object.

complain to = *say something bad about something*:
- We really should **complain to** the manager about this meal.

speak to:
- Mrs Khan **spoke to** the headmaster about her son.

Other verbs that we can use with **to** + *object* are: **say something to someone, ask someone to lunch / dinner** = *invite*, **belong to someone, invite someone to lunch / a party, write (a letter) to someone, listen to someone / something, happen to someone,** and **sentence someone to** = *decide on a punishment in a court of law*.

❹ verb + on

The following verbs can all take **on** before the object:

> **spend a sum of money / time on**:
> ▨ Let's **spend** lots of money **on** a really good meal.
> **congratulate someone on** = *tell someone they have done well*:
> ▨ I'd like to **congratulate** you all **on** a very good performance.

Other verbs that we can use with **on + object** are: **blame something on someone** = *think someone was responsible for something bad*, **spend (a sum of money / time) on**, **concentrate on**, **live on** = *survive on*, **depend on** = *trust to help*, and **rely on** = *trust or depend on*.

❺ verb + for

The following verbs can all take **for** before the object:

> **apply for** = *ask to be considered for a job or a course*:
> ▨ 200 people **applied for** the teaching job.
> **leave for** = *leave one place to go somewhere else*:
> ▨ Pam **leaves for** Florence in the morning.

Other verbs that we can use with **for + object** are: **care for** = *look after*, **look / search for** = *try to find*, **ask (someone) for** = *request*, and **wait for**.

❻ verb + of and verb + about

The following verb can take **of** before the object:

> **remind** someone **of** (= *make someone remember or look like*):
> ▨ You **remind** me **of** Madonna!

Other verbs that we can use with **of** are: **accuse someone of**, **hear of** = *know something about*, **take care of** = *look after or attend to*, **consist of** = *be made of or comprise*, and **dream of** = *imagine, or intend*.

The following verb can take **about** before its object:

> **hear (something) about** = *be told something*
> ▨ Karen hasn't **heard** the news **about** Paul!

Other verbs that we can use with **about** are: **tell someone about**, **ask (something) about** = *request information on*, **do (something) about** = *react to*, **warn someone about** = *give advice about danger* and **think about** = *consider / have an opinion*.

❼ verb + into, verb + in, and verb + from

The following verb can take **into** before its object:

> **fall into**:
> ▨ Dan nearly **fell into** the water.

Other verbs that we can use with **into + object** are: **bump / crash into** = *collide violently*, and **cut / divide / split (something) into**.

The following verb can take **in** before its object:

> **believe in** = *believe something exists*:
> ▨ Many people still **believe in** fairies!

The following verb can take **from** before its object:

> **suffer from**:
> ▨ Tom often **suffers from** toothache.

verb + preposition (look at)

A

The underlined prepositions are wrong. List the correct words below.

When I first invited Cara Andrews [0]about an interview, I wrote [1]of her at the Excelsior Hotel. They told me she had already left [2]to Mozambique. So I had to wait [3]at a year to interview her. When I finally met her, I asked her [4]to her life before she started to work at the Excelsior. She said:

'I never dreamed [5]to working in the hotel world. Things just happened [6]for me. My mother warned me [7]with all the hard work and late hours, but I didn't listen [8]for her. I did a secretarial course and then applied [9]about a job with the British Medical Association. They asked me to organise conferences and events, and that's how I got into managing functions. Then I was searching [10]to an interesting, new job and I thought [11]for working in one of the big hotels. I heard [12]for a temporary job going at the Excelsior, organising a snooker tournament. I had never heard [13]to snooker tournaments before! … But I have never suffered [14]on shyness, so I applied [15]about the job. They asked me to stay on when the tournament was over, and I stayed for three years. Then I decided to travel for a year and look [16]about the way other hotels are run. I spent far too much money [17]from hotels and good meals! Now I am starting a new job, this time in a four-star hotel in Nairobi, so I'm just home for a week. The nice thing about hotel work is you don't have to look [18]of a flat or anything – they provide you [19]for everything.'

Good luck in Africa, Cara!

0 _to_	5	10	15
1	6	11	16
2	7	12	17
3	8	13	18
4	9	14	19

(look at)

B Read the following speech and add the appropriate preposition from the box. Each one may be used more than once.

~~on~~	for	at	in	of	about	to

0 I'd like to congratulate you ......*on*...... passing your final English exams.

1 I would like to remind you .... how much you have improved this year.

2 At this time last year I would not have dreamed .... speaking .... you like this.

3 When I look .... you, I am proud of what we have achieved.

4 I haven't had to shout .... you very much, and you have listened .... everything I have told you.

5 Before you leave .... your far distant home, I'd like to say one more thing .... you.

6 I'd like to warn you .... losing self-confidence.

7 When you leave here, you will probably apply .... a new job.

8 If you are invited .... an interview, think .... what you are going to wear.

9 Your appearance is very important, so smile .... everyone.

10 Your life belongs .... you, and whatever happens .... you, keep believing .... yourself!

C Choose the best verb from the box to go in the gaps.

shouting	belong	collided	dream	~~accused~~	happened
heard	suffering	complained	listen	concentrate	

0 The police ...*accused*...... Harry Harvey of dangerous driving.

1 Harry .... to the officer at the desk.

2 He said he had never .... of such a terrible injustice.

3 The officer asked him to .... to him,

4 and stop .... at him or he would have to arrest him.

5 The officer reminded him he had .... with a bollard.

6 Mr Harvey said he had been .... from hay fever.

7 He said it could have .... to anyone.

8 The officer said it was important to .... on your driving.

9 He insisted he wouldn't .... of driving carelessly,

10 and that the car didn't even .... to him!

ANDREW: Hello Sally. **Come in**! Sit down and I'll **put** the kettle **on**. Tea or coffee?

SALLY: A coffee would be nice. You're looking a bit miserable. What's wrong?

ANDREW: Oh, nothing really. I suppose I'm a bit tired of my job. I've been teaching the same syllabus for ten years, and I just don't enjoy it any more. And Bob and Phyllis are driving me mad!

SALLY: You really should **stand up to** them. They are so lazy! I think they need to **find out** what it means to look after themselves. They don't respect you enough.

ANDREW: I know, and I'm always **tidying up** their mess. Ever since their mother died, I have been too soft on them.

SALLY: You've been a really great father to them, but you're right – it's time to **back off** now. But what about your work? You were always so keen on engineering ...

ANDREW: Oh yes, I haven't lost interest in my subject, but it's just not enough any more. I don't feel as if I have anything to **look forward to**. The kids are **growing up**; soon they'll be **going away** ... and I'm not so young any more ... I can't **carry on** like this ...

SALLY: Don't be silly! You've got years ahead of you! Maybe you need to **get out of** teaching.

ANDREW: I think you're right! But what on earth would I do? Perhaps I just need to **get away** for a while.

SALLY: No, I think you should think about a complete life change. Isn't there something you've always dreamed of? You've got enough money to take some time to **try out** some new experiences – to **find out** what you want to do.

ANDREW: Well, I've always loved motor bikes. And travelling. I've always wanted to **get out** and drive along the big highway just like in 'Easy Rider'. Sad, isn't it!

SALLY: Not at all! You've earned it! And while you're roaring through the countryside you can think about your future.

ANDREW: That sounds really cool! Oh, thank you Sally! You're a really good friend. I think I'll go and phone Graham.

SALLY: Hey, **watch out**! I don't want my husband getting any ideas!

❶ what is a phrasal verb?

Phrasal verbs consist of a **_verb + adverb_** which together have a particular meaning. It is often difficult to guess the meaning from the individual words.

There are three types of phrasal verb:

1 **_verb + adverb_** (with no object):
- Paul **stood up** and shouted at Graham.

2 **_verb + object + adverb_**:
- Anton **put** his favourite hat **on**.

verb + adverb + object / ing form:
- Anton **put on** his favourite hat.
- I've **given up** dieting.

3 **_verb + adverb + preposition + object_**:
- The hamster **got out of** its cage.

❷ verb + adverb (with no object)

verb + in:

go / **come in** = _enter a room or building_:
- Phyllis **went in** after the tennis match.
- You can **come in** now. Mr Thomas is ready to see you.

verb + on:

come on (an imperative) = _do something!_ or _accompany me!_:
- **Come on**! I think it's time to go now.

carry on = _continue_:
- You can **carry on**. You still have five minutes to finish the paper.

get on = _be good friends_:
- Phyllis and Lucy have always **got on** well.

verb + **up**:

> **stand up** = *rise to standing, stand straight*:
> ▪ We have to **stand up** when the mayor comes in.
> **get up** = *rise from your bed*:
> ▪ We never **get up** before 7.
> **sit up** = *sit in an upright position*:
> ▪ The children **sat up** and looked at the screen.
> **shut up** = *be quiet, stop talking*:
> ▪ I wish Sue would **shut up** sometimes! She talks too much.
> **wash up** = *wash dishes etc*:
> ▪ Paul **washed up** after dinner.
> **dry up** = *dry dishes etc. after they are washed*:
> ▪ Tom often **dries up** after lunch.
> **clean up** = *clean a room or other area*:
> ▪ It's important to **clean up** after painting.
> **tidy up** = *make a room or area tidy*:
> ▪ Don't forget to **tidy up** when you've finished working.
> **wake up** = *stop sleeping*:
> ▪ Sian **woke up** when the door slammed.
> **give up** = *stop*:
> ▪ Tim **gave up** college when he failed his exams.

verb + **down**:

> **sit down** = *move from standing to sitting*:
> ▪ It's best to **sit down** when you play the cello.
> **lie down** = *move to lying flat*:
> ▪ Reg **lay down** on the towel on the sand.

verb + **out**:

> **come out** = *leave a room or other place*:
> ▪ Francis **came out** before the exam was over.
> **go out** = *have a romantic relationship with someone*:
> ▪ Is it true that Frank and Carrie are **going out**?
> **go** / **get out** = *spend some time away from your home*:
> ▪ Shall we **go out** this afternoon? It's a lovely day.
> **look** / **watch out** = *be careful*:
> ▪ I told you to **look out**! That bicycle was going really fast.

verb + **away**:

> **go away** = *go on holiday* or *move to another (unknown) place*:
> ▪ Rita wants to **go away** for a while, possibly to Spain.
> ▪ Sue's **gone away**. I don't know where she is.
> **get away** = *move urgently* or *have a holiday*:
> ▪ **Get away** from the window! You'll be seen.
> ▪ We like to **get away** at least once a year.

verb + **back**:

> **come** / **get back** = *return*:
> ▪ I'll see you when I **come** / **get back** after work.

verb + **off**:

> **go off** = *to become rotten or sour*:
> ▪ I'm sure that milk has **gone off**!
> **back off** = *move back from someone or something*:
> ▪ John **backed off** when he saw the angry look in the man's face.

❸ verb + adverb + **ing** form

Some phrasal verbs can be used with an **ing** *form*. It always comes after the adverb:

> **carry on**:
> ▪ We have to **carry on walking**.
> **go out**:
> ▪ Barbara and Rory **went out dancing** last night.
> **come out**:
> ▪ It's important to **come out smiling**!
> **give up**:
> ▪ David **gave up driving** his car to work.

❹ verb + object + adverb

Phrasal verbs with an object can have the *object* after or before the adverb. If the object is one word it usually goes before:

> ▪ I really hate **washing** <u>pans</u> **up**. OR I really hate **washing up** <u>pans</u>.

If the *object* is a pronoun (**me**, **him**, **it**, **them**, **those** etc), it always goes before the adverb:

> ▪ You must **wash** <u>it</u> **up**. NOT ~~You really must wash up it~~.

verb (+ *object*) + **in**:
> **send / hand in** = *post or give something to an organisation*:
> ▪ I **sent / handed** my application form **in**.

verb (+ *object*) + **on**:
> **put on** = *dress yourself in clothes or shoes*:
> ▪ Karen wants to **put** her new shoes **on**.
> **put on** = *heat something, e.g. a kettle*:
> ▪ Would you like some coffee? Shall I **put** the kettle **on**?
> **try on** = *see if something fits you or looks nice*:
> ▪ Phyllis loves **trying on** other people's clothes.

verb (+ *object*) + **away**:
> **put away** = *put something in its correct place, e.g. in a cupboard, or drawer, or bag*:
> ▪ Ben, will you **put away** the knives and forks please?
> **take away** = *remove or take with you*
> ▪ If you take a piece in chess, you have to **take** it **away** from the board.
> **send (someone / something) away**:
> ▪ Mark's mother **sent** him **away** to school when he was seven.

verb (+ *object*) + **up**:
> **wash / clean up** = *wash the things used for a meal or clean something spilt or untidy*:
> ▪ Barbara forgot to **wash** the glasses **up**.
> ▪ Look at the mess! The boys should **clean** it **up**.
> **tidy up** = *make somewhere look neat and tidy*:
> ▪ I **tidied up** the sitting room.
> **pick up** = *lift, collect, or obtain*:
> ▪ Will you **pick up** some milk from the supermarket?
> **wake up** = *stop someone sleeping*:
> ▪ Silvia asked Mrs French to **wake** her **up** at 7.30.
> **stand up** = *make something upright*:
> ▪ Mr Davidson **stood** the skittles **up** and rolled the ball.
> **give up** = *stop doing or consuming something*:
> ▪ Kim has **given up** white sugar.

verb (+ *object*) + **out**:
> **try out** = *test a new thing*:
> ▪ Rhoda **tried** her new printer **out** this afternoon.

find out = *discover some new information*:
- Jack **found** everything **out** about his father!

send out:
- The college has **sent** a letter **out** to all the parents.

---

verb (+ *object*) + **back**:

send / bring / take / put / give back = *return something by post, or by hand*:
- Karen wants to **take** her dress **back** to the shop.
- **Put** that book **back** on the shelf, please.

---

verb (+ *object*) + **off**:

send off = *put in the post, or prepare someone to go somewhere*:
- Tom **sent** the parcel **off** this morning.
- Mrs Compton **sent** the children **off** to school early.

---

❺ verb + adverb + preposition + object

Phrasal verbs can also consist of a verb with an **adverb** and a **preposition**. The <u>object</u> always comes after the preposition:
- We've **run out of** <u>tea bags</u>.
- Jan saw her father and **ran up to** <u>him</u>.

---

verb + **up with**:

be / get fed up with = *bored and irritated by*:
- The students **are** all **fed up with** phrasal verbs.

---

verb + **in to**:

give in to = *stop resisting something*:
- Rachel said she would never **give in to** Paul's bullying.

---

verb + **out of**:

run out of = *use all of*:
- Phyllis has **run out of** coffee again.

get out of = *leave a building or institution urgently or escape from*:
- Paul wanted to **get out of** the army.

---

verb + **up of**:

made up of = *consist of, made of*:
- The coat was **made up of** bits of coloured cloth.

---

verb + **up to**:

go / walk / run up to = *approach, usually a person*:
- Greta **went up to** the guard and asked him where to go.

stand up to = *refuse to accept someone's behaviour or actions*:
- The union decided to **stand up to** the management.

---

verb + **away from**:

turn away from = *turn your back towards someone or something*:
- The teacher **turned away from** the board and looked at the class.

run away from = *escape*:
- I heard that Frank has **run away from** school again.

---

verb + **along with**:

go / play along with = *pretend to accept or agree with*:
- I wish Diane didn't always **go along with** everything you say.

---

verb + **forward to**:

look forward to = *be pleased because something is going to happen*:
- Everyone is **looking forward to** the summer holidays.

A

Choose the best adverb from the box to put in the gaps in the following conversation.

| out | on | out | up | back | up | on | up | out | up | out | up | on | out | of | up |

PHYLLIS: Come (0) ...*on*... , Jasmine. Let's go (1) .... tonight.

JASMINE: Oh no. I'm so tired I can hardly stand (2) ....

PHYLLIS: But you'll be fine once we get (3) .... Why don't you put your new dress (4) ....? I think it's great.

JASMINE: I tried it (5) .... in the shop and it looked OK, but it might be a bit too short. I think I might take it (6) .... to the shop.

PHYLLIS: Well, I thought it really suited you, and it's the fashion this year.

JASMINE: I don't know. Anyway, we have to wash (7) .... before we go. You know how annoyed Mum gets if we don't clean (8) .... after our meals.

PHYLLIS: Do we have to tidy the sitting room (9) .... as well?

JASMINE: No. I didn't make all that mess. That was Jake!

PHYLLIS: Why don't we try (10) .... the new local radio station? How do I find it?

JASMINE: I think it's 179. Oh no! We've run (11) .... (12) .... washing-up liquid! You'll have to go (13) .... and buy some.

PHYLLIS: Why don't we use shampoo? It's just the same, and we can pick (14) .... some washing-up liquid later while we're out.

JASMINE: Phyllis! You're so lazy! Just shut (15) ...., and go and get some washing-up liquid!

B

For each of the underlined phrases in this passage we could use a phrasal verb. List them below.

Stephen Cross shares a flat with his friend Bob. They usually [0]are good friends, but sometimes they get [1]bored and irritated by each other. Sometimes they get annoyed when they [2]have no more coffee or tea or milk and one of them has to [3]leave the house to [4]buy some more first thing in the morning. When Stephen [5]rises from his bed, he expects to have a nice cup of tea in a clean cup. But neither of them likes [6]washing plates and knives after their meals. If there are no clean cups, then Bob has to [7]be careful. Stephen often plays very loud music while he [8]dresses himself in his clothes, so he will be sure to [9]stop Bob sleeping. Bob usually just tells him to [10]be quiet!

0 *get on*	3	6	9 ....
1	4	7	10 ....
2	5	8	

C One of the idioms in each of the following sentences is wrong. Underline it and correct it at the end of the line.

0   Fishing is a very peaceful activity, and it's nice to get off in the fresh air for a few hours. ....*get out*....

1   Margaret Compton often sends her husband in for the day with a basket of sandwiches and his fishing gear. ....

2   He always gets down at the end of the day very calm and relaxed. ....

3   It doesn't matter very much if he doesn't catch anything, in fact, he often puts the fish off in the water. ....

4   He wanted his sons to join him, and in the end they gave out of him and went fishing. ....
....

5   James enjoyed it very much but Sam got fed out of it after an hour. ....

6   He turned up of his father and started to walk along the path by the lake. ....

7   There were lots of other fishermen all along the bank so he had to give on walking by the lake. ....

8   They got cross with him walking through their lines and sent him out. ....

9   He kicked a man's basket of worms over and he had to clean it all in. ....

10 His father decided the fishing trip was over and started to put his equipment in. ....

D Read the following sentences and rewrite each speech using a phrasal verb from the list.

pick up	~~tidy up~~	carry on	fed up with
clean up	give in to	take away	run out of
stand up	send off	put on	shut up

0   Pablo has not made the studio tidy. Tell him to do it.
' *Tidy up the studio, Pablo!* '

1   There is paint on the floor. Say you'll make it clean.
' .... '

2   There is a canvas lying on the floor. Say you think he should make it stand by the wall.
' .... '

3   A parcel is on the table. Tell him to post it.
' .... '

4   You want to remove one of the paintings.
' .... '

5   Tell him a man is coming to collect it this afternoon.
' .... '

6   Tell him he has no more money so he can't buy any paint.
' .... '

7   He must sell more pictures. Tell him he must continue painting.
' .... '

8   He says he is bored with painting the same things.
' .... '

9   You tell him to be quiet and start working.
' .... '

10 He says he will dress himself in his overalls …
' .... '

11 … and that he will finally agree to do what you say.
' .... '

GARGANTUAN GAMES

MR PATTERSON: Well, how's it going, Kim?

KIM: I'm not sure. I was quite **pleased with** the design of the last project but, actually, I'm a bit **tired of** doing warrior games. I'm quite **keen on** puzzles and adventure games ... you know, games where you have to work out clues and things.

MR P: I know. The thing is that Gargantuan Games is **famous for** its battle games. But I've been very **impressed by** your original ideas, so I'd like to give you the opportunity to be **responsible for** a whole new game project.

KIM: Wow! I thought you were a bit **cross with** me for arguing with you about the last one. I'm really **amazed at** this!

MR P: Oh no! I must say, I thought it was **stupid of** you to apply for another job without talking to me first. I'm actually really **pleased with** your work, and I'd like to give you the opportunity to try something original. I'm sure you're **capable of** it.

KIM: Well, thank you very much! I have a few ideas already if you have time to hear them ...

MR P: Not just at the moment, but we could meet again tomorrow. Will you make some notes and sketches, and then we can discuss you ideas?

KIM: Sure! This is great! I'm really **grateful to** you for giving me another chance. I feel quite **ashamed of** myself!

❶ adjective + of

After the empty subject **it** and a form of **be**, adjectives with **of** often describe *someone's behaviour*:

- It was really **nice of** John to take you home.
- It's **kind of** you to listen to my problems.
- It was **stupid of** him to miss the last bus.
- It will be **clever of** them if they win the election this time.
- It was very **rude of** Sarah to leave all her food.
- It was quite **brave of** Stanley to catch the horse.

Adjectives with **of** can often describe *how someone feels about something*:

- I'm **frightened of** snakes.
- Phyllis's father is a bit **ashamed of** her behaviour.
- Tom thinks you're **jealous of** him!
- Margaret's husband is never **suspicious of** her.
- The twins are very **fond of** each other.
- John is not **afraid of** flying.
- The students were **tired of** studying grammar. (**tired** = *bored, depressed*)

The following adjectives also go with **of**:

- The room was **full of** people.
- Bill is **short of** money at the moment. (**short** = *not having enough*)
- Are you **capable of** running a mile?

❷ adjective + **to**

Adjectives with **to** describe *a relationship to someone or something*:

- I thought Marjorie was **married to** Henry.
- Isn't Sue **engaged to** Jack?
- I'm very **grateful to** my English teacher.
- Greek yogurt is **similar to** cream.
- Your car is **different to** mine.

Note: We can also say **different from** with the same meaning:

- Your car is **different from** mine.

❸ adjective + **with**

Adjectives with **with** often describe *feelings about something*:

- Mrs Compton is **pleased with** her garden.
- Diego sometimes gets **angry with** his trainer.
- Don't be **cross with** me! I'm sorry!
- Stephen's very **happy with** his new flat.
- Be careful! The teacher will be **furious with** you! (**furious** = *very angry*)
- George was **delighted with** his new car. (**delighted** = *very happy and excited*)
- The stadium was **crowded with** football fans. (**crowded** = *very full of people or things*)

We can use **annoyed** and **bored** with **by** or **with**:

- Graham was **annoyed by** / **with** the man in the bike repair shop. (**annoyed** = *irritated*)
- I'm really **bored by** / **with** this job now.

❹ adjective + **by**

When we use verbs *describing feelings* in passive sentences, the past participles (e.g. **impressed**, **surprised**) are used like adjectives. They are followed with **by** to talk about the cause of the feeling:

- The professor was not very **impressed by** Keith's essay.
- The audience were very **excited by** the trapeze act.

(For more on passives, see unit 30.)

❺ adjective + **at** (or **by**)

Past participles with **at** describe *surprise caused by something*; we can also use **by**, instead of **at**, with these adjectives:

- Peter is always **surprised at** the number of people who attend his lectures.
- I'm quite **shocked by** the news today.
- Paul was **amazed at** how much the shoes cost.

❻ adjective + **for**

- Beyonce is **famous for** her exciting stage show.
- The manager is **responsible for** the staff.

❼ adjective + **on**

- Sabina is very **keen on** dancing. (**keen on** = *enthusiastic about*)

A Put the correct preposition in each gap.

of	with	for	at	by	on

0 The show is nearly ready to go on. The director is quite happy _with_ it.

1 Tina, the leading actress, is frightened .... the leading actor because he's famous, and she isn't.

2 It was very brave .... the director to give her that part.

3 The leading actor, Brett, is famous .... being rude to people.

4 He was very angry .... his agent for making him act with a beginner.

5 Tina is capable .... doing the part very well.

6 Brett was surprised .... how good she was.

7 The director is responsible .... giving her confidence.

8 The foyer is crowded .... people, all talking excitedly.

9 Some of them aren't very keen .... modern theatre.

10 The cast is very pleased .... the number of people in the audience.

B Rewrite the underlined sentences using the adjective in the brackets.

0 My car is very old and not very clean. <u>This makes me feel bad about my car.</u> (ashamed)
I am ashamed of my car.

1 Although my car is very slow and unreliable <u>I really like driving</u>. (keen)

....

2 My car often breaks down. <u>My car makes me angry</u>. (annoyed)
I am ....

3 Once I broke down in the middle of the high street. <u>There was a lot of traffic</u>. (crowded)

....

4 My dad bought a new Mazda recently. <u>His new car makes him very happy</u>. (delighted)
He is ....

5 It was very expensive. <u>The price really surprised me</u>. (amazed)

6 My mum didn't expect him to spend so much. <u>She did not think he had done very well</u>. (impressed)

....

7 She did not think they could afford it. <u>They didn't have much money</u>. (short)

....

8 Dad said it was great. <u>He could make financial decisions</u>. (capable)

....

9 She really thinks the car is lovely. <u>The choice was very clever</u>. (clever)
It was ....

10 I wish I could afford such a great car. <u>Mine is really depressing</u>. (tired)

....

Read the following text and choose the best adjective in the table to go in each gap.

adjectives with **in**	adjectives with **of**	adjectives with **by**	adjectives with **on**	adjectives with **for**	adjectives with **with**	adjectives with **at**
interested	full	annoyed	keen	~~responsible~~	delighted	shocked
	short			famous	crowded	surprised
	afraid					

This is a photo of the archaeological dig we visited last week.

Professor Schraff was (0) _responsible_ for the dig, which is taking place on the site of an iron age settlement in Bavaria. The site is (1) .... for its natural beauty and, at first, the local authority was (2) .... of the archaeologists ruining the environment, but now they are very (3) .... on supporting the dig. However, the local people are a bit (4) .... by the disruption. When they first discovered human remains, the area was (5) .... with curious people. Local people were (6) .... at discovering that they had been living on a graveyard. The burial pits were (7) .... of broken pottery and even some metal implements. Professor Schraff was (8) .... with what they found in one grave: the skeleton of a horse and chariot with iron wheels. The archaeologists were very (9) .... at this, because they had not found anything like it in northern Europe. Unfortunately they were very (10) .... of volunteer diggers. Are any of our readers (11) .... in coming and helping us?

For the first time in ten years Peter and Mary Ross went **on holiday**. They left the farm with their friend Tom and the staff. They went **by car**, and **on the way** to Italy through France they stopped and stayed at a campsite. They had booked **in advance on the Internet**, so they only had to put up their tent, have a meal in the camp restaurant, and go to sleep. When they left the campsite, they went **for lunch** in a little bistro in a village they were passing through and Peter found he had lost his credit card! He had to pay for his lunch **in cash**. He phoned the campsite office and they said he had left his card there **by mistake**. They had to go all the way back to collect it. He was very grateful that they were so honest, and gave them a good reference on their website **in the end**.

On the whole the journey was good, but Mary was a bit seasick **on the boat** going over to Sardinia, even though the sea was very calm. The boat was very **up to date**, with a bar and cinema and even a gym, but Mary just stayed **on deck**. Sardinia is so beautiful that they both felt the problems on the journey were worth it **in the end**; they spent a wonderful relaxing week **in the sun**. They didn't phone the farm once to find out how they were getting on!

❶ on + (article) + noun

on holiday:
■ Carol met Lucy when she was **on holiday**.

on the / a journey / trip / tour:
■ The Comptons are going **on a tour** of the harbour.

on the way (to) = *travelling somewhere*:
■ I saw Tom **on the way to** the cinema.

on time = *at the right time, not late*:
■ The dinner guests arrived **on time**.

on foot = *walking*:
■ You have to go **on foot** as there is no road.

on the / a boat / train / plane etc:
■ Hello? I'm **on the train** at the moment. Can you phone me later?

on deck = *on the top of a boat or ship*:
■ Bob loves sitting **on deck** doing nothing.

on the whole = *generally*:
■ I think I prefer Greece, **on the whole**.

on purpose = *deliberately, not accidentally*:
■ George left his credit card at home **on purpose**.

on TV / television:
■ Paul Trotman used to be **on TV**.

on the radio / the Internet:
■ What's **on the radio** at the moment?

❷ in + (article) + noun

in (good) time (for) = *before something happens*:
■ I hope we get there **in time for** Andrew's speech.

in the way = *obstructing something*:
■ I'm afraid your car is **in the way**. Can you move it?

in someone's way = *preventing someone from moving forward*:
■ The rock was **in the climber's way**.

in a way = *partly, not totally*:
■ I think he's quite shy, **in a way**.

in general = *mostly, usually*:
- People are quite impatient **in general**.

in the end = *finally*:
- It's alright because they got married **in the end**.

(right) in the middle (of):
- There is an island right **in the middle of** the lake.

in advance = *before*:
- Mr Gray prefers to book his holiday a year **in advance**.

in someone's opinion = *this is what I / you / they think*:
- **In my opinion**, that hat is too big for you.

in cash = *with notes and coins*:
- They don't take credit cards so you have to pay **in cash**.

put something **in writing**:
- They asked Tom to put his complaint **in writing**.

in ink / pencil:
- Susan often does little sketches **in ink**.

❸ by + (article) + noun

by cheque / credit card:
- The restaurant did not accept payment **by credit card**, so Paul had to pay **by cheque**.

by mistake = *not deliberately*:
- Did you touch me **by mistake**, or did you want to tell me something?

by chance = *something not planned, but good*:
- Sue met her brother in the street **by chance**.

by accident = *something bad, and not planned*:
- She bumped into him **by accident**.

by means of:
- Some native Americans used to communicate **by means of** smoke signals.

by the time = *before or at a particular time*:
- **By the time** Simon gets to Fiji, we will be in New York.

by the end (of) = *before something finishes*:
- Tom will have finished the report **by the end of** tomorrow.

❹ at + the + noun

at the (very) end (of) = *when or where something finishes*:
- They stopped singing **at the end of** the chorus.

at the (very) beginning of:
- **At the beginning of** the meal they served soup.

❺ other prepositions + noun

for example:
- David loves romantic music, **for example** Tchaikovsky.

out of date = *old-fashioned or too old to use*:
- That jacket looks really **out of date**. You've had it for 15 years!

up to date = *very modern*:
- My dad loves modern music – the more **up to date**, the better!

A Select the best phrase from the box to go in each gap in the following sentences.

> in the middle   in the end   on time   ~~on the way~~
> by mistake   in good time for   on purpose
> in their way   in her opinion   on foot
> In general   on TV

0   Annie and Josh were _on the way_ to the TV studio.

1   They had been invited to be in a game show ....!

2   They had left home very early so they would be sure to get there ....

3   They took the underground and then went .... so they wouldn't be held up by traffic.

4   ...., the underground is reliable.

5   They had just come out of the underground station and they saw a barrier right .... of the road.

6   It was ...., so they had to go by another route.

7   Josh looked at the map and, ..., decided to go left.

8   Annie said that, ..., they should go right.

9   She was holding the map upside down ....

10 She said she wasn't doing it ...., she was just nervous.

11 Fortunately, they got to the theatre .... the show.

B Choose a preposition from the box to put in each gap in the following conversation.

> on   for   in   by

Mrs Khan has just got back from the supermarket. She is talking to her husband, Qasim, in the kitchen ...

ANISHA: The supermarket was so busy! I went (0) _by_ car because it was late and I was afraid of not getting there (1) .... time before it shut. I should have planned what I was going to get (2) .... advance, because I always get more than I need if I don't have a list. (3) .... a way, it's better not taking the car, as you don't buy so much. I saw this advert (4) .... television about a special offer on tins of tuna, so I bought six. But they were so heavy that the bag broke (5) .... the way from the car to the kitchen!

QASIM: You can order food (6) .... the Internet now, and they deliver it to your home the same day. Why don't you use that service?

ANISHA: Yes, but that way you don't get all the special offers. (7) .... example, while I was there, I noticed some lovely cheap avocados so I bought six, and I know you love avocado salad. I don't buy avocados from the supermarket (8) .... general, because they are usually too hard, but these ones are nice and soft. Oh, and I had to pay (9) .... cheque as I forgot my credit card.

QASIM: That's fine. (10) .... my opinion, it's better not to use the credit card, so long as you fill in the cheque stub!

(in time, for example)

C Read the discussion and find a mistake in each speech. Circle the phrase that is wrong and write the correct phrase at the end of each speech.

0   TIM: We have to get across the river (by time) to reach the next meeting point at 3.30. How are we going to do it? ......*in time*......

1   NIGEL: At my opinion it would be best to build a raft. There's plenty of wood along the river bank. ....

2   TIM: But the current is quite strong. We might get pulled downstream by the way across. ....

3   JULIAN: Well, what about building a bridge of some sort? We've got some equipment we could use, in example this rope. ....

4   DAVID: But how can we attach it of the end? ....

5   NIGEL: And how would we support it at the middle of the river? ....

6   TIM: They taught us how to make a raft on advance. We could throw the rope over and pull ourselves across. ....

7   DAVID: There's a post on the opposite bank that looks as if it was put there in purpose. ....

8   JULIAN: Well, let's see if we have enough rope. But hurry, because at the time we get across, we will only have a few minutes to find the meeting place. ....

9   NIGEL: Oh no! I've just dropped my knife in accident into the water! ....

10 TIM: I'll try and get it. I can see it … Oh no! There's a big tree root at the way. ....

11 JULIAN: On the end, we will all wish we had never come for this stupid adventure holiday. ....

70

Pygmalion was a young sculptor from Cyprus. He didn't like women **and** thought they were wicked and stupid, **but** he loved making statues of them. He may have been trying to create the perfect woman, **who** could not exist in real life. There was one statue **that** he worked on for so long, **and** with such inspiration, **that** it became more beautiful than any woman that had ever lived **or** been carved in stone. **As** he worked on the statue's features, they became exquisitely lovely, **and** he found himself hammering **and** carving with increasing affection. **When** he finally finished the statue, there stood such a perfect woman that Pygmalion fell deeply in love.

His statue didn't seem to be made of stone, **but** of flesh. In desperate anger he embraced the cold marble girl. It was ironic that this man, who had hated **and** despised women, should fall in love with a woman who could never love him in return! He tried to pretend that she was real **and** dressed her in fine clothes, and brought her flowers and gifts, **but** he was terribly unhappy.

The goddess of love, Aphrodite, felt sorry for the young man **and**, **when** he went to her temple, she gave him a sign, **and** Pygmalion went home, wondering what the sign meant. **When** he entered his studio **and** saw Galatea, he ran to his statue **and** embraced it. Did she seem warm to his touch **or** was it just the heat from the sun that had warmed the stone? He stood back **and** looked at her. He watched in amazement **as** Galatea began to move. She turned towards him and smiled, **and**, **as soon as** she saw him, she stepped off her pedestal into his arms.

The goddess Aphrodite herself attended their wedding.

❶ what are conjunctions?

Conjunctions are words or phrases which join two or more clauses or phrases together. They show the relationship between the ideas in the clauses. There are three kinds of conjunctions: *simple*, *time*, and *logical*. Conjunctions must go at the beginning of the second clause. We can put the second clause first, except if the clause begins with **and**, **but**, or **or**.

Simple conjunctions can tell us that the second clause has additional (**and**), contrasting (**but**), or alternative (**or**) information. We can use a simple conjunction with another conjunction when there are three clauses:

1	2	3

- John went to Madrid **and**, **as soon as** he could, he phoned home.
- Paul left for the airport **but**, **before** he did, he booked his ticket first.

Time conjunctions (**when**, **as**, **while**, **as soon as**, **before**, **after** etc) can tell us about the time relationship between two or more clauses.

Some *logic conjunctions* (**so**, **because**, **unless**, **if** etc) can tell us about the logical relationship between the clauses.

Other *logic* conjunctions (**though**, **although**, **in spite of**) can tell us about a contrasting logic between the ideas in the two clauses.

(For more on logic conjunctions, see unit 71.)

❷ simple conjunctions (**and**, **but**, **or**)

We can use **and** when we *list two things*. If there are more than two things in a list, we use **and** before the last one:

▨ Can I have a cup of coffee, a glass of water, **and** a croissant, please?

Also, when we are describing something with adjectives, we use **and** before the last adjective when they are after the verb:

▨ The soldier was young **and** tall.

We also use **and** to *add more information*. We use it before the second clause or phrase:

▨ Laura told Steve to go away **and** stay away!

We use **but** when we want to give additional information which is *in contrast* with the first clause. Like **and**, it usually only goes in the middle of a sentence:

▨ Joanna liked Gail **but** she didn't really trust her.

We use **or** when we want to talk about *an alternative* to the idea in the first clause, or in a list where we are offering alternatives:

▨ I'd like to see a film **or** go to the theatre.
▨ Shall we have soup **or** pasta as a starter?

We don't usually use **and** or **but** at the beginning of a sentence, but we can do it in informal conversation and writing;

▨ **And** she gave him back his ring.
▨ **But** why did she change her mind?

❸ time conjunctions (**when**, **while**, **as**, **as soon as**, **before**, **after**, **until**)

Time conjunctions tell us about *the relationship in time* between two ideas:

▨ I'll bring some fruit **when** I come to lunch.

Note: After a time conjunction we usually use a present tense verb to talk about the future:

▨ NOT ~~I'll bring some fruit when I'll come for lunch~~.

We use **when** to say that two things happen *at the same moment*:

▨ Sam was playing football **when** I arrived at the house.
▨ **When** Jane stopped talking, silence fell over the room.

We use **while** to talk about two things which *continue together for a period of time*:

▨ Most people like to listen to music **while** they work.
▨ **While** the snow fell, the children watched through the window.

We use **as** or **just as** to talk about something that happens *while something else is happening*:

▨ The car came round the corner **just as** the dog ran out.
▨ **As** Lorna turned round, she slipped and fell.

(**As** can also mean *because*. For more on this use of **as**, see unit 71.)

We use **as soon as** to say that something happens *immediately after something else*:

▨ **As soon as** the door closed, the children started laughing.
▨ You can have some tea **as soon as** the kettle boils.

We use **before** to talk about something that happens *at an earlier time to something else*:

▨ It's best to think **before** you speak.

We use **after** to talk about something that happens *at a later time than something else*:

▨ I'm meeting James **after** I've been to the dentist.

We use **until** or **till** to talk about *something that continues for some time before something else happens*:

▨ Sarah's going to wait **until** Paul gets here.

A Read the following passage and add the best conjunction from the box in each gap.

> and   and   and   and   and   and   ~~but~~   but   but   when   as   as   as
>
> as soon as   as soon as   after   or

Anna and Sam had had a great day, walking in the country, (0) _but_ they got lost on the way home. (1) .... they walked along the road, they saw some lights in the distance. It might have been a car (2) .... a lorry. The road was very narrow (3) .... it was very dark. (4) .... they saw the lights, they immediately climbed up onto the bank (5) .... waited for it to come closer. (6) .... they left home that morning, they had forgotten to take a torch with them, so the driver would not be able to see them. (7) .... the lights got closer, they wondered if they would get splashed. The grass was very wet (8) .... their shoes were soaked. (9) .... the lights got nearer, they recognised the colour (10) .... shape of the car. It was their friend Bob's car, (11) .... he wasn't driving. It was his mate Mike at the wheel. They jumped down into the road (12) .... waved their arms. (13) .... he saw them, he stopped. He was very surprised (14) .... amazed to meet them on that road (15) .... , (16) .... they explained to him what had happened, he just laughed.

B Lucy and her friend Karen are talking about their last holidays. Read the conversation and circle which of the two underlined conjunctions is better in each case.

LUCY: Well, we went to southern Italy, but it was quite cold! I thought it would be warm at Easter (0)(but)/ or while we were there, we only had one day of sunshine. The stupid thing was that, [1]while / after we got back, it was really warm here!

KAREN: [2]Or / But was it nice anyway? I've never been there.

LUCY: Oh yes, it was fabulous [3]and / but I wish we had gone later in the year. We went to both Pompeii [4]or / and Herculaneum. It was raining [5]while / and we were there, [6]or / but it was almost better like that. There were hardly any people there, so we could walk around slowly [7]and / but peacefully, and take our time looking at the ruins. [8]While / Before we went, we bought a book about it so we knew what to look for.

KAREN: I'd love to see Pompeii. Maybe I can persuade Alan to take me [9]when / as he has his next holiday.

C Look at the following pairs of sentences. Join them with a suitable conjunction from the box to make one sentence. Sometimes you can put the conjunction at the beginning.

| before   when   but   while   and |

0   Mr Patterson is late. He decides to drive to work.
Mr Patterson is late and he decides to drive to work.

1   He goes to the garage. He gets his mobile phone from the kitchen.

2   He gets to the main road. He sees there is a lot of traffic.

3   He is waiting to turn into the main road. He decides to take another route.

4   He tries to get in the right lane to turn off. The cars won't let him in.

5   He is sitting there waiting. His mobile phone rings.

6   He doesn't have a hands-free phone. He knows the law that you can't use an ordinary mobile phone while driving.

7   The car isn't moving. There isn't a police car in sight.

8   He decides to answer it. He decides to take a risk.

9   He is talking on the phone. A police motorbike comes up beside him.

10   He puts the phone down. He doesn't put it down quickly enough!

D Look at the following sentences. Each one is missing a conjunction. Put the conjunction in brackets in the right place in the sentence.

0   The Compton family didn't have a garden *before* they moved to this house. (before)

1   Margaret Compton loves her garden works in it at the weekend. (and)

2   She is specially proud of her roses, clematis, dahlias. (and)

3   She also has a vegetable garden she doesn't like it as much as her flowers. (but)

4   Her husband helps her with the vegetables he isn't working. (when)

5   She is working in the garden she wears a big straw hat. (while)

6   This year the spring has been very wet the flowers are really lovely. (and)

7   She is trying to grow freesias this year they are quite delicate. (but)

8   Her son James has given her a book about chemical-free gardening, she is going to try not to use pesticides. (and)

9   There are lots of rose buds, she picks a big bunch of them and puts them in the sitting room. (as soon as)

10   They open, they make the room smell lovely. (as)

Gemini
Your horoscope for December

Love:

If you're looking for love, then you won't have to look far. But, **because** the astrological influences in your sign are very intense at the moment, **if** you're thinking of a calm and pleasant affair, you may be disappointed!
Obsession and revenge are in the air **so**, whoever you get involved with, you may find you get more than you expect **unless** you choose someone slow and steady. **Although** they may seem dull, in the end you will be glad you chose someone reliable.

Life:

You are probably thinking of moving office or home **because** there are a lot of suitcases in your chart this month. **Although** you might have to pay more than you want to, it will be worth it, **as long as** you think about it carefully first.
You always love travel, **because** of your adventurous nature, but don't travel alone this month **because** you may need some help in a difficult situation.

Money:

Although you are not usually very careful with money, it's important not to spend too wildly this month. **If** you have some money saved, now is the time to invest it wisely, **so** you should get some professional advice.
Although you need to try to be a bit more careful than usual this month, if you succeed, then next month you won't have any problems. **Unless** you resist throwing your money away on things you don't really need, you will have no money to enjoy next month.

❶ what are logic conjunctions?

Conjunctions are words or phrases which join two phrases or clauses together. They show the relationship between the ideas in separate clauses. There are *simple conjunctions*, *time conjunctions*, and *logic conjunctions*. (For more on simple and time conjunctions, see unit 70.)

Logic conjunctions (**so**, **because**, **as**, **unless**, **if** etc) can tell us about the logical relationship between the ideas in the two clauses. They can also tell us if there is a *contrast* or *conflict* between the information in the two clauses (**though**, **although** etc).

❷ if, even if, unless

We use **if** when we are talking about a *condition* and a *consequence*. The condition clause begins with **if**:

  ■ **If** you meet me at three, we can go to the lesson together.
  ■ Tom would pass his written exam **if** he did enough work.

(For more on conditional clauses, see units 28 and 29.)

We use **even if** when the information in the main clause is *unexpected* because of some information in the **even if** clause:

  ■ **Even if** you haven't got any money, we can still go to the cinema. I'll pay!
  ■ Dennis wants to play keyboards in the band **even if** they don't pay him.

We use **unless** to mean *if not*:

  ■ I won't know what to do **unless** you tell me the truth! (= … *if you don't tell me the truth*.)
  ■ **Unless** you hurry up, we'll be late for the lesson! (= *If you don't hurry up*, …)

❸ so (that), because, as

We use **so** at the beginning of the second clause to say that the second clause is the *consequence* of the first:

- It was raining **so** we decided not to go and play tennis.

We use **so that** to say that *something makes something else possible*:

- The Romans built aqueducts **so that** they could have fresh running water far from rivers.

We use **as** to say that something is the *cause* of something. Remember the two clauses can go in either order. If the **as** clauses comes first, we usually add a comma:

- We decided not to play tennis **as** it was raining. OR **As** it was raining, we decided not to play tennis.

We use **because** (like **as**) to explain the *cause* of something. The clauses can go in either order:

- Iannis often goes to Cyprus **because** he owns a house there. OR **Because** Iannis owns a house in Cyprus, he often goes there.

Note: We do not use both **so** and **because** in the same sentence:

- NOT ~~**Because** Iannis owns a house in Cyprus, **so** he often goes there~~.

❹ as long as, in case

We use **as long as** to say that something *depends on something else*. It has a meaning like *on the condition that*:

- Jenny wants a sandwich **as long as** there isn't any meat in it.

We use **in case** before a clause to talk about *something that may happen*. The clauses can go in either order:

- Laura's decided to take a book **in case** she gets bored.

We also use **in case of** before a ***noun phrase***:

- You should keep the doors closed **in case of** a fire.

❺ although, even though, in spite of

We use **although** when we want to show that *information that we would expect to hear in the second clause is not there*. We usually use it at the beginning of the first clause, but we can use the second clause first:

- **Although** the room was untidy, it was very clean. OR The room was untidy **although** it was very clean.
- **Although** the bag was very expensive, she bought it. OR She bought the bag **although** it was very expensive.

Though means almost the same as **although**, but it is a bit weaker. The contrast in the information is not very great. This is not often used in the first clause:

- Tom didn't think he would fail the exam, **though** he wasn't very sure.

Even though means the same as **although** but is a bit stronger:

- Helen liked Paul's house **even though** it was very small.
- **Even though** it was raining hard, they went by bicycle.

We use **in spite of** before a ***noun phrase*** to say that *something, surprisingly, did not prevent something else from happening*. We can put the two ideas in either order:

- **In spite of** the bad weather, Karen enjoyed her holiday. OR Karen enjoyed her holiday **in spite of** the bad weather.

A

Read the following story and choose the best conjunction from the list to put in each gap. Sometimes more than one answer is possible.

in case	as long as	~~so~~	unless
though	in spite of		as long as
because	so	although	because

Ahmed really wants to go to university and become a lawyer. At the moment he is working in his father's shop and studying at evening classes. He has to work (0) _so_ he can pay his university fees next year. He left school at 16 (1) .... he didn't know what he wanted to do at that time. He thought it would be easier to go into his father's business, (2) .... he was not very interested in retail management. His father was happy for him to come and help in the shop (3) .... he promised to keep studying in the evenings. He is finding the work quite hard but, (4) .... the long hours, he is doing very well. He is studying maths, history and politics at A-level (5) ...., if he gets high enough grades, he will be able to do law. He has applied to Oxford but, (6) .... he doesn't get a place there, he has also applied to Reading and York universities. He would really prefer to go back to Pakistan, (7) .... his parents are not very happy about it. His ambition is to become a barrister in the criminal courts (8) .... he has a very strong sense of justice, and he loves arguing! His teachers say he has a very good chance of doing well, (9) .... he keeps working hard. So, (10) .... something goes wrong, Mr Khan will have to find a new manager next year.

B

Make a sentence from the following pairs of sentences. Use the conjunction in the brackets.

0 It is very hot. Mrs Compton is working in her garden. (in spite of)
In spite of the heat, Mrs Compton is working in her garden.

1 She's wearing her big, straw hat. Her children hate it. (even though)

....

2 She must water the roses. If she doesn't, they will die. (unless)

....

3 You shouldn't water plants in strong sunlight. It damages the leaves. (because)

....

4 The lawn is very dry. She turns on the sprinkler in the evening. (so)

....

5 There are lots of weeds in the flower-bed. She weeds it every weekend. (although)

....

6 She must do something. The slugs will eat all her vegetables. (unless)

....

7 She won't use pesticides. It is dangerous for the birds. (as)

....

8 Someone said you should put human hair around the plants. The slugs don't like it. (because)

....

9 She isn't going to use hair. It might work. (even if)

....

10 It is a horrible job. She prefers to pull the slugs off with her hands. (even though)

....

C Match the two halves of the following sentences.

0 The Magic Café is not doing very well

1 The customers have stopped coming

2 The manager thinks they may come back

3 They thought customers who liked Greek food would stay

4 People now prefer the Globe next door

5 The café manager has decided to make some changes to the menu

6 People are suspicious of the new menu

7 The owner won't make any really big changes

8 They agree to change the name of the restaurant

9 Eventually they agree on a new name

10 Now the new restaurant is called 'Bistro Eumenides' and everyone is happy

A if the cafe reduces its prices.

B even though the old menu was very successful.

C because there are no other Greek restaurants in town.

D in spite of a lot of arguments.

E because they have lost their old chef.

F unless all the employees agree on them.

G even though the new name is hard to say!

H although the new chef is very good.

I in spite of its horrible décor.

J even though the new menu is better than the old one.

K as long as they can all choose the new name.

0 ___*E*___   3 _____   6 _____   9 _____
1 _____   4 _____   7 _____   10 _____
2 _____   5 _____   8 _____

TABLE 1   **types of words and their use**

1 nouns and pronouns

A *noun*, or naming word, has a singular and a plural form. A noun can be one word or it can be made of two or more words. Usually the plural has a final **s**, but there are many irregular plurals:

>   house, houses   party, parties
>   koala bear, koala bears   running track, running tracks

(For more on nouns, see unit 1, and for irregular noun plurals, see Table 3.)

There are two different kinds of nouns:

> *proper nouns* (which start with a capital letter) are names of places, people, or unique things:
> Hawaii   Mount Kilimanjaro   Karen   the Crown Jewels   Saturn
> *common nouns* are all the other nouns:
> book   river   man   window   science   light

Pronouns are words which are used in place of nouns. There are four different kinds of pronoun:

> *subject pronouns* – I, you, he, she, it, we, you, they:
> ■ The bird is in the back garden. **It** is singing.
> *object pronouns* – me, you, him, her, it, us, you, them:
> ■ Mrs Grant sent **me** an email.
> *possessive pronouns* – mine, yours, his, hers, its, ours, yours, theirs:
> ■ That coat is **hers**.
> *reflexive pronouns* – myself, yourself, himself, herself, itself, ourselves, yourselves, themselves:
> ■ The cat is washing **itself**.

(For more on pronouns, see unit 6. For more on possessive and reflexive pronouns, see unit 9.)

2 articles and other determiners

The *indefinite article* (**a** or **an**) before the noun tells us that *it doesn't matter*, or that *we don't know, which person or thing it is:*

> ■ **A** bird is singing. (*It doesn't matter which bird.*)
> ■ I heard **an** awful noise. (*I don't know what made the noise.*)

If we use the *definite article* (**the**) before the noun, it can tell us that *we already know which one it is:*

> ■ **The** bird is singing. (*The bird I told you about before.*)
> ■ I heard **the** awful noise of hammering. (*A noise I recognised.*)

(For more on articles, see unit 2.)

In addition to articles, there are other types of words that come before a noun, or *adjective* + *noun*. They are all called *determiners*, and they are:

> *demonstratives* – this, these, that, those (See unit 5.)
> *possessives* – my, your, his, her, its, our, your, their (See unit 7.)
> *quantifiers* – some, any, every, each, enough (See units 49–51.)

3 main verbs and auxiliary verbs

A *main verb* comes immediately, or very soon, after the subject and tells you what the subject does or what the subject feels:

subject	verb
The lion	roars.
I	understand.

Each of these examples is a *sentence*. A basic sentence has all the information needed to communicate a simple idea.

Verbs have four possible forms:

an *infinitive*:

paint, look, offer, rain etc. (often with **to**)

a *third person singular* ending after **he**, **she**, **it** etc:

paints, looks, offers, rains

an **ing** *form*:

painting, looking, offering, raining

a *past* (**ed**) *form*:

painted, looked, offered, rained

Most verbs have the same form in the infinitive and present simple, but **be** is *irregular*:

be – am, are, is

A lot of common verbs have different past participle and past simple forms:

go – been, went

(For a complete list of irregular past forms, see Table 2.)

To add meaning to the main verb, we can add an *auxiliary verb* (**do**, **have**, **will**, **be**).

We use the auxiliary **do** to make questions and negatives, and as a substitute for other verbs:

■ '**Do** you like rock music?' 'Yes, I **do**.'

■ We **don't** know how to make chapattis.

We use the auxiliary verb **have** with a past participle (**ed** *form* of the main verb) for the perfect forms:

■ I **have worked** for Gargantuan for three years.

We use the auxiliary verb **be** with the present participle (**ing** *form* of the main verb) to indicate that something continues for some time:

■ Sheila**'s playing** tennis at the club.

(For more on verbs, see units 12–26.)

Main verbs can be either *passive* or *active*. We make the passive form with **be** and the past participle:

■ Harry **is given** a lot of encouragement.

■ Don't **be tricked** by anyone!

(For more on passive verbs, see units 30 and 31.)

4 modal verbs

Modals are like auxiliary verbs, but they tell us different types of things about the main verb. They have only one form. Examples of modals are **must**, **might**, **may**, **should**, **ought to**, **will**, **have to**. After a modal verb we use the main verb in the infinitive. We use modals to say:

whether something is *necessary*:
- I **must** go now.
- They **must** pay for their meal.

whether something is *right or wrong*:
- Students **shouldn't** copy other people's work.
- Jack **ought to** stop laughing at Gail.

how *probable* something is:
- This book **will** help you pass the exam. (Note: **will** *is an auxiliary and a modal.*)
- **Shall** we try again?

how *possible* something is:
- I **might** not finish the paper in the time.
- Ahmed **may** get here this evening.

that someone is *capable of* doing something:
- Philip **can** do the tango!
- He **can't** make very good coffee.

that we are *asking permission or offering* to do something:
- **May** I talk to you for a minute?
- **Would** you like another piece of cake?

(For more on modal verbs, see units 36–44.)

5 describing words: adjectives and adverbs

To *describe* things and situations we use **adjectives**. These usually go before the noun:
- Jeffrey bought Sue a **beautiful** handbag.

We also use adjectives to *describe how something is or seems*. They usually go after the verb:
- The flowers were **bright orange**.

(Look at unit 45 for more on adjectives.)

We also use the adjectives **my**, **your**, **his / her / its**, **our**, **your**, **their**, to talk about *possession*. They go before the noun:
- Where is **your** wife?

We can give more information about actions and states with **adverbs**. They may be one word or a phrase. There are several different categories of adverbs:

adverbs of manner (or comment) – These often end in **-ly** and go after the verb:
- The British gymnast landed **awkwardly**.

adverbs of time – These usually go at the end of the sentence:
- Tom always goes to bed **very late**.

adverbs of place – These usually go after the verb:
- A large black cat ran **across the bridge**.

adverbs of frequency – These usually go before the verb:
- The prime minister **usually** has a body guard.

adverbs of probability – These usually go before the verb:
- It's **definitely** going to rain.

adverbs of focus (or emphasis) – These usually go before the verb:
- Lucy has **only** been here for two days.

adverbs of quantity (intensifiers or *diminishers)* – These usually go before an adjective:

  ■ You are **totally** wrong!

(For more on adverbs, see unit 46.)

6 prepositions

To say *where* or *when something happened* we need to use *prepositions* (**in**, **at**, **on**, **under**, **through** etc). They are at the beginning of the phrases they refer to. These phrases are called *prepositional phrases*. Usually the prepositional phrase goes after the verb, but we also sometimes put it at the beginning of the sentence, especially in written English:

  ■ There was a shed **in** the back garden. = **In** the back garden, there was a shed.

Sometimes we use a preposition on its own at the end of a sentence, especially if it is part of a *phrasal verb*:

  ■ Maria told me to put my coat **on**.

(For more on prepositions, see units 52–3, and for phrasal verbs, see unit 67.)

7 subjects

The *subject* of a clause or sentence is the person or thing who does the action or is the agent of the main verb. A subject may be:

  a noun or noun phrase:
  ■ **The old house next door** is empty.
  a determiner:
  ■ **That** smells nice!
  or a pronoun:
  ■ **We** have finished our homework.

In questions the subject goes after the auxiliary verb or **be**:

  ■ Have **you** seen my file?
  ■ Is **it** on the table?

8 objects

The *object* of a clause or sentence tells you who or what the subject acted on. The object may be a noun, or a phrase made up of a noun and other words, and it usually comes after the verb:

  ■ Nabila picked **some flowers**.
  ■ Imran watched **the grass moving in the wind**.

Not all verbs take objects:

  ■ The train left at six o'clock.

Often there are two objects in a sentence. The main object is called the *direct object* and comes after the verb. The second object is called the *indirect object* and usually comes before the direct object:

	subject	verb	indirect object	direct object
■	David	is giving	the baby	a bottle of milk.
■	Ian	threw	Jeremy	the ball.

When the indirect object goes after the direct object we add **to** / **for** etc:

	subject	verb	indirect object	preposition	direct object
■	David	is giving	a bottle of milk	to	the baby.
■	Ian	threw	the ball	for	Jeremy.

TABLE 2
irregular past forms

1 irregular past participles ending in **en**, **n** or **ne**

infinitive	past simple	past participle
be	was/were	been
beat	beat	beaten
bite	bit	bitten
break	broke	broken
choose	chose	chosen
do	did	done
draw	drew	drawn
drive	drove	driven
eat	ate	eaten
fall	fell	fallen
fly	flew	flown
forbid	forbade	forbidden
forget	forgot	forgotten
freeze	froze	frozen
give	gave	given
go	went	gone
grow	grew	grown
hide	hid	hidden
know	knew	known
lie	lay	lain
ride	rode	ridden
rise	rose	risen
sew	sewed	sewn
shake	shook	shaken
show	showed	shown
speak	spoke	spoken
steal	stole	stolen
swear	swore	sworn
take	took	taken
tear	tore	torn
throw	threw	thrown
tread	trod	trodden
wake	woke	woken
wear	wore	worn
write	wrote	written

2 irregular past participles ending with a final syllable vowel change

infinitive	past simple	past participle
become	became	become
begin	began	begun
come	came	come
dig	dug	dug
feed	fed	fed
find	found	found
get	got	got
hang	hung	hung
light	lit	lit
meet	met	met
read /riːd/	read /red/	read /red/
ring	rang	rung
run	ran	run
shine	shone	shone
shoot	shot	shot
shrink	shrank	shrunk
sing	sang	sung
sink	sank	sunk
sit	sat	sat
spring	sprang	sprung
stand	stood	stood
stick	stuck	stuck
sting	stung	stung
stink	stank	stunk
strike	struck	struck
swim	swam	swum
swing	swung	swung
understand	understood	understood
win	won	won

3 irregular past participles ending in **t**

infinitive	past simple	past participle
bend	bent	bent
build	built	built
deal	dealt	dealt
feel	felt	felt
keep	kept	kept
learn	learned / learnt	learnt
leave	left	left
lose	lost	lost
mean	meant	meant
send	sent	sent
sleep	slept	slept
spend	spent	spent
spill	spilled	spilt
sweep	swept	swept

4 irregular past participles ending in **ught**

infinitive	past simple	past participle
bring	brought	brought
buy	bought	bought
catch	caught	caught
fight	fought	fought
seek	sought	sought
teach	taught	taught
think	thought	thought

5 irregular past participles with no change

infinitive	past simple	past participle
bet	bet	bet
burst	burst	burst
cost	cost	cost
cut	cut	cut
hit	hit	hit
hurt	hurt	hurt
put	put	put
set	set	set
shut	shut	shut
split	split	split
spread	spread	spread

TABLE 3   **irregular noun plurals**

1 nouns with no change in the plural

Some nouns have the same form in the singular and the plural:

sheep	crossroads
fish	series
deer	gasworks
craft	grouse
dice	data
species	aircraft
means	salmon / trout / cod etc.
barracks	

2 en plurals

Some nouns coming from Old English have an **en** ending in the plural:

child → children
woman → women
man → men
ox → oxen

3 ouse singular → ice plural

Some nouns change from the singular **ouse** to the plural **ice**:

mouse → mice
louse → lice

4 oo singular → ee plural

Some nouns change **oo** + *consonant* to **ee** + *consonant*:

foot → feet
goose → geese
tooth → teeth

5 Latin and Greek endings

Some words coming from Latin and Greek have a different system of plural endings:

analysis → analyses
antenna → antennae (or antennas)
appendix → appendices (or appendixes)
automaton → automata
cactus → cacti (or cactuses)
crisis → crises
criterion → criteria
curriculum → curricula
fungus → fungi
medium → media (news, TV, radio etc)
nucleus → nuclei
phenomenon → phenomena
stratum → strata
thesis → theses

6 plural nouns with no singular

Some nouns are only used in the plural:

arms (weapons)	outskirts
belongings	remains
clothes	surroundings
congratulations	thanks
contents	trousers
earnings	scissors
goods	glasses (spectacles)

These plural nouns have a singular form:

police	youth
cattle	people

7 singular nouns ending in **s**

Some nouns have an s ending but are only used in the singular:

mathematics	politics
physics	gymnastics
billiards	measles
ethics	mumps

8 singular **o** → plural **oes**

hero → heroes
potato → potatoes
tomato → tomatoes

9 fe singular → **ves** plural

calf → calves
knife → knives
leaf → leaves
life → lives
loaf → loaves
self → selves
shelf → shelves
thief → thieves
wife → wives

TABLE 4

1 vowels, consonants, and phonemic symbols

The vowels of English are written as **a**, **e**, **i**, **o** and **u**. There are more vowel sounds than vowels, and some vowel sounds have more than one possible spelling. We use different phonemic symbols for each vowel sound. Dictionaries use these to help you to pronounce a new word. Here is a list of the phonemic symbols for English vowels.

/ə/ – op<u>e</u>n	/ɒ/ – h<u>o</u>t
/ɜː/ – b<u>ir</u>d	/ɑː/ – p<u>a</u>th (southern British)
/ʌ/ – t<u>u</u>g	/æ/ – b<u>a</u>d
/uː/ – sp<u>oo</u>n	/e/ – t<u>e</u>n
/ʊ/ – p<u>u</u>t	/ɪ/ – h<u>i</u>t
/ɔː/ – f<u>i</u>ll	/iː/ – f<u>ee</u>t

When two vowel sounds work together, they are called a ***diphthong***. There are phonemic symbols for each diphthong:

/əʊ/ – s<u>o</u>	/ɔɪ/ – r<u>oy</u>al	/aʊ/ – t<u>ow</u>n
/eɪ/ – s<u>ay</u>	/ɪə/ – h<u>ere</u>	/ʊə/ – f<u>ewe</u>r
/aɪ/ – cr<u>y</u>	/eə/ – f<u>air</u>	

Each consonant sound also has a phonemic symbol:

/b/ – <u>b</u>old	/l/ – <u>l</u>emon	/ʒ/ – mea<u>s</u>ure
/k/ – <u>k</u>idney, <u>c</u>ar	/m/ – <u>m</u>ood	/t/ – <u>t</u>en
/tʃ/ – <u>ch</u>urch	/n/ – <u>n</u>othing	/ð/ – <u>th</u>is
/d/ – <u>d</u>oor	/ŋ/ – si<u>ng</u>	/θ/ – <u>th</u>in
/f/ – <u>f</u>ine	/p/ – <u>p</u>it	/v/ – <u>v</u>owel
/g/ – <u>g</u>ood	/r/ – <u>r</u>ight	/w/ – <u>w</u>in
/h/ – <u>h</u>air	/s/ – <u>s</u>un	/j/ – <u>y</u>es
/dʒ/ – <u>j</u>ust	/ʃ/ – <u>sh</u>ore	/z/ – <u>z</u>en

Note the sounds of the consonants **q** and **x**:

/kw/ – <u>q</u>ueen	/ks/ – e<u>x</u>it

2 intonation

Intonation is the rise and fall of the voice in speech. In English the voice is usually high on the most important words in a sentence, and falls at the end of a statement:

Karen likes water skiing

In questions the intonation usually starts high, and then falls and rises at the end:

Would you like a newspaper?

3 pronunciation of s endings

We add **s** to the end of nouns and verbs. The pronunciation of the **s** depends on the sound at the end of the word:

1 /k, f, p, t/ + /s/:
 pic<u>ks</u>, laug<u>hs</u>, ta<u>ps</u>, pu<u>ts</u>
2 /b, d, g, l, m, n, ŋ/ + vowel sounds + /z/:
 ro<u>bs</u>, ad<u>ds</u>, bags, bo<u>ys</u>
3 /tʃ, s, ʃ, z/ + **es**, pronounced /ɪz/:
 pushes, fetches, passes, faxes

4 pronunciation of the **ed** ending

There are lots of irregular **ed** verb endings. The pronunciation of the regular endings depends on the sound of the previous syllable:

> 1 unvoiced consonant (/k,f, p, t, s/) + **ed**, pronounced /t/:
>   missed   tapped   picked   puffed
> 2 voiced consonant (/b, d, g, m, n, ŋ/) + **ed**, pronounced /d/:
>   robbed   praised   admired   nagged
> 3 vowels and liquids (**l**, **w**, **y**, **r** etc) + **ed**, pronounced /d/:
>   pulled   bored   prayed   sewed
> 4 /t/ or /d/ + **ed**, pronounced /ɪd/:
>   batted   padded   lasted   attracted

5 pronunciation of **r**

There are different pronunciations of the letter **r** in different parts of the English-speaking world. In 'standard' Southern British English we pronounce the **r** after a consonant very short and forward in the mouth, more with the lips than the tongue. We do not roll the tongue. A final **r** is not pronounced. In other regions, such as Scotland, the tongue is rolled, and in American English and the southwest of England, the **r** is 'dark', and made at the back of the mouth with the lips rounded.

Before a consonant, or between two vowels, we do not pronounce the **r**. It changes the pronunciation of the previous vowel:

park – /pɑːk/	sore – /sɔː/
port – /pɔːt/	care – /keə/
hurt – /hɜːt/	here – /hɪə/

6 weak and strong forms

Many common one-syllable words are pronounced very quickly in spoken English, and the pronunciation is different than when they are spoken slowly and clearly. The vowel is weakened, often to become /ə/ or /ɪ/. This is called the **weak** form of the word. The following is a list of some of the most common weak forms used in everyday speech:

a / an – /ə, ən/	will – /wəl/
the – /ðə/	would, could, should – /wəd, kəd, ʃəd/
some, come – /sʌm, kəm/	can, had, have – /kən, həd, həv/
at, as, am, that, than – /ət, əz, əm/	from, of, was – /frəm, əv, wəz/
you, to, should – /jə, tə, ʃəd/	them – /ðəm/
been – /bɪn/	shall – /ʃəl/
for – /fə/	

When a syllable is not stressed in a word with more than one syllable, the unstressed vowel is weakened. /iː/ becomes /ɪ/ and all the other vowels become /ə/:

partner – /pɑːtnə/	believe – /bɪliːv/
become – /bɪkʌm/	succeed – /səksiːd/
recover – /rɪkʌvə/	apply – /əplaɪ/

TABLE 5 — American English grammar

1 use of **present perfect / past simple**

The *past simple* is often used in American English when British English uses the *present perfect*:

American English	British English
■ I **gave** Sam my door key.	I**'ve given** Sam my door key.
■ Keith **didn't meet** Sue yet.	Keith **hasn't met** Sue yet.

2 use of **have / have got / gotten**

American speakers use **have** where British speakers prefer **have got**:

American English	British English
■ Cindy **has** a bad cold today.	Cindy**'s got** a bad cold today.
■ I **have** three brothers and a sister.	I**'ve got** three brothers and a sister.
■ **Do** you **have** your key?	**Have** you **got** your key?
■ **Does** Paul still **have** the blue Oldsmobile?	**Has** Paul still **got** the blue Oldsmobile?

The past participle of **get** in American English is **gotten**. In British English it is **got**:

American English	British English
■ Sheila has **gotten** very lazy recently.	Sheila has **got** very lazy recently.
■ He had **gotten** a lot of new friends.	He had **got** a lot of new friends.

3 use of **take**

American English speakers say **take a bath / shower / break / nap** etc. where a British English speaker would usually say **have a bath / shower** etc:

American English	British English
■ Steve **takes** a shower before work.	Steve **has** a shower before work.
■ Tammy has just **taken** a short break.	Tammy has just **had** a short break.
■ Let's go **take** a nap.	Let's go and **have** a nap.

4 use of **go + fetch** etc.

American English speakers use the forms **go fetch**, **go take**, **go get**, **go see** etc. where British English speakers say **go and see** etc:

American English	British English
■ Johnny, **go fetch** my slippers!	**Go and fetch** my slippers.
■ Will you **go get** a loaf of bread.	Will you **go and get** a loaf of bread.
■ I wanted to **go see** my brother.	I wanted to **go and see** my brother.

American English speakers do not use this form in the past tense:
   ■ Gail **went and got** some milk. NOT Gail ~~went get~~ some milk.

5 Prepositions

American speakers say **on the weekend**, where British speakers say **at the weekend**; American speakers say someone is **on a team**, where GB speakers use **in**:

American English	British English
■ Paul goes swimming **on the weekend**.	Paul goes swimming **at the weekend**.
■ Tim is **on the** baseball **team**.	Tim is **in the** baseball **team**.

INDEX

The numbers in this index are page numbers.